The Secret Architecture of Shakespeare's Sonnets

The Secret Architecture of Shakespeare's Sonnets

Steven Monte

EDINBURGH
University Press

Edinburgh University Press is one of the leading university presses in the UK. We publish academic books and journals in our selected subject areas across the humanities and social sciences, combining cutting-edge scholarship with high editorial and production values to produce academic works of lasting importance. For more information visit our website: edinburghuniversitypress.com

© Steven Monte, 2021, 2023

Edinburgh University Press Ltd
The Tun – Holyrood Road
12(2f) Jackson's Entry
Edinburgh EH8 8PJ

First published in hardback by Edinburgh University Press 2021

Typeset in 11/13 Adobe Sabon by
IDSUK (DataConnection) Ltd, and
printed and bound by CPI Group (UK) Ltd, Croydon, CR0 4YY

A CIP record for this book is available from the British Library

ISBN 978 1 4744 8147 2 (hardback)
ISBN 978 1 4744 8148 9 (paperback)
ISBN 978 1 4744 8149 6 (webready PDF)
ISBN 978 1 4744 8150 2 (epub)

The right of Steven Monte to be identified as the author of this work has been asserted in accordance with the Copyright, Designs and Patents Act 1988, and the Copyright and Related Rights Regulations 2003 (SI No. 2498).

Contents

Acknowledgements		vii
Note on titles, terminology, and notation		viii
Introduction: Seeing Things 'Perspectively'		1
Chapter 1	Stories in and about Shakespeare's Sonnets	10
Chapter 2	The Basic Scheme	29
Chapter 3	Poetic Rivalry in Late-Elizabethan England	62
Chapter 4	A Triptych for the Third Earl	102
Chapter 5	Competing Schemes	126
Chapter 6	The Fair-Youth Sonnets, Part 1	154
Chapter 7	The Fair-Youth Sonnets, Part 2	194
Chapter 8	The Mistress Sonnets	223
Chapter 9	Complaints of the Heart	248
Conclusion: Seeing Things Retrospectively		268
Appendices		279
Notes		302
Bibliography		318
Individual Sonnets and 'A Lover's Complaint'		329
Groups of Sonnets		331
Index		333

Thoughts tending to ambition, they do plot
Unlikely wonders.

            (Shakespeare, *Richard II*)

O learn to read what silent love hath writ!

            (Shakespeare, Sonnet 23)

Acknowledgements

My greatest debt is to David Southward and Stuart Calderwood. During the book's decade-long genesis and development, they read many versions of my work and sustained me with friendship and timely advice.

I have also been aided by friends and colleagues who perused different sections of the book: Leslie Brisman, Christopher Miller, David Rosen, and Blanford Parker read most of the work in installments; Katherine Goodland, Gerry Milligan, Harry Thorne, Matthew Greenfield, and Christopher Cuccia were especially helpful with the opening chapters.

I garnered valuable feedback from many Renaissance specialists – so many, I hope I am not forgetting anyone. By correspondence or in person, I received suggestions from Joshua Scodel, David Quint, Richard McCoy, Alastair Fowler, Brian Lockey, Heather Dubrow, Ilona Bell, and James Nohrnberg. Fellow members of the Columbia Shakespeare Seminar provided advice and inspiration: David Hershinow, Tanya Pollard, Matthew Zarnowiecki, Zoltan Markus, Steve Mentz, Laura Kolb, John Staines, Amos Rothschild, and Corey Abate. Two 'out of town' members, Richard Strier and Henry Weinfield, offered useful critiques of my introduction.

Some of the most helpful feedback came from 'non-specialists': my friends Jesse Gale, Anne Birien, Eric Lindholm, Ben Skrainka, and Dan Kimberg; my siblings Joe, Cath, Greg, Chris, and Mary; and my father and Kathy. A warm thanks to them – and a special shout-out to Alice 'Rara Avis' Scovell, for reading almost the whole book at one go, and for her down-to-earth suggestions.

I also thank the College of Staten Island (CUNY), whose sabbatical support helped make this book possible, and the readers and editors of Edinburgh Press, who have patiently steered me through to publication.

The book is dedicated to the memory of Jason Turetsky (1974–2013), a dear friend and early enthusiast for the project.

Note on titles, terminology, and notation

I treat all titles as singular proper nouns, including *Shakespeare's Sonnets* and its abbreviated form, *Sonnets*. This practice follows that of Katherine Duncan-Jones in the third Arden edition of *Sonnets*. (For readers accustomed to 'the *Sonnets*', the convention may take some getting used to.) I refer to editors and philological scholars as 'commentators'. Like many commentators, I use 'sonnet sequence' for the work's genre: it is the most common term, and 'sequence' helpfully implies that the order of the poems matters. Similarly, I refer to other commentators by surname – a scholarly practice that, at its best, is an efficient way of clarifying arguments and providing points of reference in debates. But conjured names can also be alienating, whatever one's familiarity with them; for frequently cited names, see the editorial list in the bibliography.

In quoted texts, spelling and punctuation are modernised unless rhymes or wordplay would be obscured. Against scholarly fashion, I use quotation marks, not italics, with the title of 'A Lover's Complaint', mostly to indicate that the poem is part of *Sonnets*. More in line with current trends, I refer to the first edition of *Sonnets* as Q, a designation that derives from the book's quarto format. Perhaps most crucial, I refer to the speaking voice in *Shakespeare's Sonnets* as 'the poet' or 'the *Sonnets* poet'. Though 'Will' has the authority of Sonnet 136 ('my name is *Will*'), it is not always apt; 'the poet-lover' is cumbersome; and 'the speaker' is antiseptic. Fittingly, 'the poet' refers to both Shakespeare the author and his *Sonnets* persona.

Introduction: Seeing Things 'Perspectively'

This book makes two main claims: that *Shakespeare's Sonnets* contains intricate hidden organisation, and that Shakespeare was far more engaged with other poets and with pursuing a career as a poet than is generally assumed. The first claim presupposes that the organisational schemes have been hiding in plain view for over four centuries. The second is literary-historical and biographical, because it speaks to Shakespeare's cultural milieu and personal ambitions. Although 'hidden' and 'hiding' may create the impression that Shakespeare wrote in code, the fundamental reason why his schemes have gone unnoticed is historical: within decades of his death, conventions of sonnet sequences became unfamiliar, and they have largely remained so since. The first claim might also be said to follow from the second, because the poets with whom Shakespeare engages most intensely wrote the most complex sequences. In proving these claims, the book approaches *Sonnets* as three distinct and related things: as a free-standing sequence, as a sonnet sequence among other poets' sequences, and as a work in Shakespeare's career as a poet.

Changing How We Look at *Shakespeare's Sonnets*

My interpretation of *Sonnets* is grounded in a Renaissance understanding of perspective. In Shakespeare's works, the word 'perspective' is generally associated with the art of optical illusion. This is the case in Sonnet 24, which develops the metaphor that the poet is a painter who positions and frames his art for private viewing: 'Mine eye hath played the painter and hath stelled / Thy beauty's form in table of my heart; / My body is the frame wherein 'tis held / And pérspective it is best painters' art'. The poet is saying that, like a painter, he has made a portrait of his beloved; that he has set, composed, or engraved the form of his beloved's beauty in the tablet or notebook of his heart; and that his body frames the form which, seen 'perspectively', exemplifies the art of the best painters. ('Pérspective' is an adverbial adjective – a grammatical option more available in Renaissance English.[1]) The portrait in the heart, a work of love, may seem distorted or clumsy, but when regarded from the proper perspective it is a faithful image that reveals artistic skill. Shakespeare is alluding to a type of distortion whose technical name is anamorphosis – an image whose proportional or 'true' shape can be seen only when it is viewed in a special manner, such as from an oblique angle. (A famous instance is the skull in Hans Holbein's *The Ambassadors*.[2]) Reading *Sonnets* through its schemes and its relations to other sequences is like viewing an anamorphic image from the vantage required to bring the image into focus. What at first appears haphazard emerges as a meaningful and beautiful form.

The perspective metaphor does more than signal a theme: it highlights the poet's search for undistorted views of his beloved, himself, and what is real and lasting, and it invites us to read the sequence in a manner analogous to his search. The *Sonnets* poet often presents himself as someone struggling to see things as they are: he dramatises tensions between his heart's and mind's perceptions; Hamlet-like, he points to discrepancies between appearance and reality. He also implies that what he seeks is elusive: even his own heart proves difficult to know. The world of *Sonnets* is a world of uncertainties, in which the poet's most confident assertions may in fact be pleas, provisional claims, or rhetorical gestures to ward off calamity. In this context, the sequence's structures speak to both a stable order under the chaos of appearances and a desperate attempt to save appearances – a desire for a providential narrative. In *Sonnets*' biblical language, the poet hopes to 'redeem time'. Ultimately, he looks to the future for redemption, evoking the idea of Judgement Day. In his search to gain perspective on experiences, the poet employs a narrative of transgression, judgement, and forgiveness. All of this comes into focus when the sequence's organisational schemes are taken into account.

The basic structure of *Shakespeare's Sonnets* is as straightforward as a rhyme scheme. It consists of seventeen groups of poems whose first group contains seventeen sonnets, and whose subsequent groups decrease in size incrementally from sixteen sonnets to one poem. (It also contains two other poems that mark thematic divisions.) The structure is pyramidal because the poem groups, imagined as a vertical arrangement of steps or stories – with a seventeen-unit base and a one-unit apex – form a pyramid with tapering layers. The design reinforces the conceit of poetry as a monument, and it highlights relations between poems. It also raises questions about audience:

who would have been expected to see the structure? Who might have noticed the more intricate schemes? While it is conceivable that no one outside Shakespeare's immediate circle knew of the pyramidal organisation, or that none of *Sonnets*' first readers knew of it, some Renaissance readers would have known to look for schemes, and Shakespeare may have counted on that fact – and have envisioned future readers who would look for them.

For twenty-first-century readers, the organisational schemes that I describe should offer insights into Shakespeare's sonnets and poetics. Many commentators have noted that the sequence's first seventeen sonnets urge a young man to have children. I am arguing that Sonnets 1–17 are the first group in a series of groups that clarifies a story: we are presented not with a linear narrative but a succession of viewpoints on people, events, and situations, in which the poet's concerns progressively shift. The groups also allow Shakespeare to develop modes of persuasion and to display artistry; they are thematic units with their own schemes. The third pyramid step, for example, broaches the subject of betrayal; it consists of five trios of sonnets, whose third trio speaks of a love triangle between the poet, his mistress, and his friend. Such organisation implies planning or revision. I contend that *Sonnets*' structures are similar to complex schemes in Philip Sidney's *Astrophil and Stella*, Edmund Spenser's *Amoretti*, and other Elizabethan works, and that Shakespeare was acquainted with many sonnet sequences. He knew the genre thoroughly, and he put his own stamp on it.

More fundamentally, I argue that *Sonnets*' structures are an index of Shakespeare's engagement with late-Elizabethan poets. The sonnet sequence, as derived from Petrarch's fourteenth-century *Rime*, did not become popular in England until the 1590s; within a few decades, English poets stopped writing sequences. In its heyday, the genre attracted some of the best poets – Sidney, Spenser, Shakespeare – who both imitated and reworked tradition. Elizabethan poets often portrayed themselves as latecomers and lamented that England was a poetic backwater. Such self-consciousness promoted a revisionary strain detectable in less ambitious works. The poets of the 1590s and early 1600s also faced pressure from the literary marketplace: in contrast to the courtier poets of the early sixteenth century, most of them were non-aristocratic writers competing for patronage and recognition. Although it is not certain when Shakespeare began writing his sonnets or compiling them as a sequence, he may well have been a latecomer among latecomers. Especially if he was composing his poems in the mid-1590s he would have entered a highly competitive arena. No matter when he wrote *Sonnets*, he was responding to rivals and potential competition.

Given the importance of poetic rivalry in *Shakespeare's Sonnets*, it can be argued that the emphasis on personal love is a mask for artistic and social ambitions. This line of thought is starkly represented in Arthur Marotti's 1982 article '"Love Is Not Love": Elizabethan Sonnet Sequences and the Social Order'. My book is influenced by this approach, but I do not make sharp distinctions between the kinds of love that the poet expresses: the strands of his desire are woven together, and they include affections ranging from paternal concern to sexual obsession. I also stress that *Sonnets*, on its own terms and in comparison with other sequences, is intimate in tone. This suggests that the personal situations are not mere fictions. Generic conventions also argue for autobiographical allusions, albeit of an artful sort. Especially when they are hidden, such allusions do not preclude intense personal expression. In evoking this possibility, I do not mean to suggest that *Sonnets* is a *cri de coeur* – nor to rule out that idea – but to emphasise that Shakespeare went to a great deal of trouble to construct his sequence and to conceal features of his construction. Even if *Sonnets* consisted wholly of rhetorical manoeuvres, much could be made of the feelings that prompted the monumental effort.

When we read *Sonnets*, then, we would do well to consider how it is organised, how it compares with other sequences, and what its significance was for its author. In doing so, we may experience and interpret its poems differently, especially the sonnets dubbed 'strange' or 'out of place'. Sonnet 99, for example, has fifteen lines and is generally viewed as slight because of its subject matter: the poet first accuses a flower of stealing hues and scents from his beloved, then claims that other flowers have committed similar crimes. My analysis begins by observing that the poem marks a thematic division: a transition from a time when the poet stopped writing sonnets to a moment of renewed relations with his beloved. Its form helps mark the transition, as does its inauguration of a ten-sonnet group (the eighth pyramid step). The sonnet thus performs organisational work, which militates against the notion that it is trivial or unpolished. But that is not all. Sonnet 99 echoes another sonnet, Henry Constable's 'Of his mistress upon occasion of her walking in a garden'. The echo is so clear that virtually every modern editor notes it. I argue that the poem's near-quotation of Constable is meant to be seen as brazen plagiarism, that the sonnet contains allusions to other Elizabethan poets, and that Shakespeare is commenting on poetic theft. Few poems in *Sonnets* are as allusive as 99, but Shakespeare is frequently in conversation with his contemporaries.

In drawing connections between Shakespeare and other poets, I often explore connections between Shakespeare's art and life. Here I distinguish my approach from that of scholars who, in the name of history on one hand and aesthetics on the other, guard excessively against biographical readings. In this group I include the commentators whom I admire most – notably the poet W. H. Auden, who declared that *Sonnets* is a touchstone for distinguishing readers who 'love poetry for its own sake and understand its nature' from readers who value poems as historical documents or expressions of beliefs.[3] A guarded attitude towards biographical interpretation is one with which I sympathise – up to a point. Yes, *Sonnets* was written before Romanticism, let alone confessional poetry. And yes, readers who care about art should not approach the sequence simply as a journal. But our experience of the poems is influenced by our sense of a person behind them; commentators who claim otherwise tend to belie themselves when describing the emotions in the poems. It may be that our sense of other people is inevitably fictive, and that our images of Shakespeare are inevitably mythic. Whatever our image is, when we read Shakespeare's sonnets, our understanding of them depends on our having a sense of a person who is expressing something personal. We can gain a better sense of this person and this something by paying attention to the sequence's organisation and Shakespeare's life.

Biographical interpretation is best justified by results, or at least by concrete answers to the question 'Supposing we knew, why would it matter?' With *Sonnets*, even small connections between life and art, such as the name of the youth, can make a difference. If we knew his name was William, we might regard the puns on 'will' differently; if we knew his name was Henry, we might hear a quibble on 'Hal' in 'Ev'n as when first I hallowed thy fair name' (Sonnet 108). *Shakespeare's Sonnets* invites us to consider names, even as it guards against naming names. Much more than wordplay is at stake – and wordplay is hardly trivial for someone who values poetry for its own sake. If the third Earl of Southampton was the model for the youth, we might read *Sonnets* as Shakespeare's third poetic work for him. If we knew more about Shakespeare's rivals, we might gain insight into the anxiety, contempt, indifference, or admiration expressed towards them, and we might acquire a better sense of the targeted poetry. In making the case for organisation, I present new evidence regarding Shakespeare's rivals and the styles against which the *Sonnets* poet positions himself, and I have much to say about poetic rivalry in Renaissance England. Understanding Shakespeare's milieu is as important as understanding generic conventions and organisational structures.

Reading *Shakespeare's Sonnets* after Romanticism

Shakespeare's Sonnets was published once in the author's lifetime, in 1609. (Following scholarly practice, I refer to this edition as Q.) Twenty-first-century readers are both advantaged and disadvantaged by the fact that *Sonnets* is over 400 years old: advantaged in having access to centuries of interpretations; disadvantaged in being centuries removed from the culture in which Shakespeare wrote. The advantages are clear with individual poems: many editions supply explanatory notes. For more help, readers can consult commentaries like Helen Vendler's *The Art of Shakespeare's Sonnets* (1997) and David West's *Shakespeare's Sonnets* (2007), whose detailed interpretations are interpolated between poems. But commentaries provide little or no help for reading *Sonnets* as a sequence, and many scholars cast doubt on the idea that there is design in the poems' order. One of my aims is to provide cultural-historical perspective on sequential design. The significance of this goal may be gauged against the commentary history – especially the history since Romanticism.

In England, the sonnet sequence ceased to be a living genre within a decade or two of Shakespeare's death; the last sequence of note is Mary Wroth's *Pamphilia and Amphilanthus* (1621). When John Benson published the second version of *Sonnets* in 1640 (*Poems Written by William Shakespeare, Gent*), the poems were rearranged into groups and given titles; pronouns were changed to create the impression that all sonnets addressed a woman; and seven sonnets were omitted. Bernard Lintott published a version of Q in 1711, as did George Steevens in his *Twenty Plays of Shakespeare* (1766), but there was no widely available edition retaining the 1609 order of sonnets until Edward Malone's *Supplement to the Edition of Shakespeare* (1780) – and even Malone's edition inserts *The Passionate Pilgrim* and 'The Phoenix and the Turtle' between the 154 sonnets and 'A Lover's Complaint'.[4] Although most editions since Malone's contain all of Q's sonnets in Q's order, many omit 'A Lover's Complaint' or present it as a separate work, and Q's use of Hindu-Arabic numerals did not become standard until the second half of the twentieth century. Given *Sonnets*' publication history, it is not surprising that the sequence's organisational and numeric designs have largely gone unnoticed.

By the nineteenth century, nonetheless, most editions of *Sonnets* contained all of the poems in their 1609 order, and more readers approached the poems as a collection. In the wake of Romanticism, reading *Sonnets* as a sequence often meant constructing biographical narratives that linked the poems; nineteenth-century commentators produced theories about the sonnets' narrative order and debated the identities of the youth, the mistress, and the rival. Doubts about Q's ordering inspired some readers to rearrange sonnets or to question the authorship of poems. But even those who regarded *Sonnets* as an authorial sequence made little progress on its design, perhaps because they expected a linear narrative. Still, the sequence was commonly divided into fair-youth and mistress sections. In an 1881 letter, the poet Dante Gabriel Rossetti called for 'an essential reform' in editions of *Sonnets*: 'After Sonnet 125 should occur the words "End of Part I"; [Sonnet 126] should be called "Epilogue to Part I"; then, before 127, should be printed "Part II".'[5] Such a reform would reflect the organisational structure of the sequence, but it would also make overt what was veiled.

The search for biographical and narrative design in *Sonnets* continued in the twentieth century; in some respects, it continues still, though scholars of the last five decades have tended to distance themselves from such efforts. Arthur Acheson's *Shakespeare and the Rival Poet* (1903) helped establish George Chapman as the twentieth-century's favourite candidate for the rival; debates about Southampton, Pembroke, and the youth have never really ceased; and enquiries into the mistress's identity still garner mention in periodicals like *The Guardian*. At the same time, 'anti-romantic' trends have promoted the idea that biographical interpretation of *Sonnets* is anachronistic. Twentieth-century frustration with post-romantic ideas is captured in James Joyce's *Ulysses* (1922), when Stephen Daedalus describes *Sonnets* as 'the happy hunting ground for minds that have lost their balance'; H. E. Rollins cites this line in the first paragraph of his 1944 variorum edition of *Sonnets*, alluding to a century's worth of cryptographic theories.[6] By mid-century all interpretations that posited hidden order, not simply the biographical ones, risked sceptical responses. In the century's second half, searching for hidden order fell so far out of scholarly fashion that it might be lumped with the efforts to attribute Shakespeare's works to the Earl of Oxford, which often focus on *Sonnets* and decoding. In such an atmosphere, a 'secret architecture' can come across as sensationalist.

In outlining post-romantic commentary, and in characterising discussions of hidden order as disreputable, I am not asking the reader to suspend doubts about my thesis; rather, I am emphasising that, for all my discussion of poetic structure, my approach is cultural-historical. One irony in scholarly resistance to hidden design is that analysis of sequential order has been regarded as narrowly focused on form, whereas the approach that I advocate demands enquiry into a genre whose aesthetic principles are tied to a specific milieu – the literary marketplace of 1590s England.

Scholarly Debates and Chapter Summaries

My pyramid thesis is not unprecedented. In *Triumphal Forms: Structural Patterns in Elizabethan Poetry* (1970), Alastair Fowler argues that *Sonnets* is pyramidally arranged. This idea remains a minority report, though similar arguments about structures in Spenser's *Amoretti* have gained general acceptance.[7] In analysing *Sonnets'* schemes, I defend Fowler's main thesis, especially against critics who dismiss the idea that Shakespeare is 'that kind of poet', but I am hardly calling for conspiracy theories: the smallest mistake in detailing hidden design can make the whole approach seem dubious; Fowler and the few scholars who have built on his work have mischaracterised details of *Sonnets'* pyramid. Clarifying the sequence's design is important, and clarifying why it matters is crucial. Even readers sympathetic to Fowler can come away thinking that the structure merely reinforces the conceit of book as monument. It is much more than that: the hidden organisation provides contexts for interpreting the situations and tones of individual sonnets, and for evaluating Shakespeare's relations with other poets.

My book raises questions out of the mainstream; as a result, the scholars whom I cite tend to be practical critics (interpreters of Shakespeare's words, style, and themes). While it is routine to note that *Sonnets'* 'fair youth', 'rival poet', and 'dark lady' may be modelled on real people, it is no longer fashionable to make much of these possibilities. And few recent scholars pursue the idea that *Sonnets* is an organised collection, let alone a highly organised one. Most of my cited works are editorial commentaries. This emphasis on practical criticism is necessitated by my subject: proving that *Sonnets'* schemes exist depends on interpretive pay-offs. More simply, until I have detailed the schemes, theorising about method is of limited value. I proceed under the assumption that the methodological criticism with which I am in dialogue will not be lost on readers who care about it or be missed by readers who do not, and that my own approach is best fleshed out through evidence and analysis. (For an overview of pertinent scholarship, see the prefatory note to the bibliography.)

This book has nine chapters, eight of which are paired. Chapters 1–2 are preparatory: Chapter 1 summarises common ideas about *Sonnets*, as a work in Shakespeare's oeuvre and as a sequence. Chapter 2 discusses Renaissance ideas about hidden order and provides an overview of the basic pyramidal scheme. Chapters 3 and 4 turn to other cultural-historical contexts for reading *Sonnets*: Chapter 3 focuses on poetic rivalry in 1590s England; Chapter 4, on Shakespeare's poetic career, especially on *Venus and Adonis* and *Lucrece*. Chapter 5 stands somewhat apart; it details the schemes and devices in *Sonnets* that are independent of the main pyramid. Chapters 6 and 7 focus on Sonnets 1–99 and Sonnets 100–26, respectively – the two 'halves' of the fair-youth section of *Sonnets* – analysing the poems in relation to their pyramid steps. Chapters 8 and 9 provide similar analysis of the mistress section of *Sonnets*: Chapter 8 discusses Sonnets 127–54; Chapter 9, 'A Lover's Complaint'. As this overview might suggest, I often discuss poetic form and style, though not for their own sakes. Among other things, the organisational schemes have interpretative implications for Shakespeare's 1590s plays and for Renaissance culture beyond literature. Examples of the latter include artist-patron relationships, pyramidal sight lines in the visual arts, and philosophical conceits like the Platonic World Soul.

Perhaps the best way of explaining how I intervene in scholarly debates is to describe the book as a response to the view that *Sonnets* eschews design. Paul Edmondson and Stanley Wells, for example, assert: 'To seek a pattern in these loosely connected poems is like trying to control or tidy the inevitable mess and freedom that love itself creates.'[8] Such a claim is misguided on two counts: *Sonnets* is highly designed; far from tidying love's mess, its schemes underscore desperate attempts to manage concerns. More generally, I show that *Sonnets*' organisation rewards attention. Early on, I draw few firm conclusions, partly because my subject demands careful presentation, but mostly because weighing possibilities is fundamental to Shakespeare's poetics. Sometimes I pursue an explanation that I later reject, or I ask the reader to take note of an idea that is not immediately relevant. Among other things, I stress that interpretation is a process. My exposition is guided by the belief that gradually revealing the organisation is more likely to promote understanding. The schemes have been waiting for us for more than four centuries. Let us approach them with the consideration and wonder that they deserve.

Chapter 1

Stories in and about Shakespeare's Sonnets

The Story in the *Sonnets*

It has become a scholarly custom to caution against reading *Shakespeare's Sonnets* for the plot, and understandably so: it is a sequence of poems, not a novel. Such directives should not be rigid, however: *Sonnets* encourages us to link poems and to construct narratives. For this and other reasons, it is productive to approach the sequence expecting to find some story. Let us imagine a reader with tempered expectations, paging through *Sonnets* for the first time.

A modern reader who sets out to read all of *Sonnets* will likely be familiar with some of it. The anthology sonnets are memorable for many reasons, including opening lines:

> Shall I compare thee to a summer's day?
>
> (Sonnet 18)

> Let me not to the marriage of true minds
> Admit impediments.
>
> (Sonnet 116)

> When my love swears that she is made of truth,
> I do believe her, though I know she lies.
>
> (Sonnet 138)

From such poems, it is reasonable to regard *Sonnets* as a collection of love poems – which it is, for the most part, though not always in ways that twenty-first-century readers might expect. The poet often addresses the object of his affections, but he also addresses 'Time' or 'Love', his muse or his soul, or nothing in particular, as if he were meditating or expounding general truths. He moreover presents himself as flawed; among other things, he has anxieties about growing old and has had extramarital relations with a younger woman. In ways that might be refreshing to a modern reader, he acknowledges his failings and does not idealise the woman with whom he is obsessed. With the right selection of sonnets, it is possible to present an image of the poet that squares with a popular image of Shakespeare: a tolerant person in touch with all that is human. This image may even be enhanced because the poet appears anything but godlike.

Such an image is not everyone's, of course, and reading through *Sonnets* would challenge it. More than 100 sonnets – including 'Shall I compare thee to a summer's day?' – are written to or about an aristocratic male friend. The sonnets to the mistress, fewer than thirty, are in the back of the volume. Reactions to the emphasis on the nobleman have varied widely. Some readers have downplayed the affection, claiming that male friendship was different in Shakespeare's time or that Elizabethan artists exaggerated devotion to their patrons. Others have championed Shakespeare as a gay or bisexual poet. Still others have changed female pronouns to male ones and rearranged sonnets. Given the uncertainties about when *Sonnets* was written and why it was published, such interpretations may say more about their advocates than the poetry.

Even readers with less tendentious views of Shakespeare might adjust their images as they proceed. The *Sonnets* poet is anxious about more things than growing old. One of the main events in the implied narrative is the mistress and nobleman's betrayal of the poet, alluded to in Sonnets 33–4 and reported more directly in 40–2, which colours later sonnets with suspicion. Even before the betrayal, the poet makes disparaging remarks about female infidelity; later, it is to the male friend that he speaks of a 'marriage of true minds' (116). Dramatised though such generalisations are, they might give modern readers pause. In Sonnet 20, the poet describes the young nobleman as having 'A woman's gentle heart, but not acquainted / With shifting change, as is false women's fashion'. In 135, the poet jests to his mistress that, because she is 'rich in Will' – has a voracious sexual appetite, a spacious vaginal cavity, and perhaps a few lovers named 'Will' – she should accept him and his 'will'. Misogynistic asides aside, the reader may be struck by occasional expressions of disgust with the body, especially when they are couched in religious language. Sonnet 144, for example, concludes with pointed references to hell and (as many scholars argue) venereal disease. After labelling his male friend his 'good angel' and his mistress his 'bad angel', the poet claims that he will know for sure who is sleeping with whom when the signs are fleshed out, so to speak: 'I guess one angel in another's hell. / Yet this I shall ne'er know, but live in doubt, / Till my bad angel fire my good one out'.

Because it is possible to select poems that make Shakespeare sound broad- or narrow-minded, sublime or crude, ahead of his time or merely of it, it is important to emphasise that the dramatic and rhetorical situations of any given sonnet are established not only by the poem but by the sequential context – by sonnets that are positionally proximate or thematically related. Treating *Sonnets* as a narrative is the most common way in which scholars have evoked sequential context. Indeed, it might be supposed that the genre in which Shakespeare wrote, what has come to be called 'the sonnet sequence', demands plot. Yet Renaissance sequences often frustrate narrative approaches. *Sonnets* may be particularly frustrating in that it invites us to construct a story and obscures the full version. The term 'sequence' is nonetheless apt: neither prescribing nor proscribing narrative, it indicates that the order of the poems matters.

Although the exact story that Shakespeare tells is elusive, its outlines are fairly clear through Sonnet 126. Sonnets 1–126 concern the young nobleman – 'the fair youth' or 'the friend' – who seems to have resisted his family's pleas to marry and have children. After urging the youth to beget an heir, the poet expresses personal devotion and is soon claiming that his affection is returned. Then he is betrayed by the friend, who sleeps with his (the poet's) mistress. In spite of wrongs suffered, the poet continues to express devotion to the youth, promising such things as immortality through poetry. Anxieties about fading beauty, old age, and death make their appearance, along with other fears and some hopes. Halfway through the collection, attention is drawn to rival poets: the *Sonnets* poet, it would seem, is not the only person writing for the youth. With what may be false modesty, the poet presents himself as a lesser writer but a more loving friend than his rivals. A series of farewell sonnets follow: outfaced by a rival, the poet bows out of the competition or makes a last-ditch attempt to repair the friendship via reverse psychology. Shortly before the one hundredth sonnet, a break is signalled; Sonnets 97–8 allude to a period of separation. The story does not end there, however. The friendship is renewed. The poet berates himself for being uninspired and offers new assertions of devotion and constancy. Then, in a twist almost too fitting to be true, the poet claims that he has betrayed the youth in a way that is comparable to the youth's earlier betrayal. Despite betrayals and changes, the fair-youth sonnets conclude with more assertions of devotion and with warnings about time's power.

Even as it invites us to read for plot, *Shakespeare's Sonnets* intimates that there is more to the sequence than the story. The mistress section most obviously interrupts the narrative, and the fair-youth section contains its share of disruptive poems. (How can the poet revert to praising the youth immediately after the betrayal? Why does he break off a discussion of rivals to give instructions about a gift?) Such discontinuities have led readers to question whether Shakespeare oversaw the poems' ordering and whether all poems are his. One way to come to terms with the mixed signals about narrative is to allow for more than one principle of organisation. Some poems express concerns that are more recurring than progressive, and some hidden structures may require a non-narrative approach. The organisation encourages a mode of reading that is both progressive and relational – a lyric mode.

Shakespeare's Rhetoric of Intimacy

Shakespeare's sequence can be read as an allegory of intimacy: it tells a story of closeness and knowing, and of alienation and not knowing. Whether or not he based this story on personal experiences, Shakespeare creates the impression that real events lie behind the poetry. Given the rhetoric of intimacy, the title with which the work was published is fitting, even if it is not authorial. With the possible exception of one or two religious sequences, *Shakespeare's Sonnets* is the most tonally intimate sequence of its time.

In *The "Inward" Language*, Anne Ferry shows that Shakespeare, following Philip Sidney's example, 'went beyond the expected association of the poet-lover . . . with its author', alluding in some sonnets to 'specific but unexplained incidents unknowable except to the lovers involved in them'.[1] In discussing Sidney, she cites Sonnet 93 of *Astrophil and Stella*, in which Astrophil regrets a missed opportunity to marry Stella: Sidney may be reflecting on his childhood engagement to Penelope Devereux, contracted for him by his family, from which he released her or allowed her to be released. In discussing Shakespeare, she cites Sonnet 36 of *Sonnets*, in which the poet urges the youth to maintain distance from him for reasons that are presumably clear to the youth but only vaguely disclosed in the poem: 'I may not evermore acknowledge thee, / Lest my bewailèd guilt should do thee shame, / Nor thou with public kindness honour me, / Unless thou take that honour from thy name'. 'Both sonnets', Ferry notes, 'allude to a separation which is not the kind conventional to love poetry, as the speaker in each feels the need to explain'.[2] Her point is that the sonnets are qualitatively different because we are asked to imagine overhearing speech between lovers sharing intimate knowledge. I will extend this idea and argue that, among Elizabethan love poets, Shakespeare is the most consistently intimate in tone.

In 'Scorn not the sonnet', William Wordsworth famously declares: 'with this key / Shakespeare unlocked his heart'. It would be easy to dismiss Wordsworth's claim as romantic, but many readers have felt the same, perhaps because of a simple fact: the *Sonnets* poet frequently addresses his beloved. It might be supposed that Elizabethan love sonnets mostly plead to the beloved, but in fact they infrequently do. In Thomas Watson's *Hekatompathia* and *Tears of Fancy*, the number of sonnets in which the poet addresses his mistress can be counted on one hand. In Sidney's *Astrophil and Stella*, Stella is not addressed by Astrophil until Sonnet 30 and only irregularly thereafter. Only 16 of 50 sonnets in Samuel Daniel's first edition of *Delia* address Delia, and half of them come in one series. About one third of Spenser's sonnets in *Amoretti* address the woman whom the poet is wooing, and many of them refer to her in the third person until the couplet. Henry Constable and Michael Drayton buck the trend somewhat: *Diana* (MS version) and *Idea's Mirror* begin by addressing the beloved often (in 16 of 21 sonnets and in 11 of 14 sonnets, respectively), only to drop off precipitously: less than half of each poet's total address the beloved. And *Shakespeare's Sonnets*? Over 80 per cent of the first 126 poems address the youth; over 60 per cent of the final 28 sonnets address the mistress – a figure that rises to almost 70 per cent if one formally irregular sonnet (145) and two sonnets that tell stories about Cupid (153–4) are left out of the count. All told, at least 122 of the 154 sonnets address the beloved. In such a context, even poems that do not directly address the beloved can feel as though they do.

Shakespeare's Sonnets is unusual in its manner of address; it is unique in the way that it delays the introduction of first-person singular pronouns. As MacDonald P. Jackson notes in his analysis of *Sonnets*' distribution of pronouns, the pronouns 'I', 'me', 'my', 'myself', and 'mine' do not appear in Sonnets 1–9.[3] No other English sequence opens in this fashion; the usual approach is to establish the poet's persona from the outset. This oddity may owe something to the theme on which the author may have been commissioned to write – urging a young nobleman to have children – but, even so,

Shakespeare employs pronouns in distinctive ways. I call attention to the following peculiarities:

> The first first-person singular pronoun occurs in line 9 of Sonnet 10. From Sonnet 12 on, the poet generally uses first-person pronouns.
>
> When directly addressing the mistress, mythical figures, and inanimate objects, the poet uses forms of 'thou'.
>
> When directly addressing the fair youth, the poet uses thou-forms in some sonnets and you-forms in others.
>
> One sonnet, 24, mixes thou-forms and you-forms when addressing the youth.
>
> There are many runs of poems in which the poet uses only thou-forms or only you-forms when addressing the youth.
>
> In Sonnets 63–8, the poet speaks of the youth in the third person.
>
> After Sonnet 68, you-forms predominate, though thou-forms and indirect address are used at the very end of the fair-youth section (Sonnets 122–6).

The distribution of pronouns in *Sonnets* points to design. In a later chapter, I will argue that pronoun forms point to organisational schemes; here I will focus on rhetorical effects.

Shakespeare's Sonnets begins impersonally but soon becomes intimate in tone. As Jackson explains, Sonnet 10's introduction of 'I' is momentous:

> 'O, change thy thought, that I may change my mind', the poet entreats, and then in the couplet: 'Make thee another self for love of me, / That beauty still may live in thine or thee'. The phrase 'for love of me' is the first suggestion that the poet may have some claim over the fair youth's affections. From this hint a relationship will develop.[4]

The first 'I' is meant to attract attention: it is preceded by 'O change thy thought'; it is in the ninth-line turn; and it marks a shift in mode of persuasion. The poet's outburst is presented as if it has been held in check to this point. Jackson argues for a similar shift in tone in Sonnet 13, the first you-sonnet: 'Like French "vous" in contrast to "tu", *you* was, in Shakespeare's England, potentially less intimate', but in Sonnet 13, it 'signals an *increase* in intimacy', and the poet 'goes so far as to address the youth as "love" in the opening line'.[5] In other words, Sonnet 13's exclamatory opening is reinforced by the new pronoun forms: 'O that you were yourself! But, love, you are / No longer yours'. A few sonnets later, in 18, Shakespeare shifts back to thou-forms with another dramatic opening line ('Shall I compare thee to a summer's day?'), signalling another increase in intimacy by reverting to the familiar form. The switch to thou-forms is more definitive than the switch to you-forms: Sonnet 18 inaugurates a 34-poem series in which the poet uses thou-forms when directly addressing the youth.

After turning to 'thou' with 'Shall I compare thee', the poet establishes a tone of intimacy that remains the default mode through Sonnet 125. The story of love's growth, however, climaxes in Sonnet 25, which concludes: 'Then happy I, that love and am belovèd / Where I may not remove, nor be removèd'. This couplet may imply that the poet and the youth have plighted troth. Troth or no troth, Sonnet 25 anticipates Sonnet 116, in which the poet speaks of a 'marriage of true minds' and declares: 'Love is not love [when it] bends with the remover to remove'. The poet's friendship with the youth would seem to have reached a high and stable point in Sonnet 25. Soon after, however, problems arise; the love and security of which the poet boasts are ironised by the ensuing narrative. The story of intimacy is artistically shaped: emotional outbursts and allusions to events are arranged for effect; Shakespeare often puts the reader in the position of the poet reacting in the moment. Like the poet, who learns to distrust appearances, the reader is being taught to be a suspicious interpreter.

Pairs, Trios, and Other Groups of Sonnets

Shakespeare's Sonnets contains many intensively linked poems: consecutive sonnets that signal transitions with unambiguous cues, such as coordinating conjunctions. Sonnets 15–17, for example, present arguments for poetic and biological immortality: 15 introduces the theme of poetry's power to fight Time; 16 opens with 'But' and counters 15 with a plea for procreation; and 17 synthesises 15's and 16's arguments about art and nature. Lists of linked poems are a staple of commentaries, notably those of Jackson, West, Kerrigan, Booth, and Edmondson and Wells.[6] The lists show a high degree of agreement, especially with runs of two and three sonnets (pairs and trios). Over 70 per cent of the sequence's 154 sonnets are linked to at least one directly preceding or ensuing poem. Because Shakespeare's sequence contains many clearly linked sonnets, ambiguously linked sonnets may seem connected when they are read in sequence, and sonnets that do not initially appear to be linked may be worth a second look. The moral here is twofold: sequential context matters, and it is productive to expect inter-sonnet connections. To illustrate both principles, let us turn to Sonnets 115–17. Like 15–17, these three sonnets can be read as a trio.

Popular at weddings and often anthologised, the second poem of the series has traditionally been regarded as a confident assertion about love's existence and endurance:

> Sonnet 116
> Let me not to the marriage of true minds
> Admit impediments. Love is not love
> Which alters when it alteration finds
> Or bends with the remover to remove:
> O no, it is an ever-fixèd mark
> That looks on tempests and is never shaken;
> It is the star to every wand'ring bark
> Whose worth's unknown, although his height be taken.
> Love's not Time's fool, though rosy lips and cheeks
> Within his bending sickle's compass come;
> Love alters not with his brief hours and weeks
> But bears it out, ev'n to the edge of doom.
>   If this be error and upon me proved,
>   I never writ, nor no man ever loved.

In the last half century or so, however, Sonnet 116 has increasingly been read as expressing ambivalent or negative feelings. The poem provides evidence for both interpretations, the affirming and the sceptical.

Advocates of the affirming interpretation can point to weddings and anthologies, and to readers like Wordsworth, who considered 116 among Shakespeare's finest sonnets.[7] But the endorsement of romantics (of the incurable variety or the Wordsworthian) is not likely to convince sceptics, who can argue that modern readers are influenced by the ways in which 116 has been packaged for consumption. Then again, the affirming interpretation may have been standard in the seventeenth century, to judge from a version of 116 set to music by Henry Lawes (1595–1662). Lawes's setting adds glosses, such as the couplet appended to the second quatrain:

> O no, love is an ever fixèd mark
> That looks on tempests but is never shaken;
> It is the star to every wand'ring bark
> Whose worth's unknown, although his height be taken:
>   No mountebank with eye-deluding flashes,
>   But flaming martyr in his holy ashes.[8]

Love is not some quack with eye-deceiving tricks, but a holy martyr willing to be burned at the stake for his beliefs. The couplet reinforces the poet's declaration that love is powerful and steadfast, and it suggests that the defining feature of love is constancy: 'true minds' are faithful, devoted minds. The notion that love is an unchanging thing, 'an ever-fixèd mark', may give today's readers pause, but if the poet is saying that love should endure despite change – that we should love in sickness and in health, for richer and for poorer – we need not be put off by the emphasis on love's fixed nature. The love in question is an ideal to live by.

Still, there are aspects of 116 that could reveal ambivalent feelings. Suspicious details include the legalisms (especially the oath) and the negative expressions ('Let me not', 'Love is not love', 'Love's not Time's fool'), which risk coming across as defensive. Vendler argues that the sonnet rebuts someone who has said 'I did love you once, but things have changed' and that its opening verges on sarcasm: 'Let *me* not to the marriage of true minds / Admit impediments' (Vendler's italics).[9] With similar scepticism, Kerrigan declares that 116 'has been misread so often and so mawkishly that it is necessary to say at once, if brutally, that Shakespeare is writing about what cannot be attained'.[10] Kerrigan ultimately considers an ironic interpretation 'available' rather than dominant, but he expresses more distrust than faith in the poet's declarations. Understanding the sonnet may be mostly about distinguishing tone.

Tone may be informed by context, of course. As an anthology piece, Sonnet 116 invites us to imagine its occasion (such as Vendler's scenario) or to supply our own occasion (such as a wedding). Treating 116 as a 'speech act' for an occasion has its advantages – it reminds us of artifice – but it is misleading insofar as it suggests that the poem alone creates its situation. In gauging 116's tone, it is important to hear allusions to *The Book of Common Prayer* and to take sequential context into account. Allusions to the marriage ceremony in *The Book of Common Prayer* have received attention from commentators (they will be discussed in a later chapter); the sequential context is often overlooked. Legal conceits connect the three sonnets: in 115, the poet defends himself against the accusation that his love has changed; in 116, he swears an oath in order to prove that his love is constant; and in 117, he urges his beloved to accuse him of faults, concedes that his actions have been dubious, and 'proves' his innocence by pointing to the language of his appeal. Sonnets 116 and 117 reinforce the conceits with their couplet rhymes, *proved–loved* and *prove–love*.

Rhetorical details of Sonnets 115 and 117 provide additional evidence that sequential context matters. In 115, the poet alludes to lines that he wrote previously:

> Those lines that I before have writ do lie,
> Ev'n those that said I could not love you dearer:
> Yet then my judgement knew no reason why
> My most full flame should afterwards burn clearer.
> But reck'ning Time, whose millioned accidents
> Creep in 'twixt vows and change decrees of kings,
> Tan sacred beauty, blunt the sharp'st intents,
> Divert strong minds to th' course of alt'ring things –
> Alas! why, fearing of Time's tyranny,
> Might I not then say, 'Now I love you best',
> When I was certain o'er incertainty,
> Crowning the present, doubting of the rest?
>   Love is a babe: then might I not say so,
>   To give full growth to that which still doth grow?

In earlier sonnets, the poet asserts that his love is constant and that his beloved is everything, but he never says 'I could not love you dearer' or 'Now I love you best'. (The closest analogue is 48's 'Thou best of dearest'.) Whether or not he is alluding to specific lines, his gesture is significant. He is arguing that, even if time's 'accidents' have turned his words to lies, he both told and always tells the truth about his love. Judged from the right perspective, he has been true.

Note, however, that our understanding of his pleas requires re-evaluation. The phrase 'reck'ning Time' could suggest that Time is doing the reckoning, but it turns out to mean 'taking Time into account'. 'Might I not then say' invites us to consider 'Might I not therefore say', but it must mean 'Might I not back then have said' given the 'when' clause that follows it. The couplet is similarly ambiguous: 'Love is a babe: then might I not say so, / To give full growth to that which still doth grow?' Given the 'then' in 'Might I not then say', we might hear this 'then' as 'back then', but it more likely means 'therefore': couplets promise conclusion; 'to give' points to the present; and repeating a word and changing its meaning is a common rhetorical figure in *Sonnets*.[11] And though many commentators argue that the 'so' in 'say so' refers to 'Now I love you best' or phrases like it, 'Love is a babe' is closer: 'say so' might mean 'speak in this playful fashion'. (Even the final question mark may be questioned: in Q, Sonnet 115 concludes with a period.[12]) For all the ambiguity, 115's argument is clear. Since Love (Cupid) is and always will be a baby, the poet's love is and always will be capable of growing yet full-grown. No matter when he says things like 'I can't love you more than I do now', the poet speaks a kind of truth.

Sonnet 116's declarations contrast sharply with 115's strained logic; in this light, we may read 115 as anxious and 116 as desperate. The contrasting modes of address are also telling. In 115, the poet addresses his beloved as 'you'; in 116, he does not directly address the youth. Despite the absence of second-person pronouns, he may still be addressing him: the 'please allow me' gesture in 116 chimes with the 'may I not say so' gesture in 115. Alternatively, the poet is addressing himself or no one in particular. Insofar as the sonnet turns away from the beloved to ponder or appeal to love, it is prayer-like: we might say that the poet is praying within earshot of his beloved or is appealing to his beloved's better feelings. Whatever the mode of address, Sonnet 116's connections to 115 suggest that the poet is anxious about 'alt'ring things' – changing circumstances, things that change, things that cause change – and that he is searching for a way not to feel powerless in the face of them. For such a person, 'an ever-fixèd mark' is highly desirable.

The situation is comparable to that of a man who wants badly to have his day in court but fears he will not get a hearing. In the end, he seems willing to plead guilty to all charges:

> Sonnet 117
> Accuse me thus: that I have scanted all,
> Wherein I should your great deserts repay,
> Forgot upon your dearest love to call,
> Whereto all bonds do tie me day by day;
> That I have frequent been with unknown minds
> And giv'n to Time your own dear-purchased right;
> That I have hoisted sail to all the winds
> Which should transport me farthest from your sight.
> Book both my willfulness and errors down
> And on just proof surmise accumulate;
> Bring me within the level of your frown,
> But shoot not at me in your wakened hate –
>   Since my appeal says I did strive to prove
>   The constancy and virtue of your love.

As an argument, the appeal in the couplet is weak, and commentators have taken Shakespeare to task for it. West writes:

> In the final couplet [the poet] makes an appeal in extenuation of his offences, and it is so inept, so grotesque, that a man with Shakespeare's understanding of human nature could never have made it on his own

behalf: 'I've been away and neglected you and had lots of love affairs, but I was doing it to make a strenuous attempt to test you.' Any man who spoke like this to a lover would be taking his life in his hands.[13]

In West's view, Shakespeare is 'developing the character of the offending lover and ingenious apologist', and this character is 'not a portrait of the author, but a fiction'.[14] Shakespeare may be playing a role in 117, but there is no need to insist on either/or logic: the medium of poetry may allow someone to say something to a lover that ordinary circumstances would not permit; the *Sonnets* poet may be both character and author.

Reading Sonnets 115–17 as a trio has implications for reading *Sonnets* as a sequence. Due to uncertainties about Shakespeare's role in the sequence's publication, to printing flaws, and to the lack of a straightforward narrative, commentators have tended to shy away from all but the most obvious connections between poems. One exception is West:

> This [poem] is the 116th sonnet in a collection devoted to the love between the poet and a young man. Sonnets 109–21 form a group in which [the poet] admits his infidelities and asks to be forgiven. He flatters his beloved, pleads for pity, and multiplies outrageous excuses and far-fetched arguments in an attempt to win his way back into favour . . . Read in context, [Sonnet 116's] noble expression of the constancy and strength of human love is a diplomatic manoeuvre.[15]

These observations are incisive, but similar logic could be used to argue that the context heightens the poet's sincerity. However we decide on the tone of sonnet, sequential context is crucial. In my view, 116 is affirming in a desperate way and this becomes easier to see when the poem is understood as belonging to different schemes. Sonnet 116's position near the end of the fair-youth section gives a gendered colouring to 'the marriage of true minds' and contributes to the idea that a climax is near. Its prominence is enhanced by its central position in the infidelity group to which West refers and its pivotal position among the 'marriage sonnets' that close the fair-youth section and mirror the 'procreation sonnets' at the beginning.

Sonnet Sequences and the Publication of *Shakespeare's Sonnets*

In order to set the stage for the organisational schemes, it is important to discuss the genre of the sonnet sequence and to consider traditional tales about *Sonnets*. One underlying question is how typical or unusual *Sonnets* is. There may be no simple answer to this question, but two items bear keeping in mind: much of the sequence is addressed to a man; the portion addressed to a woman expresses sexual desire openly. There is one other contemporary sequence in which a male poet's attentions are centred on a man – Barnfield's *Certain Sonnets* (in *Cynthia*, 1597) – and that work approaches its subject through a veil of pastoral conventions. Similarly, while there are other sequences in which the male poet craves physical relations with a woman – *Astrophil and Stella*, for instance, or (notoriously) *Parthenophil and Parthenophe* – *Sonnets* is atypical because the poet speaks not about winning the heart of an unattainable woman, but of an available and perhaps promiscuous woman with whom he has sexual relations. In other words, the *Sonnets* poet presents his love for a man in language traditionally employed to express love for women, and he uses distinctly physical language to express his love for a woman.

Shakespeare's Sonnets was not published until 1609, but its story might be said to begin in 1591. This is the year in which *Astrophil and Stella* first appeared in print. (To distinguish this edition from later ones, I will refer to it as A&S.) Sidney had died in 1586 of wounds received in a battle in the Netherlands, but his image as a model knight was very much alive in the 1590s. Composed around 1582, *Astrophil and Stella* circulated in manuscript among friends and family; its reputation, if not the manuscript, went beyond this circle. Early readers admired the sequence for qualities that remain appealing – its dramatic immediacy and its skilful mix of registers of speech. The author's early death also played a role in its fame. As Sidney's star rose, publishers were eager to acquire his works. In 1590, his *Arcadia* was printed under the direction of a friend, Fulke Greville, partly in response to the threat of an unauthorised edition. Greville worked with the Sidney family; the publisher of A&S, Thomas Newman, did not have the family's blessing. Newman seems to have tried to placate the Sidneys by removing indecorous verse and appealing for pardon in his dedication. Notwithstanding these efforts, Sidney's sister, the Countess of Pembroke, convinced authorities to issue an order to suppress A&S.[16]

The order did little to prevent the text and fame of *Astrophil and Stella* from spreading. Newman put out a second edition before the end of 1591, and another edition based on Newman's appeared in advance of the family-sanctioned version of 1598. By that time, sonnet sequences had become popular in England, due in no small part to Newman's editions. (For a list of Elizabethan and Jacobean sequences, see Appendix A.) Shakespeare may have been writing sonnets in the early 1590s, but he seems not to have been in the vanguard of English sonneteers. Not only is there evidence that his sonnets were influenced by sequences published in the early and mid-1590s; the *Sonnets* poet acknowledges fashion while emphasising that he does not follow it. In his plays, moreover, Shakespeare associates sonnets with lunacy and insincerity. Instead of rushing into sonnet writing, he may have come to it late, ambivalently.

Whenever Shakespeare started writing sonnets, he was influenced by Sidney and the genre that developed after A&S. Sidney's work primed readers to believe that characters and events in sequences were drawn from the poet's life: *Astrophil and Stella* drops autobiographical hints, such as references to tournaments in which Sidney jousted and puns indicating that Astrophil is Sidney and Stella is Penelope Rich. *Astrophil and Stella*'s story is distinctive not because it involves adulterous passion – adoration of a married woman is a convention of courtly love poetry, after all – but because the knight and lady were identifiable contemporaries, and because Astrophil declares that love demands physical expression: '"But ah", Desire still cries, "give me some food"' (Sonnet 71). Early readers often connected the sequence to Sidney's life, and Sidney's family and friends eventually embraced such interpretations. As a twenty-first-century editor of *Astrophil and Stella* remarks, 'five of the seven books dedicated to Penelope Rich between 1594 and 1606 connect her with Astrophil, suggesting that she happily accepted the identification'.[17]

Most Elizabethan sequences after Sidney's strike modern readers as artificial and impersonal, but the likelihood that even they were read biographically can be gauged from Giles Fletcher's introduction to *Licia* (1593). Fletcher archly notes:

> For this kind of poetry wherein I wrote, I did it only to try my humour. And for the matter of love, it may be I am so devoted to someone into whose hands these may light by chance, that she may say . . . 'Surely he is in love' – which if she do, then have I the full recompense of my labour . . . If thou muse what my Licia is, take her to be some Diana . . . or some Minerva – no, Venus (fairer far). It may be that she is learning's image . . . It may be my conceit, and pretend nothing.

Commentators have cited this passage as proof that sonnet sequences are purely fictional, but Fletcher's hint that his sonnets were being read biographically argues otherwise. In wearing its fiction on its sleeve – Licia interacts with Jove, Venus, and other mythical figures – *Licia* invites allegorical interpretations. And Fletcher's own interpretations imply that he expected readers to look for biography. Indeed, by mentioning a lady to whom he is devoted and brushing aside the idea that real experiences lie behind his sonnets, Fletcher may be baiting readers to imagine a background story, if not to read the sequence as highly personal.

If only because his sonnets are intimate in tone, Shakespeare may have held them close. A passage from Francis Meres's *Palladis Tamia* (1598) indicates that his first audience was small: 'The witty soul of Ovid lives in mellifluous and honey-tongued Shakespeare; witness his *Venus and Adonis*, his *Lucrece*, his sugared sonnets among his private friends, etc'.[18] Most commentators regard these 'sugared sonnets' as *Sonnets*' sonnets or as early versions of them. Shakespeare wrote at least some of his sequence before the turn of the seventeenth century, as evidenced by the versions of Sonnets 138 and 144 in *The Passionate Pilgrim*, a collection of songs and sonnets first published in 1598 or 1599 by William Jaggard.[19] Some remarks made by the poet and playwright Thomas Heywood, prompted by the 1612 edition of *The Passionate Pilgrim*, may indicate that Shakespeare was unhappy with the unauthorised publication: 'the author [was] I know much offended with M. Jaggard, that altogether unknown to him presumed to make so bold with his name'.[20]

Authorised or not, a book whose title page reads 'SHAKE-SPEARE'S SONNETS / Never Before Imprinted' was published by Thomas Thorpe in 1609. On the page after the title page, there is a dedication that has provoked much speculation: 'TO THE ONLY BEGETTER / OF THESE ENSUING SONNETS / MR. W.H. ALL-HAPPINESS / AND THAT ETERNITY / PROMISED / BY / OUR EVER-LIVING POET / WISHETH / THE WELL-WISHING / ADVENTURER IN / SETTING FORTH / T.T' (see Figure 1.1). Most commentators take the dedication to mean something like this: 'In setting forth on the venture of publishing this book, the well-wishing adventurer, Thomas Thorpe, wishes the only source and inspirer of the following sonnets, Mr W.H., to have all happiness and the eternity promised to him by our ever-living poet William Shakespeare.' With his layout and typography – uppercase and centred Roman letters, tapering downwards in a vaguely triangular pattern – Thorpe imitates the kind of engraved text that might be found on a monument. As Duncan-Jones notes, a similar 'mock-lapidary' dedication appears at the beginning of Ben Jonson's 1607 quarto edition of *Volpone*.[21] Thorpe also draws on themes in the sonnets, such as the poet's pleas to the young nobleman to beget children. Thorpe's fondness for wordplay is evidenced in 'setting forth' (beginning to make one's way in the world, undertaking an economic venture, printing/publishing),

TO.THE.ONLIE.BEGETTER.OF.
THESE.INSVING.SONNETS.
Mr. W. H. ALL.HAPPINESSE.
AND.THAT.ETERNITIE.
PROMISED.

BY.

OVR.EVER-LIVING.POET.

WISHETH.

THE.WELL-WISHING.
ADVENTVRER.IN.
SETTING.
FORTH.

T. T.

Figure 1.1 Thomas Thorpe's dedication to Shakespeare's Sonnets (1609)

'our ever-living poet' (the immortal Shakespeare was literally still living in 1609), and 'only begetter' (Christ as 'the only begotten son'). Whatever the dedication's exact meaning, the layout reflects a Renaissance printing practice: ending sections of books with text that is centred and tapering downwards (see Figures 1.2 and 1.3). And whatever 'Mr W.H.' signifies, it is worth pausing over 'only' in 'only begetter'. Perhaps the echo of 'only begotten' explains it. Commentators have also claimed that Thorpe is hinting that the youth is unmarried ('only' as 'single') or has yet to father a child – he has only begotten sonnets. Thorpe may be a hack, but, even so, intimations of this sort would be gauche. If Thorpe is taking his cue from *Sonnets*, he is probably alluding to the poet's recurrent claims to constancy and devotion. As the poet says of the youth in Sonnet 48: 'Thou best of dearest and mine *only* care' (emphasis added). Thorpe could also be asserting that the youth is the poet's essential source of inspiration, and that the mistress sonnets were also written for him.

There is another possibility for 'only'. Anticipating that readers might think otherwise, Thorpe is emphasising that there is only one begetter – that *Sonnets* was written for one patron or beloved, even if Shakespeare later courted another. If 'begetter' means 'inspirer', as it conventionally does in dedications, there are essentially two plausible

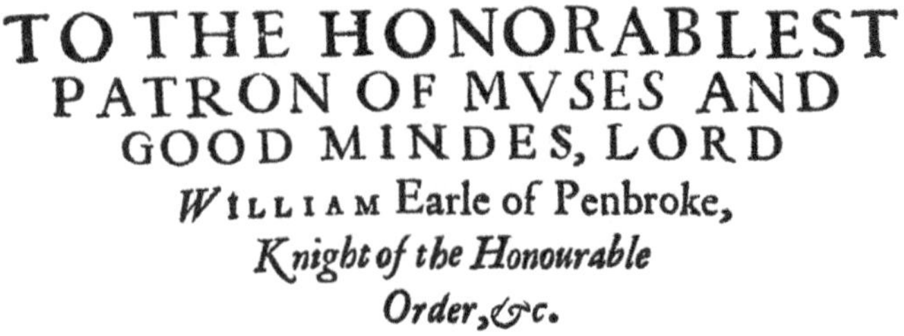

TO THE HONORABLEST
PATRON OF MVSES AND
GOOD MINDES, LORD
*W*ɪʟʟɪᴀᴍ Earle of Penbroke,
*K*night of the Honourable
Order,&c.

Figure 1.2 Conclusion to Thomas Thorpe's dedication to Pembroke in St. Augustine, Of the City of God (1610)

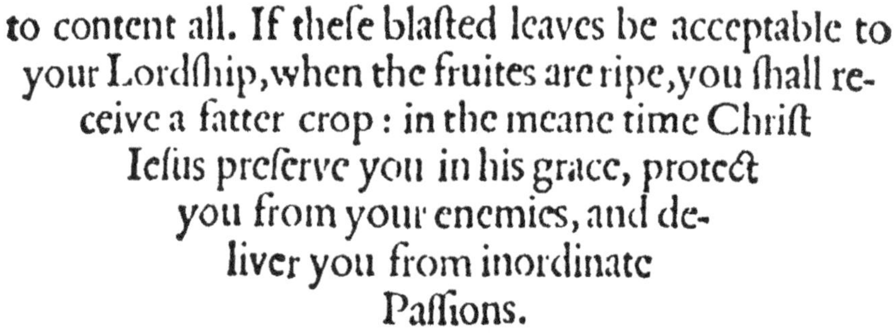

to content all. If these blasted leaves be acceptable to your Lordship, when the fruites are ripe, you shall receive a fatter crop: in the meane time Christ Iesus preserve you in his grace, protect you from your enemies, and deliver you from inordinate Passions.

Figure 1.3 Conclusion to Thomas Wright's dedication to Southampton in The Passions of the Mind (1604)

candidates for 'Mr W.H.': Henry Wriothesley, who was born in October of 1573 and became the third Earl of Southampton in 1581; and William Herbert, who was born in April of 1580 and became the third Earl of Pembroke in 1601.[22] 'Mr' ('master' or 'mister') may derive from Sonnet 20's 'master mistress'. Some commentators have stressed that 'Mr' would be a defamatory way to address an earl and might therefore disqualify both earls as the youth. But as Beeching wryly notes in his edition of *Sonnets*, commentators sceptical of the idea that a peer might be addressed as 'mister' have 'perhaps not always sufficiently considered the impossibility of dedicating [the sequence] "To the Right Honourable William, Earl of Pembroke, Lord Chamberlaine to His Majestie, etc"'.[23] If the dedication had overtly linked a living earl to the fair youth, it might well have prompted legal action against the publisher; 'Mr', by contrast, points away from high nobility and may have provided some cover for Thorpe. 'W.H.' is perhaps strategic in another way: it allows for both 'Henry Wriothesley' (reversed initials) and 'William Herbert'.

What are the consequences of assuming that Mr W.H. is one of the earls or both earls? Most immediately, dating the sonnets is at stake.

If W.H. is Southampton, Shakespeare likely began writing in the early or mid-1590s, because the sequence emphasises the nobleman's youth. Shakespeare dedicated *Venus and Adonis* to Southampton in 1593. Since the *Venus and Adonis* dedication indicates that he had no prior contact with the earl, we might take 1593 as a starting date, or even 1594: the year in which Shakespeare published *Lucrece* and promised Southampton more poetry. But if W.H. is Pembroke, Shakespeare more likely started writing sonnets in the late 1590s. Herbert's seventeenth birthday in 1597 could have been the occasion for writing: perhaps the first seventeen sonnets were composed at the request of the youth's family. If W.H. is a cipher for both earls, Shakespeare likely composed the sonnets over many years. The time frame for composition may be lengthy regardless, especially if putting the final sequence together entailed revising sonnets and writing new ones.

Dating the sonnets is complicated by topical allusions. In Sonnet 104, the poet notes that 'Three April perfumes [have into] three hot Junes burned / Since first I saw you fresh', suggesting that three years have passed since he first saw the youth. In 107, he remarks that 'The mortal moon hath her eclipse endured . . . / And peace proclaims olives of endless age', suggesting an allusion to Elizabeth as a Diana-like virgin queen. If Sonnet 104's 'Three April perfumes' refers to three years, and if 107's 'mortal moon' is Elizabeth, the case for Southampton would have to be built around an event like the queen's surviving her 'grand climacteric' (sixty-third year) in 1596–7, and the case for Pembroke built around, say, the queen's surviving the Essex Rebellion in 1601. But there is ample precedent for symbolic periods of time in sonnet collections, especially the period of three years.[24] We might suppose that Shakespeare wrote some sonnets in the year or so before he first saw the youth, and more sonnets in the year or so after the three Aprils had passed, but even a five- or six-year period is too short for many commentators, especially if 107's lines about the 'mortal moon' and 'olives of endless age' allude to Elizabeth's death and James I's peaceful succession in 1603. Under any scenario, the vagueness of topical references would be strategic.

Identifying W.H. as one of the earls has its rewards. Those who favour Southampton can make use of both his Christian name (Henry/Hal) and his surname (Wriothesley). ('Wriothesley' was probably pronounced 'RISE-lee' or 'RYE-ose-lee', though 'Rye-OAT-ess-lee', 'RIZ-lee', and 'ROSE-lee' cannot be ruled out.[25]) Some have argued for puns on 'rose' in lines like 'my rose . . . thou art my all' (Sonnet 109), but it may be more productive to look for puns relating to 'rise' – especially in the 'rising sun' language of Sonnet 33, which closely resembles Hal's 'herein will I imitate the sun' soliloquy in *1 Henry IV*. The Wriothesley family motto, *Ung par tout, et tout par ung* ('One through all, and all through one'), has been brought forward to interpret some lines, including Sonnet 105's 'To one, of one, still such, and ever so'.[26] And Southampton's 1603 release from the Tower of London has been linked to line 4 of Sonnet 107, in which the poet declares that his love has not been the casualty of a 'cónfined doom'.

Suggestive possibilities also exist for Herbert. Many commentators have called attention to puns on 'will' in Sonnets 134–6, which could indicate that more than one Will has slept with the mistress. The fact that Shakespeare and Herbert had the same Christian name, had birthdays in the same month, and were eldest sons is consistent with the poet's tendency to identify with the young nobleman, as may be evidenced in lines like ''Tis thee, my self, that for myself I praise' (Sonnet 62) and 'April's first-born flowers' (Sonnet 21). The Herbert family motto, *Ung je servirai* ('I will serve one'), may fit *Sonnets'* themes of constancy better than the Wriothesley motto. Some commentators have pointed to the fact that William Herbert's mother was Mary Herbert, Countess of Pembroke and sister of Phillip Sidney. Given her reputation for patronage and beauty, along with the possibility that she commissioned Shakespeare to write poems urging her son to marry and have children, two lines from Sonnet 3 stand out: 'Thou art thy mother's glass, and she in thee / Calls back the lovely April of her prime'.

This sort of interpretation can be extended to parallels between *Sonnets* and other works, with similar results: it would seem impossible to prove that the youth was modelled on one (or both) of the earls, and remiss not to consider the possibilities. Given the tantalising and inconclusive evidence, recent Shakespeare biographers have floated the idea that sonnets written for Wriothesley were recycled for Herbert.[27] That view will be taken up later. For now I would note that recycling poems needn't imply less emotional investment. Not only may poets feel similar love for different persons; poets who reuse poems may care greatly about the poetry that they recycle and the people for whom they intend it – as Pierre Ronsard and Samuel Daniel seem to have cared when they revised and rededicated their sequences. *Sonnets* is distinctive because of its rhetoric of intimacy, its intense concern with betrayal, and its insistence on devotion to one person along with the poet's confession of infidelity.

Chapter 2

The Basic Scheme

Shakespeare's Sonnets has a pyramidal organisation. In its basic form, the scheme invites us to see groups of poems that decrease in size incrementally: 17 sonnets, 16 sonnets, 15 sonnets, and so on. (These are the pyramid's 'steps' or 'stories'.) Shakespeare may have decided on the scheme after he had written most of his sonnets – he may have revised or added poems to fit the scheme – but when and how he composed his sequence are tangential questions at this stage. Similarly tangential is the question of whether Shakespeare had a hand in *Sonnets*' publication: it is enough to say that the manuscripts used by the publisher represented Shakespeare's intentions well. It should go without saying that the scheme is a visual conceit:

Step 17:	LC	
Step 16:	153 154	
Step 15:	150 151 152	{ Part 2 of the
Step 14:	146 147 148 149	mistress section
	[145]	
Step 13:	140 141 142 143 144	{ Part 1 of the
Step 12:	134 135 136 137 138 139	mistress section
Step 11:	127 128 129 130 131 132 133	
	[126]	
Step 10:	118 119 120 121 122 123 124 125	{ Part 2 of the
Step 9:	109 110 111 112 113 114 115 116 117	fair-youth
Step 8:	99 100 101 102 103 104 105 106 107 108	section
	[99]	
Step 7:	88 89 90 91 92 93 94 95 96 97 98	{ Part 1
Step 6:	76 77 78 79 80 81 82 83 84 85 86 87	of the
Step 5:	63 64 65 66 67 68 69 70 71 72 73 74 75	fair-
Step 4:	49 50 51 52 53 54 55 56 57 58 59 60 61 62	youth
Step 3:	34 35 36 37 38 39 40 41 42 43 44 45 46 47 48	section
Step 2:	18 19 20 21 22 23 24 25 26 27 28 29 30 31 32 33	
Step 1:	1 2 3 4 5 6 7 8 9 10 11 12 13 14 15 16 17	

'LC' stands for 'A Lover's Complaint'; the numbers signify sonnets. The three formally irregular sonnets (numbers 99, 126, and 145) mark divisions between parts.
(Because 99 is also the first sonnet in the eighth pyramid step, it is listed twice.)

This chapter explains the basic pyramidal scheme and begins to explore its implications for interpreting *Sonnets*.

The Monument Trio and Non-consecutive Organisation

Shakespeare's pyramid consists of 17 consecutive groups of poems; these steps form a series that is punctuated at three points by irregular sonnets. The sequence also contains groups of non-consecutive poems. Like the pyramid steps, these groups are hidden in plain view; their arguments tend to be metapoetic and their sonnets tend not to fit seamlessly in their immediate contexts. One such group, 'the monument trio', sheds light on the sequence's organisational and numeric principles. This trio is independent of the main structure but shares the conceit that the sequence is a monument that will outlast the pyramids.

Sonnets 55, 81, and 107 are linguistically, positionally, and thematically related. Each poem uses 'monument' once, a word that occurs nowhere else in the sequence. (For rhyme's sake, 55's 'monument' is often emended to 'monuments'.) The word also appears in distinctive locations: in 55's first line, in 81's sestet-turn line, and in 107's couplet-turn line. What is more, the first and third sonnets are equidistant from the second: 55–81 is a 27-sonnet series; 81–107 is a 27-sonnet series. The trio is easier to see when the three poems are read in tandem:

> Sonnet 55
> Not marble, nor the gilded monument[s]
> Of princes shall outlive this powerful rhyme,
> But you shall shine more bright in these contents
> Than unswept stone besmeared with sluttish time.
> When wasteful war shall statues overturn,
> And broils root out the work of masonry,
> Nor Mars his sword nor war's quick fire shall burn
> The living record of your memory.
> 'Gainst death and all-oblivious enmity
> Shall you pace forth; your praise shall still find room

Ev'n in the eyes of all posterity
That wear this world out to the ending doom.
  So, till the judgement that yourself arise,
  You live in this, and dwell in lovers' eyes.

Sonnet 81
Or I shall live your epitaph to make
Or you survive when I in earth am rotten,
From hence your memory death cánnot take,
Although in me each part will be forgotten.
Your name from hence immortal life shall have,
Though I, once gone, to all the world must die.
The earth can yield me but a common grave
When you entombèd in men's eyes shall lie.
Your monument shall be my gentle verse,
Which eyes not yet created shall o'er-read,
And tongues to be your being shall rehearse
When all the breathers of this world are dead.
  You still shall live, such virtue hath my pen,
  Where breath most breathes, ev'n in the mouths of men.

Sonnet 107
Not mine own fears, nor the prophetic soul
Of the wide world, dreaming on things to come,
Can yet the lease of my true love control
Supposed as forfeit to a cónfined doom.
The mortal moon hath her eclipse endured,
And the sad augurs mock their own presage;
Incertainties now crown themselves assured,
And peace proclaims olives of endless age.
Now, with the drops of this most balmy time,
My love looks fresh, and Death to me subscribes,
Since, 'spite of him, I'll live in this poor rhyme
While he insults o'er dull and speechless tribes –
  And thou in this shalt find thy monument,
  When tyrants' crests and tombs of brass are spent.

The trio is signalled by the correlative conjunctions in the opening sentences: 'Not . . . nor' (55), 'Or . . . or' (81), and 'Not . . . nor' (107). As a series of reflections, the sonnets develop the idea that the poet's verse has power to preserve his beloved and his love, but the emphasis shifts. In Sonnet 55, the poet speaks of his ability to give life to his beloved; in 81, he declares that, thanks to his verse, his beloved's memory will henceforth be preserved; and in 107, he speaks of how his love has endured and will endure. More specifically, in 55, the beloved is to live in 'this' (the poet's verse); in 81, the poet is to have a 'common grave'; and in 107, the poet will live 'in this poor rhyme' and the beloved will 'find' a memorial in the poetry. And as the couplets indicate, the poet promises less as his power increases: 'You live in this, and dwell in lovers' eyes'; 'You still shall live . . . in the mouths of men'; and 'thou in this shalt find thy monument'. The trio succinctly illustrates the poet's evolving stance towards the youth.

The trio also explains why 81's links to adjacent sonnets are less intense: Sonnet 81 is in the middle of the rival-poet series but is not much concerned with rivalry; Shakespeare seems to have prioritised connecting it to the other monument sonnets. As will become clear as more schemes are discussed, 81 fits a pattern: a sonnet in a group of consecutive poems and a group of non-consecutive poems tends to be less tightly linked to the consecutive group. This pattern suggests that Shakespeare inserted poems like 81 into an existing sequence. Regardless, the disruption signals a scheme. Two equations also point to design in the trio's arrangement: $81=27\times3$ and $27=3\times3\times3$. In making the eighty-first sonnet the centre poem, and in placing the other sonnets around it to form two 27-sonnet series, Shakespeare calls attention to the powers of three and evokes a specific monument – a pyramid. However he worked the trio into the sequence, he may have had to make revisions. In 55, for example, he may have removed the *S* from 'monuments' in order to help signal the trio. He may also have been attracted by the phrase 'the monument of princes', as a periphrasis for 'pyramid'.

Sonnets invites us to find groups in two senses: to encounter them and to search for them. Both meanings are present in 107's 'thou . . . shalt find thy monument'. The phrase 'find thy monument' primarily means 'come to have or receive your memorial', but if that is all Shakespeare had wished to say, 'have thy monument' would have served him better.[1] Given line 4's 'cónfined doom', line 13's 'find' may hint at liberation and vitality: unlike other poets, whose verse is lifeless, the *Sonnets* poet has built a monument in which his beloved will be more quick than dead. He may also be evoking 'border' and 'end', which are etymologically present in 'cónfined' and 'fine'.[2] Elsewhere in the sequence, 'find' gestures towards such meanings:

> So should that beauty which you hold in lease
> Find no determination: then you were
> Yourself again after your self's decease . . .
>
> (Sonnet 13)

> For through the painter must you see his skill
> To find where your true image pictured lies . . .
>
> (Sonnet 24)

> [Whatever] thy memory cannot contain
> Commit to these waste blanks, and thou shalt find
> Those children nursed, delivered from thy brain . . .
>
> (Sonnet 77)

In these examples, 'find' appears in lines whose run-on effects are meant to be felt. When he wishes to emphasise breaching boundaries, Shakespeare reaches not only for enjambments, as we might expect, but for the word 'find'. More crucial, he uses 'find' and the line breaks in order to simulate the experience of discovery or of trying to discover. In Sonnet 107, however, 'find' is not placed before or after a line break, but securely inside the first of two end-stopped couplet lines: 'And thou in this shalt find thy monument, / When tyrants' crests and tombs of brass are spent'. As it closes, then, Sonnet 107 signals containment and reassurance. After defying the claims of the world, the poet offers the beloved a different kind of space in which to rest. He may also be offering advice to the reader: look for the hidden monument in *Sonnets* and thou shalt find it.

Pyramids in Renaissance Culture

In employing a pyramidal structure, Shakespeare signals that his sequence is a memorial meant to endure. Pyramidal memorials were commonplace in Renaissance England. They ranged from material objects, such as obelisk tombstones, to shape poetry, such as the elegy for Philip Sidney in *Exequiae Illustrissimi Equitis* (1587) and the elegy for the Prince of Wales in William Drummond of Hawthornden's *Tears on the Death of Meliades* (1613)[3] (see Figures 2.1 and 2.2). The elegiac association is implicit in John Milton's 'On Shakespeare' (1630): 'What needs my Shakespeare . . . that his hallowed relics should be hid / Under a star-ypointing pyramid?' Significantly, the *Sonnets* poet is wary of creating a tomb-like monument. In Sonnet 17, he worries that his verse is 'but as a tomb'; in 83, he speaks of rival poets who 'would give life, and bring a tomb'. Ideally, his pyramid will be a living monument: whenever *Sonnets* is read, the beloved will be 'entombed in men's eyes' or 'in the mouths of men' (81).

D. Ph. Sidnæi Exequiæ.

Auferte, Ciues, marmor, & ferrum impotens, Et æs Philippo, cesset artificum labor, Peritura sæclis opera; non illi est opus Isto sepulchri genere, composito suâ Pyramide, viuus ipse quam struxit sibi, Solidâ struem virtute, quadratâ, arduâ, Ægyptiorum sola quæ superet pyras Regum superbas; nulla cui par marmoris, Ferriq̃, & æru, esse durities potest. Quam nulla venti, nulla vis imbrium, Nec fulminantis ulla tempestas poli Eruere valeat, nulla quam minuat dies. Æternâ stabit, quàm diu pietas, fides, Relligio, Musæ, fama, nobilitas erunt. Annosa tanti memoria extabit viri, Tamen vsq̃ gratâ laude florescet recens, Viresq̃, ab annis sumet, & largum sequens Addet priori gloriæ cumulum dies.

D. Ph. Sidnæi Pyramis.

Figure 2.1 Latin elegy to Philip Sidney, Exequiae illustrissimi equitis (1587)

Figure 2.2 William Drummond's elegy to the Prince of Wales, Tears on the Death of Meliades (1613)

The poet's wariness about his monumentalising project is informed by distrust of and distaste for ostentatious tombs – common reactions in humanist and Protestant discussions of monuments of fame.[4] In *Virgidemiarum* (1597), for example, Joseph Hall satirises the building of large tombs by targeting 'Osmond', a wealthy man whose name derives from Ozymandias:

> Great *Osmond* knows not how he shall be known
> When once great *Osmond* shall be dead and gone:
> Unless he rear up some rich monument
> Ten furlongs nearer to the firmament.
> Some stately tomb he builds, Egyptian-wise,

> [*King of Kings*] written on the *Pyramis*.
> . . . .
> Thy monument make thou thy living deeds,
> No other tomb than that, true virtue needs.
> (Satire III.ii, lines 1–6, 13–14)

Sonnets is influenced by criticism of lavish monuments and excessive praise, even as it finesses the question of whether its memorialised person is virtuous. Sonnet 107 concludes: 'And thou in this shalt find thy monument / When tyrants' crests and tombs of brass are spent'. The poet is alluding to emblematic tyrants like Ozymandias. Sonnet 55 also criticises costly tombs: the poet declares that his work will outlive 'the gilded monuments / Of princes'. In Sonnet 64, the poet speaks derisively of 'The rich proud cost of outworn buried age'. And in Sonnet 101, he claims that his muse has the power to make his beloved 'much outlive a gilded tomb'.

Shakespeare's pyramid is primarily linked with time and eternity, but it is informed by other associations. Egyptian pyramids were popularly believed to be storehouses for grain or treasure. While many English writers would have known that the pyramids were in fact tombs, the persistence of other explanations can be gauged by George Sandys's account of his 1610 journey in Egypt, which aims to set the record straight: 'most manifest it is, that these [pyramids at Giza], as the rest, were royal sepulchers of the Egyptians'.[5] Even as large tombs, pyramids represent great wealth: they are imposing structures built by rich rulers; they house valuables; their size suggests abundance. King James evoked such associations when he had arches with columns topped by pyramids constructed for a procession through London in 1604, an event to which Sonnets 123 and 125 may allude.[6] Storehouse imagery in *Sonnets* may also be informed by the idea that pyramids contain fabulous wealth. In using the wealth motif and expressing uneasiness about gilded monuments of princes, Shakespeare strains to distinguish his memorial, and his beloved, from discreditable wealth and excess.

In Renaissance England, the word 'pyramid' or 'pyramis' could be applied to a wide range of triangular objects, including 'taper', 'spire', and 'obelisk':

> The taper is the longest and sharpest triangle that is, and while he mounts upward he waxeth continually more slender, taking both his figure and name of the fire – whose flame, if ye mark it, is always pointed – and naturally by his form covets to climb. The Greeks call him pyramis [from 'πυρ' 'pur' or 'pyr', the word for 'fire']. The Latins in use of architecture call him *obeliscus*. (George Puttenham, *The Art of English Poesy*)[7]

Classical philosophers often speak of fire as pyramid-shaped, relating it to the tetrahedron, one of the five perfect solids.[8] And according to Hermetic writings, the heart was pyramid-shaped.[9]

In Renaissance treatises on art, pyramids were used to illustrate linear perspective. In a typical diagram, the pyramid's apex is in the viewer's eye, and the base bisects the object on which the eye is focused (see Figures 2.3 and 2.4). A verbal description can be found in Giovanni Lomazzo's *Trattato dell'arte della pittura, scoltura, et architettura* (1584), which was translated by Richard Haydocke as *The Art of Pictorial Representation* (1598):

> The visual lines ... come to our eye in a pyramidal form, the base of which pyramis resteth in the object, and the *conus* or angle thereof cometh to our eye more blunt and obtuse. And hereby we see the object more plainly and distinctly; but if the object be afar off, the *conus* or angle of the pyramis comes to the eye sharper and lesser, and then our eye cannot discern it so clearly.[10]

Pyramidal sight lines are also mentioned in Thomas Wright's *The Passions of the Mind* (1604). In discussing the five senses, Wright lists 'Problems concerning the substance of our souls': 'Twenty more problems I could set down about the manner of seeing: about the pyramis, [whose] perspectives [we] imagine necessary for every operation of seeing'.[11] Sight lines offer a productive way to regard *Sonnets*' pyramid: each step is an attempt to find perspective.

Shakespeare may have been inspired by other concepts from visual arts, such as 'pyramidal proportion'. This idea is discussed by Lomazzo:

> Michelangelo upon a time gave this observation on to the painter Marco da Sienna ... *that he should always make a figure pyramidal, serpentlike, and multiplied by one, two, and three.* In which precept (in mine opinion) the whole mystery of the art consisteth. For the greatest grace and life that a picture can have is that it express motion [and] there is no form

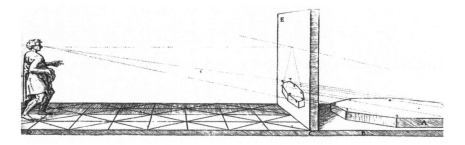

Figure 2.3 Giacomo Barozzi da Vignola, Two Rules of Practical Perspective (1583), page 55

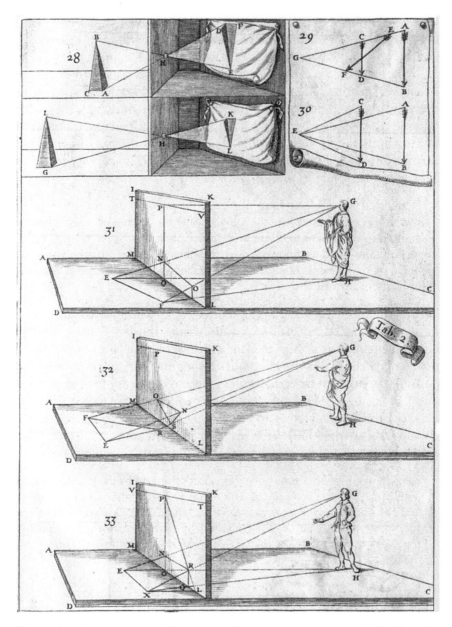

Figure 2.4 Jean-François Niceron, La Perspective curieuse (1638), Plate 2

so fit to express this motion as that of a flame of fire, which according to Aristotle . . . is an element most active of all others because the form of the flame thereof is most apt for motion, for it hath a *conus* or sharp point wherewith it seemeth to divide the air, that so it may ascend to its proper sphere.[12]

Figure 2.5 Michelangelo's and Lomazzo's serpentine figure as illustrated by Hogarth in The Analysis of Beauty (1753)

Michelangelo advises artists to paint figures in pyramidal and serpentine forms, with top, middle, and bottom widths in a 1:2:3 proportion (see Figure 2.5). Sonnet 123 may allude to this idea, if only because of its number and its use of 'pyramid', which appears nowhere else in *Sonnets*. Lomazzo moreover notes that pyramids are associated with Platonism and upward striving. According to Neoplatonic writers, sense seeks spirit: pyramidal flames want to rise to heaven.

Platonism, upward striving, and pyramids are central to Joshua Sylvester's *Divine Weeks* (1605), an adaptation of Guillaume Du Bartas's *La Sepmaine*. At one point, Sylvester exhorts Englishmen to avoid sensual love poetry, positioning himself against works like *Venus and Adonis*: 'O furnish me with an un-vulgar style, / That I by this may wean our wanton isle / From Ovid's heirs'.[13] Sylvester is showing his Puritan colours and championing a career based on Virgil and Sidney, as opposed to Ovid. In Sylvester's view, Sidney had rejected love poetry, and he was on the verge of writing a Protestant epic when he died. In a pyramidal sonnet that prefaces his translation (see Figure 2.6), Sylvester compares Sidney to a painter, a god, and a world-wonder:

> England's Apelles (rather, our Apollo,
> World's Wonder Sidney, that rare more-than-man)
> This lovely Venus first to limn began
> With such a pencil as no pen dares follow.
> How then should I, in wit and art so shallow,
> Attempt the task, which yet none other can?
> Far be the thought that mine unlearnèd hand
> His heav'nly labour should so much unhallow.
> Yet lest (that holy relic being shrined
> In some high place, close-locked from common light)
> My countrymen should be debarred the sight
> Of these divine pure beauties of the mind –
>   Not daring meddle with Apelles' table,
>   This have I muddled as my muse was able.

According to Sylvester, Sidney was the first English poet to translate *La Sepmaine*, and an artist as great as or greater than the painter Apelles. But Sidney's translation was never published: 'that holy relic [is] locked from common light'. In order not to deprive English speakers of Du Bartas's 'divine pure beauties of the mind', Sylvester has produced his own translation.

It may seem odd that a Puritan poet refers to Sidney as a god, to Sidney's translation as a 'holy relic', and to *Divine Weeks* as a 'lovely Venus'. One explanation is generic: homages call for hyperbole. Another is specific: Sidney's reputation was such that even Puritans might praise him in idolatrous terms, not least because he had died for a Protestant cause. In his pyramid-sonnet, Sylvester incorporates two icons from the Sidney coat of arms: a porcupine and a pheon (an arrow whose barbs face the shaft). In the Sidney coat, the pheon is below the porcupine and pointing down. Perhaps a symbol of zeal and ambition, the pheon is above the porcupine and pointing up. As for 'lovely Venus', it is hardly pagan: a 'lovely' Venus is not lustful; she is

ENGLAND'S
Apelles (rather
OVR APOLLO)
VVORLD'S--wonder
SIDNEY,
that 'rare more- then--man,
This LOVELY VENVS
firſt to LIMNE beganne,
VVith ſuch a PENCILL
as no PENNE dares followe:
How thē ſhold I, in Wit & Art ſo ſhalow,
Attēpt the *Task* which yet none other can?
Far be the thought that mine vnlearned hand
His heauenly Labour ſhold ſo much vnhallow,
Yet leaſt (that Holy-RELIQVE being ſhrin'd
In ſom High-Place, cloſe lockt frō cōmon light)
My Country-men ſhould bee debar'd the ſight
Of theſe DIVINE pure Beauties of the Minde;
Not daring meddle with APELLES TABLE;
This haue I muddled as my MVSE was able.

Figure 2.6 Joshua Sylvester's 'Sidney sonnet' from Divine Weeks (1605)

a representation of Love, or of God as Love. Like the upward-pointing pheon, this Venus underscores Sylvester's Christian Platonism.

The Basic Pyramidal Scheme

Sonnets' pyramid is informed by conventional associations: monument and heart metaphors, perspective lines, Neoplatonic striving, and so on. In order to gauge how relevant each is, we must analyse the pyramid's details. Again, the 153-poem pyramid is based in Sonnets 1–17, a series in which the poet urges a young man to beget an heir. This series is prominent because it opens the sequence and is large: a comparably sized group is hard to come by elsewhere. Different explanations have been offered for the procreation poems, including the theory that Shakespeare was commissioned to write them for an unmarried heir living beyond his means. A variation on this theory is that Shakespeare wrote the sonnets in search of patronage.

Alastair Fowler identifies a foundational metaphor in the opening sonnets, the base of a pyramid. His claim rests on sequential conventions, such as number symbolism; on aspects of *Sonnets* that point to organisation, such as the positions of formally distinct poems; and on the synonymous use of 'pyramid' and 'triangle' in the Elizabethan period. The 1609 *Sonnets* consists of 154 numbered sonnets and the narrative poem 'A Lover's Complaint'. Three sonnets have unusual forms, prompting commentators to question whether they are sonnets and whether Shakespeare wrote them: Sonnet 99 has 15 lines; 126 consists of six rhymed couplets; and 145 is in tetrameter verse. Sonnet 126 is often identified as a dividing line between the sonnets addressed to or concerning a young man and the sonnets addressed to or concerning a dark-eyed and black-haired mistress. Though Fowler does not draw attention to the love triangle of poet, youth, and mistress, the pyramidal organisation arguably gestures to it.

Near the start of his discussion, Fowler notes that 153 is the sum of 1 through 17 and is therefore a 'triangular number'.[14] The geometric metaphor can be illustrated by a comparison of the triangular number 15 and the square number 25:

```
            *                    15       * * * * *    21 22 23 24 25
           * *                  13 14     * * * * *    16 17 18 19 20
          * * *                10 11 12   * * * * *    11 12 13 14 15
         * * * *               6  7  8  9 * * * * *    6  7  8  9  10
        * * * * *              1  2  3  4  5 * * * * * 1  2  3  4  5
```

Diagrammed as a triangle, the number 15 has five rows. The widest row consists of five units; the narrowest, of one unit. The number 153 can also be illustrated as a series of tapering rows, with a 17-unit base and a one-unit apex. In order to account for the 154 sonnets, Fowler claims that Sonnet 136 should not count towards the total, because the poet asks his mistress if he may 'pass untold' in her 'number' of lovers. Fowler's scheme is insightful, but some details need correction. Notably, he leaves out 'A Lover's Complaint'.

Fowler argues that *Sonnets*' monument theme alludes to a pyramid. This claim is based in literary history: if we attend to triumphal forms from ancient times to the Renaissance, we should not be surprised to find such metaphors in Shakespeare. The poetry-as-monument idea is at least as old as the final ode of Horace's three-book *Odes* (23 BC):

> Exegi monumentum aere perennius
> regalique situ pyramidum altius,
> quod non imber edax, non Aquilo impotens
> possit diruere . . .

> [I have completed a monument more enduring than brass and higher than the royal structure of the pyramids, which no devouring rain, no furious north wind can destroy . . .][15]

Shakespeare would have known these verses, similar lines at the end of Ovid's *Metamorphoses*, and perhaps comparable verses by Propertius.[16] Since 'brass' and 'pyramids' are not in Ovid, some of *Sonnets*' allusions would seem to descend from Horace:

> And thou in this shalt find thy monument,
> When tyrants' crests and tombs of brass are spent.
> (Sonnet 107)

> No! Time, thou shalt not boast that I do change.
> Thy pyramids, built up with newer might,
> To me are nothing novel, nothing strange.
> (Sonnet 123)

Fowler also argues that Sonnet 125 alludes to the pyramidal organization: 'Were't ought to me I bore the canopy . . . / Or laid great bases for eternity?' (The bases may refer to pyramid steps.) Like Horace at the end of *Odes* and Ovid at the end of *Metamorphoses*, Shakespeare signals the completion of a monument. What is more, 153 has biblical significance: after the resurrection, seven disciples miraculously catch 153 fish; in one of his sermons, Augustine of Hippo interprets 153 as the sum of 1–17 and as an allegory of believers 'endowed with the Spirit'.[17]

Many commentators have greeted Fowler's pyramid with scepticism, but even the most incredulous critics allow for numberplay in *Sonnets*. Kerrigan, for example, attacks the 'stasis' of numerological schemes while granting some number symbolism in Shakespeare:

> In practice the only numerological argument that looks remotely plausible, far from offering stasis, points to a formal correlative of the anxiety about mechanical time registered in individual poems and turns of phrase. As has been recently noticed, the clock that chimes the twelve hours of the day is first invoked in Sonnet 12, and Sonnet 60 describes the 'minutes' which, in sixties, make up hours. How far this analysis may be pressed is still uncertain.[18]

The claims that Kerrigan deems plausible are those of René Graziani, who is also more interested in number symbolism than numeric organisation. Graziani finds puns relating to 'octave' in Sonnet 8, observes that Sonnet 44 'introduces a pair of sonnets on the four elements', and suggests that the poet, when writing Sonnet 100, 'is jolted into a sense of a great lapse of time that may have something do with the number'.[19] He also sees Sonnet 7's sun imagery as a possible allusion to Sunday, Sonnet 52's 'long year' as 'possibly brought into the poet's mind by . . . the weeks', and the 28 sonnets to the mistress as having 'pointed lunar associations befitting the Dark Lady and "shifting change"'.[20] In the end, though, Graziani has mixed feelings about Fowler's thesis, which he finds 'attractively apt . . . but seriously handicapped in requiring the deduction of one sonnet'.[21] Thomas P. Roche, by contrast, builds on Fowler's remarks about the grand or major climacteric – a crisis of body and soul in the sixty-third year of a human life. In Platonic number theory, the number 7 was associated with the body, and the number 9 with the mind or soul, making 49 (7×7) a crisis of body (a 'minor climacteric') and 63 (7×9) a crisis of soul and body (the 'major climacteric').[22] Sonnets 49 and 63 may thus represent moments of crisis in the *Sonnets* poet's narrative and reflections.[23]

Duncan-Jones synthesises and adds to the claims of Fowler, Graziani, and Roche. Citing Vincent Hopper's *Medieval Number Symbolism*, she suggests that Sonnet 20's emphasis on anatomy 'draws on primitive associations [of 20] with the human body, whose "digits", fingers and toes, add up to twenty', and argues that the poet's evocations of death and posthumous states in Sonnets 71 and 81 are informed by biblical adages. (According to Psalm 90, the time of our life is 'threescore and ten' years, and we may live to 'fourscore' years if we have strength.[24]) She also notes that the *Sonnets* poet takes stock of his achievements in Sonnet 108, when his sequence matches the number of sonnets in *Astrophil and Stella*.[25] With or without its Sidnean associations, the number 108 plays a role in the organisation of *Sonnets*: the fair-youth section can be divided into an introduction (1–17), a group of 108 sonnets (18–125), and a coda (126).[26] Duncan-Jones also notes that Sonnet 63 – the 'grand climacteric' sonnet – is 'exactly half-way through the "fair youth" sequence', and that 77 – a sonnet that features a mirror and a book – is exactly halfway through the 153-poem pyramid.[27] (Roche makes similar observations.) In a variation on one of Graziani's suggestions, Duncan-Jones asserts that the number of poems in *Sonnets*' mistress section, 28, 'probably alludes to the length of the lunar month'.[28] This interpretation hints at sun-moon symbolism: like Prince Hal in the *Henry IV* plays, the fair youth is associated with the sun.

Given Shakespeare's stylistic tendencies, a pyramidal arrangement should hardly be dismissed out of hand. That said, the scheme's existence needs to be more firmly established. The mere fact that *Sonnets* contains 154 numbered poems, not 153, has proved an impediment to its acceptance. Fowler's explanation for why Sonnet 136 does not count has garnered almost no support: far from being a removable sonnet, 136 would seem to belong with the 'Will' sonnets that surround it. Roche instead concentrates on 153–4 – mythological sonnets about Cupid – dubbing them 'a single sonnet moving in two directions'.[29] But if the two sonnets are so similar, and if the scheme requires only 153 poems, why did Shakespeare retain both of them? By cutting one, he would have highlighted the number 153, maintained the order of the preceding sonnets, and completed the sequence with a Cupid poem whose distinctness – balanced against the distinctness of the first 17 sonnets – would have pointed to the scheme. Besides, if no other pair is to be counted as a single sonnet, why make an exception with 153–4? Graziani arrives at 153 poems by another method. After expressing scepticism about Fowler's deduction of one sonnet from the total number, he offers his own solution, arguing in a footnote that Sonnet 146 is a 'more legitimately deductible sonnet' given its remorseful or 'palinodic' reflections.[30]

Removing Sonnet 146 from the count is dubious, but Graziani's reasoning is useful. Many sequences, most famously Petrarch's *Rime*, conclude with a palinode, a poem that recants a previously expressed view or sentiment. Petrarch's *Rime* consists of 366 numbered poems: 365 plus the palinode. In other words, the number 366 does not obscure the conceit of 365 days in a year: a seemingly superfluous poem may be integral to a sequence's design, especially if it includes retrospective commentary. So is there an extra palinodic poem in *Sonnets*? As Duncan-Jones notes, 'a more convincing way of arriving at 153, rather than 154, as the total number of sonnets, would be to omit from count the non-sonnet 126'.[31] Of the three irregular sonnets, 126 is the least sonnet-like: it consists of six couplets. Positioned at the end of the fair-youth section and commenting on the themes of time, love, and beauty, Sonnet 126 can be read as a warning about the limits of poetic consolation. It thus functions as a palinodic coda.

But neither Fowler nor Roche sufficiently takes into account 'A Lover's Complaint'. *Sonnets* opens with 17 procreation sonnets and closes with a pair of Cupid sonnets and 'A Lover's Complaint'. From this arrangement, it is possible to extrapolate an incrementally decreasing progression, starting with a seventeen-sonnet group and ending with a one-poem 'group': Sonnets 1–17 would be the pyramid's first step; the Cupid sonnets would be the sixteenth step; and 'A Lover's Complaint' would be the seventeenth step. This view implies that there are fourteen groups of sonnets between 1–17 and 153–4, as well as two poems that do not count towards the sum of 153. My argument is that the three irregular sonnets mark divisions in the sequence, and that 126 and 145 are the non-counting sonnets.

Sonnet 126 is commonly seen as a division-marker, but what about 99 and 145? Sonnet 99 is preceded by poems that dwell on a poet-youth separation, and it is followed by poems that speak of renewed relations and new inspiration. Sonnet 145 is preceded by a poem that makes a climactic statement on the love triangle of poet, youth, and mistress, and it is followed by a poem in which the poet addresses his soul. Both the fair-youth section and the mistress section may therefore be regarded as bipartite:

Sonnets   Description

1–98   First part of fair-youth series (concludes with separation)
100–25   Second part of fair-youth series (renewal of friendship)

127–44   First part of mistress series (culminates with 'Two loves I have')
146–52   Second part of mistress series (begins with an address to the soul)

The idea that the fair-youth section is bipartite is not new. Many commentators have claimed that the sequence changes at or around Sonnet 100, drawing on stylometric studies that indicate that the fair-youth sonnets after 100 are among the last that Shakespeare wrote for the sequence.[32] The idea that the mistress section is bipartite may come as a surprise. This section is often seen as messy: its narrative is hard to follow, and much of it appears to have been written early. In my view, the two bipartite schemes are thematically and temporally parallel. In each section's first part, the youth-mistress betrayal is a central event. In the fair-youth section, the first allusion to the betrayal comes in Sonnets 33–4; in the mistress section, it comes in Sonnets 133–4. In each section's second part, the poet scrutinises his actions and feelings: at the end of the fair-youth section, the poet defends his inconstancy; at the end the mistress section, he interrogates his obsession.

In brief, the scheme consists of 17 pyramid steps and the bipartite divisions. In labelling the groups 'steps', I do not mean to evoke a terraced pyramid: drawing on a Horatian tradition, Shakespeare would have envisioned an Egyptian pyramid. My label derives from Elizabethan usage. In Renaissance English, 'step' could refer to a degree of height; 'degree' could be a step of a staircase or a rung of a ladder (*degré* in French); and 'ladder' could mean a set of stairs ('the ladder' meant the steps to the gallows).[33] All of these words were associated with vertical increments if not with hierarchy ('degree' as 'rank'). *Sonnets* draws on such meanings and related conceits, including the steps of life. Whether or not he visualised the groups as 'steps', Shakespeare would have imagined a vertical series, starting at the bottom with a 17-poem base. Evidence that he assigned numeric ranks to the steps is related to evidence for the steps: the first step focuses on singleness; the second, on doubleness; and the third, on a love triangle.

My description prompts questions about organisational principles: if Sonnets 126 and 145 are non-counting poems, why did Shakespeare number them, and why did he keep 99 in the count? The short answer to both questions is that he needed the numbers and the poems to complete different schemes. If he had not numbered 126, for example, he would have thrown off the numeric and positional parallels between Sonnets 33–4 and 133–4. And if he had made 99 a non-counting poem, he would have had to extend the eighth pyramid step beyond 108 to 109, which would have foiled the allusion to Sidney's 108 sonnets. More details about numbers and positions of sonnets will be discussed in later chapters. For now, my point is that the sequence's organisational principles are consistent, and that we should look for competing schemes when we encounter an anomaly. Note, too, that it is productive to regard the fair-youth section as 125 sonnets and a coda, and the mistress section as 25 sonnets plus the Cupid sonnets and 'A Lover's Complaint'.

Questions about anomalies prompt questions about audience. Would *Sonnets*' first readers have felt that the irregular poems were strange? Sonnets with 15 lines, and sonnets in tetrameter, occur in other sequences, but they are unusual in an otherwise formally consistent collection. Sonnets 153–4 are distinct because of their 'anacreontic' subject matter: they tell fanciful explanatory tales with mythic characters. This fact helps explain why they and 'A Lover's Complaint' belong in the sequence and belong at the end. Daniel's *Delia* (1592) helped establish a tradition in which sonnets are followed by anacreontic verse and a long stanzaic poem. 'If this tradition is borne in mind', Kerrigan explains,

> Spenser's *Amoretti* (1595) no longer looks so odd. Those four slight epigrams sandwiched between the eighty-nine sonnets of the *Amoretti* and the concluding *Epithalamion* have puzzled editors; some have denied Spenser's authorship; but they have the same function in Spenser's volume as the odes in *Delia* . . . They give Spenser's book a tripartite Delian structure.[34]

'Tripartite' is misleading – the anacreontic poems are more of a transition than a separate part. More crucially, *Delia* and *Amoretti* are not isolated examples:

> Richard Barnfield's *Cynthia* appeared in 1595. [It] has twenty sonnets . . . an ode in anacreontics, and . . . the tale of Trojan Cassandra. [In] Richard Linche's *Diella* (1596), a sonnet takes the place of the ode or epigram . . . The implications of all this are clear. When those first Jacobean readers opened Shakespeare's volume in 1609, they found something perfectly familiar.[35]

Given the content of *Sonnets*, it is debatable whether Shakespeare's sequence would have been perfectly familiar to its first audience, but its format would have been typical. It would also have been typical in having circulated in manuscript before publication. The generic poems perhaps indicate that Shakespeare prepared the sequence for public consumption.

The Source of Shakespeare's Pyramid

There is growing scholarly consensus that *Sonnets* contains number symbolism. The most accepted claims regard temporal numbers –

especially 12, 52, and 60 (as evoked in Sonnets 12, 52, and 60). Claims about the climacteric years of life are more contested, perhaps because they seem obscure. They were less obscure in the Renaissance: references to them can be found in texts like Peter de la Primaudaye's *The French Academy* (1577), a popular compendium and a likely source for the 'Seven Ages of Man' in *As You Like It*.[36] Primaudaye makes a transition from the seven ages to the climacteric ages via remarks on the number 7:

> The whole time of the creation of the world is comprehended [in seven] and likewise the rest and ceasing of the work-master thereof. All the ancient writers have also noted that the number of 63, which is the multiplication of 7 by 9, carries with it commonly the end of old men: because ... in the whole course of our life we live under one only climate, which is either from seven or from nine years, except in the year of 63, wherein two terminations or climates end ... [Thus] this year is called climacterical, wherein we may note out of histories the death of many great men and the changes of estates and kingdoms.[37]

Shakespeare may have also known a tract on climacteric ages that Thomas Thorpe published five years before *Sonnets*: Thomas Wright's *A Succinct Philosophical Declaration of the Nature of Climacterical Years, Occasioned by the Death of Queen Elizabeth*. (The tract was appended to *The Passions of the Mind*.) Wright notes that '*Clymax* in Greek signifieth a stair or a ladder', that it is 'applied to the years of a man's or woman's life', and that Elizabeth I's death 'in the seventieth year of her age' argues that she was robust: she survived her grand climacteric and virtually attained the biblical age of threescore and ten.[38] A stronger constitution is measured in scores: Moses died when he was 120, and Genesis 6:3 states that the days of man 'shall be an hundred and twenty years'. In modern times, though, life is shorter: 'The number of the days of the life of men at most is an 100 years', an age only possible for those of 'solid and virile constitution'. A lifetime measured in climates of nine years is thus seen as a falling-off, even if a person lives to 9×9 years, the 'most perilous' of life's 'passages or steps'. Ideas about decline are relevant to *Sonnets*, as are suggestions that 9 falls short of the perfect number 10 and that the years of our lives are like the steps of a ladder or a stair – at the top of which is death.

Renaissance poets not only knew about the climacteric ages; they used them in their works. In 'Upon the Death of Lady Penelope Clifton' (1618), Michael Drayton cites the grand climacteric when lamenting that death did not strike women less admirable than Lady

Clifton: 'Death might have taken such, her end deferred, / Until the time she had been climactered; / When she would have been at threescore years and three, / Such as our best at three and twenty be'.[39] The full title of Drayton's 1619 *Idea* is *Idea in Sixty-Three Sonnets*, and the manuscript version of Constable's *Diana* similarly contains 63 sonnets, followed by an authorial note:

> When I had ended this last sonnet and found that such vain poems as I had by idle hours writ did amount just to the climacterical number 63, methought it was high time for my folly to die and to employ the remnant of [my] wit to other calmer thoughts less sweet and less bitter.[40]

Drayton and Constable may have been influenced by *Astrophil and Stella*, which makes an organisational allusion to the grand climacteric: its first song occurs after the sixty-third sonnet.

Like Constable and Sidney, Shakespeare makes structural use of the climacteric ages. The first sonnets of the fourth and fifth pyramid steps can be read as crisis poems:

> Against that time, if ever that time come,
> When I shall see thee frown on my defécts . . .
>
> (Sonnet 49)

> Against [that time when] my love shall be as I am now
> With Time's injurious hand crushed and o'erworn . . .
>
> (Sonnet 63)

These gestures of defiance are heightened moments in the poet's war with time. In the middle of the sixth pyramid step, the poet proclaims a triumph over time:

> Your monument shall be my gentle verse,
> Which eyes not yet created shall o'er-read,
> And tongues to be your being shall rehearse
> When all the breathers of this world are dead.
>   You still shall live, such virtue hath my pen,
>   Where breath most breathes, ev'n in the mouths of men.
>
> (Sonnet 81)

This burst of confidence could indicate that 81 is the final climacteric sonnet: the poet may be declaring that all climacteric crises have been overcome. The emphasis on breath and spirit supports this reading: 'You still shall live . . . / Where breath most breathes, ev'n in the mouths of men'. Sonnet 81's couplet echoes 18's couplet: 'So long as men can breathe or eyes can see, / So long lives this, and this gives life to thee'. And both sonnets evoke the body (physical breathing) and the soul (animating spirit) as they lay claim to poetry's power on future readers. Sonnet 81 may thus be a poem that completes 18's boast: 63 sonnets later, the poet declares that the youth will flourish in a living monument. Shakespeare signals that the poet, the youth, and the sequence have survived the major climacteric of soul and body.

In emulating predecessors, Renaissance poets sought to outdo one another. Shakespeare's pyramid is therefore likely to be informed by specific works, not merely by a generic tradition. Roche argues that Shakespeare took the idea of a pyramid scheme from Daniel, noting that Daniel, 'in adding sonnets to his sequence, reconstructed the subtext of his sequence as a Pythagorean pyramid based on the number ten'.[41] (*Delia* contains 55 sonnets in its third edition. The sum of 1–10 is 55.) He also observes that Sonnet 10 of *Delia* makes pointed use of 'triumph' and 'trophy', and that a sonnet added to the fifty-five-sonnet edition, number 17, implies that the poet is commenting on organisation: 'Why should I sing in verse, why should I *frame*, / These sad neglected notes for her dear sake?' (Roche's italics).[42] The argument is suggestive, but the evidence is inconclusive. As Roche notes, the fourth edition of *Delia* contains 57 sonnets, obscuring the numeric schemes of the earlier volumes.

Whether or not the fifty-five-sonnet *Delia* is pyramidally organised, it may allude to pyramids: Daniel published it with his drama *Cleopatra*. Set in Cleopatra's 'monument', the play's story corresponds to Act 5 of Shakespeare's *Antony and Cleopatra*. Daniel's dedication to the Countess of Pembroke also emphasises the monumental: 'Here thou surviv'st thy self, here thou art found / Of late succeeding ages, fresh in fame: / This monument cannot be overthrown / Where, in eternal brass, remains thy name' (lines 70–2). Shakespeare may have been inspired by Daniel's *Delia-Cleopatra* and attempted to outdo it. As a 153-poem pyramid, Shakespeare's sequence necessarily contains a 55-poem pyramid in its final ten steps. And Sonnet 55 is the sequence's first poem to evoke the Horatian-Ovidian claim about poetic immortality: 'Not marble, nor the gilded monument[s] / Of princes shall outlive this powerful rhyme'.

Shakespeare's 153-poem pyramid may moreover owe something to another sequence involving Daniel, the 1591 edition of *Astrophil and Stella* (A&S). A&S advertises organisation, partly because it includes 'other rare sonnets of diverse noblemen and gentlemen' (title page). As with the fifty-four sonnets in the second edition of *Delia*, Daniel's twenty-eight sonnets in A&S may represent a tribute to Sidney: they are presented as an introductory sonnet plus twenty-seven numbered sonnets (one quarter of 108). Such a tribute does not preclude other structures; indeed, A&S is packaged in ways that invite readers to look for schemes. Notably, it is divided into two bipartite sections:

107 Sidney sonnets (unnumbered)
10 Sidney songs (numbered 'first' to 'tenth')

28 Daniel sonnets (one unnumbered, the others numbered 1–27)
7 songs by 'diverse gentlemen' (five numbered in Italian, two unnumbered)

Even before the 1598 *Astrophil and Stella*, Shakespeare would likely have known that Sidney's sonnets should have totalled 108. If we include the missing sonnet, A&S can be divided into 136 sonnets and 17 songs, or 153 poems in all. The similarities go beyond the total number of poems. In A&S, Daniel's twenty-eight sonnets come after Sidney's poems; in *Sonnets*, the twenty-eight mistress sonnets come after the fair-youth section. Both sequences contain two bipartite sections, and their main sections contain similar proportions of poems: each first section is substantially longer than its second section; each section's first part is substantially longer than its second part.

Elizabethan Poets and Poetic Competition

Given the parallels among A&S, *Delia*, and *Sonnets*, Shakespeare arguably presents his pyramid as a monument that surpasses all previous poets' efforts. This claim will be fleshed out later; for now, let us turn to Sidney's 'When my good angel guides me to the place' (Sonnet 60 of *Astrophil and Stella*) and Daniel's 'Raising my hope on hills of high desire' (the final sonnet of A&S). Sidney's sonnet is the centre poem of *Astrophil and Stella* (it is the sixtieth of 119 poems); Daniel's sonnet alludes to the titanomachia (the titans' rebellion against the Olympian gods). Elizabethan poets associated the titanomachia with poetic rivalry.

In employing the conceit of climbing to a height, 'When my good angel' alludes to its central position in *Astrophil and Stella*:

> When my good angel guides me to the place
> Where all my good I do in Stella see,
> That heav'n of joys throws only down on me
> Thundered disdains and lightnings of disgrace.

> But when the rugged'st step of Fortune's race
> Makes me fall from her sight, then sweetly she
> With words, wherein the muses' treasures be,
> Shows love and pity to my absent case.
> Now I, wit-beaten long by hardest Fate,
> So dull am, that I cánnot look into
> The ground of this fierce love and lovely hate:
> Then some good body tell me how I do,
> > Whose presence absence, absence presence is;
> > Blessed in my curse, and cursèd in my bliss.

Astrophil claims that, when he is guided by his 'good angel' (virtue, conscience) to a 'place' where he can see Stella as both everything in him that is good and the sole goodness to which he aspires, then Stella, that 'heav'n of joys', looks scornfully down on him. And yet she pities him 'when the rugged'st step of Fortune's race / Makes [him] fall from her sight': when a misstep, an impediment, or the course of events removes him from her presence. Unable to see why she treats him thus or to view the essence of the matter ('I cánnot look into / The ground of this'), Astrophil turns to 'some good body' – an alternative influence, a well-meaning person – hoping to know how he is faring or how to look ('tell me how I do'). Denied love in her presence and tendered love in her absence, he concludes that he is 'blessed' in his 'curse' (looked on favourably in misfortune, given grace in damnation) and 'cursèd in [his] bliss' (damned when given grace, frustrated when favoured most). Besides playing with 'bless' and 'bliss', Sidney may be evoking *blessé*, the French word for 'wounded'.[43] The main pun, though, regards spiritual and sexual bliss; this informs Astrophil's remarks on rising and falling in Stella's eyes, his inability to look into the ground of his love, and his frustration when he is at the height of bliss. The poem questions the Platonic notion that the higher we climb the ladder of love, the less we are driven by sexual desire. In alluding to his 'good angel' in the first quatrain, Astrophil evokes its bad counterpart, which we might expect him to name next – but instead he speaks of 'Fortune'. The bad angel is both absent and present in the poem, like sexual desire in Platonic love. The sonnet functions as a thematic centre to *Astrophil and Stella* with its imagery of rising to a height and falling. Sidney transforms a common symbol of rise and fall, Fortune's wheel, into 'Fortune's race' (the direction and physical path of Fortune's flight), thereby evoking fleeting opportunity and hinting at competition. Like Jove from Olympus, Stella throws down lightning and thunder. Astrophil would seem to be climbing towards her when he falls, loses sight of her, or drops in her esteem. Sidney's sonnet may thus allude to the titanomachia.

In reworking Sidney's sonnet, Daniel more clearly evokes the titans' attack on Olympus:

> Raising my hope on hills of high desire,
> Thinking to scale the heaven of her heart,
> My slender means presumed too high a part,
> For Disdain's thunderbolt made me retire
> And threw me down to pain in all this fire –
> Where lo, I languish in so heavy smart
> Because th'attempt was far above my art:
> Her state brooks not poor souls should come so nigh her.
> Yet I protest my high-aspiring will
> Was not to dispossess her of her right:
> Her sovereignty should have remainèd still;
> I only sought the bliss to have her sight –
>   Her sight, contented thus to see me spill,
>   Framed my desires fit for her eyes to kill.

Instead of piling mountain on mountain (Ossa on Pelion), the *Delia* poet raises his hopes 'on hills of high desire', aspiring to climb the 'heaven' (Olympus) of his mistress's heart, only to be struck down by Disdain's thunderbolt. Acknowledging that Delia has a right to her own heart, the poet protests that he never intended to 'dispossess' her, but he may be protesting too much. Daniel's use of Sidney is mediated by his use of two sonnets by Luigi Tansillo, whose mythic conceit is Icarus's flight towards the sun. For Tansillo, Icarus is a figure for the poet; the doomed flight is a noble failure – the proof of a great soul.[44] Similarly laying claim to magnanimity, the *Delia* poet pleads that he has only 'sought' his mistress's 'sight' (a view of her).[45] But how high-minded are his desires? In other sonnets, the *Delia* poet's story parallels the myth of Actaeon, the hunter punished for seeing Diana naked. And in the couplet of 'Raising my hope', Delia sees the poet's desires as low-minded, perhaps because she wishes to see them that way: her 'sight' (gaze) has 'Framed [them] fit for her eyes to kill'. In other words, Delia is presented as a conventionally cruel beauty with an unconventional power: her gaze transforms the poet's desires, or it reveals them as something more carnal than he believes or would have her believe. But 'Raising my hope' is not simply concerned with amatory desire. As 'far above my art' suggests, the sonnet expresses anxiety about poetic ambition. Daniel is paying homage to Sidney, presenting himself as a nobly aspiring but less skilful poet.

Like the poet's desire for Delia, Daniel's tribute to Sidney may be more ambitious than it purports to be. 'Raising my hope' is the final sonnet of the 1591 *Astrophil and Stella* – the twenty-eighth of Daniel's twenty-eight sonnets in that volume. In the first edition of *Delia* (1592), 'Raising my hope' is again the twenty-eighth sonnet, only now it is at or near the work's centre: the sequence has fifty sonnets, a four-stanza ode, and a complaint. The titanomachia is also a major theme of Spenser's *Ruins of Rome* (1591), a thirty-three-sonnet sequence based on Joachim Du Bellay's *Antiquités de Rome*: the myth is evoked in four of the first seventeen sonnets, culminating with an allusion in the centre poem, and the sequence is at the centre of *Complaints* (the fifth of nine works).[46] Among stage dramas, the titanomachia is prominent in Marlowe's *Tamburlaine the Great*, notably in the final speech of Part 1, at the centre of the first printed edition of the play (1590). Tamburlaine, basking in the glory of his victory, expresses love for his bride and queen Zenocrate: 'As Juno, when the giants were suppressed / That darted mountains at her brother Jove, / So looks my love'. Instances like these suggest that the titan myth was associated with rivalry in the early 1590s, and that poets were contending to be Sidney's poetic heir.

Pyramid Steps and Boundary Sonnets

If the pyramid scheme foregrounds poem groups so well, why has no one suggested that every pyramid step is a group? As with the lack of enthusiasm regarding the scheme itself, there is no need for conspiracy theories. First, the number of commentators who have argued for the pyramid can be counted on one hand. Second, the commentators have mischaracterised significant details. Third and most important: as straightforward as it is to identify pyramid steps once you know what to look for, they are hidden. Every step presents 'boundary issues' – questions about where the group begins and ends. The boundary between the first two pyramid steps is clear-cut; the one between the second and third steps is less sharply defined.

The sonnets of the second step get off to a good start as a group. Consider the rhetorical effect of moving from the close of Sonnet 17 ('But were some child of yours alive that time, / You should live twice: in it, and in my rhyme') to the opening of 18 ('Shall I compare thee to a summer's day?'). In 18, the poet stops urging procreation, switches to thou-forms, and adopts a warmer manner. The contrast is not total, however: the poet continues to promise the youth immortality, telling him that his 'eternal summer' will grow in 'eternal lines'. What is more, 'Shall I compare thee . . .?' echoes 17's 'Who will believe my verse in time to come?' and can be read as a response to it. The two sonnets are related enough to make sense in sequence and contrasting enough to belong to two different series.

The next pyramid-step boundary is not immediately reassuring: Sonnet 32 hints at closure (the poet imagines his death) and 33 seems to broach a new subject (the youth's betrayal), which is continued in 34. It might be tempting to regard 32 as the second step's final sonnet. But that surmise would prove short-sighted, as a closer look at the step's first and last poems shows. In Sonnet 18, the poet evokes a summer's day; in 33, a sunny day turned cloudy. Sonnet 33 is moreover vague about the youth's fault: the depiction of the cloud-covered sun is ominous, but the poet neither addresses nor accuses the youth directly. In contrast, 34 accuses the youth-sun right away: 'Why didst thou promise such a beauteous day / And make me trávail forth without my cloak . . .?' At the end of a series about love's growth, 33 signals that something dark has come between the friends, and 34 grapples with it. As with many steps' final poems, Sonnet 33 may initially seem to inaugurate a new group, only to make more sense as a conclusion as we read on. Rather than making an exception, Shakespeare establishes a pattern.

Sonnets 18 and 33 are akin in another way: 18 inaugurates the theme of comparison; 33 foregrounds a comparison. In the second pyramid step, the poet presents comparisons as dubious figures of speech; at best, they are inadequate forms of representation. In Sonnet 18, he considers and rejects various comparisons; in 33, he addresses concerns about comparison via an extended simile whose vehicle alone takes up eight lines. Noting that the simile does not announce itself as figure of speech until line 9, Vendler remarks: 'another recurrent strategy for Shakespeare is to "mix up" the order of narration so that it departs from the normal way in which such an event would be unfolded'.[47] More precisely, *Sonnets* often plays with narrative expectations, but 33's simile is atypical, both in length and in delay in revealing itself as a figure. In his allegory of the youth's fall from grace, the poet mimics the experience of making an unwelcome discovery. He also implies that he has fallen into using comparisons now that the youth has fallen from grace.

More evidence of design can be inferred from the third step's boundary sonnets, 34 and 48. Like 18 and 33, these sonnets share a conceit. In 34, the poet describes leaving home and being overtaken by 'base clouds'; in 48, he has travelled and now fears robbery by a 'vulgar thief': 'How careful was I when I took my way, / Each trifle under truest bars to thrust, . . . / But thou, to whom my jewëls trifles are, . . . / Art left the prey of every vulgar thief'. Having equated betrayal with theft in Sonnet 40 ('I do forgive thy robb'ry'), the poet dreads a second theft. As Heather Dubrow shows in her study of domestic loss in Elizabethan England, it was common in Shakespeare's time to view thievery that violated a domestic space as more heinous than other forms of theft; in some instances, 'burglary' was applied to rape.[48] In evoking theft, the poet evokes a violation of heart and home. He also plays with boundaries, using the border between the second and third steps to allude to transgression (crossing a line), and using the third step's conclusion to signal an attempt to restore boundaries and secure his beloved.

Insofar as the border between the second and third pyramid steps is ambiguous, it is an exception that proves the rule. The themes and boundaries of steps are generally well-defined:

Step	Sonnets	Thematic description and boundary sonnets
1	1–17	*Procreation sonnets.* Sonnet 1 announces the procreation theme; Sonnet 17 synthesises 15's and 16's conclusions about preserving the youth's beauty via poetry and procreation.
2	18–33	*Growth of poet-youth friendship; initial worries about the future.* Sonnet 18 marks a shift in tone and degree of intimacy; 33 foreshadows betrayal with a story of a sunny day turned cloudy.
3	34–48	*Betrayal and its aftermath.* In 34, the poet accuses the youth of 'ill deeds'; 48 is retrospective ('How careful was I, when I took my way . . .'), pointing back to the 'trávail' of 34.
4	49–62	*Climacteric of body, struggles with appearance and reality.* This and the next step begin with a sonnet whose number and opening point to climacteric crisis (49: 'Against that time . . .'; 63: 'Against my love . . .'). 62 is retrospective and reflective: seeing signs of age in his mirror, the poet surmises that his 'sin of self-love' stems from identifying with the youth.
5	63–75	*Climacteric of soul and body, struggles with corruption and decay.* The poet seeks first to conquer his fears

about the youth's mortality and later to ease concerns (projected onto the youth) about his own mortality. This step begins by turning away from direct address: 63–8 speak of the youth in the third person. In 75, the poet summarises his situation by comparing himself to a miser.

6	76–87	*The rival-poet series.* In 76, the poet defends his verse against new fashions; in 86, he reports that the youth has favoured another poet; in 87, he bids farewell to his 'too dear' youth.
7	88–98	*Break-up and fault-finding poems.* The poet raises the possibility of a break with the youth and becomes increasingly critical. In 88, the poet offers to assume public blame for a split; in 96, he alludes to public discussion of the youth's imperfections; 97–8 speak of absence and time passing.
8	99–108	*Renewal of friendship and praise.* 99 is a formally irregular sonnet; in 100, the poet alludes to a long hiatus in writing. 108 makes a summarising statement about beauty and time.

As we will see, the ninth and tenth steps can be read as a series of seventeen marriage sonnets that recall the seventeen procreation sonnets. And with the exception of Sonnets 33–4, the boundaries between steps are demarcated by non-linked sonnets – the first sonnet of a step is not conjunctively or otherwise clearly connected to the last sonnet of the previous step. This is significant in light of the high percentage of linked sonnets in the sequence.

Evidence that Shakespeare viewed Sonnets 18–33 as the *second* step and 34–48 as the *third* step can be inferred from organisation in the steps. Sonnets 18–33 are dominated by pairs:

Pair	Description
18–19	Transitioning from the procreation poems, 18 and 19 both declare that the youth's beauty will live in the poet's verse.
20–1	In both sonnets, the poet presents the youth's beauty and inspirational power as feminine but not 'painted'.
23–4	Both sonnets employ extended conceits about art: in 23, the poet compares himself to an actor; in 24, to a painter.

25–6	In 25, the poet contrasts his secure personal friendship with the youth to the uncertain fortunes of public life; in 26, he pleads that he is not yet ready to boast publicly of his love.
27–8	These sonnets are linked through themes of sleeplessness and travel, and 28's transitional opening ('How then . . .?').
29–30	Both sonnets are framed by a distinctive rhetorical structure: *When I do X . . ., then I do Y.*
31–2	In 31, the poet speaks of the youth as the receptacle of dead loves; in 32, he imagines himself dead and the youth thinking back on the poet's love.

The only unpaired sonnets are 22 and 33, which reinforce doubleness in other ways: 22 is a mirror poem; 33 contains an extended simile; both sonnets' numbers have identical digits.

Sonnets 34–48 consist of five trios. Each trio has linked sonnets and a clear theme:

Trio	Description
34–6	In 34, the poet accuses the youth of ill deeds but claims that the youth's tears 'ransom' such acts; in 35, he gestures towards forgiveness; in 36, he suggests separation, for policy's sake.
37–9	37–9 are linked by themes of living vicariously through the youth, finding inspiration in the youth, and praising the youth.
40–2	These love-triangle poems explicitly confront the youth-mistress affair. In each sonnet, the poet excuses and blames the youth.
43–5	In 43, the poet says that he sees the youth most clearly in dreams; in 44, he wishes that his body were thought so that he might travel to the youth; and in 45, he presents his thoughts as messengers: they are sent out; they return; they are sent out again.
46–8	46–7 discuss the 'war', and then the 'league', between the poet's eye and heart. 48 concludes both the trio and the pyramid step: the poet claims that, when he left home, he locked the youth in his heart, from which he fears the youth will be stolen.

Of particular note are the love-triangle sonnets (40–2) – the third step's third and central trio.

Principles of Design in Sonnet Sequences

For Elizabethans, the possibility that a poetic scheme might be imperceptible to most readers did not make it less significant; it might even signal importance. As Derek Attridge explains in his study of English experiments in classical metres, such schemes ask us to read poetry in ways that may not feel natural:

> One characteristic of the numerological structure of many Elizabethan poems that strikes the modern reader as particularly odd is the fact that it is not directly perceptible as part of the experience of reading, but is a matter of counting and calculating in a separate intellectual operation. The conclusions reached in this operation can then be borne in mind during the reading, and related to the content of the poem; but the two cannot be simultaneously experienced in the way in which we usually demand today.[49]

Numerological structures, like the rules for determining syllable quantities, were valued because they bespoke artistic skill. Poets experimenting with classical metres sought to base vernacular poetry on a craft as difficult and demonstrable as that of Latin and Greek poetry. That aim, along with the tenet that the best art disguises its artifice, promoted the use of hidden schemes. Other attitudes to art also promoted hidden design, notably the view that 'the artist's creation of harmony is like God's creation of the universe', which is epitomised in Leon Battista Alberti's observation that the mathematical relations between a building's sections were ideals that people walking in or around the building might not be able to perceive 'correctly'.[50] Like anamorphic images, the relations might only be visible from a special perspective – or only in the mind's eye.

As noted earlier, one basis for schemes is counting poems; another is counting stanzas. *Astrophil and Stella* is a collection that mixes eleven songs among 108 sonnets. The songs have a total of 108 stanzas, which means that the sequence contains 216 'poetic units' – 108 stanzas plus 108 sonnets. Like many sonnet-sequence poets, Sidney used the totals for structural and symbolic purposes. The number 108 allows for a wide range of organisational possibilities – it can be divided by 2, 3, 4, 6, 9, and 12 – and it may allude to the 108 suitors of Penelope in the *Odyssey*.[51] Sidney also followed convention by using different kinds of verse to demarcate groups of poems. To take two examples: *Astrophil and Stella*'s first song occurs after Sonnet 63, marking the first sixty-three sonnets as a group; uninterrupted by sonnets, the fifth through ninth songs form a series of sixty-three stanzas. Although basic, such schemes point to complexity. As Fowler has shown, complex schemes in *Astrophil and Stella* are demarcated by poems with contrasting metrical forms.[52] And W. N. Parker has argued that Sidney's sequence is arranged as a series of groups whose sizes 'represent perfect musical intervals' when they are expressed as proportions relating to 108.[53] Simple principles helped poets to develop intricate schemes.

One common principle is that series have centres – measurable midpoints. The centre poem of a series is the poem that is equidistant from the series' first and last poems. (The centre poem of *Astrophil and Stella*'s 119 poems is Sonnet 60.) 'Centre poem' is a visual metaphor: distance is measured in poems. For a series to have a unique centre poem, it must have an odd number of poems. Such notions about centres inform arrangements of sonnets; among other things, poets had to find ways of marking each group's beginning and ending. One way of signaling groups is to alternate different kinds of poems – as Sidney does. In using sonnets almost exclusively of one type, Shakespeare set himself a more difficult task, perhaps because he wanted his architecture to be more secret and wanted to prove his craft. *Sonnets* has at least three important centre poems: Sonnet 63 (the centre of the 125-sonnet fair-youth section), Sonnet 77 (the centre of the 153-poem pyramid), and Sonnet 100 (the centre of the 199-unit pyramid).

The idea of multiple centres is common in Renaissance art: it can be inferred not only from poetry but from sixteenth-century buildings and gardens.[54] Preferring the term 'axis of symmetry' to 'centre', Fowler explains:

> Here the analogy with mannerist architectural façades or landscape gardening seems illuminating. [The art historian] Shearman remarks of mannerist gardens that 'nothing predominates, and there is no dramatic focus ... The successive, cumulative impression is more important' ... What we have seen of related multiple axes of symmetry [in *Astrophil and Stella*] confirms the view of mannerism as complex, intricate and undynamic.[55]

The comparisons are apt, but the argument that multiple-axis schemes are 'undynamic' is debatable. Shakespeare's schemes, at any rate, are not static. The *Sonnets* poet uses multiple centres to reinforce the idea of multiple perspectives and to express difficulty with distinguishing between appearance and reality. He creates the impression of searching for a holistic perspective that perhaps does not exist, even as he desperately wishes otherwise.

Chapter 3

Poetic Rivalry in Late-Elizabethan England

This chapter focuses on Shakespeare's poetic milieu and the rival-poet series. For all of its range and detail, the discussion is neither a comprehensive history nor a summary made solely in view of the rival sonnets. My aim is to develop a 'thick context' for understanding sonnet sequences and the ambitions of the poets who wrote them – a context capacious enough to provide perspective on the styles and careers available to poets, and specific enough to explain Shakespeare's allusions and tones. Although the opening discussion includes more information than is necessary for the analysis, without it the reader would have a less vivid sense of the goings-on of the period and less clarity about the stakes of my claims. Similarly, my discussion of historical models for the rival is both narrower and broader in scope than the subject might seem to demand: I focus on three candidates only yet assess their work in the context of their careers, not simply in relation to Shakespeare. In proceeding in this way, I hope to show that understanding *Sonnets* is as much about gaining familiarity with a cultural environment as it is about tracing lines of influence.

Elizabethan Poetry in the mid-1590s

Shakespeare may have begun writing sonnets in 1593, in the wake of such sequences as *Astrophil and Stella*, *Delia*, and *Parthenophil and Parthenophe*. By the mid-1590s, he would have had more motivation to write a sequence, and an ambitious one at that. In 1594, Daniel's *Delia-Cleopatra*, Drayton's *Idea's Mirror*, and Chapman's *Shadow of Night* were published, and Shakespeare hinted in *Lucrece* that he would write more poetry for Southampton. In early 1595, Spenser's *Amoretti*, Barnfield's *Cynthia*, and Chapman's *Ovid's Banquet of Sense* came out. Later in the year, Spenser published *Colin Clout's Come Home Again*, a work that comments on Elizabethan poetry and poets. Meanwhile Daniel had published *The First Four Books of the Civil Wars* (an epic on the War of the Roses), and Drayton had begun *The Barons' Wars* (an epic on civil war in the reign of Edward II).[1] In the mid-1590s, then, English poets were competing in print and developing ideas about Englishness and poetic careers. This is the culture in which *Sonnets* was written, even if it was not completed until shortly before its 1609 publication.

For cultural perspective, let us flesh out the story of the sonnet outlined in Chapter 1. Sir Thomas Wyatt (1503–42) is usually credited as the first English sonneteer: he started writing sonnets by translating or 'Englishing' Petrarch, often altering the Italian rhyme scheme by concluding with a couplet. Wyatt and Henry Howard, Earl of Surrey (1517–47) are generally credited as the first poets to write what are now called 'English', 'Elizabethan', or 'Shakespearean' sonnets: fourteen-line poems with six alternating rhymes and a seventh couplet rhyme.[2] This 'abab cdcd efef gg' scheme was felt to be more suitable to English, since it allowed for four rhymes in the first eight lines rather than just two. In 1575, George Gascoigne declared that he could 'best allow' sonnets to be those in which 'the first twelve lines do rhyme in staves of four lines by cross meter, and the last two rhyming together'.[3] The English-form sonnet may thus have become a norm by 1580, though it did not become the scheme of choice until the mid-1590s. The first amatory sequences, Watson's *Hekatompathia* and Sidney's *Astrophil and Stella*, contain no poems in that form, though most of their sonnets end in couplets. (The couplet is arguably the most typical feature in the period.) Watson's sonnets have eighteen lines; Sidney employs a variety of rhyme schemes. The sonnets in Greville's *Caelica* have two, three, four, or five quatrains; almost a quarter of the sonnets in *Parthenophil and Parthenophe* have fifteen lines; Spenser developed a quatrain-linking rhyme scheme that bears his name; and the sonnets in Barnfield's *Cynthia* have quatrains that rhyme 'abba cddc effe'. As latecomers, English poets may have felt pressure to do something new. Indeed, Englishness and novelty may have gone hand in hand. In his introductory sonnet to his sixty-three-sonnet *Idea*, Drayton quips: 'My muse is rightly of the English strain, / That cannot long one fashion entertain'.

With a few exceptions like *Amoretti*, English sequences published after 1593 contain mostly English-form sonnets. What brought about this shift? Besides the simple possibility that poets found the rhyme scheme amenable, Daniel's *Delia* seems to have helped popularise it. All but two of the 50 sonnets in the first *Delia* (1592) are in the English form, and a half-dozen sequences, mostly favouring that form, were published in 1592 and 1593. Together, then, Sidney's and Daniel's sequences may have sparked the sonnet vogue and helped establish its norms. But *Astrophil and Stella* and *Delia* do not explain everything. Constable's *Diana* was first published in 1592 in a twenty-sonnet edition; before then, it was circulating in a sixty-three-sonnet manuscript version. These *Diana*s and a seventy-five-sonnet edition (1594) exerted thematic and numeric influence: many later sequences have sections of 20, 63, or 75 sonnets. In Sonnet 3 of the 1599 *Idea*, Drayton invokes Constable: 'Many there be excelling in this kind, / Whose well-tricked rhymes with all invention swell. / Let each commend as he shall like his mind: / Some Sidney, Constable, some Daniël'. Drayton's triumvirate notably omits Spenser. In this respect, Drayton anticipates modern accounts of the English sequence, which typically begin with *Astrophil and Stella*.

Spenser may have paved the way for the sonnet-sequence fashion with *Ruins of Rome*, an adaptation of Du Bellay's *Antiquités du Rome*. *Ruins of Rome* is the fifth poetic work in *Complaints* (1591). With this volume, Spenser was publishing poetry written in the 1570s and 1580s and following up on his success with *The Faerie Queene*, whose first three books came out in 1590. *Ruins of Rome* is not an amatory sequence, but like *Delia* and *Sonnets*, and unlike *Astrophil and Stella* and *Diana*, it consists of English-form sonnets and is acutely concerned with the power of time and poetry. Along with *Delia*, *Ruins of Rome* promoted English-form sonnets and the theme of immortalising beauty. Spenser's *Ruins* made a strong impression on Shakespeare, to judge by verbal echoes in *Sonnets*:

> *Ruins* 27: 'which injurious Time hath quite out-worn'
> *Sonnets* 63: 'With Time's injurious hand, crushed and o'er-worn'
>
> *Ruins* 7: 'Time in time shall ruinate / Your works and names'
> *Sonnets* 10: 'Seeking that beauteous roof [your inherited traits] to ruinate'
>
> *Ruins* 7: 'your frames do for a time make war / 'Gainst Time'
> *Sonnets* 15: 'all in war with Time for love of you'[4]

With its thirty-three sonnets, *Ruins of Rome* also alludes to Christ's death in his thirty-third year; Shakespeare's thirty-third sonnet makes the same allusion.[5]

Spenser's influence is not limited to *Ruins of Rome* and *Amoretti*. The importance of *The Ruins of Time* and *Prothalamion* to 'A Lover's Complaint' has been well documented, as has *The Faerie Queene*'s impact on Sonnet 106.[6] These examples involve time and change. *Sonnets* echoes another such work by Spenser, *The Shepherd's Calendar*. Like Sonnet 126, the *Calendar*'s epilogue meditates on surviving time's ravages and consists of six couplets. Unlike the *Sonnets* poet, however, the *Calendar* poet is confident of victory: 'Lo, I have made a calendar for every year, / That steel in strength, and time in durance, shall outwear'. This confidence is reflected in the verse scheme: twelve lines of twelve syllables, a squaring of the year's months that is meant to evoke all of time.[7] Sonnet 126's verse scheme similarly gestures towards completion, only to eschew it: the poem has twelve pentameter lines and two blank lines, emblems of imperfection and uncertainty. The case for influence is strengthened if the *Calendar*'s editorial apparatus is taken into account. The first eleven eclogues are each followed by an emblem, a maxim, and editorial glosses. In this context, it is striking that no maxim appears under the December emblem. There is, however, a gloss on the missing maxim, right before the epilogue, that cites the same Latin verses that inform Shakespeare's pyramid: Horace's and Ovid's lines that boast of a monument that will outlast all other monuments. And in the epilogue itself, Spenser situates himself in a tradition of English poets, presenting Chaucer and Langland as shepherds to be followed from 'far off' rather than challenged to a contest.[8]

The variety of influences suggests that Shakespeare was familiar with Spenser's career. *The Shepherd's Calendar* was published in 1579 as a debut collection – a volume designed to recall Virgil's *Eclogues* and signal that an epic would follow. Other than new editions of the *Calendar*, Spenser published nothing in the 1580s. In 1590, he brought out the first part of *The Faerie Queene*, for which he earned a pension of £50 from Queen Elizabeth, an award that made him the de facto poet laureate if not the official one.[9] In 1591, he published *Complaints*. Soon after that, he may have been ready to publish *Colin Clout's Come Home Again*, but printing was delayed until 1595, perhaps because one poem in *Complaints*, the satiric *Mother Hubberd's Tale*, embroiled him in controversy.[10] In early 1596, he brought out the six-book edition of *The Faerie Queene*; *Four Hymns* and *Prothalamion* followed in the same year. For mid-1590s writers, then, Spenser was clearly positioning himself as the English laureate.

Spenser's laureate path did not suit Shakespeare, however. As Patrick Cheney observes, there was 'a rather large group of laureate-like authors' in late-Elizabethan England, 'from Sidney, Spenser, and

Daniel to Drayton, Chapman, and Jonson' – writers who made 'loud claims for the national value of literary art to England'.[11] By contrast, Shakespeare's mode of presentation might be called 'counter-laureate authorship', since it included 'the clear national ambitions of the Spenserian laureate without its dominant strategy of artistic self-crowning'.[12] In this view, Shakespeare follows an Ovidian career, fashioning himself as a poet who skirts writing epic poetry. (The 'Virgil vs. Ovid' binary does not extend to poetic style: Spenser is one of the poets whom Meres compared to Ovid in 1598, and Spenser's narrative strategies are Ovidian.) As Cheney suggests, an Ovidian career would have been attractive to Shakespeare as both a response to Spenser and a way of presenting himself as a poet-playwright. Among Renaissance writers, Ovid was known not only for love elegies and mythic tales but for drama; he was the author of at least one (lost) play, *Medea*.[13] Some Renaissance scholars went so far as to claim that Seneca's *Medea* was in fact Ovid's, virtually arguing that Ovid was the father of Senecan tragedy.[14]

Shakespeare's relations with Spenser were filtered through relations with Christopher Marlowe. In Cheney's formulation, 'Shakespeare processes ... the problem of being a new English poet-playwright by representing a dialogue between two oppositional aesthetics ... Spenserian and Marlovian'.[15] In contrast to Spenser, who began his career by imitating Virgil's *Eclogues*, Marlowe began by translating Ovid's first book of poetry, *Amores*. Marlowe's later works might also be called Ovidian. *Hero and Leander* is an attenuated epic, comparable to narratives in Ovid's *Metamorphoses*. *Dido, Queen of Carthage* similarly reduces the scope of epic and is Ovidian in its irreverent depiction of gods. The two parts of *Tamburlaine the Great* can be read as an ironic comment on the pastoral-to-epic career: the title character is a Scythian shepherd who conquers the world; he woos a queen in language similar to that of 'The passionate shepherd to his love' and reworks passages from *The Faerie Queene*.[16] Marlowe was an Ovidian alternative to Spenser, but because he 'could not extricate his art from the spell of the laureates', he produced a 'counter-national art'; Shakespeare 'uses the [Ovidian] frame of self-promotion to invent a frame of self-effacement'.[17]

Cheney's main ideas bear repeating: namely, that Shakespeare regarded himself as a poet-playwright, and that Spenserian-Virgilian and Marlovian-Ovidian models shaped his ideas about poetic careers. Cheney also describes Marlowe as a Lucanian poet: besides Ovid's *Amores*, Marlowe translated the first book of Lucan's *Civil War* (an anti-Virgilian, anti-imperial epic).[18] In this light, Marlowe can be seen as doubly oppositional to Spenser: his aesthetic ideas question heroic narrative; his political views question inherited privilege. Shakespeare's politics are more moderate and elusive: his history plays both acknowledge and question Tudor orthodoxies about monarchy.[19] But if, as Cheney suggests, Shakespeare is less politically opposed to Spenser than Marlowe is, he may also be less aesthetically opposed.

Spenser and Daniel

Cheney's account of Shakespeare's career underestimates the significance of 'minor' poets, notably Samuel Daniel. In light of his publications through 1595, Daniel might almost be called a Marlovian rival to Spenser. In 'Let others sing of knights and paladins', for example, Daniel distances himself from epic-romance poets, and his *Civil Wars* is Lucanian in its title and allusions. (The third stanza's encomium of the Queen stands out; it is an adaptation of Lucan's address to Nero.) But Daniel is not breaking a lance with the author of *The Faerie Queene*, or, if he is, he is not charging at full tilt to unseat his opponent. Daniel was a protégé of Spenser, or at least positioned himself as such in the mid-1590s.

Daniel's poetic career began under the shadow of Sidney, when twenty-eight of his sonnets were printed in the first edition of *Astrophil and Stella*. Daniel may have been complicit in this pirated volume; regardless, it helped his career.[20] He seized the occasion to publish *Delia*, which he dedicated to Sidney's sister, 'The Right Honourable, The Lady Mary, Countess of Pembroke'; soon after, he worked in the Pembroke household as a tutor to her son William, the future earl; and in 1594, he dedicated his *Delia-Cleopatra* volume to her.[21] Between 1591 and 1595, Daniel made a name for himself among English poets; above all, he was known for sonnet writing and 'female lament'. Before he published his *Civil Wars*, he was positioned as a more Ovidian poet than Shakespeare: he was a love poet who had published one play, a closet drama. More fundamentally, he was an heir to Sidney: he had written a sequence linked to *Astrophil and Stella*, and he had composed a tragedy along lines set forth in Sidney's *Defence of Poetry*, at the behest of Sidney's sister. In 1603, he would again link himself to the Sidney family by publishing *The Defence of Rhyme* and addressing it to William Herbert.

Daniel seems to have linked his fortunes with Spenser's at some point prior to *Delia-Cleopatra*. His dedicatory sonnet in *Delia-Cleopatra* is in Spenserian form – a rhyme scheme that he had not used before and that became his preferred form thereafter. Because the scheme would not have been widely recognised as Spenserian until *Amoretti*'s publication (1595), it is likely that Daniel read *Amoretti* in manuscript.[22] Indeed, he and Spenser may have exchanged work. In *Colin Clout's Come Home Again*, Spenser praises Daniel as an up-and-coming poet:

> And there is a new shepherd late up-sprong,
> The which doth all afore him far surpass,
> Appearing well in that well-tunèd song
> Which late he sung unto a scornful lass.
> Yet doth his trembling muse but lowly fly,
> As daring not too rashly mount on hight,
> And doth her tender plumes as yet but try
> In love's soft lays and looser thoughts' delight:
> Then rouse thy feathers quickly, Daniël,
> And to what course thou please thyself advance!
> But most, meseems, thy accent will excel
> In tragic plaints and passionate mischance.
>
> (lines 416–27)

This passage is notable on two counts: it singles out a younger contemporary as superior to 'all afore him', and contrary to generic conventions and the poem's dominant practice, it provides a surname, rather than a pseudonym. The naming is prepared by 'hight', which evokes 'high', 'height', and the archaism 'hight' (named). Spenser may be alluding to the 1591 *Astrophil and Stella*, whose final sonnet, 'Raising my hopes on hills of high desires', is followed by '*Finis*, Daniel'. By urging a young poet to pursue a Virgilian career – to fly high, as he himself had done – and by naming him, Spenser sounds as though he is naming a successor. His final praise, however, is qualified: Daniel 'will excel / In tragic plaints and passionate mischance'. The endorsement may be condescending; even so, it would have been good press for Daniel. Spenser seems to have regarded Daniel's 'Let others sing of knights' as friendly or have been willing to play along.

Relations between Spenser and Daniel were at least distantly friendly, and the two poets may have come to see themselves as natural allies. *Amoretti* provides suggestive evidence. In the thirty-third sonnet, Spenser confesses: 'Great wrong I do, I can it not deny, / To that most sacred empress, my dear dread, / Not finishing her Queen of Faëry'. In the eightieth, he pleads: 'After so long a race as I have run / Through Faery-land, which those six books compile, / Give leave to rest me'. Spenser presents *Amoretti* as a detour in his Virgilian career.

Even as a pose, this invites readers to wonder why he published *Amoretti* when he did; perhaps the sonnet-sequence vogue forced his hand. Among living writers, the poet most associated with the new fashion was Daniel, whose name was joined with Sidney's. Spenser may have regarded Daniel as both an ally and a competitor. The first edition of Sidney's *Arcadia* was published in 1590, the same year in which Spenser brought out the first edition of *The Faerie Queene*; in 1591, the pirated *Astrophil and Stella* was published; and in early 1592, the first edition of *Delia* came out. In 1592, then, Spenser and Daniel may have had common cause: getting out from under the shadow of Sidney.

In concerted effort or separately, Spenser and Daniel used Sidney's name to further their careers. The most telling publication is *Colin Clout's Come Home Again*. The title is a feint: it gestures towards Spenser's return to England in 1589–91, but the 'home' must be Ireland, to judge by the dedication ('from my house at Kilcoman') and the occasion (a return from court). In coming home, Colin asserts his independence and returns to his poetic roots (in pastoral). The book concludes with elegies to Sidney, and the title poem ends its list of contemporary writers by asserting that they are lesser poets than Sidney:

> And there, though last, not least is Aetiön –
> A gentler shepherd may no where be found –
> Whose muse, full of high thoughts' inventiön,
> Doth, like himself, heroically sound.
> All these, and many others more remain,
> Now after Astrofell is dead and gone:
> But while as Astrofell did live and reign,
> Amongst all these was none his paragon.
>
> (lines 444–51)

While 'Aetiön' could refer to Shakespeare (whose name might 'heroically sound' via a pun on 'shake spear'), it more likely refers to Drayton: he had begun his heroical epistles, and his poetic name, Roland, was associated with an epic hero.[23] (Also note that 'Drayton' ends in '-ayton'.) Spenser probably found 'Aetiön' in Lucian's *Herodotus or Aëtiön* [sic].[24] After relating how Herodotus recited from his histories at the Olympic Games and won more fame than the Olympic victors, Lucian first lists writers who followed Herodotus's example, then comes 'at last' to Aëtiön the painter. Aëtiön brought his *Marriage of Roxana and Alexander* to the Games; one judge was so impressed by it that he offered him his daughter's hand in marriage. Like Spenser,

Lucian focuses on artistic excellence, competition, and reward – and on returning to private matters after public victories. Spenser praises Aetiön 'at last' to set up his praise of Sidney, who is punningly introduced as a fallen star and a fallen king: 'Astrofell did live and reign'.

The book's elegies to Sidney are themselves unusual: three had already been published; Sidney had died a decade earlier; and Spenser's 'The doleful lay of Clorinda' is framed as a song by Sidney's sister. Spenser's elegies are also numerically distinctive: 'Astrophel' has 216 lines, alluding to the number of poetic units in *Astrophil and Stella*; 'The doleful lay' has 108 lines, alluding to the number of sonnets.[25] Spenser depicts Sidney as more poet than soldier, and most of all as sonnet writer. As a recent biographer of Spenser notes, *Colin Clout's Come Home Again* is 'designed to help foster the burgeoning legend of Sidney as the last great aristocratic poet': Spenser presents a 'changing of the guard . . . in terms of class'.[26]

Spenser's views of social class also emerge in his dedicatory sonnet to William Jones's *Nennio, A Treatise on Nobility* (1595) – a translation of Giovanni Battista Nenna's *Il Nennio*. Spenser asserts that the treatise can help its readers attain nobility:

> Whoso will seek by right deserts t'attain
> Unto the type of true nobility –
> And not by painted shows and titles vain
> Derivèd far from famous ancestry –
> Behold them both in their right visnomy
> Here truly portrayed . . .

Spenser allows for nobility by birth, but his indictment of inherited nobility is striking: he rails against 'titles vain'. Emphasising that true nobility is not an outward show, he echoes a conceit in *Amoretti*'s central mirror sonnet: that the lady's true character might be seen in the poet. In his *Nennio* sonnet and other mid-1590s publications, Spenser presents himself as a poet expressing sentiments hitherto kept hidden, as if he were finally showing his true colours.

Daniel, too, had found a new voice in 1595, one that complemented Spenser's. His sonnet in *Nennio* directly follows Spenser's and supports its claims:

> Here dost thou bring, my friend, a stranger born
> To be 'ndenised with us and made our own –
> *Nobility* – whose name indeed is worn
> By many that are great or mighty grown:
> But yet to him most natural, best known,

> To whom thou dost thy labours sacrifice
> And *in* whom all those virtues best are shown
> Which here this little volume doth comprise . . .

Daniel addresses *Nennio*'s translator, but because the sonnet has no title, it might first seem to address Spenser. The translator is praised for bringing *Nobility* (both treatise and trait) from Italy to England, so that it may be made a naturalised citizen (an endenised stranger). Like Spenser, Daniel suggests that nobility is earned and that some magnates unfortunately regard it as a mere show or garment. The 'him' to whom nobility is 'most natural' is the Earl of Essex, the translation's dedicatee, a noble by both birth and merit. As with line 1's 'friend', however, the referent is initially ambiguous: it could be anyone who might recognise his own nobility by reading the treatise. The sestet clarifies the referent and introduces mirror imagery:

> Whereon, when he shall cast his worthy eyes,
> He here shall glass himself, himself shall read:
> The model of his own perfection lies
> Here plain described, which he presents in deed.
> – So that, if men cannot true worth discern
> By this discourse, look they on him and learn.

The imagery evokes perfection and faithful representation: Essex, the mirror of chivalry, will see himself mirrored in the treatise ('himself, himself' emphasises visual reflection). The terminal position of 'look they on him and learn' recalls Sidney's 'look in thy heart and write'.

So what does all of this have to do with Shakespeare? If Shakespeare was writing his own sonnet sequence in the mid-1590s, when he also wrote *Romeo and Juliet* and *Richard II*, he was venturing into genres cultivated by Spenser and Daniel – the complaint, the sonnet, tragic love, even epic. Though Shakespeare never wrote an epic, his second 'Henriad' – *Richard II*, the two *Henry IV* plays, and *Henry V* – is epic in scope if not ambition. These plays, especially *Richard II*, were influenced by *The First Four Books of the Civil Wars*, and they in turn influenced Daniel's epic.[27] Shakespeare and Daniel may thus have been tracking each other's careers, and Daniel may have been a more direct rival to Shakespeare than Spenser was.

A Spenser-Daniel alliance might also have been a shot fired in Shakespeare's direction. The first published reference to Shakespeare is in *Greene's Groatsworth of Wit* (1592) – a pamphlet supposedly written by Robert Greene on his deathbed, which most scholars now attribute to Henry Chettle or Thomas Nashe.[28] Greene or his surrogate writes:

'there is an upstart crow [who] supposes he is as well able to bombast out a blank verse as the best of you, and [who] is in his own conceit the only Shake-scene in a country'. As an actor become playwright, Shakespeare attracted envy from university writers. These 'University Wits' included Greene, Marlowe, and Peele, non-aristocratic playwrights who had attended Cambridge or Oxford and were active in the late 1580s or early 1590s.[29] In a common version of the story, Southampton protected Shakespeare: within three months of publishing *Greene's Groatsworth of Wit*, Chettle apologised for it, declaring that Shakespeare was 'no less civil than excellent in the quality he professes', and that persons of 'worship' vouched for 'his uprightness of dealing and . . . grace in writing'.[30] Indeed, it is sometimes claimed that Sonnet 112 alludes to this incident via its reference to 'vulgar scandal' and a pun on 'green': 'what care I who calls me well or ill, / So you o'ergreen my bad, my good allow?'[31] Whether or not Southampton came to his defence, Shakespeare might have been perceived as upstart playwright and upstart poet. Like his rivals in the theatre, Shakespeare's sonnet-writing competitors were non-aristocratic and university educated. The poets who avoided writing for the stage may have been especially anxious about their social standing: Spenser made much of his family relations to the 'Spencers of Althorp'; Daniel signed his works 'Samuel Daniel, Gent'.[32] For them, as for Shakespeare, poetry could be a means to social and artistic respect.

Chapman's Marlovian Career

George Chapman has been the leading candidate for *Sonnets*' rival poet since the turn of the twentieth century; his candidacy will be discussed later in this chapter. For now I will focus on a general role that he plays in 1590s poetry. In prefaces and poems, Chapman depicts himself as a Marlovian poet who questions norms. In laying claim to Marlowe's mantle, he lays claim to a career that defines him against poets like Shakespeare.

Chapman's 1590s publications include lyric poetry, short narrative, epic, and drama:

> 1594: *The Shadow of Night* (two poetic hymns – 'To Night' and 'To Cynthia')
> 1595: *Ovid's Banquet of Sense* (title poem, ten sonnets, 'The Amorous Zodiac')
> 1598: *Hero and Leander* (by Marlowe, continued by Chapman)

1598: *Seven Books of the Iliad* (translation of Homer)
1598: *Achilles' Shield* (translation of Homer)
1598: *The Blind Beggar of Alexandria* (comedy, first performed in 1596)
1599: *A Humourous Day's Mirth* (comedy, first performed in 1597)

Chapman makes his debut with *The Shadow of Night*. In his dedicatory letter to Matthew Royden, he presents himself as oppositional, arguing for 'true Nobility' of spirit and depicting the poet as a seer who is inspired after 'invocation, fasting, watching'. Chapman develops similar ideas in *Ovid's Banquet of Sense*, which he also dedicates to Royden: 'sweet Matt . . . The profane multitude I hate and only consecrate my strange poems to these searching spirits whom learning has made noble and nobility sacred'. A coterie aesthetic does not dominate his stage writings, however, and Chapman later dedicates poems to members of the nobility.[33] His poetics and career are unusual not so much because he cultivates obscurity and interrogates inherited privilege – professing hatred of the 'profane multitude' is a conventional Horatian gesture, after all, and he was hardly alone among humanists in suggesting that true nobility was more talent than title. But Chapman advertised obscurity from the outset, and the intensity of his remarks on nobility is matched only by Marlowe in *Tamburlaine* and *Doctor Faustus*.

Chapman's difference from other poets can be measured by his sonnet in *Nennio*:

G. CHAPMAN TO THE AUTHOR

Accept, thrice noble Nennio, at his hand
That cannot bid himself well-come at home,
A thrice due welcome to our native strand,
Italian, French, and English now become.
Thrice noble, not in that used epithet –
But noble, first, to know whence nóblesse sprung;
Then, in thy labour bringing it to light;
Thirdly, in being adornèd with our tongue.
And since so (like itself) thy land affords
The right of nóblesse to all noble parts,
I wish our friend – giving the English words,
With much desert of love in English hearts –
  As he hath made one strange an Englishman,
  May make our minds, in this, Italiän.

Ex tenebris.

Drawing light or truth from darkness (*ex tenebris*), Chapman's sonnet is more obscure than the other dedications. It is also more critical of social rank. Chapman addresses 'Nennio' as author and book, but he also praises the translator, suggesting that Nennio is enriched and ennobled via translation. Chapman presents himself as an alienated Englishman: he 'cannot bid himself well-come at home'. As John Huntington argues in *Ambition, Rank, and Poetry in 1590s England*, 'By ... finding nobility in the idea, the writing, and the translating, Chapman sides with the voices in *Nennio* that attack the customary idea of inherited nobility.'[34] Because Italy recognises nobility of merit, Chapman grudgingly praises Italian values ('make our minds, in this, Italiän'). In the mid-1590s, then, Chapman looked askance at social rank. And in his continuation of Marlowe's *Hero and Leander*, he positioned himself as a countercultural poet in his own right. A salient difference between Marlowe and Chapman is the latter's moralism. In *Hero and Leander*, Chapman calls attention to the title characters' premarital sex, and he depicts their deaths as punitive; this is hardly in Marlowe's playful spirit. Chapman may be promoting poetry as a high calling, but he also expresses moralism in *The Shadow of Night* and *Ovid's Banquet of Sense* – works that respond to Shakespeare's *Venus and Adonis*. Years before he presented himself as a corrected Marlowe, Chapman presented himself as a corrected Ovidian poet.

Venus and Adonis is based on an Ovidian story, and it evokes Ovid's authority with an epigraph from the *Amores*: 'Vilia miretur vulgus; mihi flavus Apollo / Pocula Castalia plena ministret aqua' ('Let common people admire vile things; may golden-haired Apollo provide me with cups filled with Castalian waters'). In publishing sensuous verse, and in presenting himself as a serious initiate of art, Shakespeare may have infuriated Chapman. When *Venus and Adonis* was published, Chapman's ideas about poetry had not yet appeared in print, so if Shakespeare is attacking them, his knowledge comes from manuscripts or reputation. In *The Shadow of Night*, Chapman may have struck back: 'Presume not then ye flesh-confounded souls / That cannot bear the full Castalian bowls, / Which sever mounting spirits from the senses, / To look in this deep fount for thy pretences' ('Hymnus in Cynthiam', lines 162–5). Ostensibly targeting all 'flesh-confounded souls', Chapman concludes by attacking one person ('*thy* pretences'). Besides objecting to sensory experience that does not spiritually inspire, he suggests that it is easy to be deluded by the senses, and that poets who are truly inspired – the poets who can drink full cups of Apollo's intoxicating waters – possess a deep kind of knowledge.[35] Chapman's most succinct statement of his poetics occurs in 'Hymnus in Noctem': 'No pen can anything eternal write / That is not steeped with humour of the Night' (lines 376–7). Shakespeare may have taken notice of this attack and responded to it with Berowne's exclamation in *Love's Labour's Lost*: 'Never durst poet touch a pen to write / Until his ink were tempered with Love's sighs' (Act 4, Scene 3). In their mid-1590s works, Chapman and Shakespeare staked out opposing poetic territories.

In *Ovid's Banquet of Sense*, Chapman criticises all misguided heirs of Ovid, but Shakespeare is his foremost target. Chapman's title poem draws on a Platonic tradition in which feasts of the senses lead to higher, spiritual experiences. It may also be a riposte to a passage in Shakespeare's *Venus and Adonis*. When Venus pleads with Adonis for a kiss, she invokes the five senses, arguing that she would know Adonis's beauty by hearing if she could not see, by touch if she could not hear, and by smell if she could not feel. Gazing at Adonis's mouth, she exclaims:

> But O! what banquet wert thou to the taste,
> Being nurse and feeder of the other four –
> Would they not wish the feast might ever last,
> And bid Suspicion double-lock the door,
>   Lest Jealousy, that sour unwelcome guest,
>   Should, by his stealing in, disturb the feast?
>
> (stanza 75)

Sensing that Adonis is opening his mouth to rebuke her, Venus faints. Adonis tries to revive her but fails; he then 'kisses her; and she, by her good will, / Will never rise, so he will kiss her still' (stanza 80). Chapman may have felt that this scene was merely titillating, and that Shakespeare was flattering an aristocratic patron and pandering to popular taste.

The Rival-Poet Problem

The literary marketplace of Elizabethan England left its mark on *Shakespeare's Sonnets*. A useful place to begin is with the rival-poet series, which both alludes to 1590s trends and fits neatly into the pyramidal scheme (as the sixth pyramid step). From the nineteenth through the mid-twentieth centuries, commentary on the series often focused on identifying the poet who emerges victorious at the end of the series. Recent scholars tend to regard this line of enquiry as misguided, for two reasons. First, the series refers to more than one rival, and to focus on the victor is to limit our perspective; second, the main rival may be a fictional or composite figure. While many commentators grant that the series alludes to Shakespeare's contemporaries, few do more than list the usual suspects. But the problem is more tractable than it is reputed to be, and we would miss some of the spirit in which Shakespeare wrote if we avoided the question of the rival's identity.

Let us first turn to Sonnet 86 and consider whether its rival is fictional. Unlike the other sonnets in the series, this poem speaks of rival-related matters in the past tense:

> Was it the proud full sail of his great verse,
> Bound for the prize of all too precious you,
> That did my ripe thoughts in my brain inhearse,
> Making their tomb the womb wherein they grew?
> Was it his spirit, by spirits taught to write
> Above a mortal pitch, that struck me dead?
> No, neither he, nor his compeers by night
> Giving him aid, my verse astonishèd.
> He, nor that affable familiar ghost
> Which nightly gulls him with intelligence,
> As victors of my silence cannot boast –
> I was not sick of any fear from thence.
>   But when your countenance filled up his line,
>   Then lacked I matter; that enfeebled mine.

'The proud full sail of his great verse' and 'by spirits taught to write' indicate that the rival wrote in a grand style, and that he saw himself as a supernaturally inspired. The 'compeers by night' are probably spirits who taught the rival to write, though their exact status is unclear. It is also unclear who the 'familiar ghost' is; the poet says that the ghost is cramming and duping the rival with information ('gulls him with intelligence'). In general, the *Sonnets* poet suggests that there was a conspiracy against him, that the rival's verse is 'great', and that the rival's victory resulted from the youth's support of, or presence in, the rival's poetry ('your countenance filled up his line'). Sonnet 86 thus provides us with a profile for the rival, albeit a murky one.

As MacDonald P. Jackson argues, the rival poet may be 'a composite creation'. Jackson presents Chapman and Marlowe as Shakespeare's main models, adding that Ben Jonson may have contributed to the composite, along with 'Spenser, Daniel, Drayton, and other poets lauded by [Francis] Meres'.[36] His claims are consistent with the idea that the *Sonnets* poet's attitude towards the rival is not simply admiring or ironic, and they are buttressed by studies of Shakespeare's vocabulary, which assign the rival-poet series to 1598–1600. In Jackson's account, Marlowe plays a haunting role in the Marlowe-Chapman composite and the rival is 'semi-fictional'. Because he implies that the series is inspired by real people and that Chapman was the poet who outvied Shakespeare for the youth's attentions, Jackson could just have easily labelled the rival 'half-historical'. At the least, he suggests that Sonnet 86 alludes to a particular poet.

For all its virtues, the composite approach is arguably more of a pragmatic solution than an explanation grounded in Elizabethan poetics. This is not to say that it is merely pragmatic (at least not in Jackson's hands) but to stress that rival-poet arguments are conditioned by decades of inconclusive debate. To repeat three points from earlier chapters: Shakespeare creates the impression that he refers to real people and events; *Sonnets*' first readers were likely friends; and sonnet-sequence conventions favour the possibility that the rival poet is more historical than fictional in broad outlines and certain details. In short, it is *not* anachronistic to take up the matter of the rival poet's identity, and Shakespeare may have expected readers to identify the rival or to make educated guesses.

Organization and Argument in the Rival-Poet Series

Before focusing on the rival's identity, let us consider the organisation of the rival-poet series. The series might seem to begin with 78 (the first sonnet to mention a rival) and to end with 86 (the sonnet about the victorious rival), but the pyramid-step design argues that it starts with 76 (a sonnet about poetic fashion) and runs through 87 (a coda or farewell poem). Because the next eleven sonnets (88–98) address the consequences of the rival's victory, they can be read as the story's next stage. With these contexts in mind, the organisational structure becomes easier to see, especially if we focus on the eleven core sonnets (leaving out the coda):

76 (77 78 79 80) 81 (82 83 84 85) 86

Sonnet 76 is introductory (*Why is my verse so barren of new pride?*); 86 is retrospective (*Was it the proud full sail of his great verse?*); and 81 is the centre ('Or shall I live ... Or you survive'). The four sonnets that precede 81 mostly point to one rival poet; the four that follow, to more than one rival. Because 86 is preceded by sonnets that emphasise rivals (in the plural), its revelation that the youth preferred one rival is something of a surprise ending. To put it another way, the present tense in Sonnets 76–85 is rhetorical: the whole series may have been written after the events to which it alludes and retrofitted for effect.

Whenever it was written, the rival-poet series is coherent – a fact obscured by two interruptive sonnets, 77 and 81, which are more tautly linked to the gift trio and the monument trio than to their neighbouring sonnets. Sonnet 77 evokes an occasion on which the poet gives the youth a book, an event that does not seem related to the rival theme. With a little effort, though, 77 can be seen as contributing to the series. The gift may be a notebook in which the youth is to inscribe sonnets, and phrases like 'this book' could allude to a manuscript copy of *Sonnets*. The gift is moreover morally beneficial: it can be seen as an antidote to corruptive praise.

Sonnet 81 similarly requires effort to make it fit in the series:

> Or I shall live your epitaph to make
> Or you survive when I in earth am rotten,
> From hence your memory death cánnot take,
> Although in me each part will be forgotten.
> Your name from hence immortal life shall have,
> Though I, once gone, to all the world must die.
> The earth can yield me but a common grave
> When you entombèd in men's eyes shall lie.
> Your monument shall be my gentle verse,
> Which eyes not yet created shall o'er-read,
> And tongues to be your being shall rehearse
> When all the breathers of this world are dead.
> You still shall live, such virtue hath my pen,
> Where breath most breathes, ev'n in the mouths of men.

Because 80's couplet evokes the possibility that the *Sonnets* poet will be 'cast away' and the rival will 'thrive', 81's 'Or I shall live' might initially suggest 'Alternatively, I will thrive', or the entire line might suggest 'Whether it is I or he who writes your epitaph'. But by line 2, these interpretations are undone. If we remain intent on linking 80–1, we might hear the poet saying 'Because a better poet is writing for you, whatever happens from now on, your immortality is assured', but this sense is all but negated when the poet presents his verse as powerful. If we still wish to read 81 as a continuation of 80, we could say that the poet 'takes the offensive against the threat his Rival poses' (Jackson), but it is more important to see that 81 stands apart.[37] Its proclamations come from outside the frame of the rival story; the poet gestures towards eternity.

With the understanding that 81 marks a division, let us return to the series as a whole. Though it concludes with the rival's preferment and the threat of a break-up, the series does not tell much of a story. It does have two halves, however. I have said that 77–80 and 82–5 focus on one rival and more-than-one rival, respectively. That assessment needs to be qualified: what counts as singular and plural is sometimes a matter of interpretation. In Sonnet 83, for example, the poet may use the word 'others' to speak contemptuously of one rival: 'I impair not beauty, being mute, / When *others* would give life, and bring a tomb'. If singular and plural descriptors are taken at face value, the poet refers to one rival in Sonnets 79, 80, and 86; to more than one rival in 78, 82, 83, and 85; and to an unspecified number of rivals in 76, 77, 81, and 84. We need to look more closely at what is going on.

As the first poem of its pyramid step, Sonnet 76 can be understood as a preface:

> Why is my verse so barren of new pride,
> So far from variation or quick change?
> Why with the time do I not glance aside
> To new-found methods and to compounds strange?
> Why write I still all one, ever the same,
> And keep invention in a noted weed,
> That every word doth almost tell my name,
> Showing their birth and where they did proceed?
> O know, sweet love, I always write of you,
> And you and love are still my argument;
> So all my best is dressing old words new,
> Spending again what is already spent.
>   For as the sun is daily new and old,
>   So is my love still telling what is told.

Claiming to speak plain truth, the poet indulges in metaphor, referring to different modes of expression as adornment, medicine, and clothing ('new pride', 'compounds strange', and 'noted weed'). As Stephen Booth notes, Sonnet 76 'invites a reader to hunt for witty extra meanings', closing with 'gratuitous parallelisms' and a 'momentarily perceived comparison of the sun and the beloved'.[38] While hinting at complexity, the poet insists that his love is simple and constant.

In advocating a routine, 77 follows 76; in calling attention to its gift occasion, 77 threatens to interrupt the series at its outset. Sonnet 78 unambiguously invokes rivalry:

> So oft have I invoked thee for my muse,
> And found such fair assistance in my verse
> As every alien pen hath got my use
> And under thee their poesy disperse.
> Thine eyes, that taught the dumb on high to sing
> And heavy ignorance aloft to fly,
> Have added feathers to the learnèd's wing
> And given grace a double majesty.
> Yet be most proud of that which I compile,
> Whose influence is thine, and born of thee:
> In others' works thou dost but mend the style,
> And arts with thy sweet graces gracèd be.
> But thou art all my art, and dost advance
> As high as learning, my rude ignorance.

The *Sonnets* poet cites 'alien' writers who 'disperse' their poetry under the youth's name or protection. The rivals have been inspired by the youth's beauty or the promise of patronage ('fair assistance'). Though they may have written dedications to the youth or used his name to promote their works, they do not yet seem to have written about him, or at least not extensively; nor do they seem to have received special favours. His countenance has yet to fill their lines.

How many rivals are there? At first glance, they may seem legion: 'every alien pen' wants to be in the youth's good graces, and the poet claims that the youth's eyes have assisted 'the dumb', 'heavy ignorance', 'the learnèd', and 'grace' – potentially alluding to four types of poets. The couplet, however, could hint that the *Sonnets* poet is worried mostly about one rival: 'But thou art all my art, and dost advance / As high as learning, my rude ignorance'. Displaying art with a pun on 'art', the *Sonnets* poet claims that he owes everything to the fair youth; this could indicate that he was referring to himself when he spoke of heavy ignorance. Since the youth merely mends the style of other writers, 'the dumb' could also refer to the *Sonnets* poet. And because 'the dumb' and 'ignorance' are placed in parallel with 'the learnèd' and 'grace', the latter categories could refer to a poet who is both graceful and learned. Behind 'every alien pen' there is perhaps one pen in particular, the nemesis-poet.

The expression 'added feathers' merits a closer look. As West notes:

Poetic Rivalry in Late-Elizabethan England 81

> It would be wise to take [the poet's] humility with a pinch of salt. Despite the heavy load of ignorance he carries, he sings and soars aloft, but no information is given about the altitude attained by the learned. Their wing ... is a fine poetic singular ... and the beloved's eyes have added feathers to it, as a falconer imps a wing ... The sly hint is that imping is usually a treatment for a damaged bird.[39]

After explaining that *compilare* and *pilare* can mean 'plagiarise' and 'pluck', West argues that Shakespeare is 'simply plucking the feathers out of other people's work' and 'playing down his powers' in order to give 'the greater credit to the Muse who taught him to soar'.[40] More precisely, the *Sonnets* poet portrays himself as a plagiarist not so much to suggest that he is a thief as to stress that everyone steals from the youth. The phrase 'added feathers' refers to stylistic flourishes, and it may be an allusion to the 'upstart crow' passage in *Greene's Groatsworth of Wit*:

> [You are base-minded men] if by my misery you be not warned: for unto none of you ... sought those burrs to cleave – those puppets, I mean, that spoke from our mouths, those antics garnished in our colours ... Yes, trust them not: for there is an upstart crow, beautified with our feathers, that with his tiger's heart wrapped in a player's hide supposes he is as well able to bombast out a blank verse as the best of you: and, being an absolute Johannes-factotum, is in his own conceit the only Shake-scene in a country.

The stage actor is Shakespeare, whose line 'O tiger's heart wrapped in a woman's hide!' (*Henry VI, Part 3*) is parodied. itself, 'beautified with our feathers' could refer to acting, playwriting, play-doctoring, or plagiarism; combined with 'tiger's heart wrapped in a player's hide' and 'bombast out a blank verse', it suggests 'made a name for himself by composing verse he had no right to compose'. Shakespeare seems to have ruffled the feathers of some non-acting writers – perhaps the University Wits.

'Added feathers' also bears comparison to lines by Daniel and Chapman. In Sonnet 35 of the fifty-sonnet *Delia*, Daniel likens himself to Petrarch, claiming that, although he has 'less rhyme' than the Italian poet, he can 'add one feather' to Delia's fame and thus 'help [Fame's] flight throughout the fairest isle'. In the tenth sonnet of 'A Coronet for his Mistress Philosophy', Chapman criticises 'Muses that fame's loose feathers beautify, / And such as scorn to tread the theater' (lines 1–2).[41] The first line may target Shakespeare, whose fame, Chapman implies, is morally and aesthetically dubious; the second line may target Daniel, who published a closet drama, *Cleopatra*, in 1594. In this light, Shakespeare's 'Thine eyes . . . have added feathers to the learnèd's wing / And given grace a double majesty' may respond to Chapman – though Chapman is hardly a graceful poet. Beeching conjectures that Sonnet 78 refers to two rivals: a poet of learning (Chapman) and a poet of grace (Daniel).[42]

In Sonnets 79 and 80, the *Sonnets* poet has one rival in his sights – a poet of grace and grandeur. Sonnet 79 opens: 'Whilst I alone did call upon thy aid, / My verse alone had all thy gentle grace, / But now my gracious numbers are decayed / And my sick muse doth give an other place'. With 'thy gentle grace', the poet alludes to the youth's gentility and perhaps to the ducal form of address ('Your Grace'). The rival poet now seems to be in the good graces of the youth, perhaps because he wrote some gracious lines. (The sonnet may be an exasperated response to reports of the rival's 'grace'.) The *Sonnets* poet's 'numbers' are 'decayed' in a few senses: his verses have lost charm, power, vigour, financial worth; his poetic monument may be falling into ruins – he has passed the midpoint of *Sonnets*. Now that his fortunes are ebbing, he must make room for 'an other'. He argues that the rival, in praising the youth, only appears to be repaying a debt or making good on an advance payment: 'Yet what of thee thy poet doth invent / He robs thee of, and pays it thee again'. And in the couplet, he advises the youth not to be gracious or generous to the rival: 'Then thank him not for that which he doth say, / Since what he owes thee, thou thyself dost pay'. Shakespeare insinuates that the rival is mercenary.

In Sonnet 80, the poet continues to target a grandiloquent rival:

> O how I faint when I of you do write,
> Knowing a better spirit doth use your name,
> And in the praise thereof spends all his might
> To make me tongue-tied speaking of your fame!
> But since your worth, wide as the ocean is,
> The humble as the proudest sail doth bear,
> My saucy bark, inferior far to his,
> On your broad main doth willfully appear.
> Your shallowest help will hold me up afloat,
> Whilst he upon your soundless deep doth ride;
> Or, being wracked, I am a worthless boat,
> He of tall building and of goodly pride.
>   Then, if he thrive and I be cast away,
>   The worst was this: my love was my decay.

The rival poet is like a ponderous galleon; the *Sonnets* poet, like a swift manoeuvrable boat. With sexual innuendo, style is equated with poet: the *Sonnets* poet's boat is 'saucy' and 'willfully' appears on the ocean of the youth's worth; the rival's is 'of tall building and of goodly pride'. The *Sonnets* poet is likely being sarcastic, chiding the youth for valuing bad poetry. Marine imagery returns in the couplet: 'But if he thrive and I be cast away, / The worst was this: my love was my decay'. 'Cast away' means 'shipwrecked' and 'discarded'; it also hints at 'having been denied God's grace'.[43] The poet suggests that his love for the youth, or the youth himself, is both his worst sin and the source of his demise. In bringing Sonnet 80 to a close, 'my love was my decay' brings the first half of the rival-poet series to a close.

As the series' centre poem, Sonnet 81 can be read as redemptive: phoenix-like, the poet rises from the ashes of love's fire to declare that he can preserve the youth's memory. More simply, it divides the series in half. Sonnets 82–3 set the tone and agenda of the second half:

> Sonnet 82
> I grant thou wert not married to my muse
> And therefore mayst without attaint o'erlook
> The dedicated words which writers use
> Of their fair subject, blessing every book.
> Thou art as fair in knowledge as in hue,
> Finding thy worth a limit past my praise,
> And therefore art enforced to seek anew
> Some fresher stamp of the time-bett'ring days.
> And do so, love; yet when they have devised
> What strainèd touches rhetoric can lend,
> Thou, truly fair, wert truly sympathised
> In true plain words, by thy true-telling friend.
>   And their gross painting might be better used
>   Where cheeks need blood; in thee it is abused.
>
> Sonnet 83
> I never saw that you did painting need
> And therefore to your fair no painting set;
> I found, or thought I found, you did exceed
> The barren tender of a poet's debt –
> And therefore have I slept in your report,
> That you yourself, being extant, well might show
> How far a modern quill doth come too short,

> Speaking of worth, what worth in you doth grow.
> This silence for my sin you did impute,
> Which shall be most my glory, being dumb;
> For I impair not beauty, being mute,
> When others would give life and bring a tomb.
>   There lives more life in one of your fair eyes
>   Than both your poets can in praise devise.

These sonnets are linked through repetition: in 82's couplet, the poet says that 'painting' applied to the youth is misapplied; in 83's opening lines, he declares that the youth does not need 'painting'. As if keen on avoiding a desperate tone, the poet grants that his muse and the youth are 'not married', and he criticises rivals for words so 'dedicated' as to be excessive – the sort of rhetoric that is used in dedications. Sonnet 83's couplet is ambiguous: in speaking of 'both your poets', the poet is probably referring to himself and a rival poet, but the sonnet is ostensibly about many rivals, and line 12 refers to 'others'. The poet may have two rivals in mind.

Sonnets 84–5 also feature praise and plural rivals. Sonnet 84 begins: 'Who is it that says most, which can say more / Than this rich praise, that you alone are you?' Sonnet 85 ends:

> Hearing you praised, I say, ''Tis so, 'tis true',
> And to the most of praise add something more –
> But that is in my thought, whose love to you,
> Though words come hindmost, holds his rank before.
>   Then others, for the breath of words, respect;
>   Me, for my dumb thoughts, speaking in effect.

Both sonnets repeat earlier arguments: that the poet is a simple truth-teller at a loss for words; that the best way to praise the youth is to copy him in words; that the rivals are more polished but less loving than the poet; and that all poets who praise the youth steal from him. In 84, the poet does not specifically mention rivals, but he does imply that the youth likes praise so much that he accepts bad forms of it and thus devalues all the praises: 'You to your beauteous blessings add a curse, / Being fond on praise, which makes your praises worse'. In 85, the poet compares himself to an illiterate clergyman who says 'Amen' after every hymn of praise.

Given the structural divisions in the rival-poet series and the varying emphasis on one and more-than-one rival, the *Sonnets* poet may be making one or two series of reflections. In the first scenario, Sonnet 77 offers the youth a book in which worthwhile verse can be inscribed; 78 provides an overview of the rival situation; 79–80 identify a threat to the *Sonnets* poet; and 82–5 return to the overall scene with a focus on praise. In the second scenario, the rival crisis may be a two-stage affair: one rival appears; more follow. In both scenarios, 86's victorious rival may be the poet in 79–80 or a new poet emerging in 82–5. If two main rivals are in play, different pairs of poets are worth considering. We might take up Beeching's suggestion that Daniel is 'grace' and Chapman is 'learning'; we might think of a mid-1590s poet as the original rival and a turn-of-the-century poet as the victorious rival. Especially if the rival is a poet of the latest fashion, the *Sonnets* poet's indignant questions in 86 (*Was it his great verse? Was it his spirit?*) are likely incredulous as well.

Barnabe Barnes

While there may be no definitive way of identifying the model(s) for the rival poet, the question 'Who was the rival poet?' remains worth trying to answer, as I will illustrate with discussion of Barnabe Barnes, George Chapman, and Samuel Daniel. (I consider these three poets the most plausible candidates.) Barnes's first champion was Sidney Lee, who declared in his *Life of Shakespeare* (1898) that 'All of the conditions of the [rival] problem [are] satisfied' by Barnes.[44] Lee's claims were greeted with scepticism, largely because readers at the turn of the twentieth century tended to assume that the rival was a greater poet, such as Marlowe. In editions of *Sonnets* published since 1900, Barnes tends to receive brief mention; warm advocacy has seldom been renewed. One exception to the trend is Eric Sams's 'Who was the Rival Poet of Shakespeare's Sonnet 86?' (1998). Most of the details of my analysis are anticipated in Sams's discussion.

Barnes is a plausible candidate for three basic reasons: he sought Southampton's patronage around the same time that Shakespeare did; he displays learning in his poetry; and he wrote fawning praise and bombastic verse. His sequence *Parthenophil and Parthenophe* was published soon after *Venus and Adonis* and opens with a note to 'learnèd gentlemen'. In his prefatory poem 'Go, bastard orphan . . .' and his dedicatory sonnet to Southampton, Barnes makes intriguing use of the word 'countenance' (pronounced with two syllables):

> Go, bastard orphan, pack thee hence
> And seek some stranger for defence.
> . . . .

> Some goodman that shall think thee witty
> Will be thy patron and take pity,
> And when some men shall call thee base,
> He, for thy sake, shall them disgrace.
> Then, with his countenance backed, thou shalt
> Excuse the nature of thy fault.
>
> (Prefatory poem, lines 1–2, 17–22)

> *To the Right Noble and Virtuous Lord,*
>   *Henry Earl of Southampton*
>
> Receive, sweet Lord, with thy thrice-sacred hand –
> Which sacred muses make their instrument –
> These worthless leaves, which I to thee present,
> Sprung from a rude and unmanurèd land:
> Then, with your countenance graced, they may withstand
> Hundred-eyed Envy's rough encounterment.
>
> (lines 1–6)

In both poems, 'countenance' means 'support, protection, favourable regard'; it may also evoke 'face'. Infelicities include 'encounterment' and 'unmanurèd land'. In depicting his own brain as infertile soil, Barnes may have been inspired by Shakespeare's letter in *Venus and Adonis*: 'But if the first heir of my invention prove deformed, I shall . . . never after ear so barren a land, for fear it yield me still so bad a harvest'.[45] Sonnet 86's 'But when your countenance filled up his line' may in turn have been inspired by Barnes: as if parodying the idea of filling a line, 'countenance' now counts for three syllables.

Because *Parthenophil and Parthenophe* was known for its eccentricities and absurdities, Shakespeare's evocations would be sarcastic if Barnes is the model. Barnes not only resorts to trite Petrarchan similes; he writes twelve sonnets to his mistress on a zodiac theme. (His outlandish comparisons might well elicit comments like Shakespeare's in Sonnet 21: 'So it is not with me as with that muse, / Stirred by a painted beauty to his verse, / Who heav'n itself for ornament doth use'.) Also note that *Parthenophil and Parthenophe* became infamous for two poems, Sonnet 63 and Sestina 5. In Sonnet 63, Parthenophil dreams of changing shape in order to get closer to Parthenophe; the poem ends with him wishing to become her wine so that he might 'Run through her veins and pass by pleasure's part'. This scatological conceit provoked John Marston to a satiric couplet: 'Parthenophil, thy wish I will omit; / So beastly 'tis, I may not utter it' (*The Scourge of Villainy*, 1598). In Sestina 5, Parthenophil uses magic to rape Parthenophe, invoking Hecate and the Furies; this shocking ending to the sequence could account for Sonnet 86's 'spirits'. At the end of *Coelia*, Walter Percy replies: 'What, tell'st thou me by spells th'hast won thy dear?' ('Madrigal'). Percy was a friend of Barnes. To his enemies, Barnes was something of a buffoon. In *Have with you to Saffron-Walden* (1596), Thomas Nashe ridicules Barnes for wearing a 'codpiece as big as a Bolognian sausage' and being a coward when serving under the Earl of Essex. If Southampton in fact preferred Barnes over Shakespeare, sarcastic indignation would have been an apt response.

Victorious rival or not, Barnes was a poet whose work Shakespeare knew: *Sonnets* is organisationally, numerically, and thematically informed by *Parthenophil and Parthenophe*. Like *Sonnets*, Barnes's sequence contains more than 150 poems. Its ninety-first and central poem, Sonnet 77, plays on the idea of the four elements. (Shakespeare's 77 is also a centre poem, and his 44 evokes the four elements.) The sixty-sixth and central poem of the 'Sonnets' section of *Parthenophil and Parthenophe* is Sonnet 54, an anacreontic poem that may be related to Shakespeare's 154. Two of Barnes's madrigals are mirror poems whose numbers have 'doubled digits' (compare Shakespeare's 22 and 77); many of Barnes's sonnets have fifteen lines (compare Shakespeare's 99). His Sonnet 2 describes a love triangle similar to that of *Sonnets*: Parthenophil contends for his heart with an immodest woman named Laya, and he speaks of the differences between 'a mistress service and a master'. Just as the *Sonnets* poet locks up his 'sweet boy' in his breast, Parthenophil locks up his own heart, which he calls a 'tender boy'. Both Parthenophil and the *Sonnets* poet pun on 'steel' and 'steal', and both lament that their measures to prevent theft will prove ineffective. Parthenophil blames Parthenophe for stealing (Sonnet 9: 'So did she rob me of my heart's rich treasure'), and he uses a rhetorical question to accuse her of deceit (Sonnet 11: 'Why didst thou then ...?'). The *Sonnets* poet likens himself to a rich man with 'treasure' (52) and to a miser who fears that someone will 'steal his treasure' (75); in Sonnet 34, he uses a rhetorical question to accuse the youth of deceit ('Why didst thou promise ...?').

If Southampton preferred Barnes over Shakespeare, the time frame for the action may be between the publications of *Parthenophil and Parthenophe* and *A Divine Century of Spiritual Sonnets*. In publishing a spiritual sequence after his secular sequence, Barnes was making a career move similar to Shakespeare's *Lucrece* after *Venus and Adonis* – he was offering something 'serious' after a 'youthful' work. Unlike *Lucrece*, though, Barnes's second work was not written for Southampton: it is dedicated to a bishop. In 1598, Barnes was arrested for attempted murder; escaping from prison, he fled to the North of England, where he remained for many years. If Barnes was favoured by Southampton, then, 1593–5 is the likely period. In order to square that with a late 1590s dating of the rival-poet series, we might posit that Shakespeare was drawing on old events.

George Chapman

In his lifetime, George Chapman was known as a difficult poet and a translator of Homer; he also achieved some success as a playwright. His candidacy for rival relies heavily on Sonnet 86, whose 'proud full sail of his great verse' could denote the fourteener couplets in his *Iliad* translation, and whose emphasis on supernatural inspiration could allude to his claim that he was possessed by Homer's spirit. With or without 'the school of night' (an editorial crux in *Love's Labour's Lost*), 86's 'compeers by night' may refer to a coterie involving Chapman.[46] And with or without the coterie, 'compeers by night', 'by spirits taught to write', and 'affable familiar ghost' may allude to *The Shadow of Night*, in which Chapman asserts that 'Skill' will not visit readers 'without having drops of their souls like a heavenly familiar'. Chapman is an attractive candidate for the rival because he is both a talented poet and a mockable one.

But Chapman's candidacy is less attractive if we imagine that Shakespeare wrote the rival-poet series in the mid-1590s or refers to events of that time. Not only is there no clear evidence that Chapman sought Southampton's patronage in 1594–6; the second part of *The Shadow of Night*, 'Hymnus in Cynthiam', may have been written 'against Southampton'.[47] What is more, if Sonnet 21's rival ('that Muse, / Stirred by a painted beauty to his verse') is the same as Sonnet 86's rival, Chapman is not a credible model, because his mistress is not a woman of flesh but 'Philosophy', and he distances himself from poets who write of 'painted beauty'. (Sonnet 21 targets a poet inspired or aroused by a woman who wears cosmetics.) The case for Chapman seems to require a later crisis, and, even then, we might question whether he was a poet who would praise a beautiful nobleman. Chapman did write dedications to nobility, including sonnets to Pembroke and Southampton in his 1609 *Iliad*, but only a few of them date from the 1590s.[48] His general tendency in the 1590s is to champion a nobility of merit.

Though Chapman may not have been competing with Shakespeare for Southampton's patronage in 1594–6, he may have responded to *Venus and Adonis* and *Lucrece* in his works. *Venus and Adonis* was a huge success; it helped make Shakespeare a known quantity and earned him Southampton's countenance. It also helped shape Shakespeare's reputation as an amatory poet. In the second of three 'Parnassus' plays produced by Cambridge students between 1598 and 1602, the character Gullio (a naive reader) exclaims: 'I'll worship sweet Mr Shakespeare and to honour him will lay his *Venus and Adonis* under my pillow'.[49] At the turn of the seventeenth century, Gabriel Harvey wrote in his copy of Chaucer's works: 'The younger sort takes much delight in Shakespeare's *Venus and Adonis*; his *Lucrece* and his *Tragedy of Hamlet, Prince of Denmark* have it in them to please the wiser sort.'[50] But even *Lucrece* was sometimes seen as lightweight. In the third Parnassus play, the character Judicio (a mature reader) offers qualified praise of Shakespeare: 'Who loves not Adon's love, or Lucrece' rape? / His sweeter verse contains heart-robbing line, / Could but a graver subject him content / Without love's foolish lazy languishment'. As Meres's 1598 comments indicate, Shakespeare was perceived as Ovidian: 'the sweet witty soul of Ovid lives in mellifluous and honey-tongued Shakespeare; witness his *Venus* and *Adonis*, his *Lucrece*, his sugared Sonnets among his private friends'.

In *Ovid's Banquet of Sense*, Chapman criticises debased Ovidian poets, including the Shakespeare of *Venus and Adonis*. He may also be responding to *Lucrece* through stanza and verse count. *Ovid's Banquet of Sense* contains the following poems in the following order:

> Five introductory sonnets (by friends of Chapman)
> The title poem (in 117 nine-line stanzas)
> 'A coronet for his Mistress Philosophy' (a ten-sonnet corona)
> 'The Amorous Zodiac' (a poem of 30 six-line stanzas)
> 'The Amorous Contention of Phyllis and Flora' (a translation in 103 quatrains)
> Most of the Latin text of the translated poem

At a glance, the book's total number of poetic units could be 265 (the same total in *Lucrece*), and the total numbers of verses could be 1,856 (one more than the total in *Lucrece*).[51] But one of the book's themes is that appearances are deceptive, and some texts are not by Chapman. 'The Amorous Contention', for example, is a translation, likely by one of Chapman's friends.[52] Is Chapman challenging Shakespeare through numbers and numeric schemes? And assuming that he is, did Shakespeare respond?

The title page of *Ovid's Banquet of Sense* warns and guides readers (see Figure 3.1). Since Chapman's name does not appear until a few pages later, the title might initially be read as 'The Banquet of Sense, by Ovid', and 'banquet of sense' could imply that sense (reason) is the main subject. This in turn allows for the possibility that Ovid is celebrating reason or marking the occasion at which reason left him (when his sense was banqueted upon). These ambiguities are deliberate, to judge by the Latin epigraph and the emblem-like illustration. The lines from Persius can be translated: 'Who will read this stuff? Nobody, by Hercules, nobody – either a couple of people or nobody.' Chapman is pitching his book to readers who are fit though few; he expects that most will misunderstand him. The phrase above the stick with a slanted reflection ('sibi conscia recti') is from Virgil's *Aeneid*; it can be translated: '[a mind] aware of its own rectitude'. As a remark on the poet, it is a declaration of integrity. As a gloss on the image of the stick, it is a comment on truth and appearance. Chapman is warning his reader that things may not be what they seem and that our senses can mislead our sense. We should expect ambiguity.

More specifically, we should expect crafty use of optics. One example occurs in the title poem, when the poet describes a statue of Niobe as 'So cunningly to optic reason wrought / That, afar off, it shewed a woman's face, / Heavy and weeping, but, more nearly viewed, / Nor weeping, heavy, nor a woman shewed' (stanza 3). Soon after, the poet describes statues of Apollo, Diana, and Niobe's children. The gods are shooting arrows and are set in 'purple and transparent glass' atop 'two pyrámides / Of freckled marble': when sunlight passes through the glass, blood-red light falls on the children (stanza 6). Optics and pyramids are also conjoined later in the poem, after Ovid has seen Corinna naked. Inspired by this sight, Ovid muses:

> Betwixt mine eyes and object, certain lines
> Move in the figure of a pyramis
> Whose chapter in mine eye's gray apple shines,
> The base within my sacred object is:
> On this will I inscribe in golden verse
> The marvels reigning in my sovereign's bliss,
> The arcs of sight, and how her arrows pierce.
>   This in the region of the air shall stand,
>   In Fame's brass court, and all her trumps command.

(stanza 64)

Ouids Banquet of
SENCE.

A Coronet for his Miſtreſſe Phi-
loſophie, and his amorous
Zodiacke.

VVith a tranſlation of a Latine coppie, written
by a Fryer, AnnoDom. 1400.

*Quis leget hæc? Nemo Hercule Nemo,
vel duo vel nemo :* Perſius.

AT LONDON,
Printed by I. R. for Richard Smith.
Anno Dom. 1595.

Figure 3.1 Title page of George Chapman's Ovid's Banquet of Sense (1595)

Here 'chapter' means 'head' or 'top'. The pyramid consists of perspective lines; its apex is in the apple of Ovid's eye; its base is in Corinna. (But is Ovid looking up or down? Is Corinna in heaven or on earth?) On this airy pyramid, Ovid will write lines that will lead him to Elysium and fame. The arrows piercing him are perspective lines, but they also evoke Cupid's arrows and the arrows that Diana and Apollo used to punish Niobe for presumption; the whole scene alludes to the myth of Actaeon of seeing Diana naked. Ovid is being presumptuous, and his mistress and his motives are potentially base ('The base within my sacred object is').

'Ovid's Banquet of Sense' is a devious poem, but the plot, which Chapman summarises in a preface, is straightforward. In love with Caesar's daughter (Julia or Corinna), Ovid hides in the emperor's garden at the hour when she bathes there. Ovid hears Corinna sing, smells the scents from her bath, sees her naked, convinces her to let him kiss her, and 'proceeds to the fifth sense and there is interrupted'. For the most part, the poem has been read in two opposing ways – as a 'celebration of the senses as the means for a Neoplatonic ascent toward beauty', and as a satiric depiction of an Ovidian poet, whose ascent 'Chapman undermines and condemns by a combination of ironies and open moralizations'; less commonly, it has been understood as 'a kind of an optical puzzle, changing with the point from which one regards it'.[53]

Janet Levarie Smarr argues that the poem is 'a pyramid', and that 'Ovid ascends one side only to descend the other'.[54] Her main points include:

> The poem 'Ovid's Banquet of Sense' is arranged symmetrically around a centrally positioned comparison of Corinna to Elysium (stanzas 56–62).

> The order in which the senses appear does not correspond to the usual Platonic pattern of ascent. Vision, traditionally the highest sense, is the third and central sense, followed by taste and touch, the lowest senses. This suggests that the poem is arranged pyramidally, as an ascent followed by a descent.

> Like Spenser in Book 2 of *The Faerie Queene*, Chapman is evoking a 'triangle-as-body, circle-as-soul' tradition.

> The volume *Ovid's Banquet of Sense* is both informed by and critical of Ovidian love poetry. The dedicatory sonnets depict Chapman as a corrected Ovid.

There are also fifty-five stanzas on each side of the poem's centre section, and there is numeric design throughout the book – especially in 'The Amorous Zodiac', whose complexity has been analysed by Alastair Fowler.[55] 'The Amorous Contention of Phyllis and Flora' is less complex yet more devious: it contains 101 stanzas but appears to have 103. Following quatrain 53 (at the bottom of a page), the numbering skips to 56 (at the top of the next page). The misnumbering is arguably deliberate: it reinforces the theme that our senses can mislead us, and it invites us to see 'The Amorous Zodiac' and 'The Amorous Contention' as the book's second half – 133 stanzas in all, with the first stanza of 'The Amorous Zodiac' at the book's centre.

Beyond structural, thematic, and numeric parallels, *Ovid's Banquet of Sense* verbally echoes or anticipates Shakespeare. After Ovid gazes at Corinna and 'sells his freedom for a look' (stanza 50), the poet speaks of visual beauty: 'The beauty's fair is an enchantment made / By nature's witchcraft, tempting men to buy, / With endless shows, what endlessly will fade, / Yet promise chapmen all eternity' (stanza 51). Here Chapman puns on his name, which means 'merchant' or 'peddler'. The *Sonnets* poet distances himself from salesmen-poets in Sonnet 21: 'Let them say more that like of hearsay well; / I will not praise [because I] purpose not to sell'. Similar lines can be found *Love's Labour's Lost* and *Troilus and Cressida*:

> PRINCESS OF FRANCE
> Good Lord Boyet, my beauty, though but mean,
> Needs not the painted flourish of your praise:
> Beauty is bought by judgement of the eye,
> Not uttered by base sale of chapmen's tongues.
> (Love's Labour's Lost, Act 2)

> BEROWNE
> Fie, painted rhetoric! O, she needs it not:
> To things of sale a seller's praise belongs.
> (Love's Labour's Lost, Act 4)

> PARIS
> Fair Diomed, you do as chapmen do,
> Dispraise the thing that you desire to buy.
> But we in silence hold this virtue well –
> We'll not commend what we intend to sell.
> (Troilus and Cressida, Act 4)

Sonnet 21 moreover speaks of a 'muse' who uses 'heav'n itself for ornament'. Shakespeare may be alluding to Chapman's 'Amorous Zodiac', whose speaker claims that he will 'disperse' his mistress 'in heav'n, amongst those braving fires', or on earth, where her beauties, 'Bright as those flames [of heaven]', will 'glister'. The *Sonnets* poet asserts that his love is 'as fair / As any mother's child, though not so bright / As those gold candles fixed in heaven's air' (21), and that other poets 'disperse' their work under the youth's name (78).

Chapman does not seem to have praised Southampton in the 1590s nor to have won him over, but if he is the victorious poet, the likely period for victory is 1598–1600. Chapman began dedicating works to high nobility in 1598, with his Homer translations for the Earl of Essex. He may also have eyed Southampton's patronage, since Southampton was a companion of Essex. That said, would Chapman have had a reputation for 'gross painting' and flattery? Perhaps the *Sonnets* poet's accusations are exaggerations; perhaps he is alluding to verses by Chapman that have not survived. Or maybe Chapman was not the victor.

Samuel Daniel

Samuel Daniel often receives honourable mention as the rival poet. In *On the Sonnets* (1837), James Boaden announced Daniel's candidacy while arguing that Pembroke was the fair youth.[56] According to H. E. Rollins's survey of rival candidates, the next extended argument for Daniel occurs in Charles Creighton's *Shakespeare's Story of His Life* (1904).[57] This is surprising, since Daniel is widely regarded as an influence on *Sonnets* and may have been the poet laureate following Spenser's death in 1599. In *A Poetical Rhapsody* (1602), Francis Davison calls Daniel 'Prince of English Poets', claiming that Daniel's muse 'surpassed / Spenser'. In the Jacobean period, Queen Anne supported Daniel and urged him to write masques (these earned him Ben Jonson's ire). Daniel dedicated works to Southampton and Pembroke in 1603, and he may have sought their patronage earlier. As with Chapman, though, there is no clear evidence that Daniel pursued patronage with either earl in the 1590s, though he did work in the Pembroke household in 1593–4 and looked for new patrons after that.

More evidence for Daniel as the victorious rival can be gleaned from an unlikely source, Creighton's *Shakespeare's Story of His Life*. This book is among the most fantastical works in the history of *Sonnets* criticism. The following passage is typical:

> Daniel's identity is concealed under half a dozen Shakespearean witticisms, including a most ingenious anagram upon his name mingled with the names of the two necromancers [Dr. Dee and Thomas Aleyn] – namely

'*Alien* pen', the word which was printed in italics with a capital [in the 1609 *Sonnets*], making Daniel without D (Dr. Dee, who had removed to Manchester) but with Aleyn.⁵⁸

In response to this and another claim, Rollins quips, 'As Polonius might have said, "That's good!"' – but he hastens to add: 'If any real evidence were forthcoming, Daniel, an excellent poet, would make a fitting rival.'⁵⁹ Among the 'real evidence' for Daniel as rival, '*Alien* pen' may actually count, though not for the reasons that Creighton puts forward.

'Alien pen' occurs in Sonnet 78: 'So oft have I invoked thee for my muse / And found such fair assistance in my verse / As every *Alien* pen hath got my use / And under thee their poesy disperse'. Even without Q's italics and capital letter, 'alien' would be conspicuous; it primarily means 'foreign'. The poet is basically saying: 'I have called on you as my muse so often, and I have found such inspiration from your beauty, and such generous patronage from you, that strangers' pens have taken up my practice (my right) and circulated their poetry under the protection of your name'. The *Sonnets* poet presents himself as a friend or trusted servant and suggests that his claim on the youth's affections is under threat.

'Alien' as 'foreign' could point to Daniel. In the 1590s and early 1600s, Daniel was known as a poet who borrowed themes and lines from foreign writers. In the third Parnassus play, the character Judicio criticises him for his thieving tendencies:

> Sweet honey-dropping Daniël doth wage
> War with the proudest big Italiän
> That melts his heart in sugared sonneting.
> Only let him more sparingly make use
> Of others' wit, and use his own the more
> That well may scorn base imitatiön.

In 'Of honest theft: To my good friend Mr Samuel Daniel', John Harrington similarly chides:

> Proud Paulus late my secrecies revealing,
> Hath told I got some good conceits by stealing.
> But where got he those double pistolets
> With which good clothes, good fare, good land he gets?
> 'Tush, those', he saith, 'came by a man-o'-war' . . .
> Then, fellow thief, let's shake together hands,
> Since both our wares are filched from foreign lands.

An admirer of French and Italian poetry, Daniel hoped that English poetry would be more widely read. In his *Cleopatra* dedication, he laments that England is restricted by ocean and language:

> O that the ocean did not bound our style
> Within these strict and narrow limits so,
> But that the melody of our sweet isle
> Might now be heard to Tiber, Arne, and Po.
> . . . .
> O why may not some after-coming hand
> [Go] teach to Rhine, to Loire, and Rhodanus
> Our accents, and the wonders of our land?
>
> (lines 57–60 and following)

Daniel promoted the cause of English poetry and borrowed liberally from foreign writers. It would be quite cutting to refer to such a poet as an alien pen.

More evidence for Daniel can be found in Sonnet 80: 'But since your worth, wide as the ocean is, / The humble as the proudest sail doth bear, / My saucy bark, inferior far to his, / On your broad main doth willfully appear'. These lines recall the first quatrain of *Delia*'s first sonnet: 'Unto the boundless ocean of thy beauty / Runs this poor river, charged with streams of zeal, / Returning thee the tribute of my duty, / Which here my love, my youth, my plaints reveal'. In the 1590s, these lines were well known. In *Every Man in his Humour* (1598), Ben Jonson puts them in the mouth of a character who wants to impress a woman. In presenting the lines as stolen goods, Jonson insinuates that Daniel is a poetic thief. Jonson's scorn is more intense in the 1616 edition of the play, in which Daniel's lines are rewritten as parody: 'Unto the boundless ocean of thy face, / Runs this poor river, charged with streams of eyes'.[60]

Creighton's Alien-Daniel anagram may be substantive after all. As Shakespeare's 'will' and Chapman's 'chapmen' illustrate, Elizabethan poets liked to pun on their own names. Daniel is no exception: 'Delia' is an anagram of 'ideal' and 'Daniel'. (In Renaissance texts, an *A* with a tilde can represent 'an'.) Daniel, moreover, hints that his poems are like the Danaïds, the daughters of Danaus who slew their bridegrooms, and he develops the conceit that his sonnets represent self-destructive desires.[61] Shakespeare may have recognised 'Delia' as an anagram and responded with 'Alien'.

Daniel fits the rival-poet profile well. Like Chapman, his poetry is both admirable and mockable; unlike Chapman, his praise of nobility is largely unreserved. In the first three editions of *Delia*, Daniel effusively praises the Countess of Pembroke, and his sonnet in *Nennio* makes greater allowances for inherited nobility than Chapman's poem does. Daniel might also be a learned poet, and not merely because he went to university: he wrote a poem about learning – *Musophilus, Containing a Defence of all Learning* (1599). Creighton goes so far as to argue that Sonnet 85 puns on 'Musophilus' with 'mused filed': 'My tongue-tied muse, in manners, holds her still, / While comments of your praise, richly compiled, / Reserve their character with golden quill / And precious phrase by all the muses filed'.[62] This interpretation is strained – if 'muses filed' echoes another text, Francis Meres's 'the Muses would speak with Shakespeare's fine filed phrase' is a better candidate.[63] Creighton also suggests that 'Reserve their character with golden quill' alludes to Daniel. In Elizabethan English, 'reserve' typically means 'preserve', and 'character' typically means 'writing' or 'handwriting'; 'golden quill' is a conventional trope for aureate or ornamental style. Shakespeare may be alluding to a book containing calligraphic verse, like the gift copies that Daniel sent to potential patrons.[64] An allusion to calligraphy is unnecessary, however: other than Spenser, no Elizabethan poet epitomises the combination of learning and grace as well as Daniel.

Daniel was learned and graceful, but how was he taught by spirits or gulled by an affable ghost? There are at least two possibilities here. The first involves Daniel's most famous poem, 'The Complaint of Rosamond'. 'Rosamond' is a lament spoken by the ghost of Rosamond Clifford, who tells the tale of her seduction and death. Rosamond might be described as an 'affable' narrator in the sense of 'prating' (her tale is long-winded), and she is a 'gulling' spirit because she offers a dubious defence of herself and a dubious deal to the poet: if the poet tells Rosamond's story to the world, Delia may read it and sigh; if Delia sighs, the poet may be 'graced'. In Elizabethan love poetry, 'graced' is potentially a euphemism for sexual favours. In 'Rosamond', it primarily alludes to patronage: Daniel sought the good graces of the Countess of Pembroke when he first published the poem.

A second possibility for affable ghost is Spenser. His connection to the rival may be foreshadowed in 85's 'golden quill'. This phrase appears in the eighty-fifth sonnet of *Amoretti*: 'Deep in the closet of my parts entire, / Her worth is written with a golden quill, / That me with heav'nly fury doth inspire, / And my glad mouth with her sweet praises fill'. Like the *Sonnets* poet, the *Amoretti* poet asserts that his feelings are deep inside, targets outsiders who envy his love, and does so in an '85' sonnet. The *Amoretti* poet also lays claim to divine fury, and one of the sequence's dedicatory sonnets depicts

Spenser as a poet of learning and grace: 'Ah Colin', if 'in thy lovely mistress' praise / thou list to exercise thy learnèd quill: / thy muse hath got such grace, and power to please / [that all who read thee] joy their fill' (Sonnet by 'G.W.I'.). While the parallels could indicate that Spenser is the rival poet, he better fits the role of friendly ghost: Spenser promoted Daniel's career and may well have been dead when Shakespeare was writing the rival series. Creighton argues that Daniel was named laureate after Spenser's death in 1599, and that Sonnet 86 alludes to a contest for laureate that Daniel won.[65] Be that as it may, stronger evidence for Daniel can be found in Sonnet 87.

'Too dear for my possessing'

Sonnet 87 puts an exclamation point on the rival series and employs rhetorical fireworks to do so: all fourteen of its lines are end-stopped; at least six of its seven rhymes are feminine; and ten of its first twelve lines conclude with present participles, whose string of '-ing' suffixes reinforces the falling rhythm of the rhymes. In matter and manner, the poet calls attention to endings:

> Farewell, thou art too dear for my possessing,
> And like enough thou know'st thy estimate.
> The charter of thy worth gives thee releasing;
> My bonds in thee are all determinate.
> For how do I hold thee but by thy granting,
> And for that riches where is my deserving?
> The cause of this fair gift in me is wanting,
> And so my patent back again is swerving.
> Thyself thou gav'st, thy own worth then not knowing,
> Or me, to whom thou gav'st it, else mistaking;
> So thy great gift, upon misprison growing,
> Comes home again, on better judgement making.
>   Thus have I had thee as a dream doth flatter:
>   In sleep a king, but waking no such matter.

The poet declares that his relations with the youth are at an end, retrospectively portraying them as more of a business arrangement than a friendship. His bitterness comes out in 'My bonds in thee are all determinate', which implies that his claims on the youth are expired contractual obligations. The second quatrain opens with a pair of rhetorical questions, which give way to a mode of self-analysis that anticipates Sonnet 88's blame-taking rhetoric. In the third quatrain and couplet, the poet may be meditating to himself. Especially if he is echoing 'For thy sweet love remembered such wealth brings / That then I scorn to change my state with kings' (Sonnet 29), his meditation is nostalgic: 'Thus have I had thee as a dream doth flatter / In sleep a king, but waking no such matter'.

Sonnet 87's rhymes are distinctive. For most of the sixteenth century, English poets avoided feminine rhymes. As W. A. Ringler explains, Sidney brought them back into fashion:

> Surrey has at most five, and probably only two, pairs of genuine feminine rhymes in all his verse, and an analysis of the selections in a standard anthology . . . reveals only three pairs of feminine rhymes between Wyatt and Sidney. [Sidney] used feminine rhyme in all of his trochaic poems and in all of his sestinas; but he avoided it in all but three of his early sonnets – none of the *Astrophil and Stella* sonnets contains feminine rhyme, though it regularly appears in the songs.[66]

Sidney was following conventions and challenging them. Other poets made similar experiments. In *The Hekatompathia, or Passionate Century of Love* (1582), Watson only uses masculine rhymes; in *The Tears of Fancy* (1593), he often uses feminine rhyme.[67] In the wake of the 1591 *Astrophil and Stella* and the first 1592 *Delia*, more poets employed feminine rhymes. Almost every sequence published between 1592 and 1595 averages more than one feminine rhyme per sonnet.[68] A vogue for feminine rhyme coincided with the sonnet vogue.

Shakespeare was familiar with 'feminine rhyme' or 'female rhyme': in Sonnet 20, he compares the fair youth to a woman and uses all feminine rhymes. Sonnet 87's feminine rhymes are different: five of the first six rhymes end in '-ing', and the exception, *estimate–determinate*, is feminine only if the rules of French verse are applied – if each terminal 'e' is pronounced as an extra syllable. Under the same rules, *estimate–determinate* would be a 'rich rhyme'. In the Renaissance, *rime riche* was commonly defined as rhyme between words sharing three or more vowel or consonant sounds. (Rich rhyme as homophonic rhyme is mostly of a later date and is mostly an English distinction.[69]) Since 'estimate' and 'determinate' share three sounds, and the other six rhymes share at least four sounds each, all the rhymes are 'rich'. Like the fair youth, who is 'too dear' for the poet, the rhymes may be too rich: Shakespeare is mocking the use of *rime riche* and anyone who admires such rhymes.

In Elizabethan sequences, fourteen-line sonnets with six or more feminine rhymes are rare or highly uncommon. To my knowledge, only five sequences have at least one such sonnet: *Delia, Parthe-*

nophil and Parthenophe, *The Tears of Fancy*, *Idea's Mirror*, and *Fidessa*. Among these, *Delia* stands out: at least four sonnets in the fifty-sonnet *Delia* have six or more feminine rhymes (16, 17, 26, and 27). Sonnets with five feminine rhymes in '-ing' are rarer than rare. No other sonnet of the period matches Sonnet 87, though Sonnet 27 of the fifty-sonnet *Delia* comes close:

> The star of my mishap imposed this paining,
> To spend the April of my years in wailing,
> That never found my fortune but in waning,
> With still fresh cares my present woes assailing.
> Yet her I blame not, though she might have blessed me,
> But my desire's wings, so high aspiring,
> Now melted with the sun that hath possessed me;
> Down do I fall from off my high desiring,
> And in my fall do cry for mercy speedy;
> No pitying eye looks back upon my mourning,
> No help I find when now most favor need I;
> The ocean of my tears must drown me burning –
>   And this my death shall christen her anew
>   And give the cruël fair her title due.

As in Shakespeare's poem, the rhymes in '-ing' occur in end-stopped quatrain lines. Daniel's participles emphasise ongoing activities or states of feeling, especially suffering and longing; the falling rhythms reinforce the allusion to Icarus. Sonnet 28 of *The Tears of Fancy* and Amour 36 of *Idea's Mirror* also contain four feminine rhymes in '-ing'. Like Daniel's rhymes, Watson's and Drayton's rhymes complete end-stopped lines and convey suffering and longing. Sonnet 87's participle rhymes involve more active verbs: *possessing, releasing, granting, swerving, growing, making*. With its '-ing' rhymes, Sonnet 87 responds as much to languid falling rhymes as to relations gone bad: the *Sonnets* poet would break from a cycle of abjection.

Sonnet 87 arguably responds to a specific poet – Daniel. At the start of his career, Daniel frequently used feminine rhymes, especially participle rhymes; later, he used them sparingly. Though often revised, Sonnet 1 of every edition of *Delia* begins and ends with a feminine rhyme; the final sonnet of every 1590s edition of *Delia* opens with a feminine quatrain. But as he revised his sequence, Daniel changed many feminine rhymes to masculine. In the 1594 *Delia*, for example, 'The star of my mishap imposed this paining' is transformed into a sonnet that alternates masculine and feminine rhymes. In *A Defence of Rhyme* (1603), Daniel advocated against unpatterned use of masculine and feminine rhyme, and for feminine rhyme in songs, noting that his ideas evolved in response to constructive criticism:

> [To] me this change of number in a poem of one nature sits not so well as to mix uncertainly feminine rhymes with masculine, which ever since I was warned of that deformity by . . . Hugh Samford, I have always avoided it, as there are not above two couplets in that kind in all my poem of the Civil Wars, and I would willingly, if I could, have altered it in all the rest, holding feminine rhymes to be fittest for ditties, and either to be set certain or else by themselves.[70]

In short, Daniel works well as the target of 87's parody. In my view, he is the best candidate for the rival poet, and identifying him as the victorious poet clarifies the tone and wit of the series as a whole, and especially of Sonnets 80, 86, and 87. The answer to 'Who was the rival?' does not begin and end with Daniel, of course, but giving some weight to his candidacy is crucial to understanding the competitive milieu in which Shakespeare wrote. What Daniel's case shows is that poetic rivalry played out at the level of artistic craft. Among other things, this should help us see that Elizabethan sequences, for all of their generic qualities, are layered with idiosyncrasies.

Chapter 4

A Triptych for the Third Earl

It is common to suggest that Shakespeare turned to writing poems when plague forced the London theatres to close – that most if not all of his non-dramatic works stem from a need to earn a living when he could not write for the stage. Whatever the truth to that story, his career as a poet took on a life of its own, in an environment as competitive as that of the theatre. Some evidence is on display in the rival-poet series; more can be found in *Venus and Adonis* and *Lucrece*, the two poems that Shakespeare dedicated to the third Earl of Southampton. Parallels between *Sonnets* and the narrative poems argue that the three works are a triptych, and that *Sonnets*' fair youth was modelled, at least initially, on Southampton. Identifying the fair youth is significant not only in view of the poet's promise to immortalise him; it helps us see *Sonnets* as the third of three interrelated works.

Number Symbolism in Sonnets 33, 66, and 99

As 'third of three' might suggest, understanding why the youth's identity matters begins with understanding Shakespeare's poetic use of numbers. Modern commentators of *Sonnets* tend to allow for number symbolism, but few would say that Shakespeare is deeply invested in it, and many pass quickly over the subject. Like allegory, number symbolism can evoke a reductive code – a one-to-one correspondence between symbol and referent. *Sonnets* does use numbers in that way: Sonnet 44, for example, is the first of two sonnets on the four elements. But such symbolism is minor; we can take or leave most instances. Number symbolism can also speak to broad concerns. This is true of Sonnet 33, whose allusion to Christ's death in 'the thirty-third year of his age' has gone largely unnoticed.[1]

Let us look closely at Shakespeare's thirty-third sonnet:

> Full many a glorious morning have I seen
> Flatter the mountain tops with sovereign eye,
> Kissing with golden face the meadows green,
> Gilding pale streams with heav'nly alchemy,
> Anon permit the basest clouds to ride
> With ugly rack on his celestial face
> And from the forlorn world his visage hide,
> Stealing unseen to west with the disgrace –
> Ev'n so my sun one early morn did shine
> With all triumphant splendor on my brow,
> But out alack, he was but one hour mine;
> The region cloud hath masked him from me now.
>   Yet him for this my love no whit disdaineth:
>   Suns of the world may stain, when heav'n's sun staineth.

The poet describes a sunny day that turns cloudy and compares the clouds to a 'stain' on his 'sun'; he nonetheless promises forgiveness. Punning on 'son', the youth-sun figure takes on religious connotations in 'Suns of the world may stain, when heav'n's sun staineth'. The verb 'stain' is both passive ('become tainted') and active ('do wrong'); 'heav'n's sun' alludes to Christ; and the entire couplet, culminating with 'staineth', sounds biblical – like Portia's 'mercy droppeth' speech in *The Merchant of Venice*. Sonnet 33 alludes to Christ's death for man's sins; with its '33', it evokes the traditional age at which Jesus died.[2] (A similar conjunction of passion, crucifixion, and betrayal occurs 100 sonnets later, in 133, when the poet speaks of a 'torment thrice threefold thus to be crossed'.) The youth's betrayal is linked to man's fall from paradise. Original sin is what Christ's death is meant to redeem, after all, and the poet tries to see a silver lining – to think of the betrayal as a fortunate fall. Sonnet 33 marks a turning point, and its allusions to sin and redemption speak to the psychology of *Sonnets*' characters and situations.

Number symbolism in Sonnet 33 goes beyond 33: Shakespeare draws on a tradition in which 11 symbolises transgression or wrongdoing. As preliminary evidence for this claim, I cite Pietro Bongo's two-part *Numerorum Mysteria* (*The Mysteries of Numbers*), published in 1583 and 1584. According to Bongo, a number of transgression exceeds by 1 a 'stable' or 'complete' number.[3] (As the Latin *transgressus* implies, the conceptual metaphor involves stepping over or crossing a line.) In relation to 12 and 16, for example, 13 and 17 can be seen as transgressive. The most prominent number of transgression, 11, surpasses 10, a number associated with the Ten Commandments and with Christ – with God's rules, the Roman numeral X, and the Greek letter X (chi, the first letter of 'Christos'). Sonnet 33 may employ this symbolism with its lovers' triangle (3×11) and its unusual eleventh-line turn ('But out, alack . . .'). 'Overstepping' also partly explains 33's rhetorical links to 34: as a pair, Sonnets 33–34 transgress the boundary between the second and third pyramid steps.

If we think of 'transgression' as a term that denotes errors and wrongdoings stemming from deficiency and excess, Shakespeare's immediate symbolic source may be *Astrophil and Stella*. The relevant poems are Sonnets 1, 11, 22, and 33; Song 2; and Sonnets 73–83. Astrophil's errors begin in Sonnet 1, when Astrophil seeks inspiration in others' verse: '"Fool", said my muse to me, "Look in thy heart and write"'. Astrophil again evokes error in Sonnet 11, when he warns Cupid about Stella's heart: 'Fool, seekst not to get into her heart'. In Sonnet 22, he presents Stella as spotless (kissed but not stained by the sun), and in Song 2, he kisses Stella as she sleeps, only to flee and call himself 'Fool, more fool for no more taking'. In stark contrast with the sun's public kiss in daylight, Astrophil's 'stealing kiss', occurs in private and likely at night. Sonnet 33 alludes to Astrophil's/Sidney's original sin: the missed chance for marriage with Stella/Penelope. In the eleven sonnets between the second and third songs, eleven is frequently associated with violating boundaries and codes of behaviour. These sonnets speak of Stella's anger at Astrophil's kiss, and of Astrophil's desire for more kisses; 'kiss' appears a total of eleven times in the eleven sonnets, and in Sonnet 77 Astrophil lists ten attractive features of Stella and alludes to an eleventh one, of which his 'maiden Muse doth blush to tell'. In the final sonnet, 83, Astrophil threatens to wring the neck of Stella's sparrow 'Phillip' because of the kiss-like liberty ('billing') that it takes with her. His wish to kill the bird speaks to conflicting impulses to stifle his desires and to act on them. Astrophil is aware that, in Stella's eyes, he has gone too far, but he also feels that he has not gone far enough. Like the *Sonnets* poet, he is concerned with two opposing types of faults – falling short and going too far.

More evidence that Shakespeare uses 11 as a number of transgression can be found in numeric notation. Typically, notation does not affect number symbolism: the number 3, for example, can refer to a triangle whether it is written 'III' or '3'. While the number 11 can represent transgression whether it is written 'XI' or '11', the fact that multiples of eleven under 100 have identical digits in Hindu-Arabic notation allows for additional play – especially when the poet associates wrongdoing with duplicity. Like the 1598 edition of *Astrophil and Stella*, the 1609 *Sonnets* uses Hindu-Arabic numerals. Shakespeare's notation is curious, because his sequence is organised around the Horatian conceit that poetry is a monument, for which Roman numerals might seem a more natural choice. What is more, Roman numerals were the norm in sonnet sequences until at least 1598. In all sequences published through 1597 by Daniel, Barnes, Lodge, Fletcher, Percy, Spenser, Griffin, Linche, Barnfield, and Tofte, sonnets are numbered with Roman numerals. Increasingly after 1598 – in Drayton's *Idea* and William Alexander's and John Davies of Hereford's sequences – sonnets are numbered with Hindu-Arabic numerals. Whatever the trends, *Sonnets*' notation must be authorial, because the poems make symbolic use of 'doubled digits' in multiple-of-11 sonnets.

Among the multiple-of-11 sonnets, transgression is most prominent in 33, 66, and 99. As we have seen, Sonnet 33 evokes sin and redemption with its allusions to original sin and the crucifixion. Sonnet 66 lists many wrongs allowed or committed by the world:

> Tired with all these, for restful death I cry –
> As to behold desert a beggar born,
> And needy nothing trimmed in jollity,
> And purest faith unhappily forsworn,
> And gilded honour shamefully misplaced,
> And maiden virtue rudely strumpeted,
> And right perfection wrongfully disgraced,
> And strength by limping sway disablèd,
> And art made tongue-tied by authority,
> And folly, doctor-like, controlling skill,
> And simple truth miscalled simplicity,
> And captive good attending captain ill –
>   Tired with all these, from these would I be gone,
>   Save that, to die, I leave my love alone.

The form is distinctive: the sonnet's first line both stands on its own and anticipates the couplet; each of the wrongs is listed in an end-stopped line; there is no clear quatrain structure. We might say that 66 and its world are out of joint. This is not to say that there is no rationale to the form. As West observes, 'lines 2–7 describe one character in each line, each representing an ethical value, whereas 8–12 are a denser list, in which each line mentions not only the victim but also the villain'.[4] But even this structure is messy: 'And simple truth miscalled simplicity' is a villain-less verse among the victim-villain lines. Noting that Sonnet 66's 'modulation' occurs in line 8, Vendler remarks: 'It is as though the speaker in line 8 "accelerates" [by anticipating the volta], and in line 11 "overspills" his original single-figure procession of victims into his later coupled one'.[5] The form illustrates that wrongdoings are the result of shortcomings and excesses.

In Sonnet 66, the poet evokes Christ's sacrificial death and contemplates dying for the world's sins. There would be nothing redemptive in the act, however: the poet would die in despair of the world, not to save it; his beloved would be worse off. Given the tradition that Jesus died on the sixth day after six hours on the cross, Shakespeare may be alluding to the crucifixion. In judging the world and finding it wanting, he may be hinting at the Second Coming. Duncan-Jones argues that 66 is symbolic, because 'Multiples of six have adverse connotations, alluding to the biblical "beast" [whose number is 666]'.[6] Though her claim about multiples is too sweeping, she usefully calls attention to an apocalyptic subtext, which the poet uses to express desire for judgement and forgiveness. Sonnet 66's litany also lends support to the idea that 11 symbolises wrongdoing: the poet not only lists wrongs; he lists exactly eleven of them.

Like Sonnet 66, Sonnet 99 distorts the sonnet form in depicting varieties of wrongdoing:

> The forward violet thus did I chide:
> 'Sweet thief, whence didst thou steal thy sweet that smells,
> If not from my love's breath? The purple pride
> Which on thy soft cheek for complexion dwells
> In my love's veins thou hast too grossly dyed'.
> The lily I condemnèd for thy hand,
> And buds of marjoram had stol'n thy hair;
> The roses fearfully on thorns did stand,
> One blushing shame, another white despair;
> A third, nor red nor white, had stol'n of both
> And to his robb'ry had annexed thy breath.
> But for his theft, in pride of all his growth
> A vengeful canker ate him up to death.
>   More flowers I noted, yet I none could see
>   But sweet or colour it had stol'n from thee.

This sonnet is excessive in an obvious way: it has fifteen lines. As in 33, there is a volta, or a 'But', two lines before the couplet. As in 66, the opening line protrudes: there is something 'forward' about it, like the early violet. The poem also creates confusion about its addressee: in Q, there are no quotation marks around lines 2–5, and 'sweet thief' is an epithet for the youth earlier in the sequence. Sonnet 99 mentions six flowers that have stolen smells or hues from the youth: a violet, a lily, buds of marjoram, and three roses. The violet has committed two thefts; the third rose, three. In all, nine thefts are recorded, along with one punishment. Much ado is made of the flowers' wrongs, particularly the excesses of the violet and the third rose: the former flower is 'too grossly dyed'; the latter commits robberies and is punished to death by canker 'in pride of all his growth'. The couplet alludes to more flowers and thefts, of undifferentiated sort.

Through form and content, then, Sonnet 99 alludes to breaches or violations. Given the sonnet's number, the nine thefts may point to 9×11: nine times transgression. Shakespeare may also signal transgression through sequential position: like Sonnet 33, 99 marks a boundary between pyramid steps, and it can be read as a coda to the eleven sonnets that precede it (the seventh step). It moreover marks a major division in the fair-youth section of *Sonnets*: the poems before it indicate that the poet and the youth have fallen out; the poems after it speak of a renewal of relations. In short, Sonnet 99 is surrounded by sonnets that evoke an allegory of passion, death, and resurrection. This narrative closely links Sonnets 33, 66, and 99 – a scheme that may have been inspired by Spenser's *Amoretti*. As a collection of 89 sonnets, nine anacreontic stanzas, and one marriage hymn, *Amoretti* can be read as a 99-unit sequence. In the thirty-third unit (Sonnet 33), the poet confesses that he has done 'great wrong' by not finishing *The Faerie Queene*. In the sixty-sixth unit (Sonnet 66), the poet evokes Good Friday and portrays his lady as faultless except for one 'disparagement' (her willingness to receive him, a suitor of 'lowly state'). And in the ninety-ninth unit ('Epithalamion'), the poet celebrates crossing thresholds, including the doorway to the marriage chamber.

Theft in Shakespeare's Sonnets

Sonnet 99 not only discusses theft; it illustrates it. Modern editors routinely note that 99 steals from Henry Constable's 'Of his mistress upon occasion of her walking in a garden'. More precisely, lines 1–10 of 'Of his mistress' are echoed in lines 1–11 of Sonnet 99, and the final lines of the two poems are quite different. Here is Constable's sonnet:

> My lady's presence makes the roses red,
> Because to see her lips they blush for shame.
> The lilies' leaves, for envy, pale became,

> And her white hands in them this envy bred.
> The marigold the leaves abroad doth spread,
> Because the sun's and her pow'r is the same.
> The violet of purple colour came
> Dyed with the blood she made my heart to shed.
> In brief, all flow'rs from her their virtue take;
> From her sweet breath their sweet smells do proceed;
> The living heat which her eye-beams do make
> Warmeth the ground, and quickeneth the seed.
>   The rain, wherewith she watereth those flowers,
>   Falls from mine eyes, which she dissolves in showers.

Joan Grundy summarises the case for Constable's influence:

> [Both poems] treat of the same theme, the dynamic and vitalising effect which the presence of the loved one has upon the flowers and plants . . . Constable mentions the rose, lily, marigold, and violet; Shakespeare the violet, lily, marjoram, and rose. Constable's roses blush for shame; so do Shakespeare's. In each poem the lily is less white than the loved one's hand; in each the purple violet has been dyed in blood – the lover's blood, according to Constable, the loved one's according to Shakespeare. In each the flowers are said to be perfumed by the beloved's breath, although Shakespeare limits this theft to the violet, while Constable extends it to all flowers and indeed does not see it as a theft at all.[7]

As Grundy observes, 'Of his mistress' does not refer to theft. It also does not use direct address, and another sonnet by Constable, 'Of the envy others bear to his lady for the former perfections', refers to envy-induced pallor: 'When Beauty to the world vouchsafes this bliss, / To show the one whose other there is not, / The whitest skins red-blushing Shame doth blot, / And in the reddest cheeks pale Envy is'. Sonnet 99 may allude to two Constable poems.

Sonnet 99 is informed by at least one other poem, a madrigal from *Parthenophil and Parthenophe*. Barnes's Madrigal 11 uses direct address, lily-rose imagery, and a theft conceit:

> Thine eyes, mine heav'n, which harbor lovely rest
>   And with their beams all creatures cheer,
>   Stole from mine eyes their clear
> And made mine eyes dim myrrouldes of unrest.
> And from her lily forehead, smooth and plain,
>   My front his withered furrows took,
>   And, through her grace, his grace forsook;
>   From soft cheeks' rosy red,
> My cheeks their leanness and this pallid stain . . .

The poet and his beloved steal attributes from each other – or rather their eyes, foreheads, and cheeks do the stealing. In contrast with Sonnet 99, the lily and the rose are not personified; the theft conceit is most telling, along with *Parthenophil and Parthenophe*'s inclusion of many fifteen-line sonnets. Comparable imagery can also be found in Barnes's Sestina 1: blushing lilies and a rose that turns pale 'for anger' at the beauty of a 'nymph'.

Sidney is a third writer whose work informs Sonnet 99. Behind the floral poems of Constable and Barnes is a passage from Chapter 13 of the first book of *Arcadia*:

> But when the ornament of the earth, the model of heaven, the triumph of Nature, the life of beauty, the queen of love, young Philoclea appeared in her nymph-like apparel, so near nakedness as one might well discern part of her perfections, and yet so appareled as did show she kept best store of her beauty to herself: . . . with the cast of her black eyes – black indeed, whether nature so made them that we might be the more able to behold and bear their wonderful shining, or that she, goddess-like, would work this miracle with herself in giving blackness the price above all beauty – then, I say, indeed methought the lilies grew pale for envy; the roses methought blushed to see sweeter roses in her cheeks, and the apples methought fell down from the trees to do homage to the apples of her breast.[8]

This passage is narrated by Pyrocles, a Macedonian prince who has disguised himself as a woman in order to enter the house of Philoclea, an Arcadian princess with whom he is in love. His comments about lilies going pale 'for envy' and the roses blushing are similar to the *Diana* poet's lines in 'Of his mistress' and Parthenophil's lines in Sestina 1. Since Shakespeare knew Sidney's *Arcadia* well, he may be exposing Constable and Barnes as poetic thieves.[9] What is more, Sonnet 99 has parallels to floral sonnets by Spenser and Barnfield. Sonnet 64 of *Amoretti* compares eight flowers' smells to the beloved's smell, and its couplet is as oddly prosaic as Sonnet 99's: 'Such fragrant flow'rs do give most od'rous smell, / But her sweet odor did them all excel'. Sonnet 17 of *Cynthia* is a blazon of Ganymede, the poet's beloved; similar to the 'soft cheek' of 99's violet, which is dyed with the fair youth's blood, Ganymede's cheeks are dyed: 'His cheeks, the lily and carnation dyes'.[10] Sonnet 99 targets a poetic style if not specific poets – perhaps the competitors of the rival-poet series. The third rose, eaten up 'in pride of all his growth', may even allude to the victorious rival, whose verse's 'proud full sail' is mocked in Sonnet 86.

Theft is a recurring conceit in *Sonnets*. It appears in the rival-poet series:

> [Whatever] of thee thy poet doth invent
> He robs thee of, and pays it thee again.
> He lends thee virtue, and he stole that word
> From thy behavior; beauty doth he give
> And found it in thy cheek.
>
> (Sonnet 79)

As in Sonnet 99, beauty is stolen from the youth. In other sonnets, the poet worries that the youth will be stolen from him:

> But thou, to whom my jewëls trifles are . . .
> Art left the prey of every vulgar thief.
> Thee have I . . . locked up in . . . my breast . . .
> And even thence thou wilt be stol'n I fear.
>
> (Sonnet 48)

> For thee watch I, whilst thou dost wake elsewhere,
> From me far off, with others all too near.
>
> (Sonnet 61)

> And for the peace of you I hold such strife
> As 'twixt a miser and his wealth is found:
> Now proud as an enjoyer, and anon
> Doubting the filching age will steal his treasure . . .
>
> (Sonnet 75)

Anxieties about theft enter the sequence in the wake of the youth's betrayal, and they are expressed in organisationally significant places thereafter: at the end of the third pyramid step (48), near the end of the fourth step (61), and at the end of the fifth step (75). At the end of the sixth step, the poet's worst fears are realised: the youth is stolen again, this time by a rival poet.

Shakespeare associates theft with plagiarism, amatory betrayal, and poetic rivalry. But the most subtle and dangerous thief is time. Time the Thief is central to Sonnet 63, the centre poem of *Sonnets* fair-youth section:

> Against my love shall be as I am now
> With Time's injurious hand crushed and o'erworn:
> When hours have drained his blood and filled his brow
> With lines and wrinkles; when his youthful morn

> Hath trávailed on to Age's steepy night,
> And all those beauties whereof now he's king
> Are vanishing, or vanished out of sight,
> Stealing away the treasure of his spring . . .

In the long opening sentence, which extends to, if not through, the ninth-line turn, the poet steels himself against the day when his love will be old; his halting, accretive phrasing is a rhetorical barrier against advancing time. The phrasing also hints at time's stealthy movement: in apposition to 'vanishing', the participle 'Stealing away' may at first seem intransitive (beauties are furtively fleeing), but it soon reveals itself as transitive (Time is robbing the youth of youth). Time's final appearance in *Sonnets* is as a thief/creditor; in 126, the poet tells the fair youth that Nature cannot keep her 'treasure' forever, because Time will claim the youth as his due.

Wriothesley as the Fair Youth

In Chapter 1, I said that it seemed impossible to know whether Shakespeare modelled the fair youth on Southampton or Pembroke (or both earls), and that it was remiss not to consider the possibilities. With the first point, I was summarising a consensus: commentators often mention Wriothesley and Herbert as candidates for the youth, but few insist on identifying a model, let alone pursue an interpretation of *Sonnets* based on one. An angels-fear-to-tread policy may be wise with biographical interpretation, but as the rival-poet series shows, biographical enquiry can be productive even when definitive proof is elusive. I will now argue that the third Earl of Southampton was the main, and perhaps exclusive, model for the youth; that Shakespeare makes figurative use of 'Wriothesley' and *W* in *Sonnets*; and that *Sonnets* is thematically, verbally, and numerically linked to *Venus and Adonis* and *Lucrece* – the two narrative poems that Shakespeare dedicated to Southampton.

Among the weightier pieces of evidence for Wriothesley's candidacy are Shakespeare's dedications in the narrative poems. In *Venus and Adonis*, Shakespeare presents himself to Southampton as an unknown poet seeking patronage:

> I know not how I shall offend in dedicating my unpolished lines to your lordship, nor how the world will censure me for choosing so strong a prop to support so weak a burden: only, if your honour seem but

pleased, I account myself highly praised and vow to take advantage of all idle hours, till I have honoured you with some graver labour.

The *Lucrece* dedication is more personal, or at least more assured:

> The love I dedicate to your lordship is without end; whereof this pamphlet, without beginning, is but a superfluous moiety. The warrant I have of your honourable disposition, not the worth of my untutored lines, makes it assured of acceptance. What I have done is yours; what I have to do is yours; being part in all I have, devoted yours. Were my worth greater, my duty would show greater; meantime, as it is, it is bound to your lordship, to whom I wish long life, still lengthened with all happiness.

In the first dedication, 'graver labour' may refer to *Lucrece*; in the second, 'what I have to do' may hint at *Sonnets*. And both Sonnet 26 and Thomas Thorpe's *Sonnets* dedication echo the *Lucrece* dedication: in 26, the poet speaks of 'duty so great' and of being 'worthy' of his 'lord'; Thorpe wishes 'all happiness' to 'W.H'. Beginning in the impersonal mode of the *Venus* dedication and shifting to the personal mode of the *Lucrece* dedication, the *Sonnets* poet details love's growth in Sonnets 1–25; in Sonnet 26, he dedicates future efforts to the youth.

Evidence for Southampton can also be culled from the poems themselves. *Venus and Adonis* contains thematic and verbal parallels to the procreation sonnets:

Venus and Adonis	*Shakespeare's Sonnets*
Adonis is a beautiful young man.	The poet's friend is a beautiful young man.
Adonis is associated with the sun.	The friend is associated with the sun.
Adonis resists Venus.	The friend resists marriage/procreation.
Venus tells Adonis: 'Thou was begot; to get, it is thy duty' (line 168).	The poet tells the friend: 'You had a father: let your son say so' (Sonnet 13).
'Upon the earth's increase why shouldst thou feed, / Unless the earth with thy increase be fed?'	'From fairest creatures we desire increase . . . [:] Pity the world, or else this glutton be, / To eat the world's due' (Sonnet 1).

'By law of nature thou art bound to breed, / That thine may live when thou thyself art dead. /	'[Nature] carved thee for her seal and meant thereby / Thou shouldst print more, not let that copy die' (Sonnet 11).
And so in spite of death thou dost survive, / In that thy likeness still is left alive' (lines 169–74).	'And nothing 'gainst Time's scythe can make defence / Save breed to brave him when he takes thee hence' (Sonnet 12).
'What is the body but a swallowing grave / Seeming to bury that posterity / Which by the rights of time thou needs must have, / If thou destroy them not in dark obscurity?' (lines 757–60).	'Or who is he so fond will be the tomb / Of his self-love, to stop posterity? . . . But if thou live rememb'red not to be, / Die single and thine image dies with thee' (Sonnet 3).

In both works, Shakespeare may have drawn on a Latin poem presented to Southampton in 1591, John Clapham's *Narcissus*.[11] Clapham uses the Narcissus myth to warn Southampton of self-love and to urge him to marry and procreate. Shakespeare's Venus makes similar pleas to Adonis, comparing him to Narcissus (lines 161–2); the *Sonnets* poet makes similar pleas to the fair youth, comparing him to Adonis (Sonnet 53).

Like the parallels to *Venus and Adonis*, the parallels to *Lucrece* are concentrated in the early fair-youth sonnets. The most important is a conceit: rape is portrayed as theft. In the fifth stanza of *Lucrece*, Lucrece's husband Collantine is criticised for boasting of his wife's beauty and virtue and thereby tempting thieves to their home:

> Beauty itself doth of itself persuade
> The eyes of men without an orator;
> What needeth then apologies be made,
> To set forth that which is so singular?
> Or why is Collantine the publisher
>   Of that rich jewël he should keep unknown
>   From thievish ears, because it is his own?

In Sonnet 48, the poet speaks of the youth as a possession whose visibility attracts thieves: 'thou, to whom my jewëls trifles are, / . . . Art left the prey of every vulgar thief. / Thee have I not locked up [except] in my breast. / . . . And even thence thou wilt be stol'n, I fear'. Both *Lucrece* and *Sonnets* associate theft with violation of a private space. This concern is consistent with the idea that Shakespeare first circulated his sonnets among friends: the *Sonnets* poet is reticent about public praise, comparisons, and 'setting forth' matters between himself and the youth.[12]

My observations so far do not prove that the youth was modelled on Wriothesley – nor, for that matter, does an early-1590s portrait of Southampton, whose feminine depiction of the earl may inform Sonnet 20's portrayal of the fair youth.[13] But *Sonnets* contains evidence of another sort: as R. H. Winnick has argued, 'Wriothesley' is anagrammatically encoded in the sequence. Because Winnick's claim is of the sort that rolls eyes and raises eyebrows, and because, by scholarly reckoning, it is new (2009), it calls for patience. Coupled with the more traditional evidence, the anagrams go a long way towards proving the case for Southampton.

Winnick cites over twenty 'Wriothesley' anagrams and analyses 'a dozen or so' in which 'most or all of the letters needed to form Wriothesley's name occur ... within short, thematically relevant, interlinear phrases'.[14] Among his featured examples are Sonnet 17's two pairs of anagrams. In 17's first quatrain, the poet expresses fear that posterity will deem his praise a lie and challenges himself to write verse that will include all the youth's 'parts': 'Who will believe my verse in time to come, / If it were filled with your most high deserts? / Though yet heav'n knows it is but as a tomb / Which hides your life and shows not half your parts'. In the couplet, he hints that the youth, by siring children, can help him silence doubts: 'But were some child of yours alive that time, / You should live twice: in it, and in my rhyme'. In Q, line 14 lacks a colon and can therefore be construed as saying 'You will live twice in your child, and twice in my rhyme'. More telling, both line 4 and line 9 contain all twenty-two letters needed to form 'Wriothesley' twice: 'Which hides your life, and ſhewes not halfe your parts' and 'So ſhould my papers (yellowed with their age)'. Even without line 14's hint, the two pairs are unlikely to be a coincidence: among Winnick's data set of 532 sonnets by Shakespeare, Sidney, Daniel, Drayton, Constable, and Spenser, there are no other sonnets with two double-*Wriothesley* lines.[15]

Another featured example is Sonnet 126, the final fair-youth poem. In Q's spelling, the poem begins: 'O Thou, my louely Boy, who in thy power / Doeſt hold times fickle glaſſe, his fickle-hower; / Who haſt by wayning growne, and therein ſhou'ſt, / Thy louers withering, as thy ſweet ſelfe grow'ſt'. The youth holds Time's hourglass and sickle and reveals the waning vigour of his lover or lovers as he grows. All eleven letters of 'Wriothesley' occur twice in line 4: the first anagram is in 'Thy louers wither'; the second, in the remainder of the line. Given the poem's temporal theme and sequential position, Shakespeare may be saying that he grows smaller as Wriothesley and the sequence grow complete. As in Sonnet 17, the anagrams are significant because they are statistical outliers and they occur in a thematically relevant context.

The anagrams in Sonnets 81, 89, and 108 are less statistically exceptional but no less striking in context. In lines 5–6 of Sonnet 81, the poet makes a promise that he makes nowhere else – that the youth's name will endure: 'Your name from hence immortall life ſhall have, / Though I (once gone) to all the world muſt dye'. Line 6's last four words, 'the world muſt dye', contain every 'Wriothesley' letter except *I*; the first four words, 'Though I (once gone)', call attention to the removal of an *I*. With a pun on name as 'reputation', Shakespeare hints that he is protecting the youth's name while immortalising 'Wriothesley'. (The *Y* in 'dye' may also signal his removal from the world: 'I' must die for 'you'.) The pronoun-letter device is repeated in Sonnet 89: 'in my tongue, / Thy ſweet beloued name no more ſhall dwell, / Leaſt I (too much prophane) ſhould do it wronge'. Like 'the world muſt dye', 'Thy ſweet beloued name no more' has every 'Wriothesley' letter except *I*. The poet avoids open reference to his beloved's name and offers to disassociate his vulgar self – his profane 'I' – from the beloved. (Shakespeare does not want his name to stain Wriothesley's name; he may also be comparing his reputation to that of a more illustrious poet.) In Sonnet 108, the poet suggests that he has nothing left to say ('What's new to speak . . .?'), only later to note that he repeats words as if they were prayers, harking back to when he first evoked the youth's name as something holy: 'Euen as when firſt I hallowed thy faire name'. The five words leading up to 'name', 'firſt I hallowed thy faire', contain all of the 'Wriothesley' letters and 'Hal'. Echoing 'hallowed be thy name' of the Lord's Prayer, the poet idolatrously invokes the youth's name. (For more on Winnick's anagrams, see Appendix B.)

The anagrams are of a piece with *Sonnets*' pronoun puns and conceits of re-membering. (For an example of the former, see 152's 'more perjured eye'; for the latter, see 122's 'to remember thee'.) They also square with witticisms in plays.[16] In Act 1, Scene 2 of *The Two Gentlemen of Verona*, Julia rips up Proteus's love letter, gathers the pieces, and asks the wind not to blow until she has found 'each letter in the letter'. Holding a piece with Proteus's 'wounded name' on it, she declares: 'Lo, here in one line his name is twice writ'. In Act 3, Scene 6 of *Cymbeline*, Imogen claims to be 'Fidele', the page to 'Richard du Champ'. This is an allusion to Richard Field, the printer of *Venus and Adonis* and *Lucrece*: 'Fidele' is an anagram for 'Field(e)'; 'du Champ' means 'of the field'; and 'Ricardo del Campo' was Field's name in Spanish publications.[17] Citing these allusions, a recent editor of *Romeo and Juliet* suggests that Shakespeare had 'few qualms about crossing aesthetic boundaries between life and art'.[18]

The 'letter and name' witticism most relevant to *Sonnets* is in Act 2, Scene 4 of *Romeo and Juliet*:

> NURSE
> Doth not rosemary and Romeo begin both with a letter?
>
> ROMEO
> Ay, Nurse, what of that? Both with an R.
>
> NURSE
> Ah, mocker, that's the dog's name. R is for the – no, I know it begins with some other letter – and she hath the prettiest sententious of it, of you and rosemary, that it would do you good to hear it.

R was considered 'the dog's letter' because its pronunciation ('arr') was associated with a dog's growl.[19] The witticism to which the unlettered Nurse refers is based on something else, however. Whether or not we are meant to puzzle out Juliet's saying – something to do with roses, rosemary, marrying? Adding a name or doubling yourself? – Shakespeare is pointing to 'Wriothesley', a name beginning with an 'R' sound but a different letter.[20] *Romeo and Juliet* was written in the mid-1590s, around the time of the narrative poems.[21] When Juliet discovers that Romeo is a Montague, she asks 'What's in a name?' and compares her love to a rose that smells sweet. Like Romeo, Wriothesley might be called a Montague: his maternal grandfather was the first Viscount Montague.[22] Like Romeo and the fair youth, Wriothesley might be called a rose, and not merely because he was beautiful or because his name sounded like 'rosely': the shield in the Southampton coat of arms bears two red roses on a white background and one white rose on a red background.[23] In singular form, 'rose' is always capitalised in Q and is often associated with the youth; in singular and plural forms, 'rose' appears eleven times in *Sonnets*' fair-youth section.

Shakespeare's Sonnets contains a close analogue to *Romeo and Juliet*'s 'silent letter' witticism. In Sonnet 23, the poet offers unusual advice to the youth – to 'hear with eyes':

> As an unperfect actor on the stage,
> Who with his fear is put beside his part,
> Or some fierce thing replete with too much rage,
> Whose strength's abundance weakens his own heart;
> So I, for fear of trust, forget to say
> The perfect ceremony of love's rite,
> And in mine own love's strength seem to decay,
> O'ercharged with burden of mine own love's might.
> O let my books be then the eloquence
> And dumb presagers of my speaking breast,
> Who plead for love and look for recompense
> More than that tongue that more hath more expressed.
>   O learn to read what silent love hath writ:
>   To hear with eyes belongs to love's fine wit.

In Q, 'rite' is spelled 'right', and line 14's 'with' and 'wit' are spelled 'wit' and 'wiht', respectively. Typically, commentators explain 'right' as an Elizabethan variant of 'rite', and they attribute line 14's spellings to a misplaced *H*. But that mis-attends to the injunction 'hear with eyes'. In Q, the rhymes in lines 6 and 8 contain a silent *H*, and the couplet's rhymes contain a silent *W* and a silent *H*. What is more, all four silent-letter words are preceded by 'love': 'love's right', 'love's might', 'love hath writ', and 'love's fine wiht'. (To this list, 'love's strength' might be added, if the *G* in 'strength' is silent.) Shakespeare hints that, in order to hear and see love's wit, we would do well to follow 'love'. More specifically, the couplet rhyme explains Thorpe's 'W.H'.: like *writ–wiht*, Southampton's surname has a silent *W* and silent *H* in it. What is more, there is a 'Wriothesley' anagram in line 14, or there would be one if 'eyes' were not spelled 'eies'. To hear the name's sound – 'Wriotheslie' – we must hear with our eyes.

More on Number Symbolism in *Sonnets*

In order to analyse the connections between *Sonnets* and Shakespeare's narrative poems, we need more background on numbers – particularly on 6. In mathematical terms, the number 6 is a 'perfect number': the sum of its aliquot parts (its divisors other than itself). The concept of a perfect number was formulated circa 300 BCE by Euclid; in its original context, 'perfect' (*téleos*) primarily means 'complete'. The perfection of 6 is later evoked by Christian thinkers like Augustine of Hippo, who writes in *The City of God*:

> The works of creation are described as being completed in six days . . . The reason for this is that six is the number of perfection. It is not that God was constrained by the intervals of time, as if he could not have created all things simultaneously . . . No, the reason was that the completion or perfection [*perfectio*] of the works is expressed by the number six. For six is the first number that is the sum of its parts.[24]

The idea that 6 is perfect was widespread in the Renaissance. It is cited in the Geneva Bible's gloss on 666, 'the number of the beast':

> Dost thou demand how great [the number 666] is? It is so great, that it occupieth the whole man . . . Askest thou of what denomination it is? Verily it standeth of six throughout and perfectly ariseth of all the parts thereof in their several denominations . . . Therefore that cruel beast Boniface . . . doth commend [the sixth book of his *Decretals*] by the number 6 . . . *Which book* (saith he) . . . *we thought good to name 'Sextum' (the Sixth): that the same volume by addition thereof containing . . . six books (which is a number perfect) may yield a perfect form of managing things, and perfect discipline of behavior.*[25]

Here the meanings of 'perfect' include 'complete', 'faultless', and 'eternal'. Comparing the pope to the Antichrist, the commentator relates 666 to time's completion and to parts and wholes.

The symbolism of the number 6 is discussed at length in *Numerorum Mysteria*. Bongo initially follows Augustine, noting that God created the world in six days and that 6 is associated with perfection. He later points to more equivocal ideas: that man, and hence sin, was created 'on the sixth day'; that man sinned and was expelled from Eden 'on the sixth hour of the sixth day'; that David plays the penitent in Psalm 6; that the Archangel Gabriel announced to Mary 'in the sixth month' that she had conceived 'our redeemer'; that, when Christ was on the cross, darkness covered the earth at the 'sixth hour'; that the world will suffer like Christ when the 'sixth seal' is opened at the world's end. The drift of his commentary is clear: the number 6 is related to sin and redemption. His trajectory from Adam to Christ to Judgement Day points to the providential view that structures the fair-youth narrative of transgression and redemption.

In Elizabethan poems, the symbolism of 6 mostly involves faultlessness and completion. Song 6 of *Astrophil and Stella* and Sonnet 6 of *Diana*'s second section allude to moral and aesthetic faultlessness.[26] One reason that Sidney includes 216 poetic units in his sequence is to evoke unattainable perfection (6×6×6); one reason that Chapman divides *Hero and Leander* into six 'sestiads' is to signal completion of Marlowe's poem. In *Amoretti*'s final six sonnets, the poet confronts impediments to marriage in order to remove the imperfections. Barnes's use of 6 in *Parthenophil and Parthenophe* is elabourate; perfection is thematically central to the sixteen poems that conclude the 'Sonnets' section:

Poem(s)	Description
Sonnet 102	Parthenophil asks his readers to gaze on 'the sun', Parthenophe, as a model of perfection.
Madrigals 15–20	As a series, these six poems contrast perfection (heaven and the soul) with imperfection (earth and the body). The first poem begins and ends with 'Nature's pride, Love's pearl, Virtue's perfection'. In the last poem, Parthenophe is ill.
Sonnet 103	Parthenophil has a dream-vision. In it, Parthenophe has both 'An earthly body, which was framed in heaven' and eyes glazed by Urania in order to create 'divine perfection'.
Madrigals 21–6	This six-poem group is a series of blazons to Parthenophe's beauty, starting with her eyes and descending to her private parts. As in Madrigals 15–20, the poet evokes the idea of heavenly perfection at the outset, only to conclude with something more earthy.
Sestina 1	The sestina form draws attention to the number 6. The poem's theme is perfect beauty: Parthenophil wakes up in a garden, sees Parthenophe, and describes her as more beautiful than any of the other nymphs in the garden.
Sonnet 104	Parthenophil again alludes to perfect beauty, addressing Parthenophe as 'matchless mirror of all womankind'.

Barnes signals '6' with the sixteen poems, the two sets of six madrigals, Madrigal 26, and the sestina. His 'Sonnets' section moreover begins and ends with a mirror sonnet, and its sixty-sixth poem is its centre. The entire sequence concludes with six dedicatory poems.

For more perspective on 6, let us turn to the traditions of 9, 10, and 11. Bongo provides clear accounts of their symbolism. The number 10 has positive connotations: it is associated with the Commandments and Christ and is therefore 'divine'. In contrast, 9 and 11 are 'evil numbers': 'no good is to be said for them'.[27] Bongo's contempt for 9 and 11 is evident in the opening sentences of his chapters on them:

> The number 9 does not approach the perfection of 10, but is 1 less, falling short of that number, and it signals the diminution and imperfection of works, applying much more to human and worldly things than to divine things.
>
> . . .
>
> The number 11 has nothing in common with divine things or heavenly things, no attainment, no ladder reaching toward higher things, and no merit. For it is the first number that transgresses or steps beyond 10, thereby signifying those people who transgress the Ten Commandments.[28]

Bongo faults 9 for falling short of 10, and 11 for exceeding 10. Sidney draws on these ideas: in the nine sonnets between the first and second songs in *Astrophil and Stella*, Astrophil craves physical expressions of love (he feels deprived); in the eleven sonnets between the second and third songs, he suffers the consequences of his stolen kiss (of going too far). Since Shakespeare also associates 11 with going too far, we might expect him to follow Sidney's example with 9. But in fact he does not consistently associate the number 9 with deficiency.

Shakespeare tends to use 6 as the counterpart to 11. In doing so, he was not inventing a link between 6 and deficiency: according to Bongo, 6 is associated with both perfection and imperfection, and the idea that 6 falls short of 7 is as old as the number of days in a week. One prominent source of the temporal tradition is Augustine, who connects the seventh day to the sanctification of God's law. Of particular relevance is his sermon on John 21:1–11 – the one in which he explains that 153 is a triangular number. The gospel story focuses on seven disciples who spend a night fishing and catch nothing. In the morning, after Jesus appears and tells the disciples to cast their net 'on the right-hand side of the boat', they catch a miraculous load of 153 fish. Just as miraculous, their net is not torn. Augustine explains:

> This is a great mystery in the great Gospel of John: . . . inasmuch as there were seven disciples taking part in that fishing . . . they point, by their septenary number, to the end of time. For there is a revolution of all time in seven days. To this also pertains the statement, that when the morning was come, Jesus stood on the shore; for the shore likewise is the limit of the sea, and signifies therefore the end of the world.[29]

Augustine understands the story as an allegory of Judgement Day: the 153 fish are a collection of saved or perfected souls, and 7 is the completion of time. In this view, the number 6 falls short of completion even as it points to it.

Venus and Adonis, *Lucrece*, and *Shakespeare's Sonnets*

Venus and Adonis tells the story of the goddess of love and a young man: of her attempted seduction of him, his death while hunting, and her mourning for him. As commentators often point out, the poem is Ovidian. It is also numerological. This last fact has been an open secret since Christopher Butler and Alastair Fowler's 'Time-Beguiling Sport: Number Symbolism in *Venus and Adonis*' (1964), but its implications for Shakespeare remain under-appreciated. As Butler and Fowler show, *Venus and Adonis* is constructed in the astronomical mode of Chapman's 'Amorous Zodiac' and Spenser's 'Epithalamion'; it includes precise mathematical details and temporal, celestial, and mythological allusions. To take one example: the main events of the poem take place in 20 hours, and references to the passage of time indicate that 43 lines of text equate to one hour; using that formula, there are 16 hours and 25 minutes of light during the poem's day, which corresponds to the hours of light in London on the summer solstice.[30] What is more, *Venus and Adonis* was Shakespeare's first published poem: his numeric devices may have been a way of proving himself as a poet. If nothing else, they show that he was familiar with numerological conventions.

For present purposes, the most important devices are the ones involving 20 and its multiples. As Butler and Fowler argue, Shakespeare's use of 20 alludes to Southampton's twentieth year. (*Venus and Adonis* was entered in the Stationers' Register in April, 1593; the earl turned twenty in October.) Some examples require both mythological and astronomical knowledge: the hunter Adonis is traditionally associated with the sun; the planet Venus oscillates from one side of the sun to the other every 1.6 years; in 20 years, 12 full oscillations occur; in *Venus and Adonis*, Venus bestows 12 kisses on

Adonis.[31] The references to kisses are numerically patterned: Venus speaks of 'Ten kisses short as one' (line 22) and bestows 10 kisses on Adonis in stanzas 8–10; kisses in stanzas 8, 9, and 10 are matched by kisses by Venus and Adonis in stanzas 80, 90, and 100.[32] To these observations, I will add that 'kiss' appears 20 times in the poem, a device likely informed by Sidney's 11 *kiss*'s in the 11 sonnets following Astrophil's kiss of Stella. The most significant multiple of 20 is implied in the poem's total number of stanzas – 199. Adonis dies young, on the verge of adulthood; the poem comes close to, but does not reach, 200 stanzas.

The 199 stanzas are not just symbolic; they point to the poem's centre, the 100th stanza. As Duncan-Jones and Woudhuysen suggest, stanza 100 is the poem's 'non-climactic climax':

> Now is she in the very lists of love,
> Her champion mounted for the hot encounter.
> All is imaginary she doth prove;
> He will not manage her, although he mount her –
>   That worse than Tantalus' is her annoy,
>   To clip Elysium and to lack her joy.[33]

On her back with Adonis on top of her, Venus is ready for a 'hot encounter', but fulfilment proves 'imaginary'. Her torment is worse than Tantalus's because she is deprived of satisfaction while embracing paradise: 'To clip Elysium and to lack her joy'. Like *Venus and Adonis*, *Sonnets* might be said to have 199 poetic units: the pyramid's 152 sonnets and the 47-stanza complaint. Alternatively, if we count Sonnets 126 and 145, *Sonnets* has 201 poetic units. Either way, the work complements *Venus and Adonis*. The 199-unit interpretation gains support from Sonnet 100, in which the poet asks the muse to return and 'straight redeem, / In gentle numbers, time so idly spent'. Punning on 'numbers', a synonym for 'verse', the poet gestures towards a new start.

Number symbolism and numerological organisation in *Lucrece* have been worse than under-appreciated; they have gone unnoticed. *Lucrece* is a 265-stanza narrative. Like the first edition of *Venus and Adonis*, the first edition of *Lucrece* contains six stanzas on every full two-page spread – a layout that facilitates counting the stanzas. Its story offers an explanation for the founding of the Roman republic: Lucrece is raped by Tarquin, a son of Rome's king; after revealing the rape to Collantine and exhorting him to avenge the crime, Lucrece stabs herself; her suicide triggers the overthrow of Rome's monarchy. As in *Venus and Adonis*, Shakespeare takes his time telling the story:

the rape occurs almost 100 stanzas into the poem; Lucrece stabs herself in stanza 247; and Lucrece's blood encircles her body in stanza 250.

There are few overt references to numbers in *Lucrece* but much numeric organisation. In the centre stanza (133), Lucrece begins a rant on Time's injuries. In the stanzas leading up to 133, Lucrece rails against Opportunity's sins. Injury is a major theme of *Lucrece*; it is literally at the poem's centre. Lucrece's rape, however, occurs earlier – in or around stanza 99. In stanza 98, Tarquin assaults Lucrece and the poet exclaims 'O, that prone lust should stain so pure a bed!'; in stanza 99, we are definitively informed of the rape: 'But she hath lost a dearer thing than life'. After stanza 99, there are 33 stanzas leading to the poem's centre, and in stanza 166, Lucrece starts meditating on suicide: '"To kill myself", quoth she, "alack, what were it?"'. This debate signals the final stage of a process; Lucrece had the impulse to kill herself earlier but lacked the means or the resolve to do so. Like *Sonnets*, *Lucrece* develops themes of violation and suicide, and it associates them with numbers ending in '33', '66', and '99'.

Lucrece also draws on the tradition of 11 as a number of transgression. This can be seen in the stanzas between the rape and the meditation on suicide (the central stanzas):

Stanzas	Description of group
99–109	The poet speaks of the rape's immediate effects on Lucrece and Tarquin (99); Tarquin slinks guiltily away (100–7) and Lucrece anxiously awaits the morning light (107–9).
110–21	Lucrece first addresses Night, half abusing it, half praying to it (110–18). She then addresses 'unseen shame, invisible disgrace' (119) and her absent husband (120). She concludes that she is guilty of her 'honour's wrack' (121).
122–32	Lucrece meditates on imperfection (122–5) and rails against Opportunity (126–32).
133–43	Lucrece addresses Time as she earlier addressed Night – half abusively and half in prayer.
144–54	Lucrece comments on Tarquin's baseness (144–5) and realises that her words cannot provide true consolation (146–7). Seeking to turn from words to deeds and hoping to kill herself, she looks for a weapon (148–9). Like her words, her search for a weapon proves 'in vain' (150–1). Addressing her

155–65 The nightingale, Philomel, ends her song, signalling the start of day and causing Lucrece to find fault with the day and the birds that are singing (155–60). Lucrece addresses the 'mocking birds' (161) and Philomel (162–4), comparing her rape with Philomel's. The poet compares Lucrece first to a frightened deer who does not know which way to run and then to a person who is lost in a maze (165).

Five of the six groups have 11 stanzas. The exception is the second group, which has 12 stanzas: it runs from stanza 110 (11×10) through stanza 121 (11×11). This exception ensures that each group begins with a stanza whose number ends in 'doubled digits', and that Lucrece begins her extended debate on suicide in stanza 166, 99 stanzas away from the final stanza.

Venus and Adonis, *Lucrece*, and *Sonnets* are linked by more than numbers. One shared theme is 'perfection and imperfection'. In *Venus and Adonis*, this is developed in stanzas 122–5, when Venus explains to Adonis why Cynthia (the moon) is not shining. Stanzas 122–3 are especially revealing:

> 'Now of this dark night I perceive the reason:
> Cynthia for shame obscures her silver shine
> Till forging Nature be condemned of treason
> For stealing molds from heav'n that were divine –
>   Wherein she framed thee, in high heav'n's despite,
>   To shame the sun by day and her by night'.

> 'And therefore hath she bribed the Destinies
> To cross the curious workmanship of Nature,
> To mingle beauty with infirmities,
> And pure perfection with impure defeature,
>   Making it subject to the tyranny
>   Of mad mischances and much misery'.

Nature has stolen the moulds that heaven uses to stamp beauty like a coin. Venus's image of counterfeiting is likely stolen from Daniel's 'Complaint of Rosamond', which speaks of the 'treason' committed when women 'counterfeit the . . . stamp of heav'n' (use cosmetics).[34] Shakespeare is saying that earthly perfection is always mixed with imperfection. He alludes to this idea again in *Lucrece* and does so, again, in the 122nd though 125th stanzas. In stanza 122, Lucrece asserts 'But no perfection is so absolute / That some impurity doth not pollute'. In stanzas 123–5, she elabourates on how imperfection dwells within perfection or accompanies it, lamenting that 'Unruly blasts wait on the tender spring; / Unwholesome weeds take root with precious flowers; / The adder hisses where the sweet birds sing; / What Virtue breeds Iniquity devours' (stanza 125). As in *Sonnets*, the ultimate culprit is Time, who ruins perfection or reveals latent imperfection. 'Time's glory', Lucrece bitterly notes, is 'To fill with wormholes stately monuments, / To feed oblivion with decay of things, / To blot old books and alter their conténts, / To pluck the quills from ancient ravens' wings' (stanza 135).

Sonnets' counterparts to the perfection-imperfection stanzas are Sonnets 122–5, the final fair-youth sonnets. Sonnet 122 concludes a series about judgement and forgiveness; the poet tempers his ambition to immortalise the youth by offering to retain the youth's gift 'so long as brain and heart / Have faculty by nature to subsist'. Echoing 'So long as men can breathe or eyes can see' (Sonnet 18), the poet acknowledges mortal limitations. Conceding the impossibility of human perfection, he qualifies his vow to retain the youth's gift 'beyond all date' and humanises his desire to prove and preserve his love. Sonnets 123–5 are thematically linked by complaints against Time and rhetorically linked by interjections: the poet says 'No' at the start of 123's first quatrain, 124's second quatrain, and 125's third quatrain. As a series, Sonnets 123–5 begin in angry defiance and end in sorrowful pleading: in 123, the poet asserts that his heart has stayed the same, in spite of all the time passed, and in 125, he looks for private and sincere commitment: 'mutual render, only me for thee'. Acknowledging the imperfection in his beloved and his love, the poet attempts to reconcile change with constancy. This theme is at the heart of the fair-youth section if not of the whole sequence: the poet comes to realise that the seemingly perfect and steadfast youth is in fact imperfect and unfaithful, and that the flawed and overtly unfaithful mistress is not as antithetical to the youth as he initially portrays her to be.

Chapter 5

Competing Schemes

This chapter analyses organisational and numerological schemes in *Sonnets* that are not directly related to the main structure; analysis of pyramid steps begins in the next chapter and guides the remaining discussion. In view of artistic fashions of the 1590s, *Sonnets*' intricate schemes are perhaps to be expected, but their sophistication is nonetheless telling: Shakespeare both shows familiarity with Elizabethan literary conventions and exhibits ambition in his orchestration of them. Showcasing art may have been an aim; he may also have regarded his choices as suited to his subject matter and audience. Whatever their rationale, organisational and numerological schemes abound in *Sonnets*. And while it is hard to generalise about them – other than to say that Shakespeare seems to have packed them into every available space – they often comment on the basic pyramid structure, even or especially when they can exist on their own terms.

Mirror Poems and Mirror Schemes

Shakespeare alludes to mirrors in six sonnets: 3, 22, 62, 77, 103, and 126. All of these sonnets are in the fair-youth section; all are used in organisational schemes; and all feature 'glass' rather than 'mirror'. Sonnet 3 opens with an address to the youth: 'Look in thy glass and tell the face thou viewest / Now is the time that face should form another'. A century of sonnets later, in 103, the poet says something similar with a different second-person pronoun: 'Look in your glass, and there appears a face / That overgoes my blunt invention quite'. Sonnets 3 and 103 demarcate a 100-sonnet scheme, similar to that of Sonnets 33–4 and 133–4. But while the parallels between 33–4 and 133–4 suggest simultaneity – the youth-mistress affair considered from different angles – the 100-sonnet distance between 3 and 103 underscores the passage of time. This is made clear in Sonnet 104, which indicates that it has been three years since the poet first saw the youth, and which answers Sonnet 103 by declaring: 'To me, fair friend, you never can be old'.

The second mirror sonnet, 22, also belongs to a 100-sonnet scheme, the gift trio: 22-77-122. All three sonnets concern giving/exchange; with their 'doubled digits' and numeric pattern, they may allude to reciprocity and mirror imagery.[1] In Sonnet 22, the poet reminds the youth that they have exchanged hearts; in 77, he details the purpose of a gift book; and in 122, he explains why he gave away a gift book. Redeeming time is a theme of all three poems:

> Sonnet 22
> My glass shall not persuade me I am old
> So long as youth and thou are of one date,
> But when in thee Time's furrows I behold,
> Then look I Death my days should expiate.
> For all that beauty that doth cover thee
> Is but the seemly raiment of my heart,
> Which in thy breast doth live, as thine in me –
> How can I then be elder than thou art?
> O therefore, love, be of thyself so wary
> As I, not for myself, but for thee will,
> Bearing thy heart, which I will keep so chary
> As tender nurse her babe from faring ill.
>   Presume not on thy heart when mine is slain –
>   Thou gav'st me thine not to give back again.
>
> Sonnet 77
> Thy glass will show thee how thy beauties wear,
> Thy dial how thy precious minutes waste;
> The vacant leaves thy mind's imprint will bear,
> And of this book, this learning mayst thou taste:
> The wrinkles which thy glass will truly show
> Of mouthèd graves will give thee memory;
> Thou by thy dial's shady stealth mayst know
> Time's thievish progress to eternity.
> Look what thy memory cannot contain
> Commit to these waste blanks, and thou shalt find
> Those children nursed, delivered from thy brain,
> To take a new acquaintance of thy mind.
>   These offices, so oft as thou wilt look,
>   Shall profit thee and much enrich thy book.

Sonnet 122
Thy gift, thy tables, are within my brain
Full charactered with lasting memory,
Which shall above that idle rank remain,
Beyond all date, ev'n to eternity –
Or, at the least, so long as brain and heart
Have faculty by nature to subsist;
Till each to razed oblivion yield his part
Of thee, thy record never can be missed.
That poor retention could not so much hold;
Nor need I tallies thy dear love to score –
Therefore to give them from me was I bold,
To trust those tables that receive thee more.
  To keep an adjunct to remember thee
  Were to import forgetfulness in me.

Sonnet 22 opens with 'My glass'; 77, with 'Thy glass'; and 122, with 'Thy gift, thy tables'. Sonnet 22 speaks of a gift to the poet (the youth's heart); 77, of at least one gift, probably to the youth (a notebook); and 122, of a gift to the poet (a tablet or a set of bound pages). Sonnet 77 is often considered out of place: it hardly seems to fit the rival-poet series. As the centre poem of the trio and the pyramid, though, 77 is well positioned. Similarly, Sonnets 22 and 122 do not fit seamlessly in their immediate context but are nonetheless aptly positioned.

In Sonnet 22, the poet expresses love for the youth that may be more one-sided than exchanging hearts implies. The initial phrasing is awkward: 'My glass shall not persuade me I am old / So long as youth and thou are of one date, / But when in thee Time's furrows I behold, / Then look I Death my days should expiate'. Even in modern prose, this claim is odd: *As long as you are young, my mirror will not convince me that I am old, but when I see wrinkles in your face, then I will expect death to complete my days.* The awkwardness may be intentional: perhaps the poet is hinting that his relations with the youth are not as amicable as they seem. He also seems to go out of his way to say 'youth and thou' and 'expiate'. The phrase 'youth and thou' hints at 'you and thou'. This interpretation gains support from the reference to mirrors revealing changes in personal appearance, and from Sonnet 11's phrase 'when thou from youth convertest'. The word 'expiate' points to redemption: atoning for sins, paying a debt.

Sonnet 77 evokes a gift-giving occasion and features three objects: a 'glass' (a mirror), a 'dial' (a timepiece), and a 'book [with] vacant leaves' (a memorandum book). The timepiece is likely a sundial; the glass and the dial may be previous gifts or already-owned items; the poem may be understood as a letter accompanying the gift(s) or an inscription in the book.[2] If we read the poem as merely a note for an occasion, its advice is insipid: *Write down a thought a day, and you will build your character and fill up this notebook.* As a poem in a trio, however, 77 contributes to a larger story – a tale of two books (one for the youth, one for the poet) or a tale of one book (given to the youth and given back to the poet, or given to the poet and given away). The memorandum book is likely the poet's gift to the youth: in the surrounding sonnets, the poet addresses the youth; 77's tone is paternal; and 77's addressee is told that his mirror will reveal how his beauties waste away. (That said, the poet could be addressing himself.) No matter who the speaker and the addressee are, 77 urges its recipient to write. The poem's counsel is to record all memory-defying thoughts: 'Look what thy memory cannot contain' means 'Whatever your memory cannot hold'. After such 'children' are delivered from the brain, they will be nursed and they will grow; when seen again after an absence, they will be both new and familiar. The epistolary frame suggests that the speaker is writing to a loved one from whom he is, or will soon be, separated: daily writing is a method for coping with absence. With 'children . . . from thy brain', the sonnet evokes 'children of the brain', a metaphor for poetry whose best-known example is in Sonnet 1 of *Astrophil and Stella*. Sonnet 77 may thereby allude to love poetry or even to the sequence itself. Filling the book might also refer to copying verses, though 'delivered from thy brain' militates against this reading unless we construe the phrase to mean 'transcribed from memory'. If 77 alludes to copying poems, it may also allude to circulating manuscripts for copying.[3]

In light of Sonnet 122, 77's book may be a kind of ledger or account book. Sonnet 122 comes near the end of the fair-youth poems, where the theme of reckoning is prominent. It tells the story of a book that was worse than lost – of 'tables' that the poet received and gave away. The poet defends his actions on the grounds that the book's content is in his memory's tables, which are fully inscribed and will endure until doomsday – or rather, he reconsiders, will endure 'so long as brain and heart / Have faculty by nature to subsist'. If Sonnet 122's tables are 77's book, the poet may be guilty of giving away something private, such as lines by or about the youth. He suggests that the lost book is nothing to fret about: it is a 'poor retention', an inferior receptacle to his mind's and heart's tables, which are living and can better 'receive' the youth. And besides, he hints, those who truly love do not keep track of debts or think in such measured terms. In the couplet, the poet declares that he does not need 'an adjunct', an additional or external aid, to remember the youth, and that any suggestion otherwise is an insult to his feelings and his powers of memory. Sonnet 122's book is a tablet on which notes are written and erased, but it also evokes an indelible account of good and bad deeds, to be presented to God on Judgement Day.

The third mirror sonnet, 62, is especially concerned with distorted perspective:

> Sin of self-love possesseth all mine eye
> And all my soul, and all my every part;
> And for this sin there is no remedy,
> It is so grounded inward in my heart.
> Methinks no face so gracious is as mine,
> No shape so true, no truth of such account,
> And for myself mine own worth do define,
> As I all other in all worths surmount.
> But when my glass shows me myself indeed,
> Beated and chopped with tanned antiquity,
> Mine own self-love quite cóntrary I read –
> Self so self-loving were iniquity.
>   'Tis thee, my self, that for myself I praise,
>   Painting my age with beauty of thy days.

In ways that recall Sonnet 22, 62 questions self-love and self-assurance. In the earlier sonnet, the poet claimed that his mirror would not convince him he was old as long as the youth was young; in 62, he claims that he sees his self-love as a vice, or that he sees the error of his ways when his glass shows him himself as he truly is – old. As in 22, pronominal puns blur distinctions between poet and youth. The puns begin in the first line (*eye–I*), but the blurring happens later, when reflexive pronouns are introduced. This design is more apparent in Q, in which all reflexive pronouns are printed as two words ('my self' for 'myself'), as was standard Elizabethan practice.[4] Sonnet 62 also underscores reversals. The word 'cóntrary', for example, evokes 'mirror image', and its antepenultimate stress, reversing the penultimate stress that Shakespeare often uses elsewhere, gives the word extra emphasis.[5] The poet's explanation for his narcissism – that his self-love is love for his other self, the youth – seems meant to be read as ingenuous flattery; his depiction of himself as absurdly self-absorbed is not to be taken at face value. But especially in that case, the poet may be diverting blame from himself: the couplet includes 'the ugly possibilities that the [poet] praises the friend to benefit himself [and] to deceive by "Painting"'.[6]

In its flattering and overt sense, the couplet proclaims that the youth gives lustre to the poet and to the times.

Given the echoes of 22, there is little reason to believe that Sonnet 62 marks a moment when the poet has arrived at a final state of enlightenment about his love. He reworks his claim about learning from his mirror, but his history of self-assurance is not reassuring: a pattern of similar declarations can be traced back almost to the start of *Sonnets*. Sonnet 2 opens: 'When forty winters shall besiege thy brow / And dig deep trenches in thy beauty's field, / Thy youth's proud livery, so gazed on now, / Will be a tottered weed'. These 'deep trenches', dug by two-score years, foreshadow 'Time's furrows' (22) and 'Beated and chopped with tanned antiquity' (62). To put it another way: in Sonnet 2, the poet asks the youth to imagine himself as an old man; twenty sonnets later, he boasts that he will not feel old until he sees that the youth has aged; and forty sonnets after that, he recognises his age but declares that he can paint over it with the youth's beauty. Perhaps we are meant to understand that the youth is 20 or 22 years old at the start of *Sonnets*, and that the poems describe an arithmetic series whose symbolism ranges from growing old to progressing towards eternity (x+20+40+60 . . .). According to the maths, the series' next sonnet would be 122, a poem acknowledging mortal limitations after declaring that the youth's gift will be remembered 'to eternity'.

The sequence's final mirror sonnet, 126, functions as a coda to the fair-youth section:

> O thou, my lovely boy, who in thy power
> Dost hold Time's fickle glass, his sickle hour,
> Who hast by waning grown, and therein show'st
> Thy lovers with'ring as thy sweet self grow'st –
> If Nature, sovereign mistress over wrack,
> As thou go'st onwards still will pluck thee back,
> She keeps thee to this purpose: that her skill
> May Time disgrace and wretchèd minutes kill.
> Yet fear her, O thou minion of her pleasure –
> She may detain, but not still keep, her treasure!
> Her audit, though delayed, answered must be,
> And her quietus is to render thee.
>   (   )
>   (   )

Sonnet 126 offers an amicable but stern warning about the mortality of beauty. 'Time's fickle glass' is ambiguous – is it an hourglass or a mirror? It may be both, as well as an image of mutability. Time's glass is mutable because it changes – alters in appearance – as it registers change. (An hourglass changes as its sand trickles down; mirrors change as viewers return to them and see new images of themselves.) By juxtaposing 'glass' and 'sickle', the poet evokes iconic images: Father Time with his instruments; Death as the grim reaper. By juxtaposing 'fickle glass' and 'sickle hour', he again points to mutability: 'fickle' and 'sickle' differ by one letter; in Q, 'sickle' has a 'long s', which resembles an 'f'. (More proof that orthography matters can be gleaned from the two 'Wriothesley' anagrams in line 4, which depend on Q's spelling, and from the two pairs of parentheses, which arguably represent sickles or an hourglass.) 'Thy lovers with'ring' also hints at fickleness: in Elizabethan English, 'lover' can range in meaning from 'friend' to 'paramour', and 'lovers' can signify 'lovers', 'lovers'', or 'lover's'.[7] (Also note the implied conceit of the moon's waxing and waning.) In the final couplet, the youth is warned that Nature will use him to discharge her debt to Time. By placing 'though delayed' in an interruptive position in line 11, the poet expresses resistance to forward movement and the day of reckoning; by continuing with 'answered' (a trochee), he emphasises that the deadline for payment is strict. Hinting at resignation, line 12 is more fluid: 'And her quietus is to render thee'. Here 'quietus' evokes 'final rest' and 'receipt in full'. Shakespeare uses the word only once elsewhere, in Hamlet's 'To be or not to be' soliloquy, where it is also associated with time and death: 'For who would bear the whips and scorns of time ... When he himself might his quietus make / With a bare bodkin?' Sonnet 126's 'quietus' moreover evokes 'quiet', and the poem's closing pairs of parentheses, embracing blank space, reinforce the notion that the rest is silence.[8]

Sonnets' mirror schemes speak to the poet's concern with, and ideas about, perfection. Figuratively and literally, the poet adds wrinkles to the youth. We have seen how Sonnet 2 predicts 'deep trenches' in the youth's brow, how Sonnet 22 fears the day when the youth will exhibit 'Time's furrows', and how Sonnet 62 dramatises the realisation of being 'chopped' with age. Sonnet 3 speaks of how the youth, when old with 'wrinkles', will see his younger self in his child. The centre poem of the fair-youth section, Sonnet 63, protests the day when the youth's forehead with be filled with 'lines and wrinkles'. The centre poem of the 153-poem pyramid, Sonnet 77, features a mirror that reveals 'wrinkles'. And the centre poem of the 199-unit scheme, Sonnet 100, asks the muse to survey the youth's face to see 'If Time have any wrinkle graven there'. (Any line that is found, the poet argues, merely mocks aging.) In Sonnet 103, then, with 'your glass' instead of 'thy glass', and with the claim that 'much more' will show in the fair youth's mirror than 'can sit' in the verse, the poet hints that he has come to see the youth as flawed.

Shakespeare's Dialectical Schemes

There are schemes in *Sonnets* independent of the pyramid structure but in conversation with it. The 100-sonnet schemes, for example, require merely a century of poems, but Sonnets 33–4 and 133–4 also breach pyramid-step boundaries, reinforcing their theme of transgression. 'In conversation with the pyramid structure' needn't imply in agreement with it, however. Some of the independent schemes oppose the idea of an eternal monument or offer a qualified view on poetry's immortalising power. In doing so, they gesture towards an alternative way of redeeming time.

Sonnets' six mirror poems are informed by traditions in which 6 symbolises perfection and imperfection. The same is true of the six 'When I' sonnets – the six poems that begin with 'When I' or 'When . . . I' and that reflect on time and change:

> Sonnet 12
> When I do count the clock that tells the time . . .
> When I behold the violet, . . . When lofty trees I see . . .
> Then of thy beauty do I question make.

> Sonnet 15
> When I consider everything that grows . . .
> When I perceive that men as plants increase . . .
> Then the conceit of this inconstant stay
> Sets you most rich in youth before my sight.

> Sonnet 29
> When . . . I all alone beweep my outcast state,
> And trouble deaf heav'n . . . and curse my fate,
> Wishing . . . Desiring . . . I think on thee, and then,
> Like to the lark . . . [I sing] hymns at heaven's gate.

> Sonnet 30
> When . . . I summon up remembrance of things past . . .
> I sigh . . . [and I] wail . . .
> Then can I drown an eye . . . Then can I grieve.

Sonnet 64
When I have seen [Time's corruptive effects] . . .
Ruin hath taught me . . . Time will come and take my love away.

Sonnet 106
When . . . I see descriptions of the fairest wights,
And beauty making beautiful old rhyme . . .
Then . . . I see their ántique pen would have expressed
Ev'n such a beauty as you.[9]

Each sonnet is informed by a 'when I . . . then I' structure: typically a series of 'when I' phrases in the octave is answered by a 'then I' phrase in the sestet. Sonnet 12 sets the pattern; the other poems offer variations on it: 15 has a 'then' without an 'I'; 29 separates the 'I' from the 'when' and reverses the order of 'then' and 'I'; 30 introduces a series of 'then I' phrases in the octave; 64 eschews the 'then I' phrase and delays introducing the 'then' logic until line 11; and 106 avoids repeating 'when I', abruptly introducing 'then' in line 5. Like the mirror poems, the 'When I' sonnets link time with imperfection and change. With its number and its image of a tolling clock, the first 'When I' sonnet, 12, specifically evokes temporal symbolism.

The 'When I' sonnets express defiance against time and desire for redemption, but mostly they call attention to change and loss. In Sonnet 12, the poet broaches the subject of time's power over beauty; in Sonnet 15, he claims that poetry can defeat time but makes that claim only in the couplet, after expressing fear of inevitable decay. In Sonnets 29 and 30, he speaks of the youth's love as a power that can redeem time, but his redemptive proclamations only come after a litany of laments. Sonnet 64 is pessimistic: the poet acknowledges that Time will 'come and take' his love, and he experiences this thought 'as a death'. The final 'When I' sonnet, 106, equivocally evokes poetry's power in comparison with time's. The poet claims that the fair youth surpasses all beauties of former times and that he is the culmination of beauty: ancient poets saw the youth darkly, in prophetic visions; modern writers lack the art to praise him. In presenting the ancients as artists of greater skill and the moderns as witnesses to beauty's ultimate incarnation, Shakespeare finesses the question of whether his poetry has the power to preserve the youth in all his beauty.

Like the 'When I' sonnets, Sonnets 49, 64, 81, and 100 express anxiety about poetry's power to overcome time. Let us call this scheme 'the square-number series', since its sonnets' numbers are

7×7, 8×8, 9×9, and 10×10. Each sonnet repeats all or part of its opening phrase at the start of the second quatrain and the start of the third quatrain:

> Sonnet 49
> Against that time . . .
> Against that time . . .
> Against that time . . .
>
> Sonnet 64
> When I have seen . . .
> When I have seen . . .
> When I have seen . . .
>
> Sonnet 81
> Or I shall live your epitaph to make . . .
> Your name from hence immortal life shall have . . .
> Your monument shall be my gentle verse . . .
>
> Sonnet 100
> Where art thou, Muse . . .
> Return, forgetful Muse . . .
> Rise, resty Muse . . .

The pattern is evident in Sonnets 49 and 64, whose quatrains begin with the same phrases. It is also fairly clear in Sonnet 100: in each quatrain, the poet directly addresses the muse as 'Muse', posing a question or issuing a command. Sonnet 81's pattern is less distinct: each line contains 'your' (followed by a noun) and 'shall' (followed by a monosyllabic verb). This incomplete or broken repetition signals the presence of a competing scheme: the monument trio. All monument-trio sonnets start with a correlative conjunction – a requirement that complicates the task of fitting 81 in the square-number series. Sonnet 81 is also the central poem of the rival-poet series, and the third of the three climacteric sonnets. It has to fit four schemes.

Up to a point, the square-number series complements *Sonnets*' immortalising project. Sonnets 49, 64, and 81 belong to three consecutive pyramid steps, and 'squaring' might be said to resolve the dilemmas associated with the triangular pyramid. Sonnet 81 is even triumphant: 'Your name from hence immortal life shall have'. But if there is a victory over time, it is not clear-cut: in Sonnet 100, the poet calls for renewed effort and inspiration to complete the final pyramid steps of the fair-youth series. He also admits to wasted time: 'Return, forgetful Muse, and straight redeem, / In gentle numbers, time so idly spent'. Positioned at the start of the final three fair-youth steps, the fourth square-number sonnet might have been added to an original trio of sonnets: it advocates reanimating a project. Sonnets 100–25 also make allowances for imperfection. The poet is trying to reconcile immortal longings with mortal limitations.

One more scheme bears exploring here – a series of five groups across the 125-sonnet fair-youth section that offers perspectives on time and imperfection. (A possible model is William Alexander's *Aurora*, which contains 125 poems that may be divided into five 25-poem groups.[10]) The first group is the easiest to describe: Sonnets 1–25 of Shakespeare's sequence portray the growth of the poet-youth friendship, whose high point is signalled in 25's couplet: 'Then happy I that love and am belovèd, / Where I may not remove, nor be removèd'. In view of Sonnet 26, in which the poet speaks of duty to the youth and imagines a time when his guiding star will shine 'graciously', the 100 sonnets that follow 25 are potentially framed as the poet's quest to prove his worth. And in view of the first group's size, we might expect four more 25-sonnet groups, corresponding to stages in the story. But the quest is interrupted almost at its start, and none of the other groups contains exactly 25 sonnets, though all are comparable in size. I suspect that the scheme is informed by the possibility of dividing Sonnets 1–125 into five groups of twenty-five sonnets, and that the roughness of the design reinforces what the poet is saying about time's accidents and human imperfection. But first things first – what groups are we talking about, and how are their boundaries demarcated?

The five groups have 25, 26, 24, 21, and 26 sonnets, respectively:

Series   Description of the group and its boundary sonnets

1–25   The first group portrays the growth of the poet-youth friendship. Sonnet 25 ends with a triumphant couplet, in which the poet speaks of loving and being loved, and of love that will endure.

26–51   The second group begins with an epistolary sonnet in which the poet claims that he has yet to prove his worth (26); the two sonnets that follow, 27–8, and the two sonnets at the end of the group, 50–1, are pairs of poems about traveling and returning.

52–75   The third group begins and ends with sonnets that are governed by extended conceits: in 52, the poet compares himself to a rich man; in 75, to a miser. Also note that the opening lines of these sonnets echo each other: 52 begins 'So am I'; 75 begins 'So are you'.

76–96   The fourth group includes the rival-poet series and the break-up sonnets that follow from that crisis. In 76, the poet explains why he does not seek novelty or follow the fashions of the time; 96 not only marks the moment of the break but ends with a repetition of 36's couplet, which provides rhetorical closure. (Both 36 and 96 allude to an imminent separation of the poet and the youth.)

97–122 The fifth group describes the passage of time after the break (97–9), the renewal of poet-youth relations (100–8), and the poet's confessions of infidelity, pleas for forgiveness, and aspirations to a kind of marriage (109–22). The poet concludes his defence of himself in 122, which offers a strained explanation for why he gave away a book that the youth had given to him.

In the trio after 122, the poet rails against Time, employing 'No' as an interjection at the beginning of 123's first quatrain, 124's second quatrain, and 125's third quatrain.

My overview of the five groups does not prove that the scheme exists; it just illustrates that the fair-youth section of *Sonnets* can be divided into five series of roughly twenty-five sonnets each, with boundary sonnets comparable in character to those of the pyramid steps. More evidence can be gleaned from temporal allusions. The most important temporal allusion is in the final group, which consists of twenty-six sonnets and covers the interruption in the poet-youth friendship and the period after the renewal of relations, which are framed as analogous to the interim between Christ's death and resurrection and the period between Christ's resurrection and ascension. Because 99 has fifteen lines, the twenty-six sonnets have 365 lines in total – symbolising a year. Whether or not Shakespeare is referring to a particular year, he may be indicating that the renewal of friendship between the poet and the youth did not last long; this would add poignancy to the pleas for forgiveness and mutual commitment, and more anger to the railings against time in the final trio. The third group may also contain temporal allusions. Its first sonnet, 52, describes feast days as 'rare' because, like expensive jewels in a necklace, they do not come often in the string of weeks and days of the 'long year'. Although the word 'week' does not appear in the poem, many commentators have suggested that the sonnet's number alludes to the number of weeks in a year.[11] There may also be an allusion to twenty-four hours in the 24-sonnet group, which begins and ends with the image of someone vigilantly guarding valuables day and night. Temporal symbolism aside, the five groups draw attention to temporality, and the concluding trio points to eternity.

Even if they do not actively oppose the sequence's immortalising project, the 'When I' sonnets, the square-number series, and the five groups imply a dialectic between eternity and temporality, permanence and change, and perfection and imperfection. This dialectic may be inherent in the pyramidal scheme, because the pyramid is meant to be 'a living monument', a memorial that is at once enduring and vibrant if not thriving where 'breath most breathes, ev'n in the mouths of men' (Sonnet 81). Such a project is dialectical in that it seeks to include temporal aspects of beauty in timeless art. The triangular form of the monument is ambiguous, after all: the steps taper, but is the triangle pointing upward, like the top of an obelisk, or downward, like the upper bulb of an hourglass? There is similar ambiguity in the coda to the fair-youth section, whose opening lines speak of 'Time's fickle glass', and of inversely related increases and decreases: 'O thou, my lovely boy, who in thy power / Dost hold Time's fickle glass, his sickle hour, / Who hast by waning grown, and therein show'st / Thy lovers with'ring as thy sweet self grow'st'. If the 'glass' is an hourglass, it points to change or decline; if it is a mirror, it points to a perfect or exemplary type, as in the expression 'the glass of chivalry'. The ambiguity epitomises *Sonnets*' dialectic between temporality and eternity, which is figured in the trickling sand of an hourglass: as the grains fall from the upper bulb of the glass to the lower bulb, they gradually build a pyramidal pile.

Marriage and Justice

Shakespeare's Sonnets occasionally draws attention to the number 5 – with the five groups of '25' sonnets, for instance. Given the poet's symbolic use of 6, 11, and the temporal numbers, we might expect that his use of 5 is informed by symbolism. It is – and in ways as complex as of his use of 6. As Fowler explains, the number 5 has a history of symbolising marriage: 'According to Plutarch, the Pythagoreans called [the number 5] 'Marriage' because the association or addition of the first male and first female number produced it: 2+3=5'.[12] He also provides an Elizabethan example, from the fifth sestiad of Chapman's *Hero and Leander*:

> Next before her went
> Five lovely children decked with ornament.
> . . . .
> The odd disparent number they did choose
> To show the union married loves should use,
> Since in two equal parts it will not sever,
> But the midst holds one to rejoin it ever
> As common to both parts.
> . . . .
> And five [is held] in most especial prize,
> Since 'tis the first odd number that doth rise
> From the two foremost numbers' unity
> That odd and even are, which are two and three –
> For one no number is, but thence doth flow
> The powerful race of number.
> (lines 317–18, 323–7, 335–40)

Though some poets equate 8 with marriage, 5's nuptial symbolism was more common.[13] Among sonnet sequences, Alexander's *Aurora* is an example: it not only contains five groups of twenty-five poems; it concludes with the poet renouncing Cupid and Venus for Juno, the goddess of marriage.

Shakespeare's fifth sonnet contains a hidden allusion to marriage:

> Those hours that with gentle work did frame
> The lovely gaze where every eye doth dwell
> Will play the tyrants to the very same
> And that unfair which fairly doth excel:
> For never-resting time leads summer on
> To hideous winter, and confounds him there –
> Sap checked with frost, and lusty leaves quite gone,
> Beauty o'er-snowed and bareness everywhere.
> Then were not summer's distillation left
> A liquid prisoner pent in walls of glass,
> Beauty's effect with beauty were bereft,
> Nor it nor no remembrance what it was.
>   But flow'rs distilled, though they with winter meet,
>   Leese but their show; their substance still lives sweet.

In advising the youth to sire children, the poet is advising marriage; with the rosewater image, he illustrates that begetting children can preserve beauty. Shakespeare's eerie and beautiful phrase 'liquid prisoner pent in walls of glass' is inspired by a passage in Sidney's *Arcadia*, in which Cecropia talks with Philoclea about marriage:

> For believe me, niece, believe me, man's experience is woman's best eyesight. Have you ever seen a pure rose-water kept in a crystal glass; how fine it looks, how sweet it smells while that beautiful glass imprisons it? Break the prison, and let the water take his own course; doth it not embrace dust and lose all his former sweetness, and fairness? Truly so are we, if we have not the stay, rather than the restraint of crystalline marriage. My heart melts to think of the sweet comforts I in that happy time received, when I had never cause to care but the care was doubled, when I never rejoiced, but that I saw my joy shine in another's eyes ... And is a solitary life as good as this? Then can one string make as good music as a consort: then can one colour set forth a beauty. (Book Three, Chapter 4)

The *Arcadia* passage is often cited as a source, but its context is rarely analysed.[14] Philoclea is Cecropia's prisoner; Cecropia is making ad hoc arguments to which she is hardly committed. In Sonnets 1–9 (of which 5 is the central or 'pent in' sonnet), the poet similarly speaks from a parental position: in urging familial responsibility, he may be giving lip service to arguments that he was commissioned to make. (Shakespeare's 'pent' may also hint at the Greek word for 'five'.) Cecropia's speech informs the next few sonnets, especially 8, in which nuptial and musical imagery merge: 'Mark how one string, sweet husband to another, / Strikes each in each by mutual ordering, / Resembling sire, and child, and happy mother'.

The nuptial theme is more apparent if we read Sonnets 1–25 and 100–25 as related series. The sequence's first 25 sonnets chart an increase in intimacy between poet and youth, climaxing with 25's 'happy I, that love and am belovèd'. In the final sonnets of the fair-youth section, the poet tries to square accounts with the youth, hoping for forgiveness and renewed friendship. In other words, the friendship initially peaks with Sonnet 25 (5×5), then moves towards Sonnet 125 (5×5×5), with its ceremony of 'mutual render, only thee for me'. Shakespeare's design may be informed by *Astrophil and Stella*'s 6×6×6 poetic units.

Shakespeare's use of 5 is not limited to nuptial symbolism: it draws on a tradition in which 5 represents justice. As Thomas Browne explains in *The Garden of Cyrus* (1658):

> [I] cannot omit the ancient conceit of 5, surnamed the number of justice; as justly dividing between the digits and hanging in the center of 9 – [which] might be the original of that common game among us, wherein the fifth place is Sovereign and carrieth the chief intention, ... the middle point and central seat of justice.[15]

Like a king with four counsellors on each side, the number 5 is 'the center of 9'. Nine-person pageants in *The Faerie Queene* draw on this conceit, as may *Julius Caesar* in the scene of Caesar's assassination.[16] As Fowler notes, the judicial symbolism of 5 was 'reinforced in the Middle Ages by the association of the Law with the Pentateuch'.[17] Another source is the prophet Daniel's interpretation of Nebuchadnezzar's dream (Daniel 2:31–45). The Babylonian king dreams of a statue made of five materials, which Daniel sees as a symbol of five kingdoms. Renaissance exegetes glossed the final kingdom, or 'Fifth Monarchy', as the reign of Christ the Judge at the Second Coming – a Christian version of the return of Justice.[18] In Sonnet 5 of the second section of the 63-sonnet *Diana*, Constable plays with this idea, claiming that his lady deserves the 'fifth monarchy'; Spenser employs it in the fifth book of *The Faerie Queene*, 'The Legend of Artegall, or of Justice'.[19] Shakespeare evokes judgement near the end of the fair-youth section, where he connects it with marriage.

Shakespeare is not alone in conjoining nuptial and judicial conceits. In his continuation of *Hero and Leander*, Chapman draws on both traditions to emphasise that Hero and Leander must face justice for consummating their love before marriage. In Book 5 of *The Faerie Queene*, Artegall and Britomart – future spouses, principles of justice and equity – have to be reconciled.[20] The number's dual symbolism may be more rule than exception: in his study of Chapman's poetry, Raymond Waddington argues that 'justice and marriage almost invariably were conjoined in discussions of five by the commentators and in the poetic adaptations'.[21] One familiar source would have been Psalm 85, which speaks of a time of judgement when Truth and Mercy will meet as friends, and Justice and Peace will kiss. Another source may be Chapter 5 of Ephesians, to which *Sonnets* frequently alludes.[22] In Ephesians 5:1–20, Paul details ways of avoiding sin and 'redeeming the time'; in 5:21–33, he gives advice to spouses. And an iconic image of Justice – a crowned woman holding a raised sword in her right hand and a pendant scale in her left – is depicted above the shield in the Southampton coat of arms.[23]

Reckoning and Forgiving

Drawing on the tradition of 11 as a number of transgression, Shakespeare alludes to transgression in his multiple-of-11 sonnets. This is not to say that they focus exclusively on that theme – it is most prominent in 33, 66, and 99 – but they all play with numbers, and they all allude to wrongdoing. One division is implied by the narrative of redemption: the sonnets before the youth's fall/betrayal (Sonnet 33) are 'prelapsarian'; the sonnets after it are 'postlapsarian'. What is more, the sonnets after the renewal of relations (99) might be called 'post-resurrectional' and 'pre-apocalyptic', because they build towards final judgement. As a series, the multiple-of-11 sonnets show the poet learning to acknowledge imperfection and to forgive faults.

The multiple-of-11 sonnets before the betrayal, 11 and 22, have little to say about transgression, but they play with numbers. Sonnet 11 points to '11' with its conceits of copying and adding – or adding by subtracting:

>   As fast as thou shalt wane, so fast thou grow'st
>   In one of thine from that which thou departest,
>   And that fresh blood which youngly thou bestow'st
>   Thou mayst call thine, when thou from youth convertest.
>   Herein lives wisdom, beauty, and increase;
>   Without this, folly, age, and cold decay.
>   If all were minded so, the times should cease
>   And threescore year would make the world away.
>   Let those whom Nature has not made for store –
>   Harsh, featureless, and rude – barrenly perish:
>   Look whom she best endowed, she gave the more,
>   Which bounteous gift thou shouldst in bounty cherish.
>   She carved thee for her seal and meant thereby
>   Thou shouldst print more, not let that copy die.

The poem alludes to the biblical phrase 'To him whom hath, the more shall be given'.[24] The main allusion occurs in 'Look whom she best endowed, she gave the more' (line 11), which basically means 'whomever Nature endowed best, she gave the more to'. The enjambment across lines 1–2 reinforces the idea of growth; the phrases 'that which thou departest' and 'that fresh blood which . . . thou bestow'st' refer to a part of the youth – his seed – that can grow to be his child. Line 8's 'threescore year would make the world away' alludes to the proverbial limit of human life ('threescore and ten') and to an arithmetic joke: 'threescore and eleven' would transgress the limit.[25] More simply, the poem evokes 1+1=2: the youth is being asked to make a copy of himself in order to add to Nature's 'store'. Though Sonnet 11 precedes the youth's fall, wrongdoing is potentially present: the poet evokes the possibility of the world ending and chides the youth for not procreating – a sin of omission. In contrast to the postlapsarian sonnets, Sonnet 11 portrays excess positively, as bounty or largesse.

In allegory, at least, poet and youth are still living in the Golden Age. Paradise has not yet been lost.

Sonnet 22 is a mirror sonnet, in which the poet expresses strong feelings for the youth through a conceit of exchanging hearts. The two 2s in '22' reinforce the mirror imagery and underscore the theme of mutual exchange. As with Sonnet 11, a few details point to potential wrongdoings or evils. In expecting death to 'expiate' his days, the poet is not simply saying that death will complete his life: he is hinting at redemption. And in stipulating the terms of his friendship, the poet is setting himself up for betrayal, drawing a line that will soon be crossed – in Sonnet 33.

Sonnet 44 is the first of two poems on the four elements:

> If the dull substance of my flesh were thought,
> Injurious distance should not stop my way –
> For then, despite of space, I would be brought,
> From limits far remote, where thou dost stay.
> No matter, then, although my foot did stand
> Upon the farthest earth removed from thee –
> For nimble thought can jump both sea and land
> As soon as think the place where he would be.
> But, ah, thought kills me that I am not thought
> To leap large lengths of miles when thou art gone,
> But that, so much of earth and water wrought,
> I must attend time's leisure with my moan –
>   Receiving naught by elements so slow
>   But heavy tears, badges of either's woe.

'Injurious distance' suggests wrongdoing, as do 'earth' and 'water' – the elements traditionally associated with the body. Sonnet 45 begins 'The other two'. The transition is abrupt, perhaps because Shakespeare needed to clarify that both sonnets are about the four elements:

> The other two, slight air and purging fire,
> Are both with thee, wherever I abide;
> The first my thought, the other my desire:
> These present-absent with swift motion slide.
> For when these quicker elements are gone
> In tender embassy of love to thee,
> My life, being made of four, with two alone
> Sinks down to death, oppressed by melanch'ly –
> Until life's composition be re-cured
> By those swift messengers returned from thee,

>   Who ev'n but now come back again, assured
>   Of thy fair health, recounting it to me.
>   This told, I joy – but then, no longer glad,
>   I send them back again and straight grow sad.

The poet alludes to purgatorial fire and draws a contrast between life-restoring and life-injuring elements. Air and fire are the 'quicker' elements because they are more swift and more alive. Earth and water cause the poet to sink not merely to earth but 'to death', and they oppress him so much that he elides a stressed vowel – the O in the 'hol' of 'melancholy' – or he fails to keep the rhyme. (In Q, the O is not elided; there may be a pun on 'whole' and 'hole'.) In this context, the ninth-line turn points to redemption: it signals that the poet is reviving, and that his 'life's composition' is becoming whole again. The return of messengers 'from thee' is also a return of the 'ee' rhyme: as in a Spenserian sonnet, one rhyme is woven through two quatrains.[26] But though 'thee' returns as a rhyme word, the person to whom it refers remains away. It is as if the events are happening as the poet speaks, with relief and pain quickly following on each other.

Sonnet 45's rhyme-pattern may hint that Sonnets 44–5 are in dialogue with Spenser, if not specifically with Sonnet 55 of *Amoretti*:

>   So oft as I her beauty do behold
>   And therewith do her cruëlty compare,
>   I marvel of what substance was the mold
>   The which her made at once so cruël-fair.
>   Not earth (for her high thoughts more heav'nly are);
>   Not water (for her love doth burn like fire);
>   Not air (for she is not so light or rare);
>   Not fire (for she doth freeze with faint desire).
>   Then needs another element inquire
>   Whereof she might be made – that is the sky:
>   For to the heav'n her haughty looks aspire,
>   And eke her mind is pure immortal high.
>   Then, since to heav'n ye likened are the best,
>   Be like in mercy as in all the rest.

In his fifty-fifth sonnet, Spenser mentions the four elements and alludes to a fifth element. While it is conceivable that Shakespeare inspired Spenser (*Amoretti* was published in 1595), influence more likely goes in the other direction, and Sonnet 45's response may be pointed: the *Amoretti* poet is drawn 'up' to virtue; the *Sonnets* poet is pulled 'down to death'.

Shakespeare's fifty-fifth sonnet is the most triumphant of his multiple-of-11 sonnets:

> Not marble, nor the gilded monument[s]
> Of princes shall outlive this powerful rhyme,
> But you shall shine more bright in these conténts
> Than unswept stone besmeared with sluttish time.
> When wasteful war shall statues overturn
> And broils root out the work of masonry,
> Nor Mars his sword nor war's quick fire shall burn
> The living record of your memory.
> 'Gainst death and all-oblivious enmity
> Shall you pace forth; your praise shall still find room
> Ev'n in the eyes of all posterity
> That wear this world out to the ending doom.
>   So, till the judgement that yourself arise,
>   You live in this, and dwell in lovers' eyes.

In Sonnet 55, the poet presents himself as a saviour: he offers victory over Death and Time. In the octave, he speaks of Time's and War's injuries; in the sestet, of Judgement Day. Because 'that' can mean 'when' in Elizabethan English, he may be saying, 'And so, until Judgement Day, when you shall rise from the dead, you shall live in this poetry and the eyes of lovers'. If 'that' simply means 'that', he is perhaps being cagey about the youth's salvation: 'until the judgement has been given that you may rise'. 'You live in this' seems definitive, but it could mean 'May you live in this' or 'You may live in this'. Compared to the forward-driving, enjambment-rich quatrains, the couplet conveys less assurance, but the poet remains confident about his verse.

After Sonnet 66 presents a litany of the world's ills, Sonnet 77 evokes rituals of life's final accounting. Number symbolism may play a role here: 77 can be linked to redemption. In Matthew 18:21, Peter asks Jesus, 'How many times shall I forgive my brother? Up to seven times?' In most translations, Jesus answers: 'not seven times, but 70 times seven times'. In his thirty-third sermon, however, Augustine translates Jesus's answer as 'not seven times, but 77 times', claiming that 'all sins' are contained in the number 77 and that the number 7 is 'usually put for a whole, because in seven days the revolution of time is completed'.[27] Augustine also draws attention to Luke's account of the 77 generations of humans from Adam to Christ:

> When the Lord was baptised, . . . Luke has in that place commemorated the Lord's generations in the regular order, series, and line in which they

had come down to the generation in which Christ is born .., and in his reckoning he has completed 77 generations . . . from Christ up to Adam himself, who was the first sinner, and who begat us with the bond of sin . . . And, brethren, observe in this a yet greater mystery: in the number 77 is the remission of sins.[28]

In another sermon, Augustine specifically links 77 to 7×11: 'So, then, seven times eleven, . . . the transgression of righteousness, [makes] up the number seventy-seven, in which it is signified that all sins which are remitted in Baptism are contained'.[29]

Sonnet 88 passionately invokes faults and injuries:

> When thou shalt be disposed to set me light
> And place my merit in the eye of scorn,
> Upon thy side, against myself I'll fight
> And prove thee virtuous, though thou art forsworn.
> With mine own weakness being best acquainted,
> Upon thy part I can set down a story
> Of faults concealed, wherein I am attainted,
> That thou in losing me shalt win much glory –
> And I by this will be a gainer too,
> For, bending all my loving thoughts on thee,
> The injuries that to myself I do,
> Doing thee vantage, double-vantage me.
>   Such is my love – to thee I so belong –
>   That for thy right, myself will bear all wrong.

Even as he hints that he is the injured party, the poet pledges to 'bear all wrong' as proof of his devotion. As in Sonnet 66, he makes a Christ-like gesture, though he may also be threatening to *bare* all wrong. Allusions to doubling abound, from the repetitions of 'upon thy', 'do', and 'vantage' to the verb 'double-vantage'.[30]

In *Sonnets*' allegory of redemption, the poet-youth friendship revives after Sonnet 99. There is also a new numeric situation: multiples of 11 no longer end with 'doubled digits'. This does not mean that play with digits and duplicity ends. On the contrary, Shakespeare expands the possibilities, alluding to double-dealing and repetition in Sonnets 110–11 and 121–2:

> Alas 'tis true, I have gone here and there
> And made . . . old offences of affections new. (Sonnet 110)

> No bitterness . . . I will bitter think,
> Nor double penance, to correct correction. (Sonnet 111)

> No, I am that I am, and they that level
> At my abuses reckon up their own. (Sonnet 121)
>
> Thy gift, thy tables, are within my brain . . .
> [I need no] tallies thy dear love to score. (Sonnet 122)

More crucial to the redemption story, the poet evokes judgement and forgiveness in the eleven sonnets leading up to Sonnet 122 – a series that will be discussed in Chapter 7.

Sonnet 33 and the Mid-1590s

Before leaving the multiple-of-11 sonnets, let us explore how one of them may relate to Shakespeare's life. Exploring connections between art and life entails speculation, of course, but it bears attempting, and not merely because the genre of the sonnet sequence and *Sonnets* itself invite it: we can only gauge the significance of the connections if we consider them. The mid-1590s are especially worth investigating if *Sonnets* was intended as a third poetic work for Southampton: *Venus and Adonis* was published in 1593 and *Lucrece* in 1594; Shakespeare may have aspired to finish his sequence in 1595 or 1596 or have finished a version of it then.

As many commentators have noted, there are many verbal, imagistic, and thematic parallels between Shakespeare's mid-1590s plays and *Sonnets*. Here I will focus on parallels to Sonnet 33, to argue that Shakespeare's sonnet writing influenced his plays, and to connect his art to his life. As we saw in the previous chapter, Sonnet 33 alludes to the crucifixion with its imagery and its number; it also features an extended youth-sun comparison. A similar comparison can be found in Montague's speech about his son in the first scene of *Romeo and Juliet*. This speech is structured like a sonnet, as can be clarified by adding a line break after each 'quatrain':

> Many a morning hath he there been seen,
> With tears augmenting the fresh morning's dew,
> Adding to clouds more clouds with his deep sighs.
>
> But all so soon, as the all-cheering sun
> Should in the farthest east begin to draw
> The shady circuits from Aurora's bed,

> Away from light steals home my heavy son
> And private in his chamber pens himself,
> Shuts up his windows, locks fair daylight out,
> And makes himself an artificial night.
>
> Black and portentous must this humour prove,
> Unless good counsel may the cause remove.

Romeo and Juliet's final lines also feature a clouded sun and a sonnet-like structure:

> A glooming peace this morning with it brings.
> The sun for sorrow will not show his head.
> Go hence, to have more talk of these sad things.
> Some shall be pardoned and some punishèd,
>   For never was a story of more woe
> Than this of Juliet and her Romeo.

The rhyme scheme is that of a sonnet's sestet, and the couplet is summational.

Comparable images and phrases can also be found in two other plays from 1594–6:

> PHILIP (to Blanche)
> 'Tis true, fair daughter, and this blessèd day
> Ever in France shall be kept festival.
> To solemnise this day the glorious sun
> Stays in his course and plays the alchemist,
> Turning with splendor of his precious eye
> The meager cloudy earth to glitt'ring gold.
>   (*King John*, Act 3, Scene 1)

> BOLINGBROKE (to York)
> See, see, King Richard doth himself appear,
> As doth the blushing discontented sun
> From out the fiery portal of the east,
> When he perceives the envious clouds are bent
> To dim his glory and to stain the track
> Of his bright passage to the Occident.
>   (*Richard II*, Act 3, Scene 3)

In declaring that 'this blessèd day' shall 'be kept festival', Philip is responding to Blanche's approval of the marriage negotiated for her. His lines feature alchemical imagery, which is also present in Sonnet

33. The *Richard II* scene takes place at Flint Castle, where Richard, besieged by Bolingbroke, appears in regalia atop the castle (he will shortly descend to the 'base court'). Sonnet 33's 'basest clouds' are similar to Bolingbroke's 'envious clouds'; 33's sun, stealing away in 'disgrace' to the 'west' with a facial 'stain', is akin to Bolingbroke's 'discontented' sun, who eyes the clouds that would 'stain' his course to the 'Occident'.[31]

The closest parallel to Sonnet 33 is Hal's soliloquy at the end of Scene 2 of *1 Henry IV*. As with Montague's speech, added line breaks can clarify the organisation:

> I know you all, and will awhile uphold
> The unyoked humour of your idleness;
> Yet herein will I imitate the sun,
> Who doth permit the base contagious clouds
> To smother up his beauty from the world,
>
> That, when he please again to be himself,
> Being wanted, he may be more wondered at
> By breaking through the foul and ugly mists
> Of vapors that did seem to strangle him.
>
> If all the year were playing holidays,
> To sport would be as tedious as to work,
> But when they seldom come, they wished for come,
> And nothing pleaseth but rare accidents.
>
> So, when this loose behavior I throw off
> And pay the debt I never promisèd,
> By how much better than my word I am,
> By so much shall I falsify men's hopes;
>
> And like bright metal on a sullen ground,
> My reformation, glitt'ring o'er my fault,
> Shall show more goodly and attract more eyes
> Than that which hath no foil to set it off.
>
> I'll so offend, to make offence a skill –
> Redeeming time when men think least I will.

This twenty-three-line soliloquy contains rhetorical moves analogous to a sestet turn ('So, when this loose behavior I throw off') and a couplet turn ('I'll so offend . . .'). Indeed, if we were to remove the third and fifth quatrains, which do not so much advance Hal's argument

150   *The Secret Architecture of Shakespeare's Sonnets*

as amplify it, the result would be an Elizabethan sonnet (albeit with fifteen lines). Unlike the suns in the other play passages, but like the sun in Sonnet 33, Hal's sun permits clouds to cross him. In its rhetorical sweep, Hal's speech might be said to subsume all of the passages, including Sonnet 33. *1 Henry IV* was first performed in late 1596 or early 1597.[32]

Beyond Hal's speech, evidence that Sonnet 33 was written around 1596 or refers to that time can be found in parallels to *Astrophil and Stella* and *Richard II*. Sonnet 33 draws substantially on Sidney's Sonnet 22.[33] More crucial for present purposes, it contains numeric and thematic parallels to another *Astrophil and Stella* sonnet:

> Sonnet 33
> I might (unhappy word!) O me, I might,
> And then would not, or *could* not, see my bliss:
> Till now, wrapped in a most infernal night,
> I find how heav'nly day (wretch) I did miss.
> Heart, rend thy self – thou dost thyself but right:
> No lovely Paris made thy Helen his;
> No force, no fraud robbed *thee* of thy delight;
> Nor Fortune of thy fortune author is.
> But to myself my self did give the blow
> While too much wit, forsooth, so troubled me
> That I respects, for both our sakes, must show –
> And yet could not, by rising morn, foresee
>   How fair a day was near. O punished eyes,
>   That I had been more foolish, or more wise!

This sonnet is widely considered autobiographical: in 1576, when Sidney was 21 and Penelope Devereux 12, there was talk between the Sidney and Devereux families about a marriage; Sidney later released her from the bond or did not object to her being released from it.[34] Astrophil wishes that he had foreseen how 'fair a day' Stella's 'rising morn' promised. Whether his mistake was active ('would not') or passive ('could not'), he betrayed his future self, perhaps by cautiously approaching Stella or by falling in love with her. The *Sonnets* poet is betrayed by his 'other self', his sun, who has promised him 'a beauteous day'. In their thirty-third sonnets, then, Sidney and Shakespeare evoke 'original sins'.

Richard II also employs Christological symbolism. As Shakespeare's main source, *Holinshed's Chronicles*, points out, Richard came to the throne in his eleventh year, in 1377; ruled for twenty-two years, until his deposition in 1399; and died at 33, in 1400. In the play's deposition scene, Richard compares his suffering to Christ's, and in the prison scene, he delivers a sixty-six-line speech in which he cites Jesus's words in order to 'sets the word itself / Against the Word'. Evidence that the sixty-six lines are symbolic can be gathered from the sequel to *Richard II*, *1 Henry IV*: at the start of that play, Henry IV delivers a thirty-three-line speech in which he speaks of crusading in the Holy Land, where 'fourteen hundred years ago' Christ's feet 'were nailed / For our advantage on the bitter cross'.[35] Also note that *Thomas of Woodstock* – a history play that influenced *Richard II* and whose main events take place some eleven years prior to those of Shakespeare's play – contains a scene in which documents pertaining to Richard's birthdate are analysed: 'By that account, the third of April next / Our age is numbered two-and-twenty years'.[36] Like *Sonnets*, *Richard II* calls attention to multiple-of-11 numbers.

Let us consider the possibility that Shakespeare started writing his sequence with Southampton's twenty-second or twenty-third year in mind. As discussed in the previous chapter, *Venus and Adonis* alludes to Southampton's twentieth year with its multiples of 20 and its dedication that promises a 'graver' work for the earl. *Lucrece* was published a year later, when Southampton was turning twenty-one, and its dedication hints that more poetry is on the way. This progression could indicate that Shakespeare aspired to complete his sequence in 1595–6. Also note that the twenty-second sonnet of *Sonnets* may be a birthday or anniversary poem – it is the first sonnet of the 'gift trio' – and that, in the late spring, the whole summer, and the early autumn of 1596, Shakespeare was in his thirty-third year and Southampton was twenty-two.

The summer and early fall of 1596 was a momentous time for Shakespeare: he finished *Romeo and Juliet* and began the first part of *Henry IV*; in late July or early August, his 11-year-old son Hamnet died; and in October, he purchased a coat of arms for his father, giving his family gentry status. Scholarly arguments for dating *Romeo and Juliet* to late summer or early autumn of 1596 are of recent vintage; in third Arden edition of *Romeo and Juliet*, René Weis suggests that Shakespeare was influenced by Nashe's *Have With You to Saffron Walden* (which was likely circulating in manuscript over the summer of 1596), and he notes that the title page of the play's first quarto refers to performances in 1596–7 as if they were the first ones.[37] Weis also suggests that Shakespeare had his own children in mind when wrote his 'monument to the beauty and innocence of youth': Susanna (who was 13 in 1596) and Hamnet and Judith (who were twins).[38] In adapting the story, Shakespeare reduced Juliet's age to 13 from the source text's 16, and he invented 'Nurse's deceased daughter Susan, whom Nurse bore at the same time as Capulet's Wife did Juliet'. Like Judith, Juliet survives her 'twin'; like Susanna, she is 13; and 'Susan' is a form of 'Susanna'. In the play's third scene, the nurse specifies that Juliet was born on Lammas Eve (31 July) and will turn 14 in 'a fortnight and odd days'. ('Fourteen', Weis adds, 'is of course also the line-count in the sonnet, the play's most distinctive literary form', and Juliet speaks only thirteen lines in Act 5, falling just short of the sonnet line-count.) The nurse also notes that Juliet was weaned 'since the earthquake eleven years'. Citing an earthquake that took place in Kent on 4 August 1585, Weis contends that the Nurse's remarks point metapoetically to July or August 1596 and thus to the time of Hamnet's death.[39]

It is not necessary to accept all of Weis's claims to agree that Shakespeare was 'crossing aesthetic boundaries between life and art', to grant that many sonnets were written in the mid-1590s, and to allow for the possibility that Sonnets 22 and 33 were written in 1596 or refer to that time. My theory is that 33's couplet, which laments that 'suns' of earth and heaven can be eclipsed by clouds, alludes to Southampton and Hamnet. In short, Sonnets 22 and 33 point to a time when the youth is twenty-two and the 'crucified' poet is in his thirty-third year.

Hal's twenty-three-line soliloquy dates from 1596 and was perhaps written soon after Sonnet 33, as a concluding statement about suns. Some evidence for this can be inferred from an odd remark by Falstaff later in the play: 'O for a fine thief, of the age of two-and-twenty or thereabouts!' (Act 3, Scene 3). Why is Falstaff both precise and imprecise about the thief's age? His exclamation comes after he has been told that he will be an infantryman in the upcoming wars. Complaining that he will be ill-supplied in such a commission, he wishes for a spry young thief – a horse thief, no doubt – to help him meet his needs. The exchange alludes to earlier interactions. In Act 2, Falstaff is tricked in the Gad's Hill robbery: his horse is stolen from him, and he is robbed of the money he has stolen. Hal proceeds to make fun of Falstaff by encouraging him to lie about the events and then catching him in his lies. In Act 3, Scene 2, Hal pledges reformation to his father, and at the start of Scene 3 Falstaff talks to Bardolph about reformation, musing that their companionship 'this two-and-thirty years' has bankrupted and corrupted him. When Falstaff declares his desire for 'a fine thief, of the age of two-and-twenty or thereabouts', then, he is contrasting his thieving companion of 32 years with the royal thief with whom he would like to keep company.

The fact that Hal's soliloquy contains twenty-three lines may also be relevant, since Southampton was 23 years old when the play was first performed. And the period between the writing and the performance of the play may inform the phrase 'two-and-twenty or thereabouts'.

As with *Romeo and Juliet*, it is not necessary to see biography everywhere: it is enough to say that that *Sonnets* and the *Henry IV* plays are informed by mid-1590s events; that Shakespeare wrote many sonnets soon after *Venus and Adonis* and *Lucrece*; and that Shakespeare conceived of *Sonnets* as the third work in three years for the third Earl of Southampton. If Shakespeare aspired to complete his sequence in 1596–7, what prevented him from finishing it or prompted him to revise it? Duncan-Jones's musings on Shakespeare and Southampton are apropos:

> [Southampton] encouraged Shakespeare to improve his social position. But the steps Shakespeare took to do so backfired badly, leading both to the cessation of his friendship with Southampton, and to painful humiliations which were to recur for many years to come. It was most probably in the summer of 1594, rewarded handsomely by Southampton for *Lucrece*, that Shakespeare first began to lay down plans for his future. With Hamnet approaching his tenth year, it was time to set the Shakespeares of Henley Street on a better footing, one that reflected the fame and financial success he had earned in London. The transmission of inheritance and family honour had been a major theme in *Lucrece*. It is the need to prevent any possible stain on her family, should she give birth to a child of uncertain parentage, that is Lucrece's most compelling motive for suicide.[40]

In this account, Shakespeare used Southampton's money and influence to purchase a coat of arms, and complications over this action soured relations between artist and patron. Whether or not there was a falling-out, and whether or not the coat of arms was the cause of it, it is reasonable to surmise that Shakespeare was seeking respectability when he wrote and published *Lucrece*, and that his intention to purchase a coat of arms dates from that time. Hamnet was buried on 11 August 1596; the coat of arms was purchased two months later, in October.[41] If Duncan-Jones is right, Shakespeare would soon be parted from another son, Southampton. Hamnet's death at age eleven could have given Shakespeare a personal reason to associate the number 11 with the world's wrongs; a double loss could have clinched the association.

Chapter 6

The Fair-Youth Sonnets, Part 1

This chapter and the next one analyse the pyramid steps in the fair-youth section of *Sonnets*, focusing on the steps' internal organisation and on verbal and schematic allusions. While Chapters 6 and 7 form a unit – this is the introduction to both – their partition is not merely a concession to length: following the organisation of the fair-youth section, they focus on the pre-99 sonnets and the post-99 sonnets, respectively. Before proceeding, the reader may want to look back at Chapter 2, to review the pyramid diagram and the discussion of boundary poems, centre poems, and subgroups. This chapter plunges into the middle of things. Since the first pyramid step contains seventeen sonnets, Sonnet 9 is its centre poem. Sonnet 9 is unusual, and its distinctiveness is reinforced by its central position.

The Centre Poem of the First Pyramid Step

Sonnet 9 argues that the youth, by not siring children, is harming both himself and others:

> Is it for fear to wet a widow's eye
> That thou consum'st thy self in single life?
> Ah! if thou issueless shalt hap to die,
> The world will wail thee like a makeless wife.
> The world will be thy widow and still weep
> That thou no form of thee hast left behind,
> When every private widow well may keep
> (By children's eyes) her husband's shape in mind.
> Look what an unthrift in the world doth spend
> Shifts but his place – for still the world enjoys it –
> But beauty's waste hath in the world an end,

And kept unused the user so destroys it.
No love toward others in that bosom sits
That on himself such murd'rous shame commits.

As he pleads for procreation, the poet raises the possibility that the youth fears making a wife mate-less ('makeless') by predeceasing her. He alters this conceit in the sestet, alluding to the Prodigal Son and comparing the money that a spendthrift wastes, which remains in circulation, to the permanent 'waste' of beauty that threatens the youth. (Lines 9–11 might be translated: 'Whatever a prodigal man spends in the world merely shifts the money's place – because the world still enjoys what he spent – but wasted beauty ceases to exist in the world'.[1]) In this context, 'waste' denotes 'profitless expense' and 'destruction'; 'hath an end' hints at 'has a purpose'; and 'beauty's waste' may allude to the medical theory that the emission of semen shortens life.[2] The third quatrain's point is that a beautiful man destroys his beauty when he does not pass it on. The couplet's point is that a man who commits such murder on himself feels no love towards others. In arguing that the youth is hurting both himself and the world, the poet advances the arguments of Sonnets 1–8, which focused on how the youth was hurting himself.

Sonnet 9 is a variation on a theme, but it is nonetheless distinctive. As Vendler notes, the sonnet's shape 'depends on the contrast between a *sin of omission* (octave) and a *sin of commission* (sestet)'; the theological distinction is reinforced by the change in metaphor from 'a husband who leaves his widow childless' to 'a hoarder who destroys beauty and murders himself'.[3] The technical distinction may seem at odds with the sonnet's playfulness, but Shakespeare often 'plays seriously' in the tradition of *serio ludere* – a rhetorical mode for discussing religious paradoxes, used by humanists like Erasmus in the early sixteenth century.[4] Sonnets 1–17 also employ the Erasmian device of *copia* or 'the abundant style', and some of the poems echo Erasmus's 'Epistle to persuade a young man to marriage', which showcases phrasal variations and conceits of copying and copiousness.[5] (Erasmus's *De Copia*, a rhetorical handbook, illustrates *copia* for letter writing; Thomas Wilson's *The Art of Rhetoric* includes a translation of Erasmus's epistle. Shakespeare appears to have been familiar with both.[6]) In echoing Erasmus's letter, Shakespeare may be making a joke about copying others' words, in the spirit of Sonnet 1 of *Astrophil and Stella*. More generally, his rhetoric implies that he is playing the role of a wise elder.

Sonnet 9 also contains an unusual poetic device involving a letter. Vendler proposes that 'Fantasy on the Letter "W"' would be an apt title for 9, and that the sonnet arises from 'Shakespeare's fascinated observation of the shape of the word *widdow* [Q's spelling]':

> The initial and final *w*'s of *widdow* are mirror images of each other, and its middle letter is repeated – *dd* – in self-identity. The only letters in the alphabet which are mirror images of themselves are (roughly speaking, and disregarding serifs) *i, m, o, u, v, w*, and *x* . . . Shakespeare, delighted with the properties of the word *widdow*, and with the fact that *w* is double *u* . . . sets off in a flurry of *w*'s, *u*'s, and *v*'s.[7]

Shakespeare may be playing with Ws, Us, and Vs, but Vendler invokes 'fantasy', which suggests pure play, not *serio ludere*. (She also looks only at lowercase letters; in light of 'Mr W.H'., the capitals W and H could be added to her list of 'mirror image' letters.) The word 'flurry' is moreover misleading: as West points out, there are more instances of Us, Vs, and Ws in Sonnet 8, and more than forty occurrences of S in Sonnet 9.[8] Instead of speaking of a flurry of letters related to W, it is more accurate to say that the poet draws attention to W in lines 1, 4, 5, and 7. Lines 4–5 especially stand out, because of their alliteration and their anaphora: 'The world will wail thee like a makeless wife. / The world will be thy widow and still weep'.

Sonnet 9's play with *W* is informed by pronoun puns. Depicting the world as the widow of an 'issueless' youth, the poet tells the youth 'thou no form of thee has left behind'. As West observes, this phrase 'weirdly imitates [its] sense, since "thee" is another form of "thou"'.[9] Similar wordplay occurs in Sonnet 13, where 'O that you were yourself!' and 'your sweet issue your sweet form should bear' call attention to the sequence's first you-forms. Sonnet 9 may also pun on 'double you'. In Renaissance texts, *U* and *V* are often allographs; in *Sonnets*, *W* is often printed as two Vs, especially when *W* is the first letter of a poem.[10] And many of the sequence's early sonnets pun on 'use' and 'hues', or 'thou', 'you', and 'youth': 'That use is not forbidden usury' (6); 'when thou from youth convertest' (11); 'you most rich in youth' (15); 'A man in hue all hues in his controlling' (20).[11] What is more, Shakespeare was not alone in employing such wordplay. At the end of a sonnet addressed to William Herbert in 1603, John Davies of Hereford puns on *W* and 'double you': 'O then had I but single love of you, / I should be double bound to VV'.[12] Phrases like 'to double you' and 'a double of you' inform Sonnet 9 and other sonnets in which copying and mirroring are conceits.

In playing with *W*, Sonnet 9 also hints at the youth's name. The *W–double you* pun in Davies's sonnet raises the possibility that Shakespeare's *W* alludes to Herbert, but more evidence points to Wriothesley. As discussed in Chapter 4, at least a dozen poems in *Sonnets* contain thematically relevant anagrams of 'Wriothesley'. The most overt examples are in Sonnet 17, whose fourth and ninth lines contain all twenty-two letters needed to form the name twice, and whose couplet, evoking 'double you', suggests that the youth will live 'twice' in the poem. Sonnet 9 contains its own 'Wriothesley' anagram, in 'Shifts but his place, for till the world inioyes it' (Q's spelling). All eleven letters of the name are in the last four words of the line, and the first four words hint that the poet has left behind a form of the youth in the poem, which readers can find in shifted or transposed letters.[13] Also, there is at least one 'Wriothesley' anagram in Sonnet 1 (for details, see Appendix C). In other words, there are *Wriothesley*'s in the first, middle, and last sonnets of the first pyramid step.

Even if it does not allude to Wriothesley, Sonnet 9 would be significant. It is the final sonnet of a series that avoids first-person pronouns (1–9). Rhetorically, it transitions from the argument that the youth is hurting himself to the argument that the youth is hurting others. It is the centre poem of the first pyramid step. In short, Sonnet 9 is pivotal.

The Distribution of Pronouns in Organizational Schemes

Rhetorical and organisational signals often coincide in Shakespeare's sequence. Sonnet 18, for example, uses thou-forms to address the youth, whereas Sonnets 15–17 use you-forms; 18's thou-forms convey intimacy and a transition to a new pyramid step. But even when rhetorically reinforced, organisational signals can be subtle. Pronominal signals are potentially quite subtle, because they require us to notice patterns in a series of sonnets. Tracking patterns would have been a more familiar mode of reading in the Renaissance, but it would not exactly have been more natural – artifice is central to the aesthetic.

To understand pronoun schemes in *Sonnets*, it pays to begin with the third pyramid step, whose organisational scheme is straightforward. The step has five trios:

(34 35 36) (37 38 39) (40 41 42) (43 44 45) (46 47 48)

In employing trios, Shakespeare reinforces the theme of a lovers' triangle. The final sonnet, however, is tonally detached from the other poems: retrospective commentary ('How careful was I when I took my way') sets Sonnet 48 apart even as it signals closure. In this light, the diagram can be emended to illustrate the degree to which the sonnets are, and are not, linked:

(34–35–36) (37–38–39) (40–41–42) (43–44–45) (46–47 48)

The dashes represent rhetorical links. With its final, detached sonnet, the third pyramid step fits a pattern: many steps conclude with a poem that looks back on preceding poems or forward to the next step.

The step's scheme is at once typical and atypical. It is typical in that it features trios, calls attention to the centre poem(s), and is informed by the number of sonnets in the step (fifteen is divisible by three). It is atypical in being free of competing schemes and in its forms of address: every sonnet directly addresses the youth with thou-forms. With the symbol 'Th' for thou-sonnet, the diagram might be further emended:

Th Th Th   Th Th Th   Th Th Th   Th Th Th   Th Th Th
(34–35–36) (37–38–39) (40–41–42) (43–44–45) (46–47 48)

No other step in the fair-youth section consists entirely of thou-sonnets.

Now let us examine a similar diagram of the first pyramid step:

Th Th Th   Th 3rd Th   Th Th Th   Th Th Th   Y Th   Y Y Y
1 2 3   (4–5–6)   7 8 9   10 11 12   13 14 (15–16–17)

At first sight, 4–6 and 15–17 are the only unambiguous trios, and the forms of address do not seem patterned: in one sonnet, the poet uses third-person address ('3rd'); otherwise he uses thou-forms or you-forms ('Th' or 'Y'). But if we shift our focus, a possible scheme emerges:

Th Th Th   Th 3rd Th   Th Th Th
(1 2 3) (4–5–6)   (7 8 9)

Sonnets 1–9 are a series of three trios, and 9–17 are organised along similar lines. Each 'half' of the step consists of three trios, whose central trio contains a central contrasting poem.

But lest we are getting ahead of ourselves, let us pause to discuss the taxonomy of 'thou-sonnet', 'you-sonnet', and 'third-person sonnet'. In identifying all direct-address sonnets as 'thou' and 'you' types, I blur the fact that some also use third-person address. And in identifying all indirect-address sonnets as 'third-person', I blur the fact that some do not clearly refer to the beloved in the third person, and that some directly address another party. Such variations are not trivial. But recall that the *Sonnets* poet directly addresses his beloved often – in at least 122 sonnets – and that he seldom uses indirect address in consecutive poems. In sequential context, then, sonnets that mix direct and indirect address tend to come across as more direct than not, and changes in form of address tend to call attention to themselves. In short, both individually and serially the three types of sonnets are distinct enough that they might be used to demarcate schemes. Given the extensive and intensive play with pronouns in *Sonnets*, I suspect that 'thou-sonnet', 'you-sonnet', and 'third-person sonnet' are types that Shakespeare actively employed. But regardless, the taxonomy has heuristic value: it can help us find organisational structures in pyramid steps.

I have said that Sonnets 4–6 and 15–17 are unambiguous trios, and that the first step consists of two series of trios; these points call for clarification. Sonnets 4–6 are connected through financial conceits, seasonal imagery, and conjunctive expressions. Sonnet 4 addresses the youth as 'Unthrifty loveliness' and 'Profitless usurer', arguing that he 'uses' his abundant beauty (a 'sum of sums') yet cannot 'live'. Sonnet 5 provides an example of beauty's preservation. Because 'never-resting time leads summer on / To hideous winter', summer's beauty would disappear if its essence were not safeguarded like rosewater in glass; by contrast, 'flow'rs distilled, though they with winter meet, / Leese but their show; their substance still lives sweet'. And Sonnet 6 opens:

> Then let not winter's raggèd hand deface
> In thee thy summer ere thou be distilled;
> Make sweet some vial; treasure thou some place
> With beauty's treasure ere it be self-killed.
> That use is not forbidden usury . . .

Sonnet 4 introduces financial metaphors for beauty's use; 5 meditates on beauty's transience and essence; and 6 is conjunctively linked to 5 and imagistically linked to 4–5. Sonnet 5 also shifts to indirect address: the poet takes a rhetorical step back in order to press ahead in 6. And there is syllogistic quality to the pleas; Sonnets 15–17 employ a similar 'thesis, antithesis, synthesis' rhetoric: poetry will immortalise the youth (15); no, children are a better means to immortality (16); no, the best means to immortality is children and poetry (17).

Sonnets 1–3 and 7–9 do not signal transitions as obviously as 4–6 and 15–17 do, but transitions are visible on closer inspection. Take, for example, Sonnets 2 and 3. In 2's couplet, the poet summarises his case for procreation: 'This were to be new made when thou art old / And see thy blood warm when thou feel'st it cold'. Alluding to the heat of young blood, 'see thy blood warm' implies that the youth will find a warm and living form of himself in his child and will be vivified by it. Sonnet 3 follows with 'Look in thy glass and tell the face thou viewest / Now is the time that face should form another'. Though it may initially seem interruptive, 'Look' humourously follows from 'see thy blood warm'. After speaking abstractly of offspring in whom the youth will see his blood warm, the poet tells the youth to look in the mirror: such flattery might well induce a blush. The poet moreover uses antithesis to establish links between poems: 1–3 evoke opposing perspectives of age and youth, and positive and negative examples; 4–6 shuttle between personal and impersonal persuasion; and 7–9 alternate visual and aural conceits. Sonnets 7 and 8 are additionally linked by couplet rhymes; Sonnet 8 and 9, by opening rhetorical questions.

Like 1–9, Sonnets 9–17 can be read as a series of three trios:

Th Th Th   Th Y Th   Y Y Y
(9 10 11) (12 13 14) (15–16–17)

The centre sonnet's form of address contrasts with that of the adjacent sonnets: parallel to Sonnet 5 (a third-person sonnet among thou-sonnets), Sonnet 13 is a you-sonnet among thou-sonnets. And each trio is marked by a distinctive use of pronoun forms: the first trio introduces first-person-singular pronouns; the second introduces you-forms; and the third is the sequence's first series of you-sonnets. What is more, after the pronoun 'I' makes its first appearance in 10's sestet, it is prominent in 12 and 15 – the first two 'When I' sonnets and the first sonnets of their trios.

As in Sonnets 1–9, transitions in 9–17 are conveyed by antithesis. In the first trio of 9–17, the poet makes impersonal, personal, and mixed attempts at persuasion: he rebukes the youth indirectly in 9 ('No love toward others in that bosom sits'), pleads ardently in 10

('Make thee another self for love of me'), and entreats half-personally, half-impersonally in 11 ('[Nature] carved thee for her seal, and meant thereby / Thou shouldst print more'). In 12–14, he reflects on past, present, and future beauty, basically arguing: *When I see nature's beauty pass away, then I fear for your beauty* (12); *Your beauty is in danger of passing away, but it would last forever if you had children* (13); and *Your eyes tell me that Beauty and Truth will either thrive or die* (14). And in final trio, the poet invokes art in Sonnet 15 ('I engraft you new'), nature in 16 ('you must live drawn by your own sweet skill'), and the power of art and nature in 17 ('You should live twice: in [your child], and in my rhyme').

In sum, there is a 'pivot scheme' in the first pyramid step:

(1 2 3) (4 5 6) (7 8 9)
                 (9 10 11) (12 13 14) (15 16 17)

As in the third step, the basic scheme is comprised of trios and it draws attention to the centre. But while the third step's centre is a trio, the first step's centre is a pair of overlapping trios – or, more pointedly, one sonnet.

Pronoun Use in English Sonnet Sequences

The sequence's second pyramid step is not as symmetrically structured as the first step. In fact, its organisation is quite different from what we have seen so far:

(18 19) (20 21) 22 (23 24)
                 (25 26)
                            (27 28) (29 30) (31 32) 33

Pairs predominate, not trios; the opening pairs are interrupted by a non-paired poem; and a second non-paired poem protrudes at the end. In order to analyse this scheme, we should first compare Shakespeare's use of pronouns with other poets' uses.

Why *wouldn't* a poet address his or her beloved with the same pronoun form throughout a sequence, especially a poet who emphasises constancy? Even if we assume that distinctions between 'thou' and 'you' were eroding in the late-Elizabethan period, we might expect that many poets would settle on one form. But few poets do, and mixed use occasionally occurs within a poem or even within a sentence. In Song 4 of *Astrophil and Stella*, for instance, there is a 'you' in the opening line and a 'thee' in the refrain couplet:

> Only joy, now here *you are*,
> Fit to hear and ease my care;
> Let my whisp'ring voice obtain
> Sweet reward for sharpest pain:
> *Take me to thee and thee to me*.
> 'No, no, no, no, my dear, let be'.
>
> (Italics added)

There may be a rhetorical rationale for the thou-forms: perhaps Astrophil is expressing sudden ardency or quoting a song. When Henry Constable, Mary Wroth, and Giles Fletcher alter pronoun forms within a sentence, rhyme would seem to be the determining factor:

> Falsely doth envy of *your* praises blame
> My tongue, my pen, my heart of flattery,
> Because I said there was no sun but *thee*.
>
> (*Diana*, Sonnet I.ii.7, italics added)

> O strive not still to heap disdain on me,
> Nor pleasure take, *your* cruëlty to show
> On hapless me on whom all sorrows flow
> And biding make, as giv'n and lost by *thee*.
>
> (*Pamphilia to Amphilanthus*, Sonnet 6, italics added)

> But if *you* frown, I wish that none believe me;
> For, slain with sighs, I'll die before I'll grieve *thee*.
>
> (*Licia*, Sonnet 50, italics added)

Beyond rhyme, the rationales for the forms are unclear. The *Diana* poet may be highlighting differences between public and private praise. Pamphilia may be using 'thee' to appeal to Amphilanthus's better self. And the *Licia* poet may be wishing that he were on close terms with his lady and fearing that he is not. (He begins his sonnet by telling Licia to 'sigh and say 'Thou art my own', addresses her with you-forms through line 13, and ends the poem with 'thee'.) Thomas Lodge's *Phyllis* contains a rhetorically motivated use of mixed forms. Through rhyme, his twenty-sixth sonnet foregrounds 'thou' and 'you':

> I'll teach thee, lovely Phyllis, what love is.
>   It is a vision seeming such as *thou*
>   That flies as fast as it assaults mine eyes;

> It is affection that doth reason miss;
>   It is a shape of pleasure like to *you*
>   Which meets the eye and, seen, on sudden dies.
> It is a double grief . . .
>
> (lines 1–7, italics added)

The rhyme scheme of lines 1–6 is *abcabc*: 'thou' and 'you' rhyme. The references to vision and doubleness reinforce the sight rhyme: love's forms are subject to change. Like Shakespeare in Sonnet 129, Lodge emphasises that there is pain in both the pursuit and the possession of love.

Pronominal choices are sometimes influenced by considerations of style and audience. Daniel and Drayton reworked their sequences over decades. In the first versions of their sequences, they address their beloveds almost exclusively with thou-forms: the *Delia* poet addresses his lady with you-forms only in Sonnet 29; the *Idea's Mirror* poet uses you-forms only in Amour 39's sestet.[14] Daniel adds one you-sonnet to the second *Delia*, whose you-forms may refer to Delia's eyes; he adds none to later editions.[15] Drayton adds six you-sonnets to the 1599 *Idea* and changes one thou-sonnet to a you-sonnet.[16] Daniel may have disliked mixing forms; Drayton may have found rhetorical possibilities in 'you'. Both poets likely revised poems to suit new occasions: Daniel, for example, changes the colour of his beloved's hair from 'golden' to 'sable' for the 1601 *Delia*, and the number of years he has been pining for his lady from three to five. And both poets use a verse dedication – Daniel, to the Countess of Pembroke in the 1594 *Delia*; Drayton, to the Countess of Bedford in the 1599 *Idea* – in order to suggest that their dedicatees are their muses and, in a sense, their loves.

Some of Drayton's rationale for you-forms can be deduced from the thou-sonnet that he converted to a you-sonnet in the 1599 *Idea*. Drayton radically alters the opening of the poem:

> Amour 6
> In one whole world is but one phoenix found,
> A phoenix thou, this phoenix then alone,
> By thy rare plume thy kind is eas'ly known –
> With heav'nly colours dyed, with nature's wonder crowned.
>
> Sonnet 18
> *To the Phoenix*
> Within the compass of this spacious round,
> Amongst all birds, the phoenix is alone,

> Which, but by you, could never have been known –
> None like to that, none like to you is found.

Drayton's first goal may have been avoiding the repetitions of 'phoenix' and removing line 4's alexandrine. He nonetheless follows through with the pronouns: in lines 5–14, each thou-form is replaced by a you-form, and the verb forms are adjusted as needed. Oddly, though, a phantom 'thou' haunts the sonnet's 1599 *Idea* version, in line 13's '[thou] shalt to the heav'ns ascend':

> Your self . . .
> Shall spring again from th'ashes of your fame,
>   And, mounting up, shalt to the heav'ns ascend,
> So may you live past world, past fame, past end.
>
>   (Sonnet 18, lines 9, 12–14)

In the sonnet's next version (1600), 'shalt' is emended to 'shall', implying 'you shall ascend' or 'your self shall ascend'. The theme of self-transformation may have inspired Drayton to change the pronoun forms.

Unlike Drayton, Daniel seems to have avoided you-forms. One you-sonnet bedeviled him, however – number 32 of the 1594 *Delia*:

> O why doth Delia credit so her glass,
> Gazing her beauty deigned her by the skies,
> And doth not rather look on him (alas)
> Whose state best shows the force of murth'ring eyes?
> The broken tops of lofty trees declare
> The fury of a mercy-wanting storm,
> And of what force your wounding graces are
> Upon my self you best may find the form.
> Then leave your glass, and gaze your self on me . . .
>
>   (lines 1–9)

The first quatrain might be translated: 'Why does Delia put such faith in her mirror, gazing at the beauty that heaven bestowed on her, and not look at him (alas) whose state best displays the power of her murdering eyes?' The poet continues to speak of Delia in the third person until he unceremoniously introduces you-forms in line 7. Daniel is not a clumsy poet. If he is awkward here, it is perhaps because he wished to avoid the accusatory tone of his main source poem, a sonnet by Philippe Desportes ('Pourquoi si follement croyez-vous à un verre').[17]

Presumably to remove the mixture of direct and indirect address, Daniel revised his poem for the 1611 *Delia*:

> Why dost thou, Delia, credit so thy glass,
> Gazing thy beauty deigned thee by the skies,
> And dost not rather look on him (alas)
> Whose state best shows the force of murd'ring eyes?
> The broken tops of lofty trees declare
> The fury of a mercy-wanting storm,
> And of what force thy wounding graces are
> Upon my self thou best mayst find the form.
> Then leave thy glass, and gaze thy self on me:
> That mirror shows what pow'r is in thy face.
> To view your form too much, may danger be:
> Narcissus changed t'a flow'r in such a case.
>   And you are changed, but not t'a hyacint –
>   I fear your eye hath turned your heart to flint.
>
> (Sonnet 34)

This is essentially the sonnet's final version. Delia is addressed throughout, and the 'him' in line 3 is warranted: it conveys alienation. Yet in amending the mixture of direct and indirect address, Daniel introduced an assortment of thou- and you-forms. This is unique in *Delia*, and Daniel could have settled on one form, had he wished to do so. So why didn't he?

Daniel is mixing pronoun forms for rhetorical effect. Like the 'him' in line 3, the mixture evokes themes of identity and alienation. Line 11's shift to you-forms coincides with a warning: 'To view your form too much, may danger be'. This phrase suggests that the poet, expressing fear for and of his lady, has adopted an honourific form of address. Alternatively, it is an impersonal warning against vanity that lingers even when the ensuing lines clarify that the lady is being addressed. But more than anything, the poet emphasises change, signalling the moment of his lady's transformation or anticipating the otherwise abrupt 'you are changed'. (Desportes merely warns his lady that she may change.[18]) The 1594 version plays on different meanings of 'form', evoking 'image' and 'imprint' in 'Upon my self you best may find the form', and 'appearance' and 'essence' in 'To view your form too much, may danger be'. (Desportes's poem contains no close equivalent to 'form'.[19]) The 1611 version adds a metapoetic dimension: the poet may be acknowledging his obsession with revision. In brief, Daniel imitated a mirror poem, reworked his imitation, and settled on mixed address. Subject matter and writing process became linked; the theme of vision and revision became clarified and enriched.

Like the 1611 *Delia*, the 1609 *Sonnets* contains one poem with thou- and you-forms:

> Sonnet 24
> Mine eye hath played the painter and hath stelled
> Thy beauty's form in table of my heart;
> My body is the frame wherein 'tis held
> And pérspective it is best painters' art.
> For through the painter must you see his skill,
> To find where your true image pictured lies,
> Which in my bosom's shop is hanging still,
> That hath his windows glazèd with thine eyes.
> Now see what good turns eyes for eyes have done:
> Mine eyes have drawn thy shape, and thine for me
> Are windows to my breast, wherethrough the sun
> Delights to peep, to gaze therein on thee.
>   Yet eyes this cunning want to grace their art:
>   They draw but what they see, know not the heart.

The you-forms might initially seem impersonal: they are introduced in lines 5–6, which provide a general explanation of the claims made in lines 1–4. In other words, lines 1–6 might mean:

> My eye has played the painter and set your beauty's form in the tablet of my heart; my body is the frame in which the image is held and, seen from the proper perspective, the image represents the art of the best painters. For one must look *through* the painter to see his skill, to find out where one's true image lies . . . [20]

If we read on, however, the image is not a generic picture, but a portrait in the poet's heart: 'your true image . . . in my bosom's shop is hanging'. Perhaps Shakespeare wants it both ways or was unbothered by inconsistency, but there seems to be something else, or more, going on.

Like Lodge and Daniel, Shakespeare mixes pronoun forms to enhance a vision-related theme. Sonnet 24's 'pérspective' evokes an ideal or apt way of seeing an image – seeing 'perspectively'. More specifically, it alludes to a perspective glass, an optical device that brings an anamorphic image into focus or consolidates into a single image several images that are carefully arranged with respect to one another and the lens.[21] (Davies of Hereford uses the same conceit in Sonnet 1 of the second section of *Wit's Pilgrimage*, glossing his poem with 'The Trinity illustrated by a three-square perspective glass'.) The poet's eye sets and arranges images; the beloved's eye furnishes or finishes the window into the poet's breast, a window that is a perspective glass. With his perspective conceit and mixed forms, the poet suggests that he is struggling with how he sees and feels about the youth. In this interpretation, which squares with the poet's disapproval of rhetorical and cosmetic painting, the poet is not so much composing a beautiful portrait as trying to represent the youth faithfully. He may also be expressing doubts about his skill, the youth's feelings, and the youth as an ideal ('your true image . . . lies').

The combination of a 'portrait in the heart' conceit and mixed forms of address is rare if not exclusive to Sonnet 24 and 'Why dost thou, Delia': this argues that one poet influenced the other, or that there was mutual influence from different versions of the poems.[22] There are also parallels between 24 and another Daniel sonnet:

> Mine eye hath played the painter and hath stelled
> Thy beauty's form in table of my heart;
> My body is the frame wherein 'tis held
> And pérspective it is best painters' art.
>
> (Sonnet 24, lines 1–4)

> For hapless, lo, ev'n with mine own desires,
> I figured on the table of my heart
> The fairest form the world's eye admires
> And so did perish by my proper art.
>
> (Sonnet 13, first edition of *Delia*, lines 5–8)

Here the case for influence (on Shakespeare) is strong: Daniel's sonnet is from 1592; the 'table of the heart' metaphor is rare in 'portrait in the heart' poems; the phrase 'table of my heart' is even rarer; and the combined use of 'table of my heart' and 'form' is unique to these sonnets.[23] Sonnet 24 may also be influenced by a Constable sonnet that uses a mirror and a window:

> Thine eye, the glass where I behold my heart;
> Mine eye, the window through the which thine eye
> May see my heart, and there thy self espy
> In bloody colours how thou painted art . . .
>
> (Sonnet 9, 1592 edition of *Diana*, lines 1–4)

The *Diana* poet is describing two actions: seeing the reflection of a heart and 'seeing through' to a heart. Like Constable, Shakespeare begins a quatrain with an end-stopped line and enjambs the next two lines to convey looking through an eye's window at a heart's portrait: 'Now see what good turns eyes for eyes have done: / Mine eyes have drawn thy shape, and thine for me / Are windows to my breast, wherethrough the sun / Delights to peep, to gaze therein on thee'. (The lines may be informed by the Latin root of 'perspective': *perspicere*, 'to see through'.) Given the metapoetic subject matter, Shakespeare is arguably engaging with Constable and Daniel, not merely echoing them. The allusions would reinforce the point that he is musing on the difficulties of seeing through generic images to personal truths.

There is another possibility for 24's you-forms: they point to *W* and 'Wriothesley'. In Q's spelling, lines 5–6 of the sonnet are 'For through the Painter muſt you ſee his skill, / To finde where your true Image pictur'd lies'. 'Painter muſt you ſee his skill' has all 'Wriothesley' letters except *W*; the complete name can be found in 'where your true Image pictur'd lies'. Shakespeare may be hinting that there is an imperfect form of the youth in line 5 and a complete form in line 6, and that, if we see through his 'skill', we will 'find' the youth's 'true Image'. The anagrams point to the conceit that the poet carries in his heart an image of the youth.

The Centre Poems of the Second Step

The centre poems of the second pyramid step, Sonnets 25 and 26, are a pair, though 26 does not begin with a conjunctive phrase: they are a pair in the context of the step, which is filled with pairs, and because their themes are similar. Sonnet 26 can also be read as the start of a 100-sonnet scheme (26–125) and as the first poem of a self-reflective trio (26, 62, and 126). If we are familiar with how Shakespeare negotiates competing schemes, Sonnet 26's connections to other poems should not obscure the fact that it is also connected to Sonnet 25.

Sonnet 25 is one of the most joyful poems in *Sonnets*:

> Let those who are in favor with their stars
> Of public honour and proud titles boast,
> Whilst I, whom fortune of such triumph bars,
> Unlooked for joy in that I honour most.
> Great princes' favorites their fair leaves spread
> But as the marigold at the sun's eye,
> And in themselves their pride lies burièd
> For at a frown they in their glory die.

> The painful warrior, famousèd for worth,
> After a thousand victories, once foiled,
> Is from the book of honour razèd quite,
> And all the rest forgot for which he toiled.
>   Then happy I, that love and am belovèd,
>   Where I may not remove, nor be removèd.

The poet may be rejoicing to himself or the youth, to close friends or a wide audience; unlike courtiers whose public favour is precarious, he enjoys a secure love. Oddly, lines 9 and 11 do not rhyme. To remedy this, editors have emended 'worth' to 'fight' or 'might' or changed 'quite' to 'forth'. But the error may be intentional: perhaps Shakespeare is playing with the idea that the name of the dutiful and suffering warrior (the *pains*-taking knight) has been expunged from the book of honour (his 'fight' or 'might' has been removed). Sonnet 25 has another odd feature – five past participles with '-ed' suffixes pronounced as separate syllables. The suffixes in the couplet rhyme stand out most, because there is no metrical need for them.[24] Coming at the end of measured and end-stopped lines, 'belovèd' and 'removèd' might be said to shake but stay firm, or to be unshakeable. (The poet may be saying that his love is so deeply rooted it cannot be removed – that it looks on tempests and is never shaken.) Shakespeare may also be punning on his surname, which is as ostensibly absent from *Sonnets* as the names of the warrior and the youth. More simply, he is portraying himself as old-fashioned, in order to present himself as a stubbornly constant lover. (Elizabethan pronunciation of '-ed' was flexible, but by the late sixteenth century, pronouncing the suffixes of participles whose verb stems did not end in 'd' or 't' was largely archaic or poetic, as Sonnet 17's 'stretchèd meter of an antique song' suggests.[25]) In the end, the poet claims that he will neither forsake the youth nor be forsaken by the youth, in spite of the changes that time brings.

Sonnet 26 is epistolary. Addressing his 'lord', the poet takes delight in his present situation while looking to the future and confessing that he has yet to prove his worthiness:

> Lord of my love, to whom in vassalage
> Thy merit hath my duty strongly knit,
> To thee I send this written embassage,
> To witness duty, not to show my wit;
> Duty so great, which wit so poor as mine
> May make seem bare, in wanting words to show it,
> But that I hope some good conceit of thine

> In thy soul's thought, all naked, will bestow it –
> Till whatsoever star that guides my moving
> Points on me graciously with fair aspéct
> And puts apparel on my tottered loving
> To show me worthy of thy sweet respect.
>   Then may I dare to boast how I do love thee;
>   Till then, not show my head where thou mayst prove me.

Sonnet 26 has been read as a final poem, and 1–26 have been regarded as a unit.[26] But 26 is both forward- and backward-looking, and it is arguably more of a salutation than a valediction. The poet presents himself as a servant/courtier who displays wit while claiming to be only showing duty. His display is elabourate, from wordplay like 'witness . . . wit' to the conceit that his lord should 'bestow' (clothe, lodge, protect) the child of his wit. Even his rhymes are unusual: *show it–bestow it* and *love thee–prove me* are broken rhymes, which Shakespeare mostly avoids.[27] Three feminine rhymes (*show it–bestow it*, *moving–loving*, and *love thee–prove me*) encourage us to hear *vassalage–embassage* as a feminine rhyme if not to hear a French accent: the poet is mocking the language of courtiers like *Hamlet*'s Osric, who waxes eloquent about 'carriages'. (The alteration of masculine and feminine rhymes might also be French.[28]) Sonnet 26 is so extravagant that a *show it–poet* rhyme might not feel out of place in it, which may be part of the joke: the poet evokes but avoids that rhyme, as if to say that he is not yet able to show himself as his lord's poet. The final rhyme, *love thee–prove me*, is imperfect: a feminine rhyme's ultimate syllables should be homophones. The poet is portraying himself as inept, and the sonic inequality between 'thee' and 'me' parallels the social inequality between lord and poet.

Sonnets 25–6 are thematically related. In 25, the poet describes a disgraced warrior, implying that the warrior's glorious deeds – deeds of the past – have been razed from the book of honour along with his name; in 26, he portrays himself as someone who has yet to make a name for himself: the page reserved for him in the book of honour is a blank, awaiting future deeds. If we regard Sonnets 25–6 as a pair, we can read 18–24 as a series that builds towards the step's central expression of love and 27–33 as a series that anticipates darker times. If we regard the two sonnets as separate, we can read 25 as the culmination of a narrative of increasing intimacy and 26 as the start of the poet's quest to prove his love and show himself worthy of the youth. These narratives are rhetorically if not schematically reinforced by the forms of address in the two halves of the pyramid step:

Th	3rd	Th	3rd	Th	3rd?	Th	3rd
18	19	20	21	22	23	24	25

Th	Th	Th	Th	Th	Th	Th	3rd
26	27	28	29	30	31	32	33

The question mark after '3rd' denotes ambiguity in form of address. Sonnet 23 contains no thou- or you-forms, but two lines argue for direct address: 'O let my books be then my eloquence' and 'O learn to read what silent love hath writ'. The poet seems to be addressing the youth; he may also be addressing future readers. In light of 23's avoidance of second-person pronouns and the alternating forms of address in 18–25, 'third-person sonnet' may be a more apt designation than 'thou-sonnet'. Regardless, Sonnets 18–25 alternate between affectionate declarations and philosophical reflections, and they draw attention to representations of the youth. In contrast, Sonnets 26–32 focus on the poet, detailing his travels and travails, and depicting him as a social outcast and old-fashioned poet. After second-person meditations in seven consecutive sonnets, the return to the third person in Sonnet 33 is interruptive: the poet retreats into allegory, as if to fend off the coming betrayal or to delay confrontation.

Metapoetic Gestures and Allusions in the Second Step

As a bipartite scheme following the procreation sonnets, the second pyramid step can be regarded as a new stage in a story: the love between the poet and the youth grows to a new height (18–25), inspiring the poet to prove his worthiness (26–33). As is typical in *Sonnets*, though, the love story is complicated by the poetry story. Let us look again at the second step, paying more attention to metapoetic gestures.

In the step's first sonnet – 'Shall I compare thee to a summer's day?' – the poet is mostly confident as he praises the youth. Amid his joy, though, he faces a challenge: finding the right comparison. He claims that neither a summer's day nor the sun itself is adequate, and he regrets that all natural beauty fades. In the ninth-line turn, he boldly asserts that the youth's beauty is immortal: 'But thy eternal summer shall not fade'. In the couplet turn, he more boldly claims that his verse bestows immortal life: 'So long as men can breathe or eyes can see, / So long lives this, and this gives life to thee'. With this boast, the poet is not simply saying 'as long as there are people in the world'; he is placing emphasis on seeing poetry and reading it aloud – on sight and sound – and he is anticipating Sonnet 81, in which he speaks of eyes and tongues that will 'o'er-read' and 're-hearse' his verse. More broadly, the poet is challenging himself is to create a *living* monument, a memorial that will both vibrantly and faithfully preserve the youth. In Renaissance English, 'living monument' denotes an enduring memorial or a surviving mourner; metaphorically, it can refer to a memorial so well fashioned that it might seem alive.[29]

Sonnet 19 picks up where 18 leaves off, confident in poetry's power: 'Devouring Time, blunt thou the lion's paws / And make the earth devour her own sweet brood; / Pluck the keen teeth from the fierce tiger's jaws / And burn the long-lived phoenix in her blood'. Warming to his task of immortalising the youth, the poet unleashes against Time the figurative language and imagery that he was reluctant to apply in 18. (To put it another way, he rebukes Time in order to display devotion.) As if he were racing against Time, the poet employs an early volta, in line 8: 'But I forbid thee one most heinous crime'. And in the sestet, he chides Time:

> O carve not with thy hours my love's fair brow
> Nor draw no lines there with thine antique pen:
> Him in thy course untainted do allow
> For beauty's pattern to succeeding men.
>   Yet do thy worst, old Time; despite thy wrong,
>   My love shall in my verse ever live young.

The turn in line 13 is abrupt but not incongruous: drawing on the alchemical imagery of the first quatrain, the poet suggests that his verse is comparable to a philosopher's stone or an elixir of life in its transformative power.[30] But what most prevents 19's couplet from seeming out of place is its rhetorical reinforcement of 18's couplet.

Sonnets 18–19 set the stage for 20, a poem that can be read in three related ways – as an attempt to portray and praise the youth in verse, as a response to a request to 'paint' the youth, and as a reflection on a painting of the youth:

> A woman's face with nature's own hand painted,
> Hast thou, the master mistress of my passion;
> A woman's gentle heart, but not acquainted
> With shifting change, as is false women's fashion;
> An eye more bright than theirs, less false in rolling,
> Gilding the object whereupon it gazeth;
> A man in hue, all hues in his controlling,

> Which steals men's eyes and women's souls amazeth.
> And for a woman wert thou first created,
> Till Nature, as she wrought thee, fell a-doting,
> And by addition me of thee defeated
> By adding one thing to my purpose nothing.
>   But since she pricked thee out for women's pleasure,
>   Mine be thy love, and thy love's use their treasure.

The poet playfully argues that the feminine youth is ultimately defined by how he is not like a woman: Nature has 'pricked out' the youth – given him a penis and elected him 'for women's pleasure'. As many commentators point out, all seven of 20's rhymes are feminine – an allusion to the youth's femininity. But the joke is more elaborate than that. Each line contains a thing as superfluous to its metrical form as Nature's thing is to the youth's form – an unstressed eleventh syllable. Also note that the W's in 'rowling' and 'controwling' (Q's spellings) are unnecessary, as are the '-eth' suffixes in 'gazeth' and 'amazeth': Shakespeare uses 'gazes' and 'amazes' in his plays. 'Acquainted' and 'nothing' allude to female genitalia – 'quaint' and 'no thing' in Elizabethan slang.[31] 'Nature ... fell a-doting' conjures the image of a fond grandmother or fairy godmother who bestows a generous but useless gift on a child. Perhaps the most difficult line is 'A man in hue, all hues in his controlling'. It mostly suggests that the youth has a man's form and can control the colours on his and others' faces, but 'control' can also mean 'call to account', 'refute', and 'point out faults'.[32] Commentators have likened the youth's hue-based power to the nonchalant control of an ideal courtier (*sprezzatura*) and to ineffable and mysterious charm (*je ne sais quoi*).[33] His personal hue would seem to be both superficial and essential; like blood, it gives him his warm/living colour and his vitality. 'Hues' may also hint at 'use' and at 'love's use' (sex).[34] As spelled in Q ('Hews'), it potentially points to W, 'double *you*'s', and 'double use'. Some commentators have read 'Hews' as a cipher for 'Henry Wriothesley', with or without the *E* and *S* for 'Earl of Southampton'.[35] More telling, there is a 'Wriothesley' anagram in 'A man in hew all *Hews* in his controwling', and the poet may signal it with 'A man in', since the full anagram appears in the rest of the line. (For more on anagrams in 20, see Appendix C.)

Concern with figuration continues in Sonnets 21–5, with a new focus on mimesis. In Sonnet 21, the poet revisits 20's reflections on feminine beauty and painting, even as he changes the subject: 'So it is not with me as with that Muse, / Stirred by a painted beauty to his verse, / Who heav'n itself for ornament doth use / And every fair with his fair doth rehearse'. Claiming not to be inspired by a cosmetically enhanced beauty or an excessively praised one, the *Sonnets* poet questions the outlandish comparisons of another poet. Sonnets 22–4 evoke non-textual forms of representation: 22 features a mirror ('My glass shall not persuade me I am old'); 23 is theatrical ('As an unperfect actor on the stage'); and 24 draws on the visual arts ('Mine eye hath played the painter'). Sonnet 25 may therefore complete the poet's reflections on reality and appearance: the youth is true beauty, real and constant. In signalling completion, 25 also dangles the possibility of a happy ending: the poet is 'loved and belovèd' where he 'may not remove nor be removèd'. Such an ending is not to be, of course, though the raising of its possibility at the second step's centre evokes the conceit of centre as climax.

One important theme of the step's second half is travel or travail (in Q, both words are spelled 'travail'). If we read Sonnet 26 as a valediction, it initiates this theme. Sonnets 27–8 are more explicit: the poet complains of travel-induced sleeplessness. The travel theme recedes in 29–32, only to return with a vengeance in 33–4, when the poet travels forth to meet the youth and confirms the betrayal. Shakespeare may be playing a long game here: the twenty-five sonnets after 26 are a series that explores the consequences of travelling and of being absent from the youth. Like Sonnets 27–28, the sonnets at the end of the series (50–1) are a pair of poems about a round-trip journey. They are followed by a you-sonnet (52), the first since Sonnet 17.

Related to travel is the threat of outsiders, a motif originating with Sonnet 18's musings on things that are *not* the youth but might be compared to him. In Sonnet 21, the poet speaks of another poet's comparisons; and in 25, he contrasts his secure friendship with the youth with the uncertain favour of courtiers. But when he evokes outsiders in the first half of the second step, the poet underscores private friendship and mutual love, which are presented as sufficient in themselves. In the second half, he is increasingly concerned with people and things that impinge on the friendship. In Sonnet 26, he admits that he needs to make a name for himself in the world; in 27–8, he travels; and in 29, he envies 'this man's art, and that man's scope'. In Sonnet 30, he is preoccupied by missed opportunities and lost friends; in 31, he describes the youth as the repository of 'all the trophies' of his past lovers; and in 32, he pleads with the youth to read other poets 'for their style' and to read him 'for love'. Sonnet 32's pleas can be read as summational; perhaps the threat of rivals has been present all along.

Outsiders are allusively present in Sonnets 31–2: as many commentators note, 31 echoes the dedicatory sonnet of *Diana*. More precisely, 31–2 actively engage with Constable's poem.[36] To judge by wordplay, Constable's addressee is a noblewoman named 'Grace':

> Grace full of grace, though in these verses here
> My love complains of others than of thee,
> Yet thee alone I loved, and they by me
> (Thou yet unknown) only mistaken were.
> Like him who feels a heat now here, now there,
> Blames now this cause, now that, until he see
> The fire indeed from whence they causèd be –
> Which fire I now do know is you, my dear –
> Thus díverse loves dispersèd in my verse
> In thee alone for ever I unite
> And fully unto thee more to rehearse
> To Him I fly for grace that rules above,
>   That by my Grace I may live in delight,
>   Or by His grace I never more may love.[37]

Remarkably, the poet addresses Grace as if she were the Virgin Mary and admits to wooing other women; he also claims that his 'heat' for them radiated from her, and that he can now unite all previous loves in her. (The sudden and confident 'you' in 'I now do know is you' hints that Grace is his love's final form.) The poet then asserts that, in order to tell her more or simply to write more, he must 'fly' to God and win Grace or grace – succeed in his suit or renounce earthly love.

Echoing Constable's sonnet verbally and thematically, Sonnet 31 outdoes its model by claiming more significance for the beloved:

> Thy bosom is endearèd with all hearts,
> Which I, by lacking, have supposèd dead;
> And there reigns love, and all love's loving parts,
> And all those friends which I thought burièd.
> How many a holy and obsequious tear
> Hath dear religious love stol'n from mine eye,
> As interest of the dead, which now appear
> But things removed that hidden in thee lie!
> Thou art the grave where buried love doth live,
> Hung with the trophies of my lovers gone,
> Who all their parts of me to thee did give:
> That due of many now is thine alone.
>   Their images I loved I view in thee,
>   And thou, all they, hast all the all of me.

The language of 31's sestet is similar to that of 'Grace full of grace', in particular the phrase 'their parts . . . thine alone . . . in thee', which recalls 'díverse loves . . . In thee alone'. More crucially, both poets present the beloved as a messianic figure greater than the sum of her/his parts. Though it has an air of commonplace about it, this combination of conceits was far from common. As Claes Schaar observes in his survey of sonnets on the 'Platonic theme of immanent ideal beauty', the notion that the beloved is a perfect being who possesses all the best parts may not have been new in the late sixteenth century, but the idea that the poet is led to his perfect love by providential signs in the form of previous loves was very unusual.[38] Constable and Shakespeare, moreover, are the only English poets to use the latter conceit, and their non-English forbears tend to be doctrinaire Neoplatonists. And while the final lines of 'Grace full of grace' may indicate that Constable's sentiments are Platonic – Grace prompts the poet to seek a higher form of grace – Shakespeare pointedly discards Constable's setting, giving us a poem that speaks of 'holy' and 'religious' things in its octave, only to turn elsewhere in the sestet.[39] And in Sonnet 31, the beloved both compensates for loss and contains 'all the all' of the poet.

Note, too, that, unlike 'Grace full of grace', Sonnet 31 contains martial imagery – the 'trophies' of 'lovers gone'. In Elizabethan English, the word 'trophy' typically denotes an ornament hung in commemoration of a dead person's achievements, but Shakespeare draws on 'trophy' in its classical Greek and Roman sense: 'a tree or pillar or scaffold hung with the arms and treasure of a conquered enemy as a memorial of the victory'.[40] This includes the idea that the victorious warrior acquires all of the past glories of the defeated warrior – a conceit evoked in Sonnet 25, with the image of the warrior 'foiled' after 'a thousand victories', and in the fifth act of *1 Henry IV*, when Prince Hal kills his chivalric rival and foil, Henry Percy. While dying, Percy says to Hal, 'O, Harry, thou hast robbed me of my youth! / I better brook the loss of brittle life / Than those proud titles thou hast won of me'.

Martial imagery can also be found in Sonnet 32, conjoined with rivalry:

> If thou survive my well-contented day,
> When that churl Death my bones with dust shall cover
> And shalt by fortune once more re-survey
> These poor rude lines of thy deceasèd lover,
> Compare them with the bett'ring of the time,

And though they be outstripped by every pen,
Reserve them for my love, not for their rhyme
Exceeded by the height of happier men.
O then vouchsafe me but this loving thought:
'Had my friend's Muse grown with this growing age,
A dearer birth than this his love had brought,
To march in ranks of better equipage;
   But since he died, and poets better prove,
   Theirs for their style I'll read, his for his love'.

The poet presents himself as old-fashioned, conceding that improvements in poetry have been made or will be made: 'These poor rude lines ... Compare them with the bett'ring of the time'. He asks to be remembered not for his (poor) lines, but his (rich) love. His modesty may well be false; regardless, he presents himself as one poet among many whose verse might attract the fair youth. The martial imagery is in line 12: 'To march in ranks of better equipage'. 'Equipage' refers to military dress, especially the ceremonial dress of high-ranking soldiers.[41] Most of the sestet is ascribed to the youth and seems meant to evoke his manner of speaking. This is the case in lines 10–12, which might be translated: 'Over time, my friend might have improved as a poet and matched the triumphs of his betters [joined their more refined ranks], if only he had kept in step with fashion'. Given the class-inflected diction ('dearer birth', 'ranks') and the use of 'vassalage' and 'embassage' in Sonnet 26, 'equipage' likely signals irony.

'To march in ranks of better equipage' would unquestionably be ironic if Shakespeare is echoing John Marston's high-spirited introduction to the 'Satires' section of *The Metamorphosis of Pygmalion's Image* (1598):

Is not my pen complete? Are not my lines
Right in the swagg'ring humour of these times?
....
Hath not my goddess, in the vanguard place,
The leading of my lines, their plumes to grace?
And then ensue my stanzas, like odd bands
Of voluntaries and mercenarians,
Which, like soldados of our warlike age,
March rich bedight in warlike equipage,
Glittering in daubed laced accoutrements
And pleasing suits of love's habiliments.
                    (lines 7–8, 15–22; emphasis added)

Marston is satirising love poetry, including his own *Pygmalion* and Shakespeare's *Venus and Adonis*. His image of soldiers marching richly bedecked in military dress is apt in its context, whereas 'march in ranks of better equipage' is incongruous, even as imagined speech. In this light, it can be argued that Shakespeare is responding to Marston and the genre of verse satire, and that Sonnet 32 was written in the late 1590s or the early 1600s. But can we be sure of this?

Thomas Tyler thought so. In his 1880 edition of *Sonnets*, he argues that Shakespeare was influenced by Marston and that Sonnet 32 dates from 1598.[42] This view was questioned in 1898 by Sydney Lee, who maintained that 'march in equipage' was a common phrase, citing Nashe's preface to Greene's *Menaphon* (1589) and claiming that he could quote other instances.[43] Lee's view became a consensus, and references to Tyler mostly vanish after Rollins's 1944 edition of *Sonnets*. But Lee's criticism of Tyler is flawed, and not merely because 'march in equipage' may have been a more unusual phrase. Marston's and Shakespeare's uses are distinctive: both poets use the phrase in verse, to talk about verse; both employ an *age–equipage* rhyme; and both link style to social class. Verse satire was moreover a fashion in the late 1590s, and it was not simply the latest new thing: it was a 'bitter' genre that positioned itself against 'sugared' love poetry, whose epitome was the sonnet.[44] Shakespeare may well have been writing *Sonnets* after the initial vogue for sequences, if not at the height of the next poetic fashion.

The Third Pyramid Step

If written around the turn of the seventeenth century, Sonnet 32 is likely an outlier among the first seventy-five sonnets, which are commonly dated to the early or mid-1590s.[45] In view of its number symbolism and position at the boundary of the second and third pyramid steps, Sonnet 33 may be another such poem: it was perhaps written to complete a scheme. Such possibilities should remind us that *Sonnets*' order of poems, even in the parts that tell tidy narratives, does not necessarily correspond to the chronology of composition. In contrast, the sonnets of the third pyramid step might all have been written in one period (the mid-1590s), despite evidence that some of them are out of narrative order. The third step's narrative irregularities stem from its scheme of five trios, whose third trio foregrounds the youth's betrayal. The betrayal is at the centre of the step; its consequences radiate from there.

Allegorically, the youth's betrayal is also at the step's beginning: 'Why didst thou promise such a beauteous day / And make me trávail forth without my cloak, / To let base clouds o'ertake me in my way, / Hiding thy brav'ry in their rotten smoke?' (34). Because the youth's exact offence is unclear at this stage, and because the poet quickly downplays the transgression and offers forgiveness, we might initially regard the betrayal in Sonnets 40–2 as a second event. But parallels between 33–4 and 133–4 provide strong evidence that 33–4 refer to the youth-mistress affair: like 40–2, 133–4 are explicit about the affair; 33–4 and 133–4 are exactly 100 sonnets apart; 33–4 and 133–4 are the first poems to allude to betrayal in the fair-youth and mistress sections (respectively); and both pairs violate a boundary between two pyramid steps. For symbolic and expressive purposes – and at some risk of narrative confusion – 33–4 are placed at the boundary of the second and third steps, and 40–2 are 'displaced' to the third step's third trio.

Whether the result of rearranged sonnets or not, the third step's scheme is striking. With the account of the youth-mistress affair in the centre, and five trios in all, the scheme draws attention to the poet's attempts to cope with the betrayal, and to the symmetry of two trios on each side of the centre. After presenting the youth's transgression in veiled terms, the poet debates its meaning and implications, alternating between accusation and exculpation, especially in the first half of the step. By the third trio, the debate is tinged with sarcasm: the poet invites the youth to 'take' all his loves (40), excuses the youth for 'pretty wrongs' (41), and argues that the two 'loving offenders' are showing love for him (42). The poet often takes up a line of argument only to reverse his position soon after, which suggests that he is trying to rationalise his plight. While the poet's reversals can occur in the same sonnet – 34 begins with blame and turns suddenly to forgiveness in the couplet – they mostly play out across trios. In 34–6, for example, the poet confronts the youth ('Why didst thou . . .?'), reassures him ('No longer be grieved . . .'), and offers him amicable separation ('we two must be twain').

The symmetry of trios around the centre poems points to two 'halves': 34–9 and 43–8. The first two trios might be called a sextet, because their arguments are linked: at the end of 36, the poet 'confesses' that he and the youth must separate; in 37–9, he imagines what separation will be like. As he muses on possibilities, the poet claims that he will live vicariously in the youth, as a father does in a child (37), declares that, in the youth, he has all the material he needs to write poems that will 'outlive all date' (38), and questions whether he is skilled and worthy enough to write of the youth's worth, eventually concluding that absence will teach him 'how to make one twain, / By praising him here who doth hence remain' (39). Here 'twain' points to 'half' and 'two', and 'hence' points to both 'from here' and 'henceforth'. The poet suggests that what separates him and his friend can make them feel their bond more strongly, and that praising his absent friend will not only help him feel the friend is with him; it will ensure the friend's immortality. As the wordplay illustrates, the poet is evoking 'part and whole' and 'absence and presence'. The *twain–remain* couplet further links the trios, because 36 opens with the same rhyme. Like the poet and the youth, 34–6 and 37–9 are at once separated and joined.

As trios, 43–5 and 46–8 are also both distinct and connected. In Sonnet 43, the poet observes that he sees images of the youth clearest when he is asleep and dreaming at night, and he wishes that he could see the real youth in the 'living day', when he (the poet) is awake. In 44, the poet meditates on the power and impotence of his imagination, noting that if his flesh were thought, no distance would bar him from travelling instantly to the youth, but because he is 'of earth and water wrought', he must wait and shed tears. And in 45, the poet presents the 'other two' elements, 'slight air and purging fire', as his thoughts and desires. He fancies that he sends these 'swift messengers' to the youth and becomes 'oppressed with melancholy' while they are gone; when they return with news of the youth's 'fair health', he rejoices briefly, sends them out again, and 'straight grow[s] sad'. The next three sonnets, 46–8, are thematically related; the poet remains self-reflective if not trapped in his thoughts. But he is also less despondent: in 46, he speaks of a 'war' between his eye and heart over the 'sight' of the fair youth; in 47, of a 'league' between them. (The truce involves a portrait of the youth in possession of the eye, an image of the youth in possession of the heart, and visiting rights for both parties.) In contrast to the earlier images produced by restless sleep, these images are pleasurable and ever-present, or 'no farther away than . . . thoughts' (47). Sonnet 48, however, strikes a cautious note: reviewing his journeys and sufferings, the poet fears that, though he has 'locked up' the youth in his heart, the youth will nonetheless be stolen from him. Both trio and step end ambiguously.

The Fourth and Fifth Pyramid Steps

Sonnets 49–62 and 63–75 might be called the climacteric steps. Their first poems have climacteric numbers (49, 63) and hint at crises related to aging: 'Against that time, if ever that time come'; 'Against my love shall be as I am now'. In both lines, 'against' primarily means 'in preparation for', but the poet also suggests that he is fighting time and perhaps the youth or his love for the youth. As might be expected, both pyramid steps express anxiety about time, especially Time's power to harm the poet-youth friendship. Time is an enemy throughout: in the fourth step, temporal injuries are primarily physical; in the fifth, they are physical and moral. In short, the guiding conceits of the steps are, respectively, 'the climacteric of body' and 'the climacteric of body and soul'.

The fourth pyramid step is self-critical. Its opening sonnet defies time and evokes imperfection: 'Against that time . . . / When I shall see thee frown on my defécts' (49). In the closing sonnet, the poet looks in the mirror, meditates on time's ravages, and concludes that he has deceived himself by identifying with his friend: ''Tis thee, myself, that for myself I praise, / Painting my age with beauty of thy days' (62). Rhetorically, the step alternates between confident assertions and anxious questions. The poet's dialectical mode of deliberation can be gleaned from the pattern of thou-sonnets and you-sonnets:

(Th Th Th) (Y Y Y) X X (Y Y Y) (Th Th Th)
 49 50 51   52 53 54 55 56 57 58 59 60 61 62

I have put Xs over the central sonnets because 55 is mostly impersonal, addressing the youth only in its couplet, and 56 addresses both the spirit of love and the youth. In other words, both poems foreground indirect address but are ultimately neither second-person sonnets nor third-person sonnets. However we label them, there is a symmetrical pattern of you-sonnets and thou-sonnets around them. These trios vacillate between doubt and assurance.

Like many pyramid steps, the fourth step can be productively analysed as two halves. The first half builds towards a confident sonnet:

(Th Th Th Y Y Y) X
 49 50 51 52 53 54 55

> 49: 'Against that time, if ever that time come . . .'
> 55: 'Not marble, nor the gilded monument . . .'

In 50–1, the poet craves reunion with the youth, suspecting that 'grief lies onward' and 'joy behind' (50). In 52–3, he wonders about the youth and praises him for fidelity, albeit with some irony: 'But you [are] like none, none you, for constant heart' (53). Sonnet 54 alludes to marriage and poetry in its last five lines, via an image of unfruitful flowers:

> [Canker blooms] live unwooed and, unrespected, fade,
> Die to themselves. Sweet roses do not so –
> Of their sweet deaths are sweetest odors made.
>   And so of you, beauteous and lovely youth,
>   When that shall vade, my verse distills your truth.

Echoing Sonnet 5's image of rosewater and anticipating 55's declarations about poetry's power, these lines point to the number 5 and to nuptial symbolism. The final line has provoked editorial debate: Q prints 'by verse', not 'my verse'. The phrase 'by verse' potentially evokes drop-by-drop distillation: 'When your beauty/youth goes away, your truth will be transmitted to posterity by lines of poetry'. 'My verse' speaks more to the poet's power: 'When your beauty/youth goes away, my poetry will distill your truth'. Either way, the 'truth' that the poet distils cleanses and idealises the beloved.

The step's second half begins on a high note, falls off, and ends self-consciously:

X (Y Y Y Th Th Th)
56 57 58 59 60 61 62

56: 'Sweet Love, renew thy force . . .'
62: 'Sin of self-love possesseth [me] . . . / But when my glass shows me myself . . .'

Launching the second half, Sonnet 56 looks to future love: 'Sweet Love, renew thy force'. It may also point to the poet's renewed commitment to proving his worth. The implied pledge of love is short-lived, however: in 57–58, the poet represents himself as a slave straining not to think ill of his master, and in 59 he meditates on the idea that there is nothing new under the sun, ambiguously noting that the ancients praised 'subjects worse' than the youth. Sonnet 60 complements 59; the poet again meditates on time and praise, offering an optimistic conclusion: 'to times in hope, my verse shall stand / Praising thy worth, despite [Time's] cruël hand'. In its rededication to poetry's power, the sonnet functions as a stay against time's injuries and the anxiety attendant on them. But anxiety returns in ensuing sonnets. In 61, the poet wonders whether his nights are sleepless because the youth is sending a jealous spirit to watch him, only to conclude that he is the one keeping a jealous vigil; in 62, he deduces that his praise of the youth is a form of self-praise. In the step's second half, then, the poet calls for a renewal of love and is inspired to praise the youth in ways that will stand the test of time, but he ultimately presents the friendship as one-sided and his praise as suspect. The fourth step begins with meditations on the youth's absence and essence and concludes with the poet wondering whether he is projecting virtue onto the youth. This self-reflective quality is underscored by the final mirror poem and by the pattern of address pronouns, whose symmetry may allude to a mirror image: 'Th Th Th Y Y Y X | X Y Y Y Th Th Th'.

The fifth step's pattern of pronouns is not as symmetrical, but it too demarcates halves:

(3rd 3rd 3rd   3rd 3rd 3rd)   (Th Th   Y Y   Th Th)   Y
  63–64–65   66–67–68   69–70 71–72 73–74   75

The step consists of two six-sonnet series and a coda. The first series can be divided into two trios; the second, into three pairs. (With its retrospective matter, Sonnet 75 stands apart, like Sonnet 48 in the third step.) Throughout the step, the number 6 is prominent, starting with the six third-person sonnets, whose numbers are all in the 60s. Here, as elsewhere in *Sonnets*, traditions in which 6 symbolises perfection and imperfection inform the use of 6 and its multiples.

The six third-person sonnets pack a rhetorical punch. Their form of address indicates a determination to gain perspective on the youth and a turn from self-obsessed reflections. At the end of the previous step, the poet presented himself as older if not wiser, and he pledged to cure himself of narcissism. Now, at the midpoint of the fair-youth section, he suggests that he is more earnestly pursuing the task of immortalising his beloved: 'For such a time do I now fortify / Against confounding Age's cruël knife, / That he shall never cut from memory / My sweet love's beauty, though my lover's life' (63). Having examined time's injurious effects on himself, the poet turns to examine time's injurious effects on the youth.

The fifth step also turns to time's corrupting effects on spirit. Initially, the poet focuses on physical decay: in Sonnet 63, he speaks against the day when the youth's forehead will be filled with lines, promising to keep the youth's beauty 'green' in 'black lines'; in Sonnets 63–5, he suggests that his love will miraculously 'shine bright' in 'black ink'. But after laying claim to poetry's immortalising power, the poet questions whether his friend should bother to live in a foul and fallen world: 'Ah, wherefore with infection should he live . . . ? Why should he live . . . ?' (67). In Sonnets 66–8, he wonders whether the youth might be better off dying now, before the evils of the age corrupt him, and he hints that the youth has already been morally corrupted and perhaps physically infected. In 67–8, the poet add a further twist: he avoids both first- and second-person pronouns, reinforcing the homiletic tone of his questions and comments.

The second half of the fifth step begins with the poet insisting that he is looking beyond himself. Sonnets 69–70 avoid first-person pronouns, and their tone is paternal. The poet evokes the outside world ('Those parts of thee that the world doth view'), finds fault in the company kept by the youth ('thou dost common grow'), and offers Polonius-like counsel ('So thou be good, slander but doth approve / Thy worth the greater'). Similarly concerned with the world's view of the youth, Sonnets 71–2 are linked by verbal repetition:

> Sonnet 71
> . . . .
> But let your love ev'n with my life decay –
>   Lest the wise world should look into your moan
>   And mock you with me after I am gone.
>
> Sonnet 72
> O, lest the world should task you to recite
> What merit lived in me that you should love,
> After my death, dear love, forget me quite . . .

Along with first-person pronouns, self-centred anxieties return. The poet not only alludes to his own death but attempts to induce pity with passive-aggressive rhetoric.

In Sonnet 73, the poet asks the youth to think of him not as dead but as dying:

> That time of year thou mayst in me behold
> When yellow leaves, or none, or few, do hang
> Upon those boughs which shake against the cold,
> Bare ruined choirs, where late the sweet birds sang.
> In me thou seest the twilight of such day
> As after sunset fadeth in the west,
> Which by and by black night doth take away,
> Death's second self, that seals up all in rest.
> In me thou seest the glowing of such fire

>That on the ashes of his youth doth lie
>As the deathbed whereon it must expire,
>Consumed by that which it was nourished by.
> This thou perceiv'st, which makes thy love more strong,
> To love that well which thou must leave ere long.

The poet claims that the youth already sees him as a dying man and therefore loves him more strongly, but his assertion is rhetorical: he wants to move the youth. As a sonnet structured by three images developed across three quatrains, Sonnet 73 is climactic. In depicting a crisis of growing old, it is climacteric. Indeed, Sonnet 73 may allude to the major climacteric with its image of a ruined church (understood as a figure for physical and spiritual decay) and its links to 74 (73 reflects on the poet's body; 74, on the poet's spirit). It may also echo the couplet of 49, the minor climacteric sonnet: 'To leave poor me, thou hast the strength of laws, / Since why to love, I can allege no cause'. Sonnet 73's final line, 'To love that well which thou must leave ere long', basically means 'To love that person well whom you will lose before long'. (Compare it to 64's 'weep to have that which it fears to lose'.) But 'leave' does not simply mean 'lose'. Many commentators argue for a pun on 'leaves' (line 2) and an allusion to bloom and decay: the poet may be warning the youth about the transience of youth.[46] More simply, he expresses fear of abandonment: *You will leave me soon.*

Sonnet 74 is an anticlimactic continuation of 73. Counselling the youth not to mourn him, the poet speaks more directly: 'But be contented when that fell arrest / Without all bail shall carry me away'. At the same time, his argument is platitudinous: because his spirit belongs to the youth, the youth should not be upset about his death ('My spirit is thine, the better part of me'). As the step ends, then, the poet focuses on the soul, though perhaps the soul has been present all along: the project, after all, is to create a monument in which the beloved is preserved in all his beauty. Fearing for his monument and for the youth, the poet turns self-defensive and inward, even as he evokes a public world: 69–70 consider the youth from an outside perspective; 71–2 urge the youth to forget about the poet (in order to avoid unwanted attention from 'the world'); and 73–4 urge the youth to love the poet more because the poet is about to leave the world.

Sonnet 75 functions as a coda to the fifth step's meditations:

>So are you to my thoughts as food to life
>Or as sweet seasoned showers to the ground,

And for the peace of you I hold such strife
As 'twixt a miser and his wealth is found:
Now proud as an enjoyer, and anon
Doubting the filching age will steal his treasure;
Now counting best to be with you alone,
Then bettered that the world may see my pleasure;
Sometime all full with feasting on your sight,
And by and by clean starvèd for a look,
Possessing or pursuing no delight
Save what is had or must from you be took.
  Thus do I pine and surfeit day by day –
  Or gluttoning on all, or all away.

As at the end of other pyramid steps, the poet takes stock of his friendship with the youth. The sonnet's terminal position, subject matter, and syntax might tempt us to read 'So' as 'To sum up' or 'Therefore', but 'So' is a correlative conjunction in an 'as . . . so' formula, initiating a series of comparisons. With the phrase 'So are you' and the miser simile, the poet echoes Sonnet 52, which begins with 'So am I' and a rich-man simile. This echo links the fifth and fourth steps. Anxiety about theft provides another link: 'Doubting the filching age will steal his treasure' echoes lines from sonnets at or near the end of the two previous steps: 'And even thence thou wilt be stol'n, I fear' (48) and 'For thee watch I . . . with others all too near' (61). Suspense is building towards the sixth step, in which the youth will be stolen from the poet for a second time.

The Sixth and Seventh Pyramid Steps

The sixth pyramid step is the rival-poet series; its schemes were analysed in Chapter 3. The step has eleven sonnets (76–86) and a coda (87). The eleven-sonnet series consists of two four-sonnet sections preceded by an introductory sonnet (76), separated by a monument sonnet (81), and followed by the victorious rival sonnet (86). Patterned use of pronouns reinforces the design:

Y (Th Th Th Y)   Y   (Th Y Y Y)   Y
76   77 78 79–80   81   82–83–84–85   86

The three punctuating poems are you-sonnets. The four-sonnet sections consist of three thou-sonnets followed by a you-sonnet, and of a thou-sonnet followed by three you-sonnets. In terms of content, the first section's sonnets mostly allude to one rival; the second section's sonnets, to more than one rival. Forms of address are moreover used for rhetorical effect. In six of the seven sonnets before 87, the poet addresses the youth with you-forms; in 87, he reverts to thou-forms, to reinforce a point. After a rival poet wins over the youth, the *Sonnets* poet is angry and threatens a break: 'Farewell, thou art too dear for my possessing', he tells the youth, insinuating that their friendship is transactional, and that it has cost the poet dearly. In adopting thou-forms, which were once a sign of intimacy with the youth, the poet expresses contempt.

Sonnet 87's thou-forms also help the poet transition to the seventh step, which consists mostly of thou-sonnets. The step begins with three trios and ends with a self-reflective pair:

Th Th Th   Th Th Th   3rd Th Th   Th Y
(88–89–90) (91–92–93) (94–95–96) (97–98)

Thematically and rhetorically, the trios are tightly linked:

Trio	Description
88–90	The poet strives to show his love for the youth by offering to accept scorn (88), blame (89), and hate (90). At the end of 88, he offers to 'bear all wrong'; 89 begins: 'Say thou didst forsake me'. At the end of 89, he vows to fight against himself because he refuses to love anyone whom the youth hates; 90 begins: 'Then hate me when thou wilt; if ever, now'.
91–3	In contrast to 88–90, the poet pleads for love. In expressing how much the youth means to him, he notes that he can be made 'most wretchèd' if he loses the youth's love (91), that the youth may be false for all he knows (92), and that the youth's beauty would be like 'Eve's apple' if the youth lacks virtue (93). At the end of 91, the poet recognises that the youth has power to make him miserable; 92 begins: 'But do thy worst'. At the end of 92, the poet grants that he may be naive in believing that the youth is true; 93 begins: 'So shall I live, supposing thou art true'.
94–6	In contrast to 91–3, the poet begins with third-person address, speaking of people who 'have the power to hurt and will do none' (94). He then develops the theme that the youth has faults that might yet be corrected (95–6). 94–5 are linked together by their couplets: the final lines of 94 and 95 are

proverbs. 94–6 are strongly linked to 91–3: all six poems plead for love and discuss the youth's perfections and imperfections; the opening lines of 91 and 96 echo each other ('Some glory in their birth, some in their skill'; 'Some say thy fault is youth, some wantonness').

Sonnets 97–8 can be read as a continuation of the trios or an addendum to them: the poet depicts a period of separation from the youth, which follows from the events to which 88–96 allude and marks an end to a stage in the poet-youth friendship. Like a couplet rhyme after three quatrains, the pair provide closure to the three trios:

> Sonnet 97
> How like a winter hath my absence been
> From thee, the pleasure of the fleeting year!
> What freezings have I felt, what dark days seen!
> What old December's bareness everywhere!
> And yet this time removed was summer's time,
> The teeming autumn big with rich increase,
> Bearing the wanton burden of the prime,
> Like widowed wombs after their lords' decease:
> Yet this abundant issue seemed to me
> But hope of orphans and unfathered fruit;
> For summer and his pleasures wait on thee,
> And, thou away, the very birds are mute –
>   Or, if they sing, 'tis with so dull a cheer,
>   That leaves look pale, dreading the winter's near.

> Sonnet 98
> From you have I been absent in the spring,
> When proud pied April, dressed in all his trim,
> Hath put a spirit of youth in every thing,
> That heavy Saturn laughed and leapt with him.
> Yet nor the lays of birds, nor the sweet smell
> Of different flow'rs in odor and in hue,
> Could make me any summer's story tell,
> Or from their proud lap pluck them where they grew.
> Nor did I wonder at the lily's white,
> Nor praise the deep vermilion in the rose;
> They were but sweet, but figures of delight,
> Drawn after you, you pattern of all those.
>   Yet seemed it winter still, and, you away,
>   As with your shadow I with these did play.

Both sonnets imply that the poet-youth separation, portrayed as imminent since Sonnet 87, has come to pass, though its duration is unclear. In 97, the poet writes in autumn about a summer absence – a period that could range from three months to almost nine months, depending on how late it is in autumn and whether 'summer's time' refers to summer or spring-summer. (The nine-month period may gain support from the childbearing imagery.) And as Burrow notes, 98's springtime draws out the absence in one of two directions – 'forwards' (to the spring after 97's autumn) or 'backwards' (to the spring before 97's autumn) – and may thus extend 'to a whole year, spring to spring'.[47] In the more probable scenario (spring to autumn), 98 would refer to 97's period of time from a reverse perspective.

Sonnets 97–8 are a pair, but how are they connected? Vendler sees 98 as 'a simpler version' of 97 and finds it 'tempting to think that 98 . . . was written first'.[48] 'Simpler' is misleading, especially if it implies 'aesthetically inferior'. Consider Sonnet 98's negative litany of beauties, as in the lines 'Nor did I wonder at the lily's white, / Nor praise the deep vermilion in the rose'. Besides depicting himself as emotionally numb, the poet is saying that he has refrained from making typical observations and uttering conventional expressions. While his imagery and phrasing do not cease being generic because they are framed as such, their effect is complex. To begin with, the litany may be a critique of other poets. More crucially, the list is in tension with the argument that the spring's arrival fails to inspire new song: the poet keeps registering in verse the presence of beautiful things, even as he claims that they are 'but sweet, but figures of delight'. His mode of presentation effectually conveys his alienation, and it arguably restores beauty to familiar images and phrases.

Taking a different approach to 97–8, Evans identifies verbal and pronominal parallels such as *thou away/you away* and *From thee/ From you*.[49] More telling is that 97 is a thou-sonnet and 98 is a you-sonnet, and that 98 contains *you/youth*, *you/hue*, and *you-you/ double-you* puns. The poet is developing two related conceits: that he must play with 'figures' of the beloved while the beloved is absent, and that all forms of beauty are shadowy reflections of the beloved. In shifting from 'thou' to 'you', he may also imply that his representations of the beloved have become less personal and immediate as time has passed. As we might expect, the poet's figures point to the youth's name, especially at the end of Sonnet 98:

> They weare but fweet, but figures of delight,
> Drawne after you, you patterne of all thofe.

190   *The Secret Architecture of Shakespeare's Sonnets*

> Yet feem'd it Winter ftill, and, you away,
> As with your fhaddow I with thefe did play.
>
>   (lines 11–14, Q's spelling)

Reinforcing the conceit of mimesis, all four lines contain at least one double-letter word; line 12's 'you, you' points to *W*; and there are 'Wriothesley' anagrams in lines 11 and 14. The poet is playing with figures 'drawn after' the youth. So ends the seventh pyramid step. So ends the first part of the fair-youth section.

Sonnet 99 and the Turn of the Century

As I discussed in the last chapter, there is evidence that Shakespeare wrote the bulk of his sonnets in the mid-1590s, and that he aimed to finish his sequence a year or so after *Lucrece*. But something – call it life – must have intervened, because there is also evidence that he wrote sonnets around the turn of the century, to say nothing of the Jacobean period. One sonnet, 99, may even be a 'dating poem'. As G. R. Ledger suggests:

> [Sonnet 99 perhaps] refers us explicitly to the year 1599 . . . For this sonnet the crucial number is found by taking its unique fifteen lines and this number is joined with the sonnet number 99 to give the date 1599 . . . In favour of the adoption of this theory I should mention the predominant theme of this sonnet, that of theft, which links closely to the publication by William Jaggard in 1599 of stolen copies of two of the sonnets, 138 and 144, in *The Passionate Pilgrim*.[50]

Like Ledger, I consider the allusion speculative but worth exploring.

Shakespeare and other Elizabethans would have had good reason to be calendar-minded in the 1590s. England remained on the Julian calendar even though most of Europe had switched to the Gregorian calendar in the 1580s: it was common knowledge that England was ten days behind the continent. The scheduling of moveable feasts could point up greater discrepancies: 'True Easter' and 'Observed Easter' sometimes fell on days five weeks apart. Many saints' days, moreover, no longer counted as holy days or had been removed from the calendar entirely. *Julius Caesar* – Shakespeare's 1599 play about the person distantly responsible for the calendar that England was still using – often alludes to confusion about dates and times. The second line of the play – 'Is this a holiday?' – may have been intended as a joke.[51]

The fact that *Julius Caesar* was first performed in 1599 points to another context that may be relevant – millennialism. Historians in the Renaissance are more likely to situate periods with respect to monarchs' reigns than calendar years, but the turning of the calendar from 1599 to 1600 prompted some discussion of revolutionary change. John Weever comments ironically on such change in his satire 'A Prophecy of This Present Year, 1600', beginning with his epigraph: 'Who lives past ninety-nine, / Shall afterward speak of a blessèd time'.[52] Since the queen turned 66 in 1599 and had yet to name a successor, Elizabethans would not have needed a new century to be concerned about radical change, and English history provided them with a relevant anniversary that did not go unnoticed: Richard II was deposed by Henry Bolingbroke in 1399 and died in 1400. The 1599 publication of Sir John Hayward's *The First Part of the Life and Reign of King Henry IV* was perhaps timed with the anniversary in mind. The book sold well, attracted the attention of authorities for its content and its dedication to the Earl of Essex, and landed its author in prison. Less than two years later, in February, 1601, some of Essex's followers paid to have Shakespeare's company stage *Richard II* at the Globe Theatre; the day after the performance, Essex staged a rebellion against Elizabeth for which he lost his head.

But to return to millennialism: after Sonnet 99, Shakespeare's sequence increasingly refers to final judgement; the Southampton poems may allude to it in their total number of stanzas and poems. The number of poetic units in *Venus and Adonis*, *Lucrece*, and *Sonnets* is 665, or one short of 666; this figure may point to Judgement Day and to falling short of perfection. The total number of lines is 5,533, or 22 less than 5,555; '5533' and '5555' may represent two dates in the Anno Mundi or 'year of the world' calendar – dates that would be in the sixteenth century in the Anno Domini or 'year of our lord' calendar. More specifically, the dates may refer to the year of Southampton's birth (1573 AD) and to the year in which Southampton was 22 years old (1595–6 AD), and the numbers may be informed by Christological symbolism. Let us explore these possibilities.

Among Renaissance exegetes, there was limited consensus about when God created the world: most sixteenth- and seventeenth-century chronologists proposed dates between 3949 BC (Julius Caesar Scaliger) and 4004 BC (James Ussher).[53] Depending on the degree of approximation of 'almost', Shakespeare may hint at an older date in *As You Like It*, when Rosalind tells Orlando: 'The poor world is almost six thousand years old'. The world's exact age aside, Rosalind is alluding to a millennial number: the Second Coming is supposed to occur after six millennia, and the world is supposed to end a millennium after that. Whether or not Shakespeare believed that he was living in the world's latter days, he employs the Christian narrative of redemption in his sequence, especially in Sonnets 33, 66, and 99. In this allegory, the Christ-figure can be both the youth (33's sun) and the poet (33's crucified lover). With the first date that I have put forward, 5533 AM, '33' could symbolise redemption: Shakespeare depicts Southampton as his redeemer, perhaps with a buried pun on 'year of my lord'. With the second date, 5555 AM, '55' could allude to the Platonic World Soul (I will explore this idea in Chapter 9), and the Christ-figure is primarily Shakespeare, whose sufferings would include the infidelity of his 22-year-old patron and the death of his 11-year-old son.

In linking 1573 AD to 5533 AM and 1595–96 AD to 5555 AM, Shakespeare would have been selecting a chronology that fell within Elizabethan norms; he would also have been following norms if he rounded off the numbers for symbolic purposes. Although Renaissance calculations of the world's age vary, most of them place 5555 AM in the 1590s AD: one Elizabethan almanac, for example, establishes 1593 AD as the 5,555th year of creation.[54] And some histories, like *Holinshed's Chronicles*, supply both Anno Mundi and Anno Domini dates in their accounts. In the Holinshed account of Cymbeline, for instance, Christ's nativity is listed as '3966 AM', which not only highlights '66' but points to 3999 as the year of the crucifixion and resurrection. (Shakespeare's play *Cymbeline* notably features Imogen's 'resurrection'.) Working within the paradigm that Christ was born approximately 4,000 years after the world's creation, *Holinshed's Chronicles* employs a chronology that symbolically aligns Christ's birth and death years, reinforcing a providential view of history.

In *Sonnets*, Shakespeare similarly hints at a providential story – one that moves towards the turn of the seventeenth century. If the most of the fair-youth sonnets were written in the 1590s or refer to events of that time, and 99–100 mark the turn of the century, 97–8 may also be 'dating' poems. Southampton was in France in the spring, summer, and autumn of 1598, during which time he was separated for all but a few days from Elizabeth Vernon, a woman whom he had impregnated and to whom he was married in late August or early September.[55] In late March of 1599, he left for Ireland; in late September, he returned to England; and in October he was frequenting London playhouses.[56] Sonnets 97–8 may therefore allegorise Southampton's three-season absence in 1598 and/or 1599. And taken together, 97–9 may evoke the end of a poetic era:

they are among the sequence's most allusive sonnets, and most of the poets to whom they allude were dead or otherwise absent by the end of 1599 – Watson, Spenser, Barnes, and Constable. (For more on absent poets and 1599, see Appendix D.)

In the end, analysis of Shakespeare's numerology is most redeemed by the conceit of redeeming time. Playing with figures, reckoning with numbers, gesturing towards the idea that everything adds up – such actions suggest that the *Sonnets* poet is hoping against hope for redemption. The mindset of someone who posits a future, no matter how imminent, in which everything can finally be set right, is the mindset of someone who has already lost or fears that he is losing, especially if he is fighting for the love of an individual (as opposed to, say, rallying troops). This is the predominant mindset of the *Sonnets* poet, which may explain why he gravitates towards devices and expressions that evoke final judgement, and why he insists that time can be redeemed, even as it is slipping away.

Chapter 7

The Fair-Youth Sonnets, Part 2

Figuration and Allusion in Sonnets 97–9 (with a glance at Sonnet 96)

Just as Sonnet 9 acts as a pivot in the first pyramid step, providing transition between two halves, Sonnet 99 is pivotal in the fair-youth section, marking a transition between poems before a break in the poet-youth friendship and poems after the renewal of relations. And like Sonnet 9, Sonnet 99 can be seen as straddling two parts: it connects to preceding sonnets through its floral imagery and its indeterminate time (it seems to take place in the limbo between break-up and reunion), and it connects to ensuing sonnets through its conceit of stealing beauty from the youth, its structural position as the first poem of the eighth step, and its abrupt opening. Before analysing 99 and the eighth step, then, it helps to examine 99's connections to the sonnets that precede it, especially 97–8.

Sonnets 97–9 can be read as a trio that covers the interim between separation and reconciliation. In 97–8, the poet relates that he has been away from the youth for many months and that, during the time, he has played with 'figures' that are 'drawn after' the youth; at the end of 98, he despondently notes 'As with your shadow, I with these did play'. Although 'these' seems to refer to 'figures', editors have suggested changing the punctuation at the end of the sonnet from a period to a colon, in order to indicate that 'these' looks forward to 99's allegory of flowers that have stolen beauty from the youth. Such an intervention would be too intrusive: besides shifting the referent of 'these', it would spoil the poem's gesture towards closure, and it would unambiguously link 98 to 99. Still, it is not difficult to understand why editors have considered the change: Sonnet 99 is imagistically connected to Sonnets 97–8; in all three poems, the poet is concerned with figuration. In my view, Shakespeare wants it both ways, for two schemes: 97–8 are a pair that closes the seventh step, and 97–9 are a trio that alludes to the interim period. In this light, it becomes easier to see how 97–122 might comprise a series of sonnets that covers the entire period after the break in the poet-youth friendship, as I claimed in Chapter 5 when analysing the fair-youth section's five-group scheme.

Additional evidence that Sonnets 97–9 are a trio can be gleaned from allusions to Thomas Watson's *The Tears of Fancy* (1593), specifically to three of Watson's sonnets:

> Sonnet 46
> My mistress, seeing her fair counterfeit
> So sweetly framèd in my bleeding breast,
> On it her fancy she so firmly set,
> Thinking herself, for want of it, distressed;
> Envying that any should enjoy her image,
> Since all unworthy were of such an honour,
> Though 'gan she me command to leave my gage –
> The first end of my joy, last cause of dolor.
> But it so fast was fixèd to my heart,
> Joined with inseparable sweet commixture,
> That naught had force or power them to part:
> 'Here take my heart', quoth I, 'with it the picture'.
> But oh, coy dame! intolerable smart!
>   Rather than touch my heart or come about it,
>   She turned her face and chose to go without it.

> Sonnet 47
> Behold, dear mistress, how each pleasant green
> Will now renew his summer's livery:
> The fragrant flow'rs, which have not long been seen,
> Will flourish now ere long in bravery.
> But I, alas, within whose mourning mind
> The grafts of grief are only giv'n to grow,
> Cannot enjoy the spring which others find,
> But still my will must wither all in woe.
> The lusty *Ver*, that whilome might exchange
> My grief to joy and my delight increase,
> Springs now elsewhere and shows to me but strange –
> My winter's woe therefore can never cease.
>   In other coasts his sun doth clearly shine
>   And comfort lend to every mold but mine.

Sonnet 48
The tender buds whom cold hath long kept in
And winter's rage enforced to hide their head
Will spring and sprout, as they do now begin,
That everyone will joy to see them spread.
But cold of care so nips my joys at root
There is no hope to 'cover what is lost:
No sun doth shine that well can do it boot,
Yet still I strive but lose both toil and cost.
For what can spring that feels no force of *Ver*?
What flower can flourish where no sun doth shine?
These balls, dear love, within my breast I bear,
To break my bark and make my pith to pine.
  Needs must I fall, I fade both root and rind –
  My branches bow at blast of every wind.

Like Shakespeare's 97–8, Watson's 47–8 are about a springtime that is winter-like because the poet and beloved are separated; like Shakespeare's 99, Watson's 46 is a fifteen-line sonnet. In other words, 97–8 are followed by a fifteen-line sonnet, and 47–8 are preceded by one: the order is inverted. Inversion is a theme for both poets: 97–8 describe the period of absence from reverse perspectives; 47 inverts expected seasonal order by putting 'summer's livery' first and 'spring' later. Watson also refers to the spirit of spring as 'Ver' (Latin for 'spring'). Among other things, Watson is punning on 'Vere', the surname of his patron.[1] The artist-patron situation in 97–8 is similar to that of 47–8, and Shakespeare uses similar devices to refer to his patron's surname: 98's use of W and 'Wriothesley' anagrams.

Beyond these parallels, Watson's 46 may be echoed in Shakespeare's 24 – the sonnet that mixes thou-forms and you-forms and describes a picture of the beloved in the poet's heart:

> Mine eye hath played the painter and hath stelled
> Thy beauty's form in table of my heart;
> My body is the frame wherein 'tis held
> And pérspective it is best painters' art.
> For through the painter must you see his skill,
> To find where your true image pictured lies . . .

As noted in the last chapter, the first quatrain of Shakespeare's 24 resembles one of Daniel's quatrains, and the third quatrain resembles one of Constable's quatrains. Sonnet 24 also contains parallels to Watson's 46, namely the word 'image' and the idea of a framed and fixed painting, which is evoked in the first quatrain and developed in the second: 'My eye hath . . . stelled / your beauty's form . . . / My body is the frame wherein . . . your true image pictured lies'. In short, Shakespeare's Sonnet 24 may allude to three poets in three quatrains. In this respect, it is almost as allusive as 99 – a sonnet whose echoes of Constable, Barnes, and other poets border on plagiarism and point to an allegory of poetic theft. Finally, in the numeric counterparts to Watson's sonnets, Shakespeare's 46–8, the *Sonnets* poet speaks of a war between his eyes and heart (46), of a truce between his eyes and heart (47), and of the beloved being locked in his breast/chest (48). Both Shakespeare's and Watson's allegories involve a picture, a heart, and a theft. Watson makes his theft conceit explicit right before his trio: in Sonnet 45, the *Tears* poet says that he showed his lady 'the picture of her beauty', and that she, aghast, reacted as if his heart had 'robbed' her.

The parallels between Watson's and Shakespeare's sonnets are conceptual, imagistic, and verbal, but more than anything else they are schematic: Shakespeare appears to have reworked a device or pattern in another poet's sequence. A similar allusion may inform the poem right before the interim trio, Sonnet 96. Sonnet 96 repeats verbatim Sonnet 36's couplet, and the repetition closely resembles something in *Amoretti*: Sonnets 35 and 83 of Spenser's sequence are almost identical poems. While Elizabethan poets sometimes repeat lines of poems – last lines as first lines, as in a corona – repetitions of more than one line in non-consecutive sonnets are so unusual that modern editors have wondered whether *Amoretti*'s and *Sonnets*' repetitions are printing mistakes.[2] They are in fact purposeful: Spenser and Shakespeare are signalling changes in perspective. Both schemes call for a closer look.

In Sonnet 35 of *Amoretti*, the poet is so intent on his lady's beauty that he accuses his own eyes of 'covetize' (covetousness). Though he remains intent on the lady's 'fair sight' in 83, the verbal differences hint at change, as a combined version of the two poems helps to illustrate:

> My hungry eyes, through greedy covetize
> Still to behold the object of their paine/**payne**,
> With no contentment can themselves suffize,
> But having, pine, and having not, complaine/**complayne**.
> For lacking it, they cannot life sustayne,
> And having/**seeing** it, they gaze on it the more:
> In their/**theyr** amazement like Narcissus vaine/**vayne**
> Whose eyes him starved. So plenty makes me poor.
> Yet are mine/**myne** eyes so fillèd with the store

> Of that faire/**fayre** sight, that nothing else they brook:
> But loathe the things which they did like before
> And can no more endure on them to look.
>   All this world's glory seemeth vain to me
>   And all their/**theyr** shows but shadows, saving she.

There are two significant differences between the sonnets: 'having' becomes 'seeing' in line 6; seven words whose spelling features an *I* in 35 have a *Y* in 83. The shift from 'having' to 'seeing' suggests that the poet was initially too keen on possessing his lady or that he mistakenly believed that winning her was a given.[3] In Sonnet 83, he engages in a mode of seeing that is more Platonic and less narcissistic: the 'things' that his eyes 'did like before' could refer to features of outward beauty that he was coveting in 35; the shift from *I* to *Y* suggests that the poet has become less self-centred – less oriented towards 'I' and more towards 'you'. Support for this interpretation can be inferred from the puns on 'I' (as in the *hungry eyes–covetize* rhyme) and the fact that the word 'fair', which appears seventy-seven times in *Amoretti* in all of its variants, appears only once with an *I* in the sonnets after 35.[4] (The spelling 'faire' last appears in Sonnet 55; 'fayre' conspicuously appears three times in 56 – at the start of each quatrain.) While we may question whether the poet is any less interested in physical beauty or any less idolatrous in the second half of *Amoretti*, the allegorical scheme points to a change of heart. Something similar might be said about *Sonnets*' narrative.

Shakespeare's 36 and 96 have the same couplet, whose meaning shifts with context: 'But do not so; I love thee in such sort, / As thou being mine, mine is thy good report'. In both instances, the poet addresses the youth and 'report' connotes 'reputation'.[5] The first couplet might be translated: 'But don't consort with me or honour me; I love you in such a way that – because you are mine – I cherish your good name as if it were mine (I don't want you to be tarnished by associating with me)'. The second couplet basically means: 'But don't use your looks to lead anyone astray; I love you in such a way that – because you are mine – my good name depends on yours (I may be tarnished by your actions)'. Sonnet 36 comes in the wake of the youth's betrayal, which taints the poet and the youth: the poet is advising separation. Sonnet 96 precedes a break in relations and concludes a series of poems critical of the youth: the poet is warning about abuse of power. In 36, then, the poet is mostly worried about the youth's reputation; in 96, his own 'report' is central and 'mine is thy good report' is double-edged: the poet may be hinting that the youth's good name is merely the poet's good account of the youth.

With 35 and 83, Spenser frames a series of 49 sonnets, perhaps evoking the climacteric of body (7×7 years). With 36 and 96, Shakespeare frames a series of sonnets that increasingly refers to the youth's imperfections, whose centre sonnet is 66, and whose framing sonnets' numbers are multiples of six (6×6 and 6×16). The emphasis on '6' points to perfection/imperfection. Number symbolism aside, the repetition of 36's couplet provides rhetorical closure. Separation follows.

The Eighth Pyramid Step

The eighth pyramid step begins and ends by delineating thresholds. The first poem, Sonnet 99, divides the fair-youth series into two parts: the sonnets before it portray a period of separation between poet and youth; the sonnets after it speak of renewed relations. The final sonnet, 108, marks an end to the poems of praise – a series that arguably begins with Sonnet 18, a poem that both praises the youth and questions the possibility of praising him adequately. The eighth step also evokes the end of an era and makes pointed allusions to other poets, continuing a trend that started in the seventh step and has links to the rival-poet series.

As its own scheme, the eighth step can be regarded as Sonnet 99 plus three trios:

Th   3rd 3rd   Y   Y   Y   3rd   Y   Th   Th
99   (100–101 102) (103–104 105) (106–107 108)

The trios' pronouns are less telling than their 'linked pair plus conclusion' structure:

Trio   *Description*

100–2   In 100–1, the poet addresses his muse and questions her silence. In 102, he claims that, although his love may seem 'more weak', it has in fact 'strengthened' over time. 102 completes the trio by turning to address the youth, and by using the conjunctive adverb 'therefore' in the couplet: 'Therefore . . . I sometime hold my tongue, / Because I would not dull you with my song'.

103–5   Continuing to address the youth, 103 returns to discussing the muse: the poet derides his muse for bringing forth 'poverty' and tells the youth to look into the mirror – there the youth will find 'much more' than what is in the poetry. 104 similarly focuses on the youth's appearance: the poet declares that the youth's beauty is as 'green' as ever, and he addresses future generations: 'Ere you were born was beauty's summer dead'. In 105, the poet may still be addressing the future: he begins by declaring or imploring 'Let not my love be called idolatry' and proceeds to describe the youth as the only beloved in history who has been 'Fair, kind, and true'.

106–8   In 106, the poet continues the theme of the beloved's place in history: meditating on the beauties praised in 'the chronicle of wasted time', he declares that all previous expressions of praise 'are but prophecies' of the youth. In 107, he criticises the world's 'prophetic soul', which predicted an end to his love. In 108, he returns to the step's opening theme that there is nothing new to say about the youth, declaring that he will keep saying the same things as if he were saying prayers.

Like the seventh step's trios, the eighth's might be called a trio of trios: they are interconnected.

The eighth step's final sonnet, 108, broadly gestures towards closure:

> What's in the brain that ink may character,
> Which hath not figured to thee my true spirit?
> What's new to speak, what new to register,
> That may express my love or thy dear merit?
> Nothing, sweet boy, but yet, like prayers divine,
> I must each day say o'er the very same,
> Counting no old thing old: thou mine, I thine,
> Ev'n as when first I hallowed thy fair name.
> – So that eternal love in love's fresh case
> Weighs not the dust and injury of age,
> Nor gives to necessary wrinkles place,
> But makes antiquity for aye his page:
>   Finding the first conceit of love there bred,
>   Where time and outward form would show it dead.

The poet argues that there is nothing more to say about the youth – that all he can do is repeat words like daily prayers. Besides completing a trio that evokes past beauty, present peace, and eternity, 108 recalls the step's opening sonnets, in which the poet berated himself for not singing the youth's praises. In revisiting arguments about needing and not needing to speak, the sonnet rounds off the eighth step. As the final poem of seven consecutive trios, it rounds off the seventh and eighth steps – a group linked by 97–9. Sonnet 108 also caps a group of thirty-three sonnets going back to the rival-poet series: in 76, the poet asks 'Why write I still all one, ever the same?' and calls the youth 'sweet love'; in 108, he questions whether there is anything 'new to speak' and calls the youth 'sweet boy'. In different ways, then, Sonnet 108 completes the eighth step, the seventh and eighth steps, and the sixth through eighth steps.

As if that were not enough, Sonnet 108 looks back to the start of the fair-youth section and forward to its end. In the sestet, the poet asserts that 'eternal love ... makes antiquity ... his page', and that it does so by finding 'the first conceit of love' in an unexpected place – in an 'outward form' such as a wrinkle. In arguing that anyone whose love is eternal can always look at the beloved and see love's first conceit there, the poet is playing with different senses of 'conceit': the figurative expression of a thought, the apprehension of an idea, and the creation of a child. The third sense recalls the seventeen procreation sonnets and anticipates the seventeen marriage sonnets at the end of the fair-youth section. With 'sweet boy', 108 anticipates 126, in which the poet calls the youth 'lovely boy'. 'Sweet boy' is used in Shakespeare's plays 'by fathers to their sons, and makes great claims to intimacy'.[6] Near the end of *2 Henry IV*, for example, Falstaff calls Hal 'sweet boy', imagining that he is on intimate terms with the new king:

> FALSTAFF
> God save thee, my sweet boy.
>
> HENRY V
> My Lord Chief Justice, speak to that vain man.
>
> CHIEF JUSTICE
> Have you your wits? Know you what 'tis you speak?
>
> FALSTAFF
> My king! my Jove! I speak to thee, my heart!
>
> HENRY V
> I know thee not, old man.

Falstaff's inappropriate overtures prompt his banishment. Whatever its exact claim to intimacy, 108's 'sweet boy', like 126's 'lovely boy', signals an end. And in asserting that his poetry written for the youth will endure forever on the printed page, the poet employs two conceits involving boys: that Time is the page-boy for his lord Love, and that Love is a boy (Cupid).

Sonnet 108 also gestures towards completion with an allusion to Sidney. As Duncan-Jones explains, when the poet reaches 'the total number of sonnets in Sidney's *Astrophil and Stella*', he 'takes stock of his achievements'.[7] Like other poets of his era, Shakespeare seems to have associated the number 108 with Sidney and have regarded it as a limit.[8] For Sidney, 108 would have been useful in at least two ways: as a number divisible by 2, 3, 4, 6, 9, and 12, it facilitates schematic partitioning; as the number of suitors to Penelope in Homer's *Odyssey*, it is symbolic.[9] More crucial to *Sonnets* is the fact that *Astrophil and Stella* contains 108 sonnets and 108 stanzas, or 216 units in all (6×6×6): both Sidney and Shakespeare associate 108 with perfection and completion, even as they evoke imperfection.

Containing Rivals: Poetic and Temporal Allusions in the Eighth Pyramid Step

Shakespeare echoes other poets throughout his sequence, but allusions increase in the wake of the rival-poet series and are especially prominent in the eighth pyramid step. I have argued that the final poems of the sixth step allude to at least two poets (Spenser and Daniel), that the final poems of the seventh step echo at least one poet (Watson), that the first poem of the eighth step echoes at least two poets (Constable and Barnes), and that poems at the border of the seventh and eighth steps refer to the passage of time. Poetic and temporal allusions continue through the eighth step. Sonnet 106's poetic allusions are as distinct as 99's: Shakespeare draws on at least three poets. Overt temporal allusions occur in 104 and 107: 104 refers to a three-year period of acquaintance with the youth; 107 refers to a time when prophecies of doom were proved wrong. With the allusions, Shakespeare develops two related themes: that the youth contains all previous beloveds, and that *Sonnets* contains all previous sequences.

In the centre poem of the eighth step's centre trio, the poet reassures the youth:

> Sonnet 104
> To me, fair friend, you never can be old,
> For as you were when first your eye I eyed,
> Such seems your beauty still. Three winters' cold
> Have from the forests shook three summers' pride,

> Three beauteous springs to yellow autumn turned
> In process of the seasons have I seen,
> Three April perfumes in three hot Junes burned
> Since first I saw you fresh, which yet are green.
> Ah yet doth beauty, like a dial hand,
> Steal from his figure, and no pace perceived;
> So your sweet hue, which methinks still doth stand,
> Hath motion, and mine eye may be deceived –
>   For fear of which, hear this, thou age unbred:
>   Ere you were born was beauty's summer dead.

The poet begins by proclaiming that the youth never grows old. As he develops this idea in the octave, he overflows three pairs of lines with three expressions for three years: 'Three winters' cold / Have . . .'; 'Three beauteous springs . . . / In process'; and 'Three April perfumes . . . / Since'. The enjambments set up a short declaration ('I saw you fresh, which yet are green'), and the entire octave underscores the discrepancy between time passing and beauty remaining. But even as he conveys devotion, the poet betrays doubts. Uncertainty is expressed more openly in the sestet. With the image of a sundial's shadow or a clock's hand stealing away from the numeral it passes, the poet suggests that Time is a thief. By emphasising 'still' in 'still doth stand', by separating 'your sweet hue' from 'Hath motion', and by punning on 'I' in 'eye may be deceived', he undercuts his reassurances, perhaps hinting that the youth is unfaithful. In the couplet, he addresses unborn readers, proleptically announcing beauty's passing. His gesture to the future may conceal a more immediate fear – that beauty's truth or the youth's fidelity is already gone. This interpretation gains support from Sonnets 14 and 41, which express similar concerns. In 14, the poet predicts that the youth's death will be 'truth's and beauty's doom'; in 41, he concludes that the youth has used his beauty to break truth and troth.

    Even if we suppose that Sonnet 104 expresses wholehearted devotion to the youth, the poet is ambiguous about time. How much time has passed since he 'first' saw the youth, and what does 'saw you fresh' mean? The poet may simply be saying that three years have passed since he first met the youth in person, when the youth was in his first bloom. But a literal three-year period is hard to square with a time frame in which Southampton is the youth (or Pembroke, for that matter), especially if the poem dates from the Jacobean period: Shakespeare would have first seen him long before 1603. Shakespeare may of course be telescoping events for poetic purposes. Alternatively, 'When first I saw you fresh' could mean something like 'the first time that I saw you in all your glory'. Yet another possibility is the period when Southampton was imprisoned in the Tower – from February 1601 to April 1603 – and perhaps some months before and after that time. (In Sonnet 107, the poet says 'now my love looks fresh' and boasts that his love is not 'forfeit to a confined doom'.[10]) Finally, there is the remote possibility that the three references to three years denote a nine-year period. Whatever the exact chronology, the renewal of the friendship is presented as a resurrection or Second Coming. For that reason alone Shakespeare may have alluded to three years, as an analogue to Christ's three days in the tomb.

Sonnet 106 likens the youth to Christ by portraying him as the fulfilment of prophecies:

> When in the chronicle of wasted time
> I see descriptions of the fairest wights
> And beauty making beautiful old rhyme
> In praise of ladies dead and lovely knights,
> Then in the blazon of sweet beauty's best,
> Of hand, of foot, of lip, of eye, of brow,
> I see their ántique pen would have expressed
> Ev'n such a beauty as you master now.
> So all their praises are but prophecies
> Of this our time, all you prefiguring,
> And for they looked but with divining eyes,
> They had not skill enough your worth to sing;
>   For we, which now behold these present days,
>   Have eyes to wonder, but lack tongues to praise.

The youth is a messianic beauty who surpasses beauties of former times. Modern writers lack the art to praise him; ancient writers saw him but darkly. In Q, 'skill enough' is 'still enough': Shakespeare may be suggesting that the ancients did not see enough of the youth to sing about his worth, or that they lacked the means to sing about all his worth. He may also be hinting that 'not still enough your worth' has every 'Wriothesley' letter except one *E*, and that 'we, which now behold these present days' has all eleven letters.[11] Sonnet 106 describes the youth as the sum of all previous beauties and the sum of the most beautiful parts of beauties.[12] It is also the last of the 'When I' sonnets – six poems that take up the theme of perfection and imperfection.

Sonnet 106 not only presents the youth as the sum of all previous beauties; it implies that *Sonnets* is the culmination of all previous sequences. Note that the poem alludes to at least three poets – Spenser,

Constable, and Daniel. As Patrick Cheney has shown, 106's allusions to Spenser are both extensive and intensive. 'Wight' is a common archaism in *The Faerie Queene*, and 'lovely knights' is a 'Spenserian repetition'; it appears in conjunction with 'ladies' in Book 5 of *The Faerie Queene* ('Fit for such ladies and such lovely knights'), as it does in 106.[13] 'Ladies dead' similarly recalls Spenser, in that Spenser likes to invert the standard adjective-noun syntax and employ a postpositive 'dead' in contexts relating to Queen Elizabeth and poetry's immortalising power. A notable example occurs in Sonnet 33 of *Amoretti*, where the phrases 'Queen of Faëry' and 'praises dead' appear in close order: 'Great wrong I do, I can it not deny, / To that most sacred Empress, my dear dread, / Not finishing her Queen of Faëry, / That might enlarge her living praises dead'.[14] Elizabeth, of course, may have been literally dead when Shakespeare wrote Sonnet 106.

Cheney also cites the Proems to Books 1 and 5 of *The Faerie Queene*:

> Lo I the man, whose Muse whilome did mask
>   (As Time her taught) in lowly shepherd's weeds,
> Am now enforced a far unfitter task –
> For trumpets stern to change mine oaten reeds
> *And sing of knights' and ladies' gentle deeds;*
> *Whose praises having slept in silence long,*
> Me, all too mean, the sacred Muse areeds
> *To blazon* broad amongst her learnèd throng:
> Fierce wars and faithful loves shall moralise my song.
>   (stanza 1 of the Proem to Book 1, italics added)

> So oft as I, with state of *present time*,
>   The image of the *ántique* world compare
>   (Whenas man's age was in his freshest prime
>   And the first blossom of fair virtue bare),
>   Such odds I find twixt those, and *these* which are,
>   As that, through long continuance of his course,
>   Me seems the world is run quite out of square
>   From the first point of his appointed source
> And, being once amiss, grows daily worse and worse.
>   (stanza 1 of the Proem to Book 5, italics added)[15]

The Proem to Book 1 sets a literary agenda: Spenser is a Virgilian poet progressing from pastoral to epic. The Proem to Book 5 sets a historical and ethical agenda: modern times are less virtuous than ancient times; the world is growing worse. Cheney argues that 'ladies and knights' in Sonnet 106 'more clearly recalls' Spenser's lines about ladies and knights than Daniel's 'knights and paladins', and that Shakespeare is deeply engaged with Spenser's epic and a tradition going back to Virgil.[16] In his view, Shakespeare intervenes in the tradition in a radically Ovidian way, employing Spenser's 'counter-Petrarchan' discourse but rejecting Spenser's Virgilian model. Spenser and Shakespeare are 'counter-Petrarchan' rather than 'anti-Petrarchan': they would avoid Petrarchan excess while expressing a Petrarchan preference for love poetry over war poetry. But unlike Spenser, Shakespeare favours lyric and dramatic poetry over epic. In brief, Cheney regards 106 as a poem that primarily targets Spenser, especially Spenser's idea of a poetic career.

As helpful as Cheney's analysis is, it gives short shrift to the Constable and Daniel allusions in Sonnet 106. The most clearly echoed Constable poem is 'To his mistress, upon occasion of a Petrarch he gave her, showing her the reason why the Italian commentators dissent so much in the exposition thereof':

> Miracle of the world! – I never will deny
> That former poets praise the beauty of their days,
> But all those beauties were but figures of thy praise,
> And all those poets did of thee but prophesy.
> Thy coming to the world hath taught us to descry
> What Petrarch's Laura meant, for truth the lip bewrays
> Lo! why th' Italians, yet which never saw thy rays,
> To find out Petrarch's sense such forgèd glosses try!
> The beauties which he in a veil enclosed beheld
> But revelations were within his surest heart
> By which in parables thy coming he foretold.
> His songs were hymns of thee, which only now before
>   Thy image should be sung; for thou that goddess art
>   Which only we without idolatry adore.

Shakespeare borrows more than a theme: the phrasing 'all their praises are but prophecies . . . all you prefiguring' is close to 'all those beauties were but figures of thy praise', and the idea that older poets looked with 'divining eyes' and 'had not skill enough your worth to sing' is analogous to the Italian commentators' failure to decipher Petrarch's Laura. (Also note that both Shakespeare and Constable use a *days–praise* rhyme, and that 'only we without idolatry adore' is similar to Sonnet 105's 'Let not my love be called idolatry'.) Sonnet 106 responds to a sonnet about the Petrarchan tradition and develops a messianic conceit. Shakespeare places himself at the end of a tradition: he, not

Constable, is the final poet-prophet. Like the allusions to *The Faerie Queene*, the allusions to 'Miracle of the world' point to poetic competition and genre.

So what might Constable have meant to Shakespeare? Sir Henry Constable (1562–1613) was a gentleman who had friends and relations in English and Scottish high nobility.[17] In 1591, Constable left England and converted to Catholicism; he did not return to his native land until 1603. While he was gone, his poetic reputation flourished. Editions of *Diana* appeared in 1592 and 1594; another version circulated in manuscript. In Drayton's 1599 sonnet 'Let each command as best shall like his mind', Constable is cited as one of the age's best sonnet writers. For English poets, then, Constable was a living and worthy heir to the Petrarchan tradition. This may simply mean that he was a convenient figure for Shakespeare's presentation of himself as the final poet-prophet, but if Sonnet 106 was written after 1603 the allusions could be inflected by Constable's Jacobean reputation. Through his connections to court, Constable obtained permission to return to England in 1603, but he wore out his welcome by seeking to secure policies of tolerance for Catholics. From April to July of 1604, he was imprisoned in the Tower, after which he was placed under house arrest; in subsequent years, he was imprisoned again. The Jacobean Constable, then, would have been known for his conversion to Catholicism and his efforts on behalf of Catholics; in situating Constable in a series of poet-prophets, Shakespeare could be employing an allegory 'old faith' and 'new faith'.

Let us turn now to the Daniel sonnet to which Sonnet 106 alludes:

> Let others sing of knights and paladins
> In agèd accents and untimely words,
> Paint shadows in imaginary lines
> Which well the reach of their high wits records –
> But I must sing of thee, and those fair eyes
> Auténtique shall my verse in time to come,
> When yet th' unborn shall say, 'Lo where she lies,
> Whose beauty made him speak that else was dumb'.
> These are the arks, the trophies I erect,
> That fortify thy name against old age;
> And these thy sacred virtues must protect
> Against the dark and Time's consuming rage.
>   Though th' error of my youth they shall discover,
>   Suffice they show I lived and was thy lover.

The attack on epic-romance appears to have a specific target – *The Faerie Queene*, a poem known for its archaisms ('untimely words'). Both Sonnet 106 and 'Let others sing of knights' imply that *The Faerie Queene* is an old-fashioned poem whose matter and manner distance its poet from authentic modern beauty. Shakespeare uses 'wights' and 'ántique' to emphasise old-fashionedness; Daniel uses 'agèd' and 'auténtique' to convey that his own poetry and Delia's beauty are the opposite of old and imaginary. (The verb 'auténtique' means 'make vivid, real, authoritative'.) With 'those fair eyes / Auténtique shall my verse', Daniel is saying that his poetry will show the future how beautiful Delia's eyes are ('my verse shall make those eyes vivid') and that Delia's eyes will give lasting power to his poetry ('those eyes shall make my verse vivid').[18] Like the *Sonnets* poet in Sonnet 78, the *Delia* poet claims that he would not be able to write sonnets without the beloved's inspiration.

'Let others sing of knights' is notably echoed elsewhere in Shakespeare's sequence – in Sonnets 17 and 31. In three non-consecutive lines of Sonnet 17, Shakespeare draws on three consecutive lines of Daniel's 'Let others sing of knights':

> But I must sing of thee, and those fair eyes
> Auténtique shall my verse in time to come,
> When yet th' unborn shall say, 'Lo where she lies . . .'
> (Daniel, lines 5–7)

> Who will believe my verse in time to come?
> If I could write the beauty of your eyes,
> The age to come would say, 'This poet lies . . .'
> (Shakespeare, lines 1, 5, and 7)[19]

Shakespeare has taken parts of 'Let others sing of knights' and recombined them, a gesture that squares with the idea that the poet is re-membering the youth by gathering the youth's parts. (Sonnet 17 contains two pairs of 'Wriothesley' anagrams.) The *Sonnets* poet fears that future readers will see his praise of the youth as proof that he 'lies'; authentication for his verse will not simply come from the beloved's eyes. Later in the poem, he speaks of 'The stretchèd meter of an antique song', echoing Daniel's 'agèd accents' with a reference to outdated versification and with a use of a participle whose '-ed' pronunciation was already old-fashioned in the 1590s.

As noted in the last chapter, Shakespeare draws on Constable's sonnets 'Grace full of grace' and 'Miracle of the world' in 31's octave. He draws on Daniel's poem in the sestet:

> Thou art the grave where buried love doth live,
> Hung with the trophies of my lovers gone,
> Who all their parts of me to thee did give:
> That due of many now is thine alone.
>   Their images I loved I view in thee,
>   And thou, all they, hast all the all of me.

'Trophies' does not appear in the Constable sonnets, but it does appear in Daniel: 'These are the arks, the trophies I erect'. As in Sonnet 106, Shakespeare comments on tradition while alluding to other poets. And in both 31 and 106, Daniel emerges as his most immediate antagonist. In redeploying Daniel's martial image of a trophy, Shakespeare underscores poetic competition.

The Ninth and Tenth Pyramid Steps

Sonnets' fair-youth section concludes with a pair of pyramid steps in which the poet confesses infidelity to the youth, asks to be regarded as true, and defies time's power. These seventeen sonnets can be read as a nuptial series that parallels the procreation series: in 109–25, the poet confess to misdeeds in order to remove impediments to love, and he concludes with a request for 'mutual render, only thee for me'. But the series is not focused entirely on marriage: nuptials are linked to judgement and Judgement Day. As the poet attempts to effect a permanent reconciliation with the youth, complications arise.

The ninth and tenth steps' nuptial scheme belongs to a larger redemptive scheme. After the break in the poet-youth friendship, at least three seasons pass before the poet renews friendship with the youth and promises to 'redeem, / In gentle numbers, time so idly spent' (100). With literary and temporal allusions, the eighth step evokes redeeming time through verse-writing. But the poet also seeks forgiveness, if not a renewal of love through formal recommitment. Time is running out, though – like sand in an hourglass, the pyramid steps are shrinking. The poet's last chance to make things right is conveyed by Sonnets 97–122. These sonnets contain 365 lines, perhaps symbolising a year of renewed friendship between poet and youth. If Shakespeare is alluding to an actual 365-day period, it might be one of the years soon after James I came to the throne and Southampton was released from prison: 1603–4 or 1604–5. In the 1604–5 Christmas season, Shakespeare's company revived an old play for private performance at Southampton's house in London – *Love's Labour's Lost*.[20]

Given that the seventh and eighth steps both contain a trio of trios, we might expect the nine-sonnet ninth step to continue the trend. But it does not:

Th   Th   Y   Y   Y   Y   Y   3rd   Y
(109–110) (111–112) (113–114) (115 116 117)

One reason why the step initially avoids trios can be gleaned from Sonnet 111, the first you-sonnet in a series of 11 'transgression' sonnets that will be discussed shortly: in order to inaugurate the series with a poem whose number ends in '11' and close it with a poem whose number is 11×11, Shakespeare may have had to make adjustments with subgroups and forms of address. As its own group, the ninth step consists of three pairs and a trio. In each pair, the poet both admits to mistakes and refers to mitigating circumstances:

Pair	Description
109–10	In 109, the poet exclaims: 'O never say that I was false of heart, / Though absence seemed my flame to qualify'. In 110, he admits that he has 'gone here and there', but adds that 'all is done'; he 'never more will grind' his 'appetite' on 'newer proof'.
111–12	In 111, the poet asks the youth to excuse his 'public manners' and to pity him; in 112, he asserts that the youth's 'love and pity' remove the mark that 'vulgar scandal' stamped on him.
113–14	In 113, the poet claims that he sees the youth everywhere and that his 'true mind' is what makes him see the images. In 114, he wonders about the source of his mind's ability to transform even 'monsters' into images of the youth, eventually deciding that his mind is flattered by his eyes, which see what they want to see.

The impulse to name and excuse faults is also present in Sonnets 115–17: this trio is linked via its legal conceits. In Sonnet 117, the poet even proclaims that he will plead guilty to all charges, provided that his motive – to test the youth – is taken into account.

While the tenth step could be analysed by itself (as two four-sonnet halves), the poet's continued efforts to clear himself suggests that the ninth and tenth steps are linked. Like 117, Sonnet 118 refers to a test of love, only this time the poet is testing himself:

> Like as to make our appetites more keen,
> With eager compounds we our palate urge;
> As to prevent our maladies unseen,
> We sicken to shun sickness when we purge –
> Ev'n so, being full of your ne'er-cloying sweetness,
> To bitter sauces did I frame my feeding;
> And, sick of welfare, found a kind of meetness
> To be diseased ere that there was true needing.
> Thus policy in love, t'anticipate
> The ills that were not, grew to faults assurèd
> And brought to medicine a healthful state,
> Which rank of goodness would by ill be curèd.
>   But thence I learn and find the lesson true:
>   Drugs poison him that so fell sick of you.

In evoking 'appetite', the poet echoes Sonnet 110: 'Mine appetite I never more will grind / On newer proof'. He also uses a double simile: he compares his wayward actions to sharpening the appetite and to preventing illness. His evocation of 'eager compounds' recalls his criticisms of 'compounds strange' (76) and 'couplement[s] of proud compare' (21). Having broken amatory faith, the poet is now breaking stylistic faith. In the tenth step's final sonnet, 125, the poet strains to return to a mode of unadulterated love and writing: he criticises 'dwellers on form and favor' who forgo 'simple savor' for 'compound sweet', and he asks the youth to accept his offering as a gift that 'is not mixed with seconds' and that 'knows no art'.

The infidelities to which the poet refers seem personal, but what are they exactly? In Sonnet 109, the poet speaks of absence rather than active misdeeds; in 120, he compares his infidelity to the youth's: 'if you were by my unkindness shaken / As I by yours, you've passed a hell of time, / And I, a tyrant, have no leisure taken / To weigh how once I suffered in your crime'. His unkindness seems equivalent to the youth's crime of sleeping with the mistress. But if he is guilty of sleeping with one of the youth's lovers, his claim that he may have hurt the youth as much as the youth hurt him is strained, even if he imagines that the youth is equally invested in the friendship. More to the point, the infidelities are not clearly amatory. In Sonnets 110 and 111, the poet refers to public behaviour if not specifically to acting: 'I have . . . made myself a motley to the view'; 'Fortune [gave me] public means which public manners breeds'. In 112, he speaks of a 'vulgar scandal', and in 118–19, he confesses to a harmful regimen for preventing love's illnesses and to drinking 'Siren tears'. The poet may be alluding to several wrongdoings, such as keeping dubious company, womanising, and contracting a disease.

Whatever the infidelities are, they are framed in terms of judgement and marriage. This is especially true of the eleven-poem transgression series, whose central sonnet is 116:

> Let me not to the marriage of true minds
> Admit impediments. Love is not love
> Which alters when it alteration finds
> Or bends with the remover to remove:
> O no, it is an ever-fixèd mark
> That looks on tempests and is never shaken;
> It is the star to every wand'ring bark
> Whose worth's unknown, although his height be taken.
> Love's not Time's fool, though rosy lips and cheeks
> Within his bending sickle's compass come;
> Love alters not with his brief hours and weeks
> But bears it out, ev'n to the edge of doom.
>   If this be error and upon me proved,
>   I never writ, nor no man ever loved.

The poet speaks of a 'marriage of true minds' and a love that lasts until Doomsday. In stressing that marriage is a lifelong pact, he is echoing the language of the standard marriage ceremony:

> I require and charge you (as you will answer at the dreadful day of judgement, when the secrets of all hearts shall be disclosed) that if either you do know any impediment why ye may not be lawfully joined together in matrimony, that ye confess it. For be ye well assured, that so many as be coupled together otherwise than God's word doth allow are not joined of God; neither is their matrimony lawful. ('Form of Solemnization of Matrimony', *The Book of Common Prayer*[21])

This passage is often cited in notes to 116, though most commentators omit the parenthetical admonishment, with its 'day of judgement' and 'secrets of all hearts'. Along with this warning, there is legal language. Such language is prominent in the accompanying instructions:

> At which day of marriage, if any man do allege any impediment why they may not be coupled together in matrimony, [he] will be bound . . . to the parties . . . to prove his allegation: then the solemnization must be deferred unto such time as the truth be tried.

The poet evokes a trial of truth. In this light, 116's legalisms are neither incongruous nor defensive. The same might be said of the negative expressions: Shakespeare draws on a tradition of defining God and Love in terms of things that they are not. One such definition is still read at weddings: 'Love does not envy, it does not boast, it is not proud. It does not dishonour others, it is not self-seeking, it is not easily angered, it keeps no record of wrongs' (1 Corinthians 13:4–6).[22]

Sonnet 116 is organisationally and thematically central to the transgression series:

```
Y      Y       Y    Y       Y   3rd  Y     Y   3rd    Y    3rd
(111–112)  (113–114)  (115  116  117)  (118–119)  (120  121)
```

Preceded by two pairs of you-sonnets that admit to wrongdoing and ask for understanding, the central trio continues in that defensive mode with altered tactics: in 115, the poet confesses to 'lying' about not being able to love the youth more; in 116, he switches to third-person address and attempts to define love; and in 117, he claims that his dubious actions were meant to test the youth. In other words, instead of pleading mitigating circumstances, the poet maintains that his misdeeds are not misdeeds at all. The remaining sonnets add a twist to this rhetorical strategy. The poet argues first that his missteps served a greater good, claiming that he had hoped 'to anticipate . . . ills' (118) and that 'better is by evil still made better' (119). He then alludes to the youth's earlier betrayal, which 'now becomes a fee' for anything the poet might have done wrong (120). Finally, he suggests that he is only 'vile' in reputation and that people who accuse him of wrongdoings 'reckon up their own' (121). Employing indirect address in two of the last three sonnets, the poet distances himself from blame.

In the transgression series, 116 is the first sonnet to use indirect address and the first to link missteps and marriage; the poet's pleas after it are both more personal and more impersonal. They are more personal because they appeal for forgiveness and offer commitment. They are more impersonal because they resort to indirect address and evoke an imaginary marriage. And while the conceit of a trial continues after 117, the poet's defence is directed more to an outside jury. In 118–21, he pleads again for forgiveness, but he addresses the youth only in the couplet of 118, and he does not address the youth at all in 119 and 121. After 121, there are four sonnets in the tenth pyramid step: one in which the poet defends giving away a book, and the 'No' trio. The trio addresses Time, no one in particular, and the youth. Again, the rhetorical effect is distance. The poet appeals to judgement beyond the youth: to his friends, God, posterity.

Sonnet 125 is the poet's last vigourous attempt to move the youth:

> Were't aught to me I bore the canopy,
> With my extern the outward honouring,
> Or laid great bases for eternity,
> Which proves more short than waste or ruining?
> Have I not seen dwellers on form and favor
> Lose all and more by paying too much rent,
> For compound sweet, forgoing simple savor,
> Pitiful thrivers, in their gazing spent?
> No! Let me be obsequious in thy heart,
> And take thou my oblation, poor but free,
> Which is not mixed with seconds, knows no art
> But mutual render, only me for thee.
>   Hence, thou suborned informer! A true soul,
>   When most impeached, stands least in thy control.

Duncan-Jones suggests that first quatrain alludes to James I's procession in 1604, a festivity in which eight knights bore a canopy over the king and for which a triumphal arch with pyramids was erected.[23] The poet distances himself from pageantry, evoking marriage and communion as simple sacraments. J. W. Lever argues that 'oblation' is 'the traditional bride-cake of pure flour', and that 'mixed with seconds' hints at ' ulterior motives' and 'time-serving'.[24] Booth notes that 'many particulars ... pertain to Holy Communion', and that, before the consecration of the host, the priest speaks of Christ's death as 'a full, perfect, and sufficient sacrifice, oblation, and satisfaction for the sins of the whole world'.[25] The 'suborned informer' can be read as historical, fictional, or historical-fictional; as the youth or an unknown, as Time or Slander. In all cases, 'Hence, thou suborned informer!' is abrupt. If we read Sonnet 125 as a closing argument in a trial that has been in session since Sonnet 109, the informer is the latest devil's advocate. In a sense, the poet has suborned his own accuser – and now dismisses him.

Shakespeare's and Spenser's Marriage Plots

The parallels between *Amoretti* and *Sonnets* are structural, conceptual, imagistic, and verbal. For present purposes, what matters is *Amoretti*'s marriage plot. To appreciate this plot and its impact on *Sonnets* requires some familiarity with *Amoretti*'s organisation. Spenser uses the total numbers of poems and stanzas of his sequence to construct a variety of schemes. The relevant scheme consists of 117 poetic units – the eighty-nine sonnets, the four anacreontic poems, and the twenty-four stanzas of 'Epithalamion':

Sonnets 1–28   Sonnets 29–56   (Sonnets 57–61)   Sonnets 62–89   Non-sonnets
  28 poems   28 poems   28 poems   28 units

At the centre of this scheme are Sonnets 57–61, in which the poet portrays the end of his 'war' with his lady: in 57, the poet queries, 'Sweet warrior, when shall I have peace with you?'; in 60, he cites 'Mars' for the last time; and in 61, he promises that 'henceforth' he will not dare 'accuse [his lady] of pride' or 'rashly blame' her. The lovers have come to an understanding about good courtship and may have made private vows. More simply, the poet has learned something from his lady. This can be gleaned from the two pairs of 28 units. In Sonnet 1, the poet calls his lady 'My soul's long-lackèd food'. Sonnet 29 is the first poem in which the lady speaks: she tells the poet that the laurel is not won by poets but by 'victors'. Sonnet 62 alludes to 'Lady Day' (the feast of the Annunciation) and announces a new year. And the first poem of the non-sonnet group, 'In youth, before I waxèd old', dramatises a misstep: when the poet first fell in love, he was stung when he tried to 'grope for honey'. With its four different groups, then, the 117-unit scheme hints that the lady teaches the poet lessons in love, thereby nourishing his soul. *Sonnets* similarly includes a lady-oriented series of 28 sonnets, except the mistress's lessons are more carnal, and the sequence casts doubt on whether anyone learns from love.

The three sonnets at the scheme's centre – 58–60 – are important for *Sonnets*. The first two are a pair:

Sonnet 58

By her that is most assured to her self

Weak is th'assurance that weak flesh reposeth
In her own power and scorneth others' aid:
That soonest falls when as she most supposeth
Her self assured and is of naught afraid.
All flesh is frail and all her strength unstayed
Like a vain bubble blowen up with air;
Devouring time and changeful chance have preyed
Her glory's pride, that none may it repair.
Ne none so rich or wise, so strong or fair,

But faileth trusting on his own assurance;
And he that standeth on the highest stair
Falls lowest – for on earth naught hath endurance.
  Why then do ye proud-fair misdeem so far
  That to your self ye most assurèd are?

Sonnet 59
Thrice happy she that is so well assured
Unto herself and settled so in heart
That neither will for better be allured
Nor feared with worse to any chance to start –
But, like a steady ship, doth strongly part
The raging waves and keeps her course aright,
Nor aught for tempest doth from it depart,
Nor aught for fairer weather's false delight.
Such self-assurance need not fear the spite
Of grudging foes, nor favor seek of friends –
But in the stay of her own steadfast might
Neither to one herself nor other bends.
  Most happy she that most assured doth rest;
  But he most happy who such one loves best.

Sonnet 58 has a superscription: 'By her that is most assured to her self'. 'By her' could mean 'near her' or 'concerning her' – the latter has precedents in George Gascoigne – but the least strained sense is 'spoken by her', just as the least strained sense of 'that' is 'who'.[26] If the lady is speaking, 'ye proud-fair' would seem directed at other women. But this interpretation does not resolve all ambiguities: 'Spoken by her who is most assured to her self' could mean that the speaker is addressing her self or herself, that she is self-assured, that she is confident about the state of her soul, or that she is betrothed to herself. (In Elizabethan English, 'assured' commonly means 'betrothed'.[27]) Baffled by the superscription, some modern editors argue that it was meant for Sonnet 59.[28] The ambiguities might be resolved if a soul were speaking: souls are often gendered female, and the speaker makes a case against the flesh. But the best solution is that the ambiguity is meant to linger. Like the *Sonnets* poet, who accuses the youth of being 'contracted' to his own eyes (Sonnet 1), the *Amoretti* poet argues that to be too self-assured or too betrothed to oneself is to be less secure and less fulfilled, and he blurs distinctions between himself and his lady, anticipating their union. In *Sonnets*, too, there is ambiguity at the heart of the sequence: in Sonnet 77, it is not clear who is addressing whom and whether the poem's gift book is Sonnet 122's book. Shakespeare may have learned this mode of ambiguity from Spenser.

A series of parallels between Sonnet 59 and Sonnet 116 points strongly to influence:

Sonnet 59, *Amoretti*	Sonnet 116, *Shakespeare's Sonnets*
Thrice happy she that is so well assured / Unto herself, and settled so in heart / That neither will for better be allured / Nor feared with worse to any chance to start –	Let me not to the marriage of true minds / Admit impediments. Love is not love / Which alters when it alteration finds / Or bends with the remover to remove:
But, like a steady ship, doth strongly part / The raging waves and keeps her course aright, / Nor aught for tempest doth from it depart . . .	O no, it is an ever-fixèd mark / That looks on tempests and is never shaken; / It is the star to every wand'ring bark . . .
Such self-assurance need not fear the spite / Of grudging foes, nor favor seek of friends – / But in the stay of her own steadfast might, / Neither to one herself nor other bends.	Love's not Time's fool, though rosy lips and cheeks / Within his bending sickle's compass come; / Love alters not with his brief hours and weeks / But bears it out, ev'n to the edge of doom.

The similarities are conceptual and rhetorical. Each first quatrain argues that there is virtue in holding to a principle in adversity, and this point is reinforced with counter-examples and with phrasing that expresses resistance to deviating movement: 'to start' and 'to remove' are at once syntactically displaced words, verbs of motion, and the final words of their lines. Each second quatrain features a ship-in-storm conceit and a 'tempest'. And each third quatrain invokes an inimical figure ('the spite . . . of foes', 'Time') and draws a distinction between constancy and bending. Both poems, moreover, make pointed use of rhetorical turns and negative expressions.

Sonnet 60 provides comic relief. The *Amoretti* poet notes that skilled observers of the heavens know that every planet has its 'year', and he proceeds to propose that the planet Cupid takes forty years to circle the earth, lamenting that he has languished in Cupid's 'sphere' for forty years. Spenser's exact birth year is unknown, but he would have been roughly forty years old when courting Elizabeth Boyle – the lady whom *Amoretti* commemorates – and Boyle would have been twenty to twenty-five, 'perhaps even younger'.[29] This suggests that Spenser is alluding to his age in a self-deprecating manner. In Sonnet 60, the *Sonnets* poet more earnestly alludes to time's passage, declaring that 'our minutes hasten to their end' like waves towards a shore, and that 'Time . . . delves the parallels in beauty's brow'. He is also more earnest when he uses forty years as a benchmark for old age (Sonnet 2's 'forty winters') and when he sees himself as old (Sonnet 73's autumnal portrait). Both the *Amoretti* poet and the *Sonnets* poet acknowledge an age gap with their beloveds, and both regard differences in age and in worth as impediments to 'marriage'.

After the central section of sonnets, the *Amoretti* poet still has work to do, but he senses that his suit is progressing. By Sonnet 83 – the second 'hungry eyes' sonnet – his wooing would seem complete and his sight would seem perfected, but six sonnets remain. In order to complete the nuptial plot, the poet must remove all impediments to marriage: he must publicly and privately prepare for a change in life. In Sonnet 84, he announces his betrothal or 'election', rejoicing in new sights of his lady and telling himself to behold her 'rare perfection'; in 85–6, he encounters envy and slander, hinting that someone was hired to defame him; and in 87–9, he is separated from his lady, wandering 'as in darkness' and mourning like a mateless dove on a 'barèd bough'. *Sonnets*' fair-youth story is similar, though it refers only obliquely to marriage and is more concerned with forgiveness and accepting imperfection. Like *Amoretti*'s betrothal sonnet ('Let not one spark of filthy lustful fire / Break out'), *Sonnets*' most overt nuptial sonnet opens with a gesture to ward off evils ('Let me not to the marriage of true minds / Admit impediments'). And in a manner much like that of the *Amoretti* poet cursing his slanderer (86), the *Sonnets* poet berates a procured witness (125). As their stories come to a close, both *Amoretti* and *Sonnets*' fair-youth section gesture towards imminent marriage. The *Sonnets* poet's marriage is essentially symbolic and private. It may just be wishful thinking.

My larger point is that Shakespeare revises Spenser's marriage plot. Both poets draw on a tradition in which the poet-lover is a negative example: in most sequences, the male poet does not get the girl and his motives are dubious throughout. Unusually, the *Amoretti* poet learns from experiences and is rewarded with marriage. The *Sonnets* poet learns from the youth and the mistress, but his marriage to the youth is of an imaginary sort, and his feelings for the mistress are portrayed as diseased. *Sonnets* moreover conjoins conceits of marriage and justice. While both conceits are present in *Amoretti*, *Sonnets* pointedly evokes Judgement Day. As the fair-youth series comes to a close, the poet depicts himself as a man trying to clear his name and clear the way for marriage. In his imagination, at least, he gets his day in court.

The 'Vulgar Scandal' and the Poet's Infidelities

Before leaving the fair-youth section, let us consider the post-99 sonnets in relation to Shakespeare's life after 1600. Dating Sonnets 100–25 to the early Jacobean years is attractive: stylometric analysis assigns them to that time, and Sonnet 107 can be read as alluding to James's coronation and the release of Southampton from the Tower. The chronology could also tally with the poet-youth separation and with a delay in publishing *Sonnets*: if Shakespeare had completed a version of his sequence by 1600, it would have been difficult to see it to print given Southampton's situation. But what about the 'vulgar scandal' to which sonnets after 108 refer? And why does the poet emphasise that he has been unfaithful? Besides the explanations already offered – an allusion to venereal disease or to the low company that the poet keeps – at least two possibilities are worth exploring: that Shakespeare was embroiled in a scandal relating to the coat of arms that he had purchased for his father, and that he was unfaithful to Southampton because he had courted another patron.

To judge by Sonnet 111's octave, Shakespeare's scandal may have something to do with his theatrical profession:

> O, for my sake do you with Fortune chide –
> The guilty goddess of my harmful deeds –
> That did not better for my life provide
> Than public means, which public manners breeds.
> Thence comes it that my name receives a brand,
> And almost thence my nature is subdued
> To what it works in, like the dyer's hand;
> Pity me, then, and wish I were renewed.

Since the eighteenth-century, commentators have suggested that Sonnet 111 refers to the low esteem in which actors were held in Renaissance England. Burrow notes that woad-based dyes produced indelible stains on those regularly exposed to them, and that Shakespeare's father, a glover, likely worked with dyes.[30] Duncan-Jones explores the possibility that Shakespeare's 1599 attempt to have the Arden coat of arms quartered with the Shakespeare coat reflected 'his painful awareness that the patent that he acquired so expensively in 1596 was highly questionable, and well known to be so'.[31] The herald who granted the coat, William Dethick, was a dubious character: branded in the thumb for an act of violence, he came under suspicion for issuing questionable patents. As Duncan-Jones tells the story, the hearing to which Dethick was summoned for his irregular patents occurred in 1602, but the link between 'branded' 'vulgar scandal' may be rooted in earlier times:

> On the day of his attempted coup Essex said, when told to obey the Herald, 'I see no herald here but that branded fellow [Dethick], whom I took not for a herald'. [Shakespeare too] had been 'branded'. As a mere 'player', he should never have sought arms, in the view of many authorities. But worse than that, he was unlucky enough to acquire his patent from a herald who himself was disgraced . . . The three sonnets 110–12, all dealing with the speaker's poor reputation and the 'brand' [that] 'vulgar scandal stamped upon [his] brow' . . . make good sense as agonised commentaries on Shakespeare's misery in finding that all his efforts to improve his social status have resulted, instead, in shame.[32]

Difficulties with the coat of arms have weighed on Shakespeare for years. In Sonnet 112, he may be pleading for renewed protection when he says that the youth can 'o'er-green' all faults.

A coat-of-arms scandal may shed light on Sonnets 111–12 but it applies less well to the poems about infidelity. Perhaps Southampton had backed the acquisition of the coat of arms, and Shakespeare had promised to prove worthy of the honour. In that case, Shakespeare may have felt unfaithful because he had betrayed a trust and sullied Southampton's name. Alternatively, he may have courted a new patron – an action that might well qualify as an infidelity. In Sonnet 110, the poet declares ''tis true, I have gone here and there' and exclaims 'but, by all above, / Those blenches gave my heart another youth'. With 'gave my heart another youth', the poet is saying 'made me feel young again', but he could also be alluding to a second patron.

The most plausible candidate for a second youth is William Herbert (Pembroke), who can be seen as Wriothesley's mirror image: he was a third earl, and the initials of his first and last names are Wriothesley's initials reversed. What is more, Herbert was available to be courted: because he did not participate in the Essex rebellion, he was spared imprisonment or worse. He was also a lover of the arts, and when he became Lord Chamberlain in 1615, he effectively became Shakespeare's patron (the 1623 First Folio is dedicated to him and his brother). Finally, he wrote love poetry, including lines that were likely influenced by Shakespeare:

> If her disdain least change in you can move,
>   you do not love –
> For while your hopes give fuël to your fire,
>   you sell desire.
> Love is not love, but given free;
> And so is mine, so *should* yours be.

These are the first lines of the second sonnet of Herbert's *Poems* (1660). The phrase 'Love is not love' can be found in two of Shakespeare's works, *Sonnets* and *King Lear*:

> Let me not to the marriage of true minds
> Admit impediments. Love is not love
> Which alters when it alterations finds . . .
>
> (Sonnet 116)

> What say you to the lady? Love is not love
> When it is mingled with regards that stand
> Aloof from th'entire point . . .
>
> (Act 1, Scene 1)[33]

Both Shakespeare and Herbert use 'Love is not love' to argue that true love is constant, at the risk of suggesting that they may not have lived up to their ideal. (Herbert may have had a reputation for womanising: he is the model for Amphilanthus, the unfaithful lover of Mary Wroth's sequence *Pamphilia and Amphilanthus*.) My point is this: the *Sonnets* poet's confession of infidelity may stem from Shakespeare's seeking Pembroke's patronage prior to 1603.

Even if he did not seek Pembroke's patronage, Shakespeare may have been pricked by guilt for 'abandoning' Southampton – a feeling that he may express in 'The Phoenix and the Turtle', his two-part poem about constancy that was published in *Love's Martyr* (1601).[34] *Love's Martyr* is a volume dedicated to Sir John Salisbury: its title poem is by Robert Chester, and supporting poems by Shakespeare and others are in the back.[35] The book celebrates Salisbury for his fidelity and his knighthood, which he received for helping suppress the Essex rebellion. If we read 'The Phoenix and the Turtle' as a poem about Elizabeth and Salisbury, the allegory would go something like this: the Queen is as singular as the phoenix; the Knight is as true as a turtledove to its mate. But it also seems to be informed by Shakespeare's personal situation. In contributing their verse, Shakespeare and the other poets may have been demonstrating loyalty to the Queen, a gesture that would have been expedient for anyone associated with Essex's circle, as Shakespeare was in two respects: his theatrical company came under suspicion for staging *Richard II* on the eve of the rebellion; his current or former patron Southampton had rebelled alongside Essex. Shakespeare may have had no choice but to contribute some verse; willing contributor or not, he may have felt that he was effectively renouncing Southampton.

With its imagery and its two-part structure, 'The Phoenix and the Turtle', hints at a marriage that preserves or includes separateness – not unlike the fair-youth section of *Sonnets*, whose second part moves towards a 'marriage of true minds'. And as in various fair-youth sonnets, the poet makes pointed use of the words 'compound', 'simple', and 'twain':

> So between them love did shine
> That the Turtle saw his right
> Flaming in the Phoenix' sight;
> Either was the other's mine . . .
>
> Reason, in itself confounded,
> Saw division grow together,
> To themselves yet either neither –
> Simple were so well compounded
>
> That it cried, 'How true a twain
> Seemeth this concordant one'.
>
> (lines 33–36, 41–46)

'The Phoenix and the Turtle' is perhaps strategically obscure: Shakespeare may be expressing overt loyalty to the Queen and covert loyalty to Southampton. In this light, the outlandish claim that the *Sonnets* poet makes in 109–25 – that he has stayed faithful to the youth, despite obvious evidence to the contrary – may not be so outlandish after all.

Chapter 8

The Mistress Sonnets

In a 1930 lecture, J. W. Mackail dubbed the mistress sonnets a 'miscellaneous and disorderly appendix'.[1] His assessment remains common. My argument is that these sonnets are highly organised: 127–44 consist of three pyramid steps; 145 is a division marker; and 146–54 consist of three more steps. (*Sonnets*' final step, 'A Lover's Complaint', can be regarded as part of the mistress section or as something apart.) With slight differences, the mistress poems are organised along the same lines as the fair-youth poems. Why there are slight differences, and why the sequence's conclusion is ambiguous, are guiding questions in this and the next chapter.

Stories in and about the Mistress Sonnets

'Mistress section' or 'mistress series' is a useful label for the sonnets after 126. The poet refers to his beloved as 'mistress' in Sonnet 127, and 127–54 can be read as pertaining to her. Besides being the poet's term, 'mistress' is less scented with Victorian societal romance than 'Dark Lady', even granting that it could mean 'mistress of the house'. And though it does not typically denote an extramarital lover in Elizabethan English – in sonnet sequences, it generally refers to the woman to whom the male poet is devoted – that meaning is useful: the *Sonnets* poet hints that he and his mistress are married to others. Meanwhile, 'section' or 'series' allows for narrative development without insisting on it. But beyond pertaining to the mistress, what is the section about, and what is it doing in a sequence mostly weighted towards the youth?

Let us first consider whether the mistress is modelled on an actual person. According to the poet, the mistress is at once black and beautiful (127, 131). This minimally means that she has black hair and eyes; she may also have a dark complexion and a reputation for promiscuity. She seems to be musical: in Sonnet 128, she is depicted as woman who can play the virginal (a keyboard instrument) while being herself the opposite of virginal. Unlike Shakespeare's wife Anne Hathaway, who was seven or eight years older than him, the mistress is younger than the poet, to judge by a remark in Sonnet 138: 'she knows my days are past the best'. Like the poet, the mistress appears to be married to someone else: both poet and mistress have 'Robbed others' beds' revénues of their rents' (142); both are 'forsworn' (152); and she has broken a 'bed-vow' (152).[2] The details that the poet provides about the mistress are at once generic and specific, as they are in *Astrophil and Stella* and *Amoretti* – which is to say that they are probably based on someone Shakespeare knew.

While many scholars allow that the mistress may be modelled on an Elizabethan woman, they tend to assume that her identity is lost to time – that the names gathered in her name hardly amount to a list of suspects, especially compared to the usual suspects for the youth. Largely agreeing with this view, I nonetheless draw attention to three women: Samuel Daniel's sister (whose name is unknown), Lucy Negro, and Emilia Lanier. Daniel's sister may have been the wife of John Florio; Florio may have been Daniel's tutor in Italian and French at Oxford and a model for Holofernes in *Love's Labour's Lost*. Lucy Negro or 'Black Luce' operated a brothel in London: her name 'appears in a list of bawdry entertainments – the Gray's Inn Christmas entertainments of 1594 – and in a few plays and literary texts of the period'.[3] Emilia Lanier (née Bassano) came from a family of Jewish and Venetian origin; her father was a court musician. Before she was married off to another court musician, she was the mistress of Lord Hunsdon.[4] (From 1594 until his death in 1596, Hunsdon was the patron of the Lord Chamberlain's Men, the company for which Shakespeare wrote and acted.) All three women could have met Shakespeare and Southampton in the mid-1590s, and all fit the mistress profile. Daniel's sister and Lanier, for example, both came from musical families of Italian heritage, which arguably increases the odds that they were brunettes who could play the virginal.

While none of the candidates is a sure bet, the three in question have generated instructive stories. Jonathan Bate, for example, tells the following story about Daniel's sister:

> My dark lady ... is John Florio's wife, who happens to have been the sister of Samuel Daniel, the sonneteer ... As for Florio himself, he was not a poet but he was in the 'pay and patronage' of Southampton ...

Shakespeare introduces the theme of rival writers in sonnet 78 with the phrase 'every *Alien* pen'. 'Alien'... had a very specific meaning in Elizabethan English: it referred to a foreigner. The Italian Florio was the only writer of Shakespeare's acquaintance who was an 'alien'. Could he have been the initial rival who inspired Shakespeare to imagine a series of greater rivals in the sequence through to 86?[5]

In this account, Mrs Florio and Shakespeare had a brief affair. Because the Florios were sometime members of the Southampton household, Bate wonders whether the plot could be complicated 'by proposing Daniel as the "rival poet"'.[6] Bate does not develop this idea – he eventually argues that Marlowe is the rival, only to propose John Davies of Hereford in a later book – but the implications of his mistress-rival conjunction are potentially significant: if the mistress is modelled on a relation of the rival poet, the mistress-youth affair might be emotionally charged in ways that scholars have yet to explore. (But where does the *Sonnets* poet suggest that his mistress is the rival's sister?) More significant than the mistress theory is the possibility that Daniel had an entrée to Southampton through his sister's marriage. As for Lucy Negro, her name and profession have been brought forward to explain the emphasis on blackness and venereal disease. Puns on 'Negro' would be consonant with the wordplay on the youth's name, and a 'mistress as madam' conceit could add meaning to sonnets like 143, in which the mistress is portrayed as maternal.

The case for Lanier also offers interpretive possibilities. If nothing else, Lanier's musical background and unhappy marriage make her a plausible candidate. Her maiden name and heritage could moreover connect her to *The Merchant of Venice*, a play that depicts sixteenth-century Jewish culture in more detail than Shakespeare might be expected to have, and whose musical imagery is extensive. The play also features a love triangle between an older man (Antonio), a younger man (Bassanio), and a woman (Portia). 'Bassano' could be spelled 'Bassanio' or 'Bassany', and related French and Italian words – *basannée* and *basana* – can be translated 'black lady' or 'dark lady'.[7] Lanier may be the best candidate for the mistress, but the evidence is hardly conclusive. She does however illustrate that identifying a model has interpretive implications, and she reminds us that *Sonnets* invites us to consider Shakespeare's biography.

This brings us to Shakespeare's life in the mid-1590s. According to stylometric analysis, many mistress sonnets were written before the fair-youth sonnets, in the early or mid-1590s. More evidence that Shakespeare began writing those sonnets in that period can be inferred from the opening sonnet of the series, 127:

> In the old age, black was not counted fair,
> Or if it were, it bore not Beauty's name;
> But now is black Beauty's successive heir
> And Beauty slandered with a bastard shame –
> For since each hand hath put on Nature's power,
> Fairing the foul with Art's false borrowed face,
> Sweet Beauty hath no name, no holy bower,
> But is profaned if not lives in disgrace.
> Therefore my mistress' eyes are raven black,
> Her brows so suited, and they mourners seem
> At such who, not born fair, no beauty lack,
> Sland'ring creation with a false esteem.
>   Yet so they mourn, becoming of their woe,
>   That every tongue says beauty should look so.

Shakespeare is not the first poet to describe his lady's beauty as the opposite of that of the blonde-haired, blue-eyed Petrarchan type; nor is he the first to rail against cosmetics: both gestures have Renaissance and classical precedents.[8] In Shakespeare's own work, the idea of a black-haired, black-eyed beauty is developed in *Love's Labour's Lost*, in which Berowne not only notes that Rosaline has 'two pitch-balls stuck in her face for eyes' but exclaims: 'O, if in black my lady's brows be decked, / It mourns that painting and usurping hair / Should ravish doters with a false aspéct; / And therefore is she born to make black fair' (Act 4, Scene 3). *Sonnets* contains many parallels to *Love's Labour's Lost*, including some as verbally close as those in Sonnet 127.[9] The play dates from the early or mid-1590s.

Regardless of when they were written, what stories do Sonnets 127–54 tell? The mistress sonnets are harder to reduce to a narrative than the fair-youth sonnets. Perhaps this is to be expected, especially if Shakespeare wrote them before he had envisioned writing a sequence on the youth or writing a sequence at all. In broad outline, the narrative goes something like this: the poet falls for a woman whose beauty and morals he questions; lust plays a problematic role in his feelings; the poet believes that the mistress is sleeping with other men; the mistress seduces the fair youth; the poet wrestles with love and hatred of the mistress; unable to break from her, he seeks an elusive cure for his 'disease'. But the real story may be the poet's swings in emotion and his meditations on his heart, body, and soul.

The Basic Scheme of the Mistress Sonnets

The mistress narrative is elusive, but the series has a clear beginning, middle, and end, and these parts fit snugly in the pyramidal scheme. There are nonetheless significant differences between fair-youth and mistress sonnets. Only the first and last pyramid steps of the mistress section have clearly demarcated boundary sonnets, and structure-within-structure design is harder to discern. The differences may be due to logistics: Shakespeare was perhaps trying to fit old poems in a new scheme, and the small pyramid steps at the top of the scheme provide less room to work with. But Shakespeare did not simply cram the mistress poems into the fair-youth framework; he created new schemes and put the two sections in conversation with each other.

The first mistress step (the eleventh altogether) has clear boundaries. The opening sonnet presents the mistress as a new kind of beauty in the world and a new kind of beauty in the sequence. The closing sonnet similarly announces something new while gesturing back to the fair-youth section:

> Sonnet 133
> Beshrew that heart that makes my heart to groan
> For that deep wound it gives my friend and me!
> Is't not enough to torture me alone,
> But slave to slav'ry my sweet'st friend must be?
> Me from myself thy cruël eye hath taken,
> And my next self thou harder hast engrossed:
> Of him, myself, and thee I am forsaken;
> A torment thrice threefold thus to be crossed.
> Prison my heart in thy steel bosom's ward,
> But then my friend's heart let my poor heart bail;
> Whoe'er keeps me, let my heart be his guard;
> Thou canst not then use rigor in my jail.
>   And yet thou wilt; for I, being pent in thee,
>   Perforce am thine, and all that is in me.

This is the first mistress sonnet to refer to the love triangle between poet, youth, and mistress – a subject first broached in Sonnet 33. Like Sonnet 33, Sonnet 133 alludes to the crucifixion ('thrice threefold thus to be crossed'). It also contains imagery of a heart inside another heart: offering his own heart as bail for the youth's, the poet asks the mistress to lock it in her 'steel bosom's ward'. In the couplet, though, the poet acknowledges that he is pleading in vain: because he is 'pent' in his mistress – imprisoned by her, obsessed by her, physically inside her – she possesses him and everything in him, including his heart and the youth's heart. Metaphors from earlier sonnets – of the youth's heart locked in the poet's chest (48), and of the youth as the sum and container of previous loves (31) – acquire new meanings.

In echoing the second pyramid step's final sonnet, 133 is a fitting conclusion to the eleventh step. The parallel is confirmed by 134 ('So now I have confessed that he is thine'), which continues discussing the infidelity in ways that recall 34's continuation of 33: both pairs of sonnets cross pyramid-step boundaries. This suggests that the mistress steps are constructed on principles similar to those of the fair-youth steps. But the poet never addresses the mistress with you-forms; groups of sonnets are not demarcated via thou- and you-forms. Even the poet's use of direct and indirect address is not obviously patterned:

3rd   Th   3rd   3rd   Th   Th   Th
127   128   129   130   131   132   133

If there is a pattern here, it has to do with getting personal. The step opens with a background story ('In the old age, black was not counted fair'), turns flirtatious ('How oft, when thou, my music, music play'st'), and returns to general reflections ('Th'expense of spirit in a waste of shame'). After another generalising sonnet ('My mistress' eyes are nothing like the sun'), the step ends with three thou-sonnets. By 133, matters have grown quite personal.

If we view the eleventh step as an introduction plus a six-sonnet group, a more specific scheme comes into focus: after describing his mistress as a black beauty and claiming that she has changed the world's idea of beauty, the poet alternately expresses positive and negative feelings about her. In Sonnet 128, he observes her playing the virginal. As the keys 'leap' and 'kiss' her hands, he first wishes that his lips could change places with the keys; by the sonnet's end, he wants more of her: 'Give [others] thy fingers, me thy lips to kiss'. This playful sonnet is followed by a description of lust's painful and corruptive effects: 129 asserts that lust's promises of bliss are 'bait / On purpose made to make the taker mad', that everyone knows this, and that, regardless, no one knows how 'To shun the heaven that leads men to this hell'. Even if we read 129 as general commentary on desire, the poet is lashing out. Sonnet 130 returns to playfulness: the poet describes his mistress's imperfections, only to conclude that she is as 'rare' a love as any woman praised with false comparisons.

Sonnet 131 shifts back to harshness: 'Thou art as tyrannous', the poet asserts, 'As those whose beauties proudly make them cruël'. Now the mistress's imperfections are thrown back at her: the poet accuses her of being black in her deeds. Then in Sonnet 132, the poet is tender again. Perhaps taking his cue from 130's 'My mistress' eyes are nothing like the sun', he begins by saying 'Thine eyes I love'. Perhaps offering amends for 131's slander, he offers to swear that 'Beauty herself is black'. When he berates the mistress in 133 ('Beshrew that heart . . .'), he is continuing the 'eye vs. heart' conceit of 131–2, and he is completing the series of emotional extremes. For all of its apparent chaos, the first mistress step is quite organised, to a degree if not a quality comparable to fair-youth steps.

Now let us turn to some unusual sonnets in the middle of the mistress section, 144–6: none of these poems directly addresses the mistress. Sonnet 144 can be read as a summary of the poet's state of affairs to this point:

> Two loves I have, of comfort and despair,
> Which like two spirits do suggest me still.
> The better angel is a man right fair;
> The worser spirit, a woman coloured ill.
> To win me soon to hell, my female evil
> Tempteth my better angel from my side
> And would corrupt my saint to be a devil,
> Wooing his purity with her foul pride.
> And, whether that my angel be turned fiend,
> Suspect I may, yet not directly tell,
> But being both from me, both to each friend,
> I guess one angel in another's hell.
>   Yet this shall I ne'er know, but live in doubt,
>   Till my bad angel fire my good one out.

In Sonnet 133, the poet accused the mistress of stealing the youth from him; in 144, he admits to uncertainty – he has suspicions but can only confirm them when his 'bad angel' (the mistress) fires out his 'good angel' (the youth). The expression 'fire him out' has at least three possible meanings in Elizabethan English: 'smoke him out', 'discard him after using him', and 'infect him with a venereal disease'.[10] In turning to third-person narration and summarising the situation, the poet concludes a series stretching back to Sonnet 133 and ultimately to 127: both 144 and 127 are explanatory third-person sonnets, and 144 can be read as an update on the dark woman who was introduced in 127.

Sonnet 145 is the sequence's only tetrameter poem: like 99, it is formally distinct and positioned at a boundary between two steps, and it marks a division between the two parts of its section. The parallels to the fair-youth section argue that the sonnets after 145, like those after 99, are written after a hiatus. The bipartite parallel is especially close if we treat the first pyramid step as an introduction to the fair-youth sonnets, and the seventeenth step ('A Lover's Complaint') as a coda to the mistress sonnets. This leaves us with nine fair-youth steps and six mistress steps:

Fair-youth section (pyramid steps 2–10)

The section has two parts, divided by 99. 6 pyramid steps + 3 pyramid steps (3 pairs of steps + 3 steps)

Mistress section (pyramid steps 11–16)

The section has two parts, divided by 145. 3 pyramid steps + 3 pyramid steps (3 steps + 3 steps)

The '3+3' design in the mistress series sheds light on its fair-youth counterpart. To argue that steps 2–7 are three pairs requires no special pleading: the second and third steps are linked by the announcement of betrayal; the fourth and fifth steps open with climacteric sonnets; and the sixth and seventh steps describe the rival-poet crisis and its aftermath.

The third unusual poem in the middle of the mistress series is also the only sonnet in which the poet addresses his soul:

Sonnet 146
Poor soul, the center of my sinful earth,
[Pressed by] these rebel powers that thee array,
Why dost thou pine within and suffer dearth,
Painting thy outward walls so costly gay?
Why so large cost, having so short a lease,
Dost thou upon thy fading mansion spend?
Shall worms, inheritors of this excéss,
Eat up thy charge? Is this thy body's end?
Then soul, live thou upon thy servant's loss,
And let that pine to aggravate thy store;
Buy terms divine in selling hours of dross;
Within be fed, without be rich no more:
  So shall thou feed on Death, that feeds on men,
  And Death once dead, there's no more dying then.[11]

Initially, perhaps, we might interpret 'Poor soul' as the mistress, but it soon becomes clear that the poet is debating with himself. The octave consists of pointed questions, as if the poet were berating himself for being wasteful and for allowing his soul to serve his body. The sestet shifts modes, offering advice in the form of commands: the poet tells his soul to let the body pine, to buy 'terms divine', to be fed 'within', and to cease being rich 'without'. These actions will allow the soul to 'feed on Death, that feeds on men, / And Death once dead, there's no more dying then'. In its immediate context, Sonnet 146 is unusual because it evokes Christian redemption. After it, religious language and imagery recede, but the poet still presents himself as diseased in soul and body, seeking a cure. Like 127 and 144, 146 is an explanatory assessment. The two sonnets that close the mistress series are similarly explanatory: in telling a mythic origin story, 153–4 recall 127's tale of Black's beauty.

The Twelfth and Thirteenth Pyramid Steps

If the mistress section of *Sonnets* merely had a clear beginning, middle, and end, it would be more structured than it is reputed to be. Closer examination reveals more organisation: the schemes in the twelfth and thirteenth pyramid steps not only rival the fair-youth schemes in complexity; they echo them, and in doing so they develop conceits about sin and redemption. One reason why the mistress section can seem less structured is that it contains fewer poems linked by conjunctive words or phrases. Indeed, there is only one such pair, 133–4. Sonnet 133 upbraids the mistress for making the fair youth her 'slave'; Sonnet 134 begins: 'So now I have confessed that he is thine'. The uniqueness of 133–4 could indicate that Shakespeare wrote the second sonnet later, or that he revised it later, in order to set up the parallels between 33–4 and 133–4.

The scarcity of conjunctive links should not imply a lack of organisation, however. As Jackson demonstrates in his study of rhyme and organisation in *Sonnets*, the mistress section contains many consecutive poems that share rhyme words – including 'one exceptional run of *sixteen* rhyme-linked sonnets' (131–46).[12] According to Jackson, the run 'cannot be explained as a chance result', and the 'formal connecting device' goes 'some way toward countering any impression of heterogeneity and disorder'.[13] Just as crucial, the twelfth and thirteenth pyramid steps contain most of the rhyme-linked series, and these steps invite us to read them as a unit. The first sonnet, 'So now I have confessed that he is thine', and the last sonnet, 'Two loves I have, of comfort and despair', frame 134–44 as a series about the poet's feelings after the youth-mistress affair.

And the two sonnets in the middle of the series are rhetorically and thematically linked:

> Sonnet 139
> O call me not to justify the wrong
> That thy unkindness lays upon my heart –
> Wound me not with thine eye, but with thy tongue;
> Use power with power, and slay me not by art.
> Tell me thou lov'st elsewhere, but in my sight,
> Dear heart, forbear to glance thine eye aside –
> What need'st thou wound with cunning, when thy might
> Is more than my o'erpressed defence can bide?
> Let me excuse thee: ah, my love well knows
> Her pretty looks have been mine enemies,
> And therefore from my face she turns my foes,
> That they elsewhere might dart their injuries.
>   Yet do not so; but since I am near slain
>   Kill me outright with looks and rid my pain.
>
> Sonnet 140
> Be wise as thou art cruël; do not press
> My tongue-tied patience with too much disdain,
> Lest sorrow lend me words and words express
> The manner of my pity-wanting pain.
> If I might teach thee wit, better it were,
> Though not to love, yet, love, to tell me so –
> As testy sick men, when their deaths be near,
> No news but health from their physicians know.
> For if I should despair, I should go mad,
> And in my madness might speak ill of thee;
> Now this ill-wresting world is grown so bad,
> Mad sland'rers by mad ears believèd be.
>   That I may not be so, nor thou belied,
>   Bear thine eyes straight, though thy proud heart go wide.

While Sonnet 139 can be read as a final poem of the twelfth step, its links to 140 are strong: both sonnets feature prohibitory commands ('O call me not to justify the wrong', 'do not press / My tongue-tied patience'); both ask the mistress to alter her manner of speaking and especially her manner of looking ('Kill me outright with looks', 'Bear thine eyes straight'); and 140's 'That I may not be so' answers 139's 'Yet do not so'. The sonnets are also linked through rhyme, not just through the word 'pain': line fourteen of Sonnet 139 rhymes with line two of Sonnet 140. Linking poems with a 'carried over' rhyme is a variation on another device in *Sonnets*: repeating words from a couplet in the next sonnet's opening lines.

Carried-over rhymes are uncommon in *Sonnets*: there are four in each section.[14] The first example in the mistress section occurs near the beginning of the twelfth step:

> Sonnet 135
> ....
>   Let no unkind, no fair beseechers kill;
>   Think all but one, and me in that one *Will*.
>
> Sonnet 136
> If thy soul check thee that I come so near,
> Swear to thy blind soul that I was thy *Will*.

Will–Will, an identical rhyme, connects the poems, though it is less significant than *Will* itself: the word 'will' is capitalised and italicised seven times in Sonnet 135 and three times in 136. The second carried-over rhyme, *pain–disdain*, occurs in Sonnets 139–40; it links the twelfth and thirteenth steps. The third rhyme occurs at the end of the thirteenth step:

> Sonnet 143
> ....
>   So will I pray that thou mayst have thy *Will*,
>   If thou turn back and my loud crying still.
>
> Sonnet 144
> Two loves I have, of comfort and despair,
> Which like two angels do suggest me still.

The poet ends Sonnet 143 by asking the mistress to 'still' his cries and comfort him; he begins 144 by admitting to loves 'of comfort and despair', who even now ('still') tempt him and urge him to action. The *still–still* rhyme is a more effective than *Will–Will* because the rhyme words are more distinct – the first 'still' is a verb; the second, an adverb – and because 144's 'still' implies continuation, a meaning reinforced by the rhyme.

The carried-over rhymes at the beginning, middle, and end of Sonnets 134–44 point to organisational design; so do the parallels to 111–21. As discussed in the last chapter, 111–21 are a series featuring wrongdoing, judgement, and marriage. As a series, 134–44 are framed by two sonnets that allude to the youth-mistress betrayal; the rest focus on sin and excessive desire. Both series have eleven sonnets, and both evoke transgression through subject matter and number symbolism. It is also telling that the eleven-sonnet series in the mistress section contains eleven capitalised and italicised instances of 'will'. Shakespeare may have been inspired by an eleven-poem series in *Astrophil and Stella*: Sonnets 73–83. Sidney's sonnets detail Astrophil's attempts to obtain kisses from Stella; the word 'kiss' appears eleven times, and the final sonnet speaks of a sparrow named 'Philip', who playfully pecks at Stella. 'Will', in the sense of 'sexual desire', is as excessive in 134–44 as kisses are in the *Astrophil and Stella* series, and Shakespeare's pun resembles Sidney's pun. Neither Phil nor Will can contain himself.

The Becoming of Things III (the Fourteenth, Fifteenth, and Sixteenth Steps)

If we accept that Sonnet 145 marks a division in the sequence's pyramid but is otherwise outside the scheme, we can read the mistress section in different ways: it can be understood as an eighteen-sonnet series plus a nine-sonnet series, as two sets of three pyramid steps, or as a series of twenty-five sonnets plus two Cupid sonnets. There is also a fourth possibility:

Sonnets	*Step(s)*	*Description*
127–33	11	Introduction and six sonnets (6, perfection/imperfection)
134–44	12–13	Transgression series (11, exceeding the mark)
146–54	14–16	Redemption series (9, falling short of the mark)

This scheme basically consists of one, two, and three pyramid steps. The eleventh step calls attention to the number 6 and to perfection/imperfection; the twelfth and thirteenth steps call attention to the number 11 and to transgression; and the fourteenth, fifteenth, and sixteenth steps form a redemption series, which depicts the poet as diseased in soul and body, longing for a cure. Its nine sonnets may symbolise falling short.

The first sonnet of 146–54 evokes Christian redemption; the final sonnets suggest that the poet is beyond cure; throughout the series, the poet is chronically ill. At first, he seems trapped by his condition: in 147, he is a patient 'past care' not following the 'prescriptions' of Reason, his doctor; in 148, he is blinded by Love. Then in 149–50, he shows some fight. Arguing with the mistress and rallying himself, he poses intense rhetorical questions:

Sonnet 149
Canst thou, o cruël, say I love thee not,
When I against myself with thee partake?
Do I not think on thee, when I forgot
Am of myself, all-tyrant for thy sake? . . .

Sonnet 150
O, from what pow'r hast thou this pow'rful might,
With insufficiency my heart to sway?
To make me give the lie to my true sight
And swear that brightness doth not grace the day? . . .

In 149, the poet responds to the accusation, imagined or real, that he does not love the mistress. He says that he is fighting selflessly against himself, and he emphasises this with three quatrains' worth of questions and an enjambment whose awkwardness expresses disregard for self: 'I forgot / Am of myself'. The questions in 150 run through line 10; they underscore the power of love to distort judgement and the poet's resistance to love's distorting influence.

As if to show that he has not lost his ability to make reasoned judgements, the poet changes the tone if not the tenor of his argument in the next pair of sonnets:

Sonnet 151
Love is too young to know what conscience is,
Yet who knows not conscience is born of love?
Then, gentle cheater, urge not my amiss,
Lest guilty of my faults thy sweet self prove . . .

Sonnet 152
In loving thee thou know'st I am forsworn,
But thou art twice forsworn, to me love swearing . . .
But why of two oaths' breach do I accuse thee
When I break twenty? I am perjured most . . .

Sonnets 151–2 are more explanatory than 149–50: they pose only one question each. They are also less recriminatory: in 151, the poet calls the mistress 'gentle', an epithet generally reserved for the youth; in 152, he acknowledges his culpability, proclaiming that his faults are greater than the mistress's. Though the poet ultimately falls short of finding a cure for his soul and body, and though he never pursues reconciliation with the mistress as urgently as he does with the youth, 146–52 progress towards self-knowledge. In that sense, the series moves towards redemption.

Schematically if not historically, Sonnets 146–54 come after a break in writing, which could mean that they were written or revised in the seventeenth century. Regardless, they share themes with Shakespeare's later plays, as can be illustrated with the word 'become'. In the plays, 'become' (in all its forms) appears most often in *Antony and Cleopatra* (1606) and *The Winter's Tale* (1610–11), and next most often in *Henry IV, Part 2* (1597–8), *Coriolanus* (1607–8), and *Cymbeline* (1609–10).[15] All five plays feature transformation, and four of the five date from within a few years of 1609. The noun 'becoming' occurs only twice in Shakespeare's works – in Sonnet 150 and *Antony and Cleopatra* – and the adjective 'becoming' occurs only in Sonnet 127 and five plays: *Love's Labour's Lost*, *Pericles*, *Cymbeline*, *The Winter's Tale*, and *Henry VIII*. This is to say, the adjective occurs in one sonnet, one mid-1590s play, and four plays from no earlier than 1607. While Sonnet 127 may be from the 1590s – its language parallels Berowne's description of Rosaline in *Love's Labour's Lost* – the same cannot as easily be said of Sonnet 150. It is also telling that, in *Antony and Cleopatra*, Shakespeare puns on different meanings of 'become': 'make appealing', 'befit', and 'transform into'. In Act 3, Scene 12, for example, Octavius commands a follower to observe 'how Antony becomes his flaw'.

Beautification and transformation inform Sonnet 150's use of 'becoming':

> O, from what pow'r hast thou this pow'rful might,
> With insufficiency my heart to sway?
> To make me give the lie to my true sight
> And swear that brightness doth not grace the day?
> Whence has thou this becoming of things ill
> That in the very refuse of thy deeds
> There is such strength and warrantize of skill
> That in my mind thy worst all best exceeds?
> Who taught thee how to make me love thee more,
> The more I hear and see just cause of hate?
> O, though I love what others do abhor,
> With others thou shouldst not abhor my state.
>   If thy unworthiness raised love in me,
>   More worthy I to be beloved of thee.

Line 5's 'this becoming of things ill' primarily means 'this power of making bad or diseased things seem appealing', but it also suggests that the mistress is transforming into 'things ill' before the poet's eyes. Similar puns apply to Cleopatra in *Anthony and Cleopatra*. In the play's first scene, Antony tells Cleopatra that she is a queen 'Whom everything becomes – to chide, to laugh, / To weep; whose every passion fully strives / To make itself . . . fair and admired'. In the third scene, Antony captiously remarks that Cleopatra is 'idleness itself'; she responds: '"Tis sweating labour / To bear such idleness so near the heart / As Cleopatra this. But, sir, forgive me, / Since my becomings kill me, when they do not / Eye well to you'. Cleopatra is saying that her graceful qualities 'kill' her when they stop appealing to Antony and especially when they are cited in reproof. And in Act 2, Scene 2, Enobarbus says of Cleopatra:

> Age cannot wither her, nor custom stale
> Her infinite variety. Other women cloy
> The appetites they feed, but she makes hungry
> Where most she satisfies; for vilest things
> Become themselves in her.

Part of Cleopatra's appeal is her variety, her power of becoming. Like Cleopatra, the mistress possesses the mysterious power to make all manner of things seem appealing. And in the final sonnets, the mistress's changing nature potentially becomes a positive quality, or at least ceases to be associated solely with inconstancy.

In a related vein, the final sonnets depict the mistress as more like the youth. Sonnet 151, for example, contains two phrases that we might expect to find in a fair-youth sonnet, 'gentle cheater' and 'rising at thy name':

> Love is too young to know what conscience is,
> Yet who knows not conscience is born of love?
> Then, gentle cheater, urge not my amiss,
> Lest guilty of my faults thy sweet self prove.
> For, thou betraying me, I do betray
> My nobler part to my gross body's treason;
> My soul doth tell my body that he may
> Triumph in love; flesh stays no farther reason,
> But, rising at thy name, doth point out thee
> As his triumphant prize. Proud of this pride,
> He is contented thy poor drudge to be –
> To stand in thy affairs, fall by thy side.
>   No want of conscience hold it that I call
>   Her 'love', for whose dear love I rise and fall.

'My . . . flesh . . . rising' refers to an erection, and the enjambments in lines 5–10 reinforce the image of an involuntary physical reaction.

'Rising' moreover points to metaphors of rebellion and conjuring: Mercutio uses a similar conceit in *Romeo and Juliet*, when he tells Benvolio that he will 'conjure' Romeo in the 'name' of Romeo's mistress Rosaline and thereby 'raise him up' (Act 2, Scene 1). Some commentators have suggested that the mistress's name is hidden in Sonnet 151, especially if 'at thy name' means 'when I hear your name'.[16] While a pun on 'Rosaline' is conceivable, 'at thy name' could simply mean 'when you call' – or pun on the poet's name ('at your Will'). More crucial, the fair youth is the person whom the poet has hitherto associated with roses and rising.

Sonnet 151 clarifies a trend in the final sonnets: that the poet's experiences have caused him to rethink assumptions about mistress and youth. But for all his acknowledgement of faults and for all his reappraisals, his approach to the mistress remains harsher than his approach to the youth. This can be seen in the last sonnet in which the poet directly addresses the mistress:

> Sonnet 152
> In loving thee thou know'st I am forsworn,
> But thou art twice forsworn, to me love swearing –
> In act thy bed-vow broke and new faith torn,
> In vowing new hate after new love bearing.
> But why of two oaths' breach do I accuse thee,
> When I break twenty? I am perjured most.
> For all my vows are oaths but to misuse thee,
> And all my honest faith in thee is lost;
> For I have sworn deep oaths of thy deep kindness –
> Oaths of thy love, thy truth, thy constancy –
> And, to enlighten thee, gave eyes to blindness
> Or made them swear against the thing they see.
>   For I have sworn thee fair – more perjured eye,
>   To swear against the truth so foul a lie.

While confessing he is more perjured than the mistress, the poet asserts he has lost all faith in her; in the couplet, he hints that she is completely foul. He is hardly exonerating her, and, insofar as he is suggesting that he, unlike she, has acted out of love, his reasoning is as awkward as the phrase 'more perjured eye': the poet rationalises his perjuries as necessary if not magnanimous; while admitting to wrongs, he does not express a willingness to forgive. This ending is a striking contrast with the conclusion of the fair-youth sonnets, in which the poet bends over backwards to take blame and ask forgiveness. The poet's spiritual progress in 146–54 is limited.

A more sympathetic way to interpret Sonnet 152 is to regard the end as provisional, and to see the poet as striving to correct his vision. Sonnet 152 is not the final poem, after all: 153–4 back away from 152's allegations, and they are followed by 'A Lover's Complaint', a lament that identifies with a female perspective. We might also compare the nine-sonnet series at the end the mistress section to the eleven-sonnet series at the end of the fair-youth section. As a transgression series, 111–21 are more comparable to 134–44, but, as a nuptial series, the closer parallel is 146–54. Sonnet 154 concludes with a *prove–love* rhyme, which connects it both to the mistress sonnets leading up to it (151 and 153 have *love–prove* rhymes) and to several fair-youth sonnets – notably 116 (*proved–loved*) and 117 (*prove–love*). But while 116 aspires to absolutes, and the poet swears to his definitions of love by using 'prove' in the sense of 'demonstrate the truth' ('If this be error and upon me proved, / I never . . . loved'), 154 is a fable about the nature of love in which the poet shifts the meaning of 'prove' towards 'experience a truth' ('this by that I prove –/ Love's fire heats water; water cools not love'). In their tone and their recognition of experience as a corrective to fixed ideas, 153–4 present a more becoming idea of being human.

The nuptial parallels between 111–21 and 146–54 also suggest the poet is questioning his feelings about the mistress, and that his feelings towards her and the youth are mutually constitutive. The most overt nuptial poem of 111–21 is the centre sonnet: 116 evokes the language of the standard marriage service. The central poem of the nine-sonnet series, 150, similarly evokes the service's language. Sonnet 116's loudest echo is the word 'impediment', which is used by the priest to ask the couple for reasons why they should not be married. Sonnet 150's loudest echo is 'just cause', which is used by the priest to ask the congregation if there is a reason why the couple should not be married:

> . . . if any man can show any just cause why they may not lawfully be joined so together, let him now speak, or else hereafter forever hold his peace. (*The Book of Common Prayer*)

> Who taught thee how to make me love thee more,
> The more I hear and see just cause of hate?
> (Sonnet 150, lines 9–10)[17]

At first glance, it might seem that Sonnet 150's situation could not be more different than 116's: instead of indirectly addressing his beloved and making a series of declarations about love, the poet directs a series of intense questions at his beloved, who is a source of hate. But the sonnet's conclusion indicates that the poet has been pulling out all the rhetorical stops in an attempt to retain a love he fears he is losing: 'O, though I love what others do abhor, / With others thou shouldst not abhor my state. / If thy unworthiness raised love in me, / More worthy I to be beloved of thee'. Even if he is only referring to sexual love – the pun on 'whore' in 'abhor', the double entendre of 'raised love in me' – the poet is similarly desperate to win over his beloved and to establish a more stable, if not a more healthy, state of affairs.

Shakespeare's Contemporaries and the Mistress Sonnets

The clearest poetic echoes in *Sonnets* tend to occur at or near the boundaries of pyramid steps. Sonnet 99, for example, echoes at least two poets (Constable and Barnes). Other instances include Sonnet 17 (Daniel), Sonnets 31–2 (Constable and Marston), and Sonnets 106–7 (Daniel, Constable, and Spenser). The echoing sonnets in the mistress series may not signal design as clearly, but they too occur at the boundaries of steps or groups – at the beginning, middle, and end of Sonnets 127–54.

The first mistress sonnet resembles Sonnet 7 of *Astrophil and Stella*:

> When Nature made her chief work, Stella's eyes,
> In colour black why wrapped she beams so bright?
> Would she in beamy black, like painter wise,
> Frame daintiest luster mixed of shades and light?
> Or did she else that sober hue devise
> In object best to knit and strength our sight,
> Lest, if no veil these brave gleams did disguise,
> They, sun-like, should more dazzle than delight?
> Or would she her miraculous power show,
> That, whereas black seems beauty's contrary,
> She ev'n in black doth make all beauties flow?
> Both so and thus – she, minding Love should be
>   Placed ever there, gave him this mourning weed
>   To honour all their deaths who for her bleed.

Like the *Sonnets* poet, Astrophil tells an origin tale, observes that black is not considered beautiful, and concludes that his lady's eyes are wearing mourning clothes. The 'black yet beautiful' idea has precedents, but the 'mourning clothes' conceit is rare. In his study of Renaissance sonnets, Schaar lists only four examples – Sidney's sonnet, Shakespeare's 127 and 132, and Poem 58 of Greville's *Caelica*.[18] Poem 58 was not published until 1633. While Shakespeare could have read *Caelica* in manuscript, Greville does not refer to black as beauty's opposite; in that respect, the parallels between Sonnet 127 and Sidney are more striking.[19] Even if Shakespeare is drawing on Greville, Jacobean readers would have been more likely to hear echoes of Sidney's Sonnet 7 and regarded them as a knowing nod to Sidney.

The parallels between Sonnet 144 ('Two loves I have, of comfort and despair') and Drayton's 'An evil spirit, your beauty, haunts me still' could also have been noticed by early readers, though who was echoing whom may have been no clearer to them than it is us. 'Two loves' ends the first half of the mistress section; 'An evil spirit' is Sonnet 22 of the 1599 *Idea*:

> An evil spirit, your beauty, haunts me still –
> Wherewith, alas, I have been long possessed –
> Which ceaseth not to tempt me to each ill
> Nor gives me once but one poor minute's rest.
> In me it speaks, whether I sleep or wake,
> And when by means to drive it out I try
> With greater torments, then it me doth take
> And tortures me in most extremity.
> Before my face it lays down my despairs
> And hastes me on unto a sudden death –
> Now tempting me to drown myself in tears,
> And then, in sighing, to give up my breath.
>   Thus am I still provoked, to every evil,
>   By this good wicked spirit, sweet angel-devil.

Parallels include the good and bad angels, the rhymes *still–ill* and *evil–devil*, and 'suggest me still' and 'tempt me to each ill'. As Schaar notes, 'Drayton's imagery and phraseology fall outside [sonnet] convention'; 144 is the closest parallel.[20] Since a version of 144 was published in *The Passionate Pilgrim* in 1599, and since Drayton may have been one of the friends with whom Shakespeare circulated his sonnets, a good case can be made that Drayton was influenced by Shakespeare.[21] For 1609 readers, though, 144 may have seem haunted by Drayton's sonnet.

The first poem of the mistress series' second half, 'Poor soul, the center of my sinful earth', may be also be haunted by another poem – Sonnet 28 of Griffin's *Fidessa* (1596):

> Well may my soul, immortal and divine,
> That is imprisoned in a lump of clay,
> Breath out laments until this body pine,
> That from her takes her pleasures all away.
> Pine then, thou loathèd prison of my life,
> Untoward subject of the least aggrievance –
> O let me die! Mortality is rife;
> Death comes by wounds, by sickness, care, and chance.
> O Earth, the time will come when I'll resume thee,
> And in my bosom make thy resting place:
> Then do not unto hardest sentence doom me;
> Yield, yield betimes – I must and will have grace!
>   Richly shalt thou be entombed, since for thy grave,
>   Fidessa, fair Fidessa, shalt thou have.

Griffin's subject is 'the common one of the poet's desire to die because of hopeless love, but the way in which this theme is expressed is anything but common'.[22] His claim that the poet's body will entomb earth ('in my bosom make thy resting place') is unusual, as is the way in which he uses religious language to plead for sex. In asking his body to let him 'die', the poet expresses a desire for sexual release, presumably inside Fidessa. As in Shakespeare's 146, the poet instructs the body to 'pine' as a means to an end, and he plays with the idea that the soul is confined in the body. Both poems, moreover, use 'pine' twice and 'divine' once, and 'Griffin's preceding sonnet', as Kenneth Muir observes, 'begins with the words "Poor worm", while Shakespeare begins with "Poor soul" and mentions worms in line 7'.[23] Because the religious resignation of Griffin's opening clashes with the 'grace' demanded at the end, Schaar and Muir conclude that Griffin is the 'debtor'. They may be correct – Griffin often borrows eclectically from other poets – but it is not safe to assume, as they do, that Shakespeare's 146 dates from the 1590s.

Griffin aside, Sonnet 146 likely echoes Daniel's verse. In 146, the poet tells his soul to 'live upon thy [body's] loss / And let that pine to aggravate thy store'. Here 'aggravate thy store' would seem to mean 'increase your stock of goods', but this positive sense of 'aggravate' is unusual, particularly in light of the etymological pun (*aggravare*, 'to make heavy').[24] A close negative parallel can be found in the second book of Daniel's *Civil Wars*, in a scene in which Richard II is threatened by siege: Richard rails at the 'sins' of the rebel Bolingbroke before exclaiming 'O injurious Land, what dost thou gain, / To aggravate thine own affliction's store?'[25] Another echo of Daniel can be heard in 146's description of the soul surrounded by and afflicted by 'rebel powers': 'these rebel powers that thee array'.[26] 'Rebel powers' is used in an analogous context in Daniel's *Cleopatra*, when Cleopatra speaks of her 'flesh and blood' as 'rebel powers': they are forces that threaten her resolve to commit honourable suicide.[27] This echo gains support from the parallels between various mistress sonnets and *Antony and Cleopatra*.

Sonnets' final two sonnets almost certainly echo other poets, though their proximate source is uncertain. Sonnets 153–4 tell an origin story that involves Cupid, a nymph, and a bath:

> Sonnet 153
> Cupid laid by his brand and fell asleep.
> A maid of Dian's this advantage found,
> And his love-kindling fire did quickly steep
> In a cold valley-fountain of that ground –
> Which borrowed from this holy fire of Love
> A dateless lively heat, still to endure,
> And grew a seething bath, which yet men prove
> Against strange maladies a sovereign cure.
> But at my mistress' eye, Love's brand new-fired;
> The boy for trial needs would touch my breast.
> I, sick withal, the help of bath desired
> And thither hied, a sad distempered guest,
>   But found no cure – the bath for my help lies
>   Where Cupid got new fire: my mistress' eye.
>
> Sonnet 154
> The little Love-god lying once asleep
> Laid by his side his heart-inflaming brand,
> Whilst many nymphs that vowed chaste life to keep
> Came tripping by; but in her maiden hand
> The fairest votary took up that fire
> Which many legions of true hearts had warmed –
> And so the general of hot desire
> Was, sleeping, by a virgin hand disarmed.
> This brand she quenchèd in a cool well by,
> Which from Love's fire took heat perpetual,

> Growing a bath and healthful remedy
> For men diseased; but I, my mistress' thrall,
>   Came there for cure and this by that I prove –
>   Love's fire heats water, water cools not love.

In both poems, a virginal nymph steals Cupid's 'brand' while Cupid sleeps, plunging it into cold water to snuff out its powers; the water is transformed into a hot medicinal bath; and the poet goes to the water for a cure but finds none. With a pun on 'nether eye', 153's couplet suggests that the poet's sole hope for a cure is to resume sexual relations.[28] By telling the same story twice, the poet alludes to alternative perspectives. And like the epilogue to *Troilus and Cressida*, which refers to a sweating cure, 153–4 allude to a 'hot bath' treatment for venereal disease.[29]

The Cupid story ultimately derives from a sixth-century Greek epigram:

> Here beneath these plane trees, exhausted Love was sleeping softly. He had entrusted his torch to the Nymphs. But the Nymphs said to one another, 'Come on, why are we waiting? Let's put out the torch and with it quench the fire in human hearts'. But the torch set light even to the waters, and the Nymphs of Love have filled the bath with hot water ever since.[30]

Since the epigram does not mention the medicinal transformation, Shakespeare may have found that detail in a later adaptation. In his source study, James Hutton notes that there are two traditions of the story – one with mineral springs, one without – and that there is 'interplay' between the traditions in 153–4.[31] A simple way of explaining the sources is to say that Shakespeare read the Greek text or a Latin translation of it, along with Sonnet 27 of Fletcher's *Licia*:

> The crystal streams, wherein my love did swim,
> Melted in tears, as partners of my woe;
> Her shine was such as did the fountains dim –
> The pearl-like fountain, whiter than the snow.
> Then, like perfúme, resolvèd with a heat,
> The fountain smoked as if it thought to burn:
> A wonder strange to see the cold so great
> And yet the fountain into smoke to turn.
> I searched the cause and found it to be this:
> She touched the water, and it burnt with love.
> Now, by her means, it purchased hath that bliss,
> Which all diseases quickly can remove.

> Then if, by you, these streams thus blessèd be,
> Sweet, grant me love, and be not worse to me.

Fletcher's sonnet and the epigram are all that Shakespeare would have needed to write 153–4.

Shakespeare may have also drawn on other sources. One possibility that has escaped commentators is a pair of sonnets in Barnes's *Parthenophil and Parthenophe*:

> Sonnet 54
> When I was young, endued with Nature's graces,
> I stole blind Love's strong bow and golden arrows,
> To shoot at redbreasts, goldfinches, and sparrows;
> At shrewd girls; and at boys, in other places.
> I shot when I was vexèd with disgraces;
> I pierced no skin, but melted up their marrows.
> How many boys and girls wished mine embraces!
> How many praised my favor, 'bove all faces!
> But, once, Parthenophe, by thy sweet side sitting,
> Love had espied me, in a place most fitting.
> Betrayed by thine eyes' beams (which make blind see),
> He shot at me and said, 'For thine eyes' light,
>   This daring boy that durst usurp my right –
>   Take him, a wounded slave, to Love and Thee!'
>
> Sonnet 55
> Nymphs, which in beauty mortal creatures stain,
> And satyrs, which none but fair nymphs behold –
> They, to the nymphs, and nymphs to them, complain,
> And each, in spite, my mistress' beauty told;
> Till soundly sleeping in a myrtle grove,
> A wanton satyr had espied her there –
> Who, deeming she was dead, in all haste strove
> To fetch the nymphs, which in the forests were.
> They, flocking fast in triumph of her death,
> Lightly beheld, and, deeming she was dead,
> Nymphs sang, and satyrs dancèd out of breath.
> Whilst satyrs, with the nymphs, *la volta* led,
>   My mistress did awake! Then they which came
>   To scorn her beauty, ran away for shame!

Like Shakespeare's 153–4, Barnes's 54–5 are an unusual pair of anacreontic poems. Their numeric position and subject matter also seem significant: 54 is the sequence's sixty-sixth poem; it tells the story of the poet's original sins, and its theme of erring is reinforced with a defective Petrarchan rhyme scheme and a feminine-rhymed octave, in which the poet's ill-advised theft and misplaced pride are detailed. The narrative similarities are also striking: in 54, Cupid is robbed of a love-wounding instrument; in both 54 and 55, someone who belongs to a group of hurt lovers encounters a sleeping or reclining person who is the focus of the group's ill feelings; and in 55, a defunct love is revived or threatened to be revived, and hopes are raised and dashed about assuaging grief. While some details diverge – brand vs. bow, nymphs vs. nymphs and satyrs, and so on – the matching details are suggestive.

The most telling similarities are stylistic. Both Shakespeare and Barnes use enjambments that pivot around action verbs: 'A maid . . . his . . . fire did quickly steep / In a cold . . . fountain' (153); 'many nymphs . . . / Came tripping by' (154); 'They . . . strove / To fetch the nymphs' (55); 'they . . . came / To scorn her beauty' (55). In three of the four sonnets, the last sentence of the third quatrain flows into the couplet: 'I . . . hied, a sad distempered guest, / But found no cure' (153); 'I, my mistress' thrall, / Came there for cure' (154); 'Whilst satyrs . . . *la volta* led, / My mistress did awake' (55). And both Barnes and Shakespeare use participles ambiguously. Barnes employs ambiguous referents: 'But, once, Parthenophe, by thy sweet side sitting, / Love had espied me' (Parthenophil, not Love, is sitting next to Parthenophe); 'They . . . my mistress' beauty told; / Till soundly sleeping in a myrtle grove, / A wanton satyr had espied her there' (Parthenophe is sleeping, not the satyr). Shakespeare's reserves his ambiguities for Sonnet 154:

> The little love-god lying once asleep
> Laid by his side his heart-inflaming brand . . .
>
> (lines 1–2)

> And so the general of hot desire
> Was sleeping by a virgin hand disarmed.
>
> (lines 9–10, Q's punctuation in line 10)

In light of 153's opening ('Cupid laid by his brand and fell asleep'), 154's first lines seem meant to convey that Cupid laid his torch aside before sleeping, not after, but the phrasing hints at postcoital detumescence.[32] In a similar vein, Sonnet 154 invites bawdy interpretations with 'general of hot desire', 'sleeping by a virgin', 'by a virgin hand disarmed'. Shakespeare may have been inspired by Greek or Latin participles, which are more fluidly ambiguous than English participles, but also seems to owe something to Barnes: 'Laid by his side' and 'sleeping by a virgin hand' resemble 'sleeping in a myrtle grove' and 'by thy sweet side sitting'.

All of the sonnets feature robbery; if Shakespeare is echoing Barnes in 153–4, he is likely doing so in a spirit similar to that with which he echoes Barnes in another theft sonnet, 99. Both 99 and 153–4 advertise that they echo a non-Barnes text, and both require us to listen past that echo to hear Barnes. Shakespeare's 99 is a transitional poem that allegorises poetic theft; 153–4 are similarly transitional, but their allegory seems to have more to do with sexual addiction than with poetry: by sleeping with the mistress, the poet contracts a 'love disease' for which there is no cure, or rather the cure is uncertain, since it 'lies' in his mistress's eye. But if we link 153–4 to 99, a poetic allegory emerges: in hinting that his disease stems from sleeping with someone who slept with many people, the poet suggests that he has been stylistically and conceptually infected by a common mode of love poetry. The poet's cure is to seek again his mistress's eye. In the end, he evokes a conventional Petrarchan image but adds a sexual twist, as if aiming to refresh the image.

Chapter 9

Complaints of the Heart

> Nor gives it satisfaction to our blood
> That we must curb it upon others' proof.
>
> (Shakespeare, 'A Lover's Complaint')

The Proof of Others in 'A Lover's Complaint'

As a final poem of a sequence, 'A Lover's Complaint' is both conventional and unusual. It is conventional because it is a lament by someone other than the poet, whose allegory relates obliquely to preceding sonnets. It is unusual because its title is ambiguous, its characters are nameless, and its narrative and meaning are open-ended. The title might lead us to expect that the poet will be the plaintant, since 'lover' in Renaissance English typically denotes a man, but a maid does most of the 'plaining'.[1] The lamenter's identity is further complicated because the maid quotes her seducer's pleas at length, and because the title could refer to more than one lover. (Q's 'Lovers' could mean 'Lovers''.) Schematically, the complaint invites the reader to be a suspicious interpreter: two narrative frames that are opened at the outset are not closed at the conclusion, and the moral of the story is unclear – the maid is regretful, but her regret is no proof against falling again for her seducer.

Modally if not narratively, 'A Lover's Complaint' begins *in medias res*:

> From off a hill whose concave womb reworded
> A plaintful story from a sist'ring vale,
> My spirits to attend this double voice accorded,
> And down I laid to list the sad-tuned tale;
> Ere long espied a fickle maid, full pale,

> Tearing of papers, breaking rings atwain,
> Storming her world with sorrow's wind and rain.

The verb 'reworded' means 'echoed' or 'rephrased'; it may also hint at 'rewarded' and frame the poem as redemptory. Portraying the maid's lament with feminine imagery ('womb', 'sist'ring'), the poet suggests that the poem is a female response to his sonnets and the maid is his double. He is drawn to hear her story and remains as spellbound as a conjured ghost: his 'spirits' agree to 'attend'. He also evokes a dream-vision: his lying down is a kind of ritual action, and his sighting of the maid soon follows – or follows in almost no time, to judge by the interruptive manner in which it is introduced: 'down I laid to list ... the tale; / Ere long espied a ... maid'. Like Cupid, who lays aside his brand and falls asleep in Sonnets 153–4, the poet lies down to listen, as if he were laying aside his lyre to hear someone else sing or closing his eyes to imagine a scene inspired by sad song: 'And down I laid [sic] to list the sad-tuned tale'. The maid herself is ghostlike: 'full pale'. She is also 'fickle'. 'Fickle' could describe her temperament ('moody' or 'distraught', with a hint of 'unreliable'), or it could be a transferred epithet (from her faithless seducer); it could even describe her appearance (flickering?).[2] From the start, then, 'A Lover's Complaint' blurs meanings and identities and evokes doubles and echoes.

The poem also opens with a prepositional phrase: 'From off a hill'. This is itself an echo that links the complaint to the first poem (Sonnet 1, 'From fairest creatures, we desire increase'), and perhaps to a central poem (Sonnet 98, 'From you I have been absent in the spring'). More crucial, it rewords Daniel's 'The Complaint of Rosamond', which similarly begins with a double preposition:

> Out from the horror of infernal deeps,
> My poor afflicted ghost comes here to plain it,
> Attended with my shame that never sleeps,
> The spot wherewith my kind and youth did stain it.
> My body found a grave where to contain it.
> A sheet could hide my face, but not my sin,
> For fame finds never tomb t'enclose it in.

Shakespeare's 'From off' echoes Daniel's 'Out from'. Both poems begin *in medias res*; both are in rhyme-royal stanzas; and both use 'attend' in line 3. Daniel's 'Rosamond' is moreover allusive in its own right: with his ghost-speaker, it draws on a convention popularised by *A Mirror for Magistrates*, whose plaintive 'Shore's Wife' (by

Thomas Churchyard) Rosamond later invokes.[3] In echoing the first stanza of 'Rosamond' in his first stanza, Shakespeare signals that he is writing in a genre that is steeped in competition – a type of poem in which the speaker is one 'complainer' among many – and that he is responding to Daniel.

The importance of 'Rosamond' goes beyond its influence on 'A Lover's Complaint'. Shakespeare draws on Daniel's poem in three mid-1590s works: *Romeo and Juliet*, *Venus and Adonis*, and *Lucrece*. Romeo's address to Juliet's lifeless body echoes Rosamond's account of her poisoned body and Henry II's address to Rosamond's body.[4] *Venus and Adonis*'s stanzas on perfection and imperfection, especially the lines about 'stealing molds from heav'n', resemble Rosamond's diatribe against women who use cosmetics.[5] In *Lucrece*, clear verbal and situational echoes of 'Rosamond' can be found in the passages describing Tarquin and Henry as they approach, respectively, Lucrece's bedroom and Rosamond's bedroom, and in the passages in which Lucrece and Rosamond interpret mythical art.[6] More subtle but no less significant are *Lucrece*'s numeric and thematic parallels to Daniel's poem. The 1594 version of 'Rosamond' contains 129 stanzas. The 'sin and fall' portion of Rosamond's story is told in stanzas 61–6 and is most emphasised in stanza 65 (the poem's centre), which not only begins 'Now did I find myself unparadised', but contains falling feminine rhymes that bolster the biblical allegory (*beginning–sinning*, *loathing–nothing*). *Lucrece* employs similar numeric symbolism: at the poem's centre is a series of stanzas divisible into six '11 stanza' groups, in which Lucrece meditates on Tarquin's sin (rape) and later considers a potential sin of her own (suicide). In short, Shakespeare drew heavily on 'Rosamond' in the mid-1590s. This may indicate that he wrote a version of 'A Lover's Complaint' at that time and revised it later: among Shakespeare's works, the complaint is stylistically closest to *Cymbeline* (1609–10).[7] Even if he wrote the entire poem shortly before 1609, he may have been returning to 'Rosamond' and other materials that were seminal to him when he began writing *Sonnets*. As we will see, this includes Sidney's *Arcadia*.

Stripped of its framing devices, Shakespeare's plot can be summarised as follows: near a river into which she has thrown love tokens, a sobbing woman tells how she was seduced by a young nobleman of dubious reputation, who confessed his faults and expressed submission by giving her the love tokens that he had received from his conquests; now abandoned, the woman is regretful but unreconciled – she would fall again for her seducer, despite what she knows about him. In Book 2, Chapter 18 of *Arcadia*, Dido tells a similar story. Dido was seduced by Pamphilus, a young nobleman who did not hide the fact that he seduced many women and played the women off one another: '[he would be] making us now jealous; now envious; now proud of what we had, desirous of more; now giving one the triumph to see him . . . ; now with an estranged look making her fear the loss [of him]'.[8] Like *Sonnets*' fair youth and the complaint's male seducer, Pamphilus is feminine in appearance and unmasculine in behaviour: 'never was there man that could . . . with a more unmanlike bravery use his tongue to her disgrace, which had lately sung sonnets of her praises'. Joan Rees describes the *Arcadia* episode as close to 'A Lover's Complaint' in characterisation and mood: both women 'know the wooer is not be trusted. Both exclaim that the example of others' downfall has no power to deter; both describe their seducer as young, noble, handsome, and gifted; and [moral] ambiguity attaches to both of them'.[9] Rees also argues that, later in Book 2, Sidney enhances and purifies the character of Dido and further vilifies Pamphilus, and that 'Shakespeare makes no use in his poem of the later pages of the Dido story'.[10]

Shakespeare in fact engages with the entire episode, including its narrative frames. Dido's tale is a story within a story within a story. In the chapter before the one in which Dido tells her tale, the Macedonian prince Pyrocles, dressed as a woman, is weeping by a stream. The Arcadian princess Philoclea overhears his plaints and watches him inscribe verses in the sand, which describe how he 'laid' his face down to see his woes reflected in the stream; how his griefs, given to the air, rebound with 'Echoes' force'; and how his cares, written in sand, foretell his lamentable situation. Philoclea then reveals herself to Pyrocles, who kisses her and reveals to her his true identity: he is not the maid Zelmane, but the prince whose story he partly told her. After Philoclea expresses affection for him more than she 'minded to have done', Pyrocles reassures her of his sincerity and nobility by giving her 'some jewels of right princely value, as some little tokens of his love and quality', and by showing her 'letters from his father, King Euarchus'. She 'little needed these proofs', the narrator tells us, and, after she eagerly accepts his marriage proposal, she is wary of his and her own desire for embrace – and therefore commands him to tell the rest of his story. 'Sweet princess of my life', Pyrocles resumes, 'what trophies, what triumph, what monuments, what histories might ever make my fame yield so sweet a music to my ears, as that it pleaseth you . . . ?' Within this story, Pyrocles will recount how Dido told him her story.

In his complaint, then, Shakespeare draws details from Dido's story and its narrative context, especially the Philoclea-Pyrocles frame. Beyond the generic images – a weeping lover by a stream, a lover laying his head down to listen to laments – he seems to have been influenced by the use of jewels as love tokens, and by the idea that the tokens and letters are 'proofs'. (His own maid casts away such items.) He may also owe something to Sidney's 'trophies'. In stanza 33, Shakespeare's male seducer refers to tokens from other women as 'trophies': '"Lo, all these trophies of affections hot, / Of pensive and subdued desires the tender, / Nature hath charged me that I hoard them not, / But yield them up where I myself must render"'. As Duncan-Jones notes, these lines echo Sonnet 1, 'with its account of the addressee as *niggarding*', and Sonnet 126, 'with its anticipation of the time when nature must *render* the youth up to death'.[11] They also recall Sonnet 31, in which the poet tells the youth: 'Thou art the grave where buried love doth live, / Hung with the trophies of my lovers gone'. Sidney's 'trophies' are not quite the same as Shakespeare's – the 'winner takes all' conceit is not present – but Pyrocles can be seen as a seducer: besides disguising himself to gain access to Philoclea and telling her stories to win her over, he has abandoned women in the course of his adventures. When he resumes his story at the end of Chapter 17, he confesses that Erona, a queen whose throne he helped restore, was overthrown by her husband soon after he left her.

The Dido-Pamphilus episode and the narratives framing it develop two other themes relevant to 'A Lover's Complaint': triangular desire and doubling. When Philoclea finds Pyrocles weeping by the stream, she is on a mission from her father, who is in love with 'Zelmane' and has asked Philoclea to plead for him. The episode parallels *Sonnets*' love triangle with its old man, its young man who can pass as a woman, and its intervening woman. It also parallels the narrative frame of 'A Lover's Complaint': a maid tells an old man how a young man seduced her. Alternatively, the situations in *Arcadia* and 'A Lover's Complaint' can be said to involve four people, since Philoclea's mother is also in love with Pyrocles, and Shakespeare's poet overhears the story that the maid is telling. Whether they involve three or four (or more) people, the plots are governed by a logic of triangular desire: desire for another person begins or increases when the person is desired by a third party. In a related vein, the plots feature deceit (disguise) and doubling (a second beloved who is eerily similar or antithetical to the first). Sidney's doubling is extreme: near the end of the Philoclea-Pyrocles frame, interlaced with the later part of the Dido-Pamphilus story, is the story of the original Zelmane (Chapters 21–3). Zelmane was a princess who fell in love with Pyrocles and disguised herself as a man in order to serve him as his page; pining away in his service, she died. Pyrocles confesses that he adopted her name and her dress in his pursuit of love, and that his love for Philoclea was inspired by a portrait of Philoclea that reminded him of Zelmane. The issues raised in this account have close parallels in *Sonnets*: both Sidney and Shakespeare suggest that love is a compensatory and idealising response to loss – that our love for another person correlates with the feeling that the beloved gives us back someone, perhaps imaginary, whom we have lost.

Arcadia is a significant influence on 'A Lover's Complaint', but Daniel's 'Rosamond' is a more pointed one. All three works tell stories within stories within stories, but Daniel's and Shakespeare's poems are complaints in rhyme royal, and their pairs of narrators and addressees (poet to reader and woman to man) are schematically identical. What is more, their narrative frames are inversely related. 'Rosamond' begins with the speech of an unknown person and ends with a clear demarcation of narrators and speakers: Rosamond reminds the poet to tell Delia her story; the poet addresses the reader. 'A Lover's Complaint', by contrast, quickly establishes two narrative frames but does not return to them: the poem ends abruptly with the maid's unreconciled plaints. Shakespeare subverts generic expectations and inverts Daniel's structure, and in doing so suggests that his complaint is as much about poetry as love.

The complaint's parallels to Spenser are less pointed but no less significant. Spenser's *Complaints* begins with *The Ruins of Time*. This poem's speaker is female (Verlame), but the complaint is not amatory: Time is the culprit, not a male seducer. Like 'A Lover's Complaint', the poem begins with an encounter between a male speaker and a lamenting woman. As John Kerrigan notes, such encounters are 'commonplace in late medieval and Tudor literature', but the overlap between the poems is 'unmistakable'; this is partly because *The Ruins of Time* is in the same stanza form as 'A Lover's Complaint', but mostly because Verlame, like Shakespeare's maid, sits on a bank, weeps tears that resemble the stream she borders, is initially nameless, and has untucked hair.[12] What is more, *The Ruins of Time* calls attention to 'the transience of beauty, the violence of Time, and the importance of poetry as a means to immortality'.[13] In light of Shakespeare's monument trio, one of Spenser's stanzas stands out:

> Thy lord shall never die, the whiles this verse
> Shall live, and surely it shall live forever:
> Forever it shall live and shall rehearse

His worthy praise and virtues dying never –
Though death his soul shall from his body sever.
And thou thyself herein shalt also live:
Some grace the heav'ns do to my verses give.

(*Ruins*, stanza 37)

In Sonnets 55, 81, and 107, the fair youth is the man who 'shall live' as long as there are readers to 'rehearse' the lines. In *The Ruins of Time* stanza, the 'lord' is the deceased brother of the Earl of Leicester, who may have been Spenser's patron: Spenser is fulfilling a duty to Leicester's family and transitioning to a subject of more concern to him – society's neglect of poetry and poets.[14] After tracing family connections from Leicester to the Countess of Pembroke, Spenser arrives at Sidney, for whom he will now, belatedly, write an elegy. The Sidney elegy is the poem's climax; among other things, it is a plea for respect and recognition of poets. Spenser makes a similar plea in *Prothalamion* – another lament-filled work that may have influenced 'A Lover's Complaint'.[15] In that poem, Spenser situates himself on the banks of the Thames in late 1596. *Prothalamion* ostensibly celebrates a double wedding, but the festive mood is undercut by a melancholy refrain or countermelody ('undersong'), which hints that the poet is reflecting on his life and career.[16] In echoing other poets, Shakespeare reflects on similar matters.

The allusions in 'A Lover's Complaint' are legion, but none underscores poetic ambition as intensely as the Sidney, Spenser, and Daniel examples do. In drawing on these poets, Shakespeare places himself in high company, in a line descending from Sidney. The Echo myth is also prominent in Spenser and Daniel. *Amoretti* traces a progression from Narcissus to Echo, or rather from Narcissus to Narcissus and Echo, which culminates in the 'Eccho' refrain in 'Epithalamion' – Spenser combines the Italian word 'ecco' (behold) with the English 'echo', in order to convey the union of sight and sound. In 'An Ode', Daniel cites Echo as someone who knows the name of his beloved; and in the final stanza of 'Rosamond', he portrays himself as Echo-like: now that the world has heard his laments, he must live unseen. Like the *Amoretti* poet and the *Delia* poet, the *Sonnets* poet attempts to move beyond narcissism and concludes his sequence with a poem that emphasises echoing.

'A Lover's Complaint' may also echo or anticipate Shakespeare's own writings, from the 'Willow Song' in *Othello* to Imogen's lament in *Cymbeline*.[17] The parallels to *Lucrece* matter most here. Note that the post-rape stanzas of *Lucrece* are in the mode of a complaint, and that stanza 1 has parallels to the opening of 'A Lover's Complaint':

> From the besieged Ardea, all in post,
> Borne by the trustless wings of false desire,
> Lust-breathed Tarquin leaves the Roman host
> And to Collatium bears the lightless fire –
> Which, in pale embers hid, lurks to aspire
> And girdle with embracing flames the waist
> Of Collatine's fair love, Lucrece the chaste.

Tarquin's haste is conveyed by enjambments and a run-on sentence. Shakespeare echoes this stanza twice at the beginning of 'A Lover's Complaint' – with 'From' in the first line, and with the entrance of the 'reverend man' in the ninth stanza:

> A reverend man, that grazed his cattle nigh,
> Sometimes a blusterer, that the ruffle knew
> Of court, of city, and had let go by
> The swiftest hours observèd as they flew,
> Towards this afflicted fancy fastly drew,
> And, privileged by age, desires to know
> In brief the grounds and motives of her woe.

Despite his age, the reverend man swiftly accosts the maid, and his speed is emphasised with enjambments and the observation that he 'had let go by / The swiftest hours observèd as they flew'. Even in the passing and misspent hours of his youth, it would seem, he reflected on time and profited from his reflections. The hurrying figures of Tarquin and the reverend man evoke different temporal perspectives in relation to love: a *carpe diem* mentality and a long-term religious perspective.

The 'hurrying' motif also connects *Lucrece* and 'A Lover's Complaint' to *Venus and Adonis*. *Venus and Adonis* concludes in the mode of a complaint (Venus mourns Adonis), and its final stanza consists of a sentence that employs enjambments to convey brisk movement – Venus's hurrying away:

> Thus weary of the world, away she hies,
> And yokes her silver doves, by whose swift aid
> Their mistress mounted through the empty skies
> In her light chariot quickly is conveyed –
> Holding their course to Paphos, where their queen
> Means to immure herself and not be seen.

Like Echo, Venus will be unseen but perhaps heard. Her hurrying away is itself an echo of the poem's first stanza, in which Adonis hurries to join the hunt and Venus hastens to seduce him:

> Even as the sun with purple-coloured face,
> Had ta'en his last leave of the weeping morn,
> Rose-cheeked Adonis hied him to the chase –
> Hunting he loved, but love he laughed to scorn;
> Sick-thoughted Venus makes amain untó him
> And, like a bold-faced suitor, 'gins to woo him.

The image of the 'weeping morn' foreshadows Venus's lament at the end; Venus's appearance is as abrupt as the fickle maid's in 'A Lover's Complaint'. All of the hurrying figures and the references to time illustrate that *Venus and Adonis*, *Lucrece*, and *Sonnets* are thematically linked.

In completing a poetic triptych, 'A Lover's Complaint' more immediately completes *Sonnets*, and it is thematically linked to the sonnets that precede it. As Duncan-Jones observes, the complaint's youth provides a strong link: he seems to be a 'wealthy and promiscuous courtier' who is 'as universally admired and sought after as the fair youth'; he is 'fascinatingly unreliable'; and his unreliability is 'conveyed in terms of spring weather'.[18] The maid, meanwhile, has 'much in common with the poet-speaker of the sonnets': she is 'in the grip of an obsessive devotion to a fair youth' and 'betrayed by the very words she uses'.[19] To put it another way, she is a figure for the poet, and the poem offers an alternative perspective on the situations in the sonnets. As Duncan-Jones also observes, 'A Lover's Complaint' can be divided into four parts: in the first ten stanzas, the poet sets the scene; in the next fifteen, 'the maid describes her attraction to the young man'; in the fifteen after those, the man's 'wooing speeches are reported'; and, in the final seven stanzas, 'the maid exclaims at the irresistibly beguiling power of the youth's words and tears, to which she would willingly submit once more'.[20] Given the poet's opening remarks and description of the reverend man, 'A Lover's Complaint' might lead us to expect two more parts:

Part	Stanzas	Description
1	1–10	The poet sets the scene and establishes the narrative frames.
2	11–25	The maid describes the young man and her attraction to him.

3	26–40	The maid reports the speeches of the young man.
4	41–47	The maid confesses that she would fall again for the young man.
5	–	(The reverend man responds to the maid.)
6	–	(The poet addresses the reader.)

In leaving two narrative frames open, Shakespeare suggests that the maid is incompletely repentant and that his sequence is imperfect.

Meanwhile, the numeric and thematic centre of 'A Lover's Complaint' is stanza 24:

> 'Nor gives it satisfaction to our blood
> That we must curb it upon others' proof,
> To be forbode the sweets that seem so good
> For fear of harms that preach in our behoof.
> O appetite, from judgement stand aloof!
> The one a palate hath that needs will taste,
> Though reason weep and cry "It is thy last!"'

Here the maid explains why she was unable to resist the young man despite having good reasons to reject him. As she notes two stanzas earlier, even 'proofs new-bleeding' (recently deflowered women) did not give her adequate emotional defence. Now generalising about 'others' proof', she claims that no one can curb passion by observing others' fates. According to the maid, seeing harms may instill some fear in us but ultimately they are ineffective warnings: we can only hope that 'appetite' (desire) will stay away from 'judgement' (reason); once we acquire a taste for the forbidden, we will taste it (because our appetite will have infected our judgement). The maid's view is comparable to that of the *Sonnets* poet, who sees himself as governed by his desires.

The maid's statement about love potentially doubles as a statement about poetry: as in Sonnets 153–4, Shakespeare suggests that love and poetry are infectious diseases. At the end of the poem, images of infection are coupled with images of art and tears:

> For lo, his passion, but an art of craft,
> Ev'n there resolved my reason into tears;
> There my white stole of chastity I doffed,
> Shook off my sober guards and civil fears,
> Appeared to him as he to me appears –
> All melting – though our drops this diff'rence bore:
> He poisoned me, and mine did him restore.
>
> (stanza 43)

> O that infected moisture of his eye!
> O that false fire which in his cheek so glowed!
> O that forced thunder from his heart did fly!
> O that said breath his spongy lungs bestowed!
> O all that borrowed motion, seeming owed,
> Would yet again betray the fore-betrayed,
> And new pervert a reconcilèd maid.
>
> (stanza 47)

The youth's tears are those of an actor and are therefore fake, but they cause the maid to shed tears, and they perhaps excite her. Their moisture, carrying infection, poisons her, and though the youth is temporarily restored by his sexual encounter, he has already been infected by a 'love disease': like the maid, the youth may be aroused by his effect on another person. (Unlike her, however, he seeks to produce an effect, which suggests that he is mostly enamored of his art.) As a poet seeking to show both love and art, Shakespeare is both maid and youth: he cannot curb his passions based on 'others' proof', yet he must draw on others to prove himself as a poet.

The Pyramid at the Heart of the Pyramid

One way in which Shakespeare proves himself as a poet is by adapting conventions. This includes drawing on other poets' devices and schemes, as I have noted throughout the book. In my discussions, however, I have deferred examining one scheme, which in manifest and subtle ways is central to *Sonnets*: a fifty-five-sonnet pyramid hidden within the 153-poem pyramid. To borrow a phrase from Hamlet, this is *Sonnets*' 'heart of hearts'. The scheme is so well-hidden that even readers apprised of the main pyramid might not find it: discovering it presupposes familiarity not only with the sequence's organisational principles, but with Platonism in Renaissance poetry.

Like other Elizabethan poets, Shakespeare needn't have been deeply versed in Platonism to employ its conceits. Generic instances abound in *Sonnets*:

> Then thou, whose shadow shadows doth make bright –
> How would thy shadow's form form happy show
> To the clear day with thy much clearer light,
> When to unseeing eyes thy shade shines so?
>
> (Sonnet 43)

> What is your substance, whereof are you made,
> That millions of strange shadows on you tend? –
> Since everyone hath, every one, one shade,
> And you, but one, can every shadow lend?
>
> (Sonnet 53)

As Stephen Booth notes, words like 'shadow', 'form', and 'substance' are Platonic:

> In the work of Renaissance Platonists, *substance* and *shadows* were used as technical terms. [Sonnet 53] is not in any way an exposition of the philosophic ideas to which it alludes, but the mere presence of the two Platonic terms in lines 1 and 2 establishes the Platonic doctrine of 'ideas' or 'forms' as a basis from which Shakespeare can expand.[21]

Shakespeare plays with two contrary meanings of 'form': 'essence' and 'appearance'. Sometimes the fair youth represents an ideal form; sometimes, a deceptive sensory form.

Sonnets also features more abstruse Platonic conceits, such as 'the Great Year' and 'the World Soul'. In Sonnet 59, the poet wishes that he could 'with a backward look, / Ev'n of five hundred courses of the sun', find the fair youth's image 'in some ántique book'. With 'five hundred courses', he alludes to a cyclical view of history if not to the Great Year – the period of time that it takes for the heavens' bodies to return to their original positions.[22] He tries to gain perspective on beauty and truth, hoping to find a record of the youth's form and to read what the ancients said about the world's wonder. In Sonnet 107, he speaks of 'the prophetic soul / Of the wide world'. He is partly referring to gloom-and-doom predictions of common opinion, but the phrasing and the context point beyond mundane matters to the World Soul – the life force with which the universe was endowed by its creator. The *Sonnets* poet often associates the youth with the cosmos. As he says in Sonnet 109, 'For nothing this wide universe I call / Save thou, my rose: in it thou art my all'. As he says in Sonnet 112, 'You are my All-the-world'.

In the *Timaeus*, Plato describes the World Soul in mathematical terms:

> God created the soul [and] he composed it in the following way . . . He first marked off a section of the whole, and then another twice the size of the first, next a third, half as much again as the second and three times the first, a fourth twice the size of the second, a fifth three times the third, a sixth eight times the first, a seventh twenty-seven times the first.[23]

In short, God created the soul in a geometrically precise fashion. The *Timaeus* formulation was later called 'the Platonic lambda' or 'the lambda formula' because it resembles the Greek letter lambda (Λ) in its standard diagram:

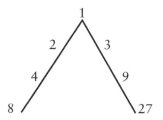

The soul's parts are expressed as a series of seven numbers: 1, 2, 3, 4, 9, 8, 27. (In the lambda diagram, start from the top and read across and down the rows.) They are also expressed as two series of four numbers: 1, 2, 4, 8, and 1, 3, 9, 27. (Start from the top of the diagram and read down the left side; start again and read down the right side.) The sum of the seven numbers is 54; the sum of the eight numbers is 55. Either sum can be regarded as a representation of the World Soul, or as a marriage of numbers related to 2 and 3.

The 55-part formula for the world soul is discussed at length by the Italian humanist Marsilio Ficino.[24] In the late fifteenth century, Ficino translated and commented on Plato's works, including the *Timaeus* and the *Symposium*. In the *Timaeus* commentary, he includes a pyramidal diagram of the soul in his chapter 'On the composition of the soul, and why the soul needs five elements for its constitution' (see Figures 9.1 and 9.2). He explains that the number 5 'accords with the composition of the soul' for three reasons:

> The first reason is that, as 5 consists of the first even number and the first odd number, so the soul consists of the divisible nature and the indivisible nature ... The second reason is that the natures by which God compounds everything are five in number ... (Indeed, the soul is deemed the mean of all things, for the special reason that it consists of the five qualities of all things.) The third reason is that, since the soul is the mean of the universe, it naturally assumes the number 5, the mean of universal number. For 5 is the perfect mean of 10, since if we duly divide 10 five ways, the justly spaced mean in each division is 5.[25]

Ficino's first reason is the standard explanation for 5's nuptial symbolism: as the sum of 2 and 3, 5 represents the joining of 'female' and 'male' principles. His second and third reasons are illustrated in

Complaints of the Heart 261

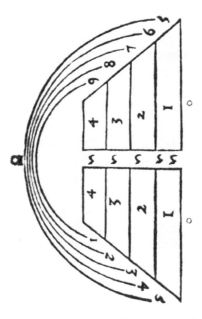

Figure 9.1 Marsilio Ficino's pyramidal illustration of the soul in his commentary on Plato's Timaeus

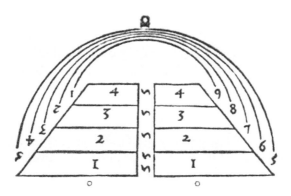

Figure 9.2 Ficino's image, rotated 90 degrees counterclockwise

his diagram: by placing a row of 5s at the pyramid's centre and five numeric pairs around the pyramid, Ficino aims to show that 5 is 'the mean of the universe'. The omega above the pyramid signifies the world soul or 'All'; the human soul is a microcosm of the World Soul (as Ficino says later, 'our soul contains all of the proportions contained in the World Soul').[26] Notably, the pyramid lacks an apex and has only four levels, despite its five 5s and its five pairs of numbers.

Ficino associates the four levels with the four elements, emphasising that 'the power of the soul extends from the central position and fills the universe'.[27] In other words, he suggests that 'the fifth element' – the element above the terrestrial elements – is the missing apex.

As arcane as the Platonic lambda may seem, there is good evidence that Renaissance poets were familiar with it. In his study of Philip Sidney and the Sidney circle, Tom W. N. Parker shows that the fifty-four-part formula informs *Astrophil and Stella*'s structure: Sidney alludes to the World Soul with poem groups whose sizes correspond to the formula.[28] Parker also shows that sequences by Fulke Greville, Robert Sidney, and Mary Wroth contain groups that are informed by the lambda numbers. In a manuscript of Robert Sidney's sequence, for example, there is an authorial note explaining that the sizes of groups correspond to the row totals of the formula.[29] The centre poem of Greville's *Caelica* is Sonnet 55, and a major division in Wroth's *Pamphilia to Amphilanthus* comes after the fifty-fifth poem. Henry Constable alludes to the World Soul in the fifty-fifth sonnet of *Diana* – 'To Sir Philip Sidney's Soul' – in which he portrays Sidney's death as the world's loss, and he presents Sidney's soul as the sum of all virtues.[30] With its pyramid shape and description of Sidney as the 'world's wonder', Joshua Silvester's elegy in *Divine Weeks* arguably alludes to the World Soul. Chapman may allude to the fifty-five-part soul in the title poem of *Ovid's Banquet of Sense*, via the pyramidal organisation and the fifty-five-stanza sections that precede and follow the central Elysium section.[31] Spenser likely alludes to the World Soul in Sonnet 55 of *Amoretti* (via its 'fifth element'), and in the fifty-five stanzas of *The Faerie Queene*'s first canto (via the allegory of holiness/wholeness). Perhaps emulating Spenser, later poets gravitated to 55 as the World-Soul number. At least one surviving copy of Drayton's *Idea's Mirror* has fifty-five poems because two Spenserian pastorals have been appended to it, and Drayton's 1599 *Idea* has fifty-five sonnets.[32] Daniel's 1594 *Delia* contains his first Spenserian sonnets and fifty-five numbered sonnets.

As *Sonnets*' first monument poem, Shakespeare's Sonnet 55 may allude to the fifty-five-part soul, as may the sequence's total number of poems, 155. But the most important allusion to the World Soul is a fifty-five-sonnet pyramid contained within the 153-poem pyramid. Like many schemes in *Sonnets*, this 'pyramid within the pyramid' comments on the main scheme – or rather it relates to it obliquely, like an anamorphic image in a corner of a painting. It is a figure for the inmost heart or soul. In light of Sonnet 22's conceit of exchanged hearts, the pyramid-heart may be that of the poet, the fair youth, or both poet and youth; in light of Sonnet 24's portrait in the heart, it may be an image of the beloved in the poet's heart.

But first things first – the pyramid is composed of Sonnets 21–75:

Step 10:	75
Step 9:	73 74
Step 8:	70 71 72
Step 7:	66 67 68 69
Step 6:	61 62 63 64 65
Step 5:	55 56 57 58 59 60
Step 4:	48 49 50 51 52 53 54
Step 3:	40 41 42 43 44 45 46 47
Step 2:	31 32 33 34 35 36 37 38 39
Step 1:	21 22 23 24 25 26 27 28 29 30

The series begins with a sonnet that alludes to another poet and whose first word is 'So' (21), and it ends right before the rival-poet series, with a sonnet that compares the poet to a miser guarding his treasure, whose first word is 'So' (75). As in the 153-poem pyramid, the steps exhibit thematic and structural coherence, and boundaries between steps are demarcated by non-linked sonnets. (A step's first sonnet is not conjunctively or otherwise clearly linked to the previous step's final sonnet.) The themes and boundaries are especially apparent in the first three steps:

Step	Sonnets	Description of boundary sonnets
1	21–30	21 is the sequence's first sonnet to mention another poet and use the word 'muse'. 29–30 are a pair of 'When I' sonnets. Like a couplet rhyme, the repetition of the 'When I' formula signals rhetorical closure.
2	31–9	In 31–2, the poet mentions other poets and uses 'muse' for the second time, describing the youth as the epitome of previous lovers, and asking the youth to read other poets 'for their style' and his own verse for 'love'. In 38–9, he uses 'muse' for the third time and admits that his praise of the youth is inadequate; he cites the age's 'curious' demands and argues that the youth will 'teach' him to redeem time by inspiring him to a new type of praise.
3	40–7	40–2 are the 'betrayal trio': the poet alternately blames and excuses the youth for the affair with the mistress. 46–7 are a linked pair: 46 speaks of a 'war' between the poet's eyes and heart, and 47 speaks of a 'truce'.

Five of the first six steps have boundary sonnets that refer to verse writing, and the fifth step begins with a monument sonnet (55) and ends with a meditation on time (60). The final three steps also have distinctive content: the eighth step focuses on the youth's future reputation; the ninth step concerns the poet's imminent death; the tenth step returns to the present impasse.

The fifty-five-sonnet pyramid is constructed on the same principles as the main pyramid and is hidden within it – a remarkable feat of design. To put this in perspective, imagine a sequence in which half of the poems are clearly linked to the next poem: the probability that a randomly selected fifty-five-poem series will have non-linked poems at the correct intervals for a ten-step pyramid is less than a tenth of a per cent; even with an exception, the probability is less than two per cent.[33] With a sequence like Shakespeare's, the probabilities would be smaller yet: not only is *Sonnets* distinct in containing many unambiguously linked sonnets; more than half of the sonnets in the fair-youth section are linked to the next sonnet, and many non-linked sonnets are already 'spoken for' – they demarcate boundaries in the 153-poem pyramid. In short, the pattern of linked and non-linked sonnets in the series beats very difficult odds: non-linked sonnets demarcate eight of the nine pyramid-step boundaries, and the exception – Sonnets 69–70 – arguably confirms the rule. (For details on 69–70, see Appendix E.)

The most crucial evidence is the centre poem of the series:

>Sonnet 48
>How careful was I when I took my way,
>Each trifle under truest bars to thrust,
>That to my use it might unusèd stay
>From hands of falsehood, in sure wards of trust!
>But thou, to whom my jewëls trifles are,
>Most worthy comfort, now my greatest grief,
>Thou best of dearest, and mine only care,
>Art left the prey of every vulgar thief.
>Thee have I not locked up in any chest,
>Save where thou art not, though I feel thou art,
>Within the gentle closure of my breast,
>From whence at pleasure thou mayst come and part;
> And even thence thou wilt be stol'n I fear,
> For truth proves thievish for a prize so dear.

The poem's conceits of travelling and securing valuables are informed by its terminal position in the main pyramid's third step and its central position in the fifty-five-sonnet series. The terminal position reinforces the retrospective theme: the poet is thinking back on the travel and travail of the third step. The central position hints at a variety of figures: the human heart's position in the chest, a heart that has been 'stolen' or 'locked up', and deep and precious feelings. Sonnet 48's imagery also looks back to Sonnet 24, in which the poet claims to have 'stelled' or 'steeled' the youth in his heart, and forward to Sonnet 75, the pyramid's apex, in which the miser-like poet is afraid that 'the filching age will steal his treasure'.

As a representation of a heart, the fifty-five-sonnet pyramid may speak to personal love, but it also speaks to poetic ambition: figuratively, the pyramid points to the rival-poet series. In the first poem of the rival-poet series, the *Sonnets* poet looks askance at new trends and perhaps especially at hyphenated compound words, a common feature of verse satire: 'Why is my verse so barren of new pride, / So far from variation or quick change? / Why with the time do I not glance aside / To new-found methods and to compounds strange?' (76).[34] The first poem of the fifty-five-sonnet pyramid similarly evokes a style antithetical to that of the *Sonnets* poet:

> Sonnet 21
> So is it not with me as with that muse,
> Stirred by a painted beauty to his verse,
> Who heav'n itself for ornament doth use,
> And every fair with his fair doth rehearse –
> Making a couplement of proud compare
> With sun and moon, with earth and sea's rich gems,
> With April's first-born flow'rs and all things rare
> That heaven's air in this huge rondure hems.
> O let me, true in love, but truly write,
> And then, believe me, my love is as fair
> As any mother's child, though not so bright
> As those gold candles fixed in heaven's air.
>   Let them say more that like of hearsay well –
>   I will not praise, that purpose not to sell.

As in Sonnet 76, the poet tries to distinguish his simple and true verse from poetry of overblown praise and strained use of compound words or double comparisons. The apparent allusion to a specific poet – 'that muse' – has prompted commentators to suggest that Sonnet 21 belongs in the rival-poet series. But as the first sonnet of a series that points towards the rival-poet series, 21 fits well where it is.

The broader sequential context also points to poetic ambition. In the poems leading up to the fifty-five-sonnet pyramid, the poet first pleads to the youth to sire a child, eventually concluding that the best way to insure the youth's immortality is through both progeny and poetry (17). He then considers and rejects comparisons to the youth, asserting that the youth's beauty 'will not fade' once it is grafted onto his verse (18) and pledging that the youth will 'ever live' in his poetry (19). Finally, perhaps in response to a request to paint the youth in verse, the poet argues that the youth was painted by 'nature's own hand' and therefore needs no more painting (20). In this context, Sonnet 21 represents a new stage in argument: the poet rejects another poet's 'painted beauty' and far-fetched comparisons. As the first sonnet of the hidden pyramid, 21 also underscores the poet's desire to create a worthy portrait/monument worthy, hinting that the best portrait is a secret one: because he wants to keep, not sell, the youth, the poet does not lavishly praise him. In short, the fifty-five-sonnet pyramid seems meant as a private monument. To judge by the rival-poet series, though, the offering proves insufficient. More evidence that Shakespeare intends a link between this pyramid and the rival series can be deduced from the two sonnets that frame them, 20 and 87. These are the sequence's two feminine-rhyme sonnets; in between them there are sixty-six sonnets: the pyramid sonnets and the core sonnets of the rival-poet series.

The fifty-five-sonnet pyramid is an extreme case; as such, it raises new questions about audience. Notionally, the pyramid would seem intended for Southampton, but is it reasonable to argue that he would see it without being told details that run counter to the conceit of an intimate understanding? Among Shakespeare's contemporaries, friends and fellow poets would be more likely to discover the pyramid, but in that case, we might regard it as a product more of poetic competition than of personal devotion. The truth may lie somewhere in between, especially if Shakespeare enhanced schemes and devices for himself. If he did, that could help explain why the sequence is teeming with them. The impulse to enrich every line was common in sixteenth- and seventeenth-century poetry. It is dramatised in George Herbert's 'Jordan (II)', in which the poet first attempts to find the most elaborate words and inventions, 'Decking the sense, as if it were to sell'. (Compare Sonnet 21's 'I will not praise, that purpose not to sell'.) Eventually, the poet hears a 'friend' whisper in his ear: 'How wide is all this long pretence! / There is in love a sweetness ready-penned: / Copy out only that, and save expense'. The conceits are Shakespeare's and ultimately Sidney's. A tension between finding the best figures of speech and speaking from the heart is writ large on *Sonnets*: on one hand, the poet cannot offer enough poetic fireworks; on the other, he hides or allows them to fade into the background as if they paled before basic truths.

If we approach *Sonnets* as ambitious poetry, we may discover additional schemes and devices. To take one example: in light of the fifty-five-sonnet pyramid and *Sonnets*' use of W and doubled digits, Shakespeare may play with the Roman numeral V, figuring 55 as 'VV' (rather than, or in addition to, 'LV'). This would be in line with other fanciful emblems for the youth. Also, with the major exception of the fifty-five-sonnet pyramid, the schemes and devices that I have analysed are largely independent: each can be evaluated on its own. This is not to say that they are unrelated – they may well corroborate one another. In Chapter 6, for instance, I observed that the number of lines in *Venus and Adonis, Lucrece*, and *Sonnets* is 5,533, and I explored the possibility that 5,533 and 5,555 allude to dates in the Anno Mundi calendar. This claim gains support from the lambda formula and the fifty-five-sonnet pyramid. What is more, if *Sonnets* is linked to the 5,555th year of creation, it is not the only pyramidal monument linked to that year. In the mid-1590s, Sir Thomas Tresham built an edifice now known as the Rushton Triangular Lodge, a three-sided construction whose walls are 33 feet long and whose entrance, windows, and gables are superscribed with four-digit numbers. The number above the entrance, '5555', is believed to refer to the Anno Mundi year in which the lodge's construction was begun (1593?) or completed (1595?); it may also represent four five-letter words, such as 'Jesus Maria, Salus Mundi'.[35] Shakespeare's symbolism is akin to that of Tresham's pyramidal edifice. The *Sonnets* poet sees the fair youth as the saviour of his world. My point is twofold: such possibilities are worth exploring on their own terms; at the current stage in our understanding of *Sonnets*, there is more to be gained in testing limits than in issuing warnings about going too far.

Conclusion: Seeing Things Retrospectively

A Matter of Priorities

To reword my opening line, this book claims that *Sonnets* is intricately organised, and that Shakespeare was an ambitious poet who engaged with other poets in his works. Most of my analysis has been devoted to the first claim, whose evidence and arguments can be summarised as follows:

> Elizabethan sonnet sequences are often highly organised. Conventions of the genre include numerological structures and a final stanzaic poem. 'A Lover's Complaint' is integral to *Sonnets*.

> In *Sonnets*, three formally unusual sonnets signal divisions (99, 126, and 145). The sequence can be divided into a fair-youth section (1–126) and a mistress section (127–54). 'A Lover's Complaint' can be regarded as the concluding poem of the mistress section or as a reflection of and on both sections. Each section is bipartite: the fair-youth sonnets divide at 99; the mistress sonnets, at 145.

> *Sonnets* is pyramidally organised. With two division-marking sonnets left out of the count, the remaining 153 poems consist of seventeen groups, starting with Sonnets 1–17 and ending with 'A Lover's Complaint'. Because they decrease in size incrementally, the groups can be visualised as a pyramid.

> The groups or 'pyramid steps' are internally organised. The third pyramid step, for example, has five trios of sonnets, the third of which pertains to the love triangle of the poet, the youth, and the mistress. In these and other schemes based on a series of poems, centre poems tend to be important, along with first and last poems.

> Beyond the two bipartite sections and the 153-poem pyramid, *Sonnets* contains many organisational and numerological schemes. They include groups of non-consecutive sonnets, such as the 'monument' trio (55,

81, and 107), and groups of consecutive sonnets, such as the 'No' trio (123–5).

Sonnets is thematically and schematically linked to *Venus and Adonis* and *Lucrece*.

To this list can be added a few observations less related to organisation:

Sonnets contains a high percentage of poems that directly address the beloved, and a high percentage of rhetorically linked poems (especially pairs and trios).

Sonnets contains many puns involving pronouns. Some schemes are signalled or reinforced by patterned use of pronoun forms.

Often in combination with wordplay, *Sonnets* employs letterplay and numberplay. There are puns on *W* and 'double you', for example, and there is figurative use of 'doubled digits' in sonnets whose numbers are multiples of 11.

Many examples of letterplay and numberplay are associated with Southampton, including *W* puns and 'Wriothesley' anagrams. Southampton is the primary or exclusive model for the fair youth.

The events and situations in *Sonnets* are informed by an allegory of Christian redemption. (In some sonnets, like 33, the poet is a Christ figure; in others, like 106, the youth is the Saviour.) Sin and forgiveness are common themes. Passion and death, resurrection, and final judgement are common reference points.

Taken together, these claims speak to a broader claim: that reading *Sonnets* as a sequence means approaching it with a radically new (and old) set of expectations.

Beyond the basics, there are schemes and devices that may be easier to countenance in retrospect. At the end of the previous chapter I proposed one possibility: that allusions to the Anno Mundi years 5533 and 5555 might become more plausible in view of the 'World Soul' pyramid (and vice versa). To say that the scheme and the device corroborate each other is not to say that the proof is complete, of course, and neither claim is basic. But the calendrical allusions and the fifty-five-sonnet pyramid clarify each other and are stylistically akin to other examples in *Sonnets*. In short, they are Shakespearean; instead of relegating them to footnotes, we should bring them into the light of examination.

More generally, many examples merit a second look. Here I will focus on one – number symbolism – partly because it is prevalent and partly because it tends to provoke scepticism. *Sonnets* incorporates much more number symbolism than it is reputed to contain, even among commentators who allow for it. Temporal versions include:

Sonnet and line(s)   *Symbolism*

7: Lo, in the orient, when the gracious light   Sunday, seven days
12: When I do count the clock that tells the time   12 hours
60: Like as the waves ... So do our minutes ...   60 minutes

49: Against that time, if ever that time comes   climacteric of body
63: Against my love shall be as I am now   climacteric of body
81: Or shall I live, your epitaph to make   and soul climacteric
                                                       of soul

52: So am I as the rich [miser], whose ... feasts   52 weeks (and 24
    ... seldom coming in the long year ...   hours as the first
                                                       sonnet of 52–75)

33: Full many a glorious morning have I seen ...   The thirty-third
    ... Suns of the world ... heaven's sun ...   year of the Son
                                                       of God

The first three instances are essentially witticisms: as with many Shakespearean puns, we can take them or leave them. The climacteric examples are of a different order, because they are linked to schemes: 49 and 63 are the first sonnets of consecutive pyramid steps, and 81 is the centre sonnet of the monument trio. There is also a schematic element to 52's symbolism: besides alluding to the number of weeks in the year, the poem inaugurates a twenty-four-sonnet series whose first and last poems evoke twenty-four-hour vigilance. Sonnet 33's allusion to Christ's thirty-third year is of a different order yet: it is central to the sequence's theme of sin and redemption.

Other symbolic numbers point to less familiar themes:

Number(s)   *Symbolism*

1   unity, wholeness (Elizabethans did not consider 1 a number)
2, 3   (the first 'female' number and the first 'male' number)
2   doubleness, duplicity
3   triangle, trinity
5   marriage, justice
6   perfection, imperfection
10   Christ (X), the Law (ten commandments)
11   transgression, exceeding the mark (fault of excess)

Both columns of this chart could be expanded: in the left column, more room might be made for multiples of 11 and powers of 2 and 3; in the right, more items might be added, along with some notes warning that symbolism is not a reductive code. The chart summarises discussions that occur throughout the book and illustrates ways in which Shakespeare draws on traditional material and makes it his own. Of particular note are his uses of 5, 6, and 11. With 5, he conjoins nuptial and judicial symbolism (a traditional pairing), alerting us to two of the sequence's crucial themes. With 6, he combines positive and negative symbolic traditions (an unusual pairing) and links moral perfection to temporal completion. And with 11, he uses a 'number of transgression' tradition in concert with conceits of duplicity, false comparisons, and doubled digits. At once conventional and idiosyncratic, *Sonnets*' number symbolism underscores the poet's aspiration for, not achievement of, final and eternal meaning. Far from narrowing the poetry's meanings, it suggests that there is more depth to them.

Like my analysis of number symbolism, my discussion of Shakespeare's poetics and poetic career is scattered among chapters. To comprehend the range and depth of Shakespeare's engagement with his contemporaries, it helps to compile *Sonnets*' parallels to other poets' works. The following list is conservative; it includes only the loudest and clearest verbal echoes:

Sonnet(s)	*Echoed poet(s)*	*Echoed poem(s) or work(s)*
5, 8	Sidney	*Arcadia* (Cecropia's argument for marriage)
15	Spenser	*Ruins of Rome* 7 (war against Time)
17	Daniel	*Delia* 46 (1592)
24	Daniel, Constable	*Delia* 13 (1592); *Diana* 9 (1592)
30–1	Constable	*Diana*, 'Grace full of grace'
31	Daniel	*Delia* 46 (1592)
32	Marston	Introductory poem to *Certain Satires*
33	Sidney	*Astrophil and Stella* 22
63	Spenser	*Ruins of Rome* 27 ('injurious Time')
97–9	Watson	*Tears of Fancy* 46–8
99	Constable, Barnes	*Diana* 17 (1592); Madrigal 11 of *Parthenophil and Parthenophe*
106	Spenser	*The Faerie Queene* (proems to Books 1 and 5)
106	Constable, Daniel	*Diana*, 'Miracle of the world'; *Delia* 46 (1592)

116	Spenser	*Amoretti* 59
127	Sidney	*Astrophil and Stella* 7
146	Daniel	*Civil Wars*; *Cleopatra*
153–4	Fletcher, Barnes	*Licia* 27; *Parthenophil and Parthenophe* 54–5

Shakespeare not only echoes many poets but often does so in pointed ways. These tendencies run counter to the view that he differs from his contemporaries in not writing through sources; more important, they show that he knew the genre well and that he drew heavily on certain poets – Sidney, Spenser, Constable, Barnes, and Daniel.

Organisational parallels point to engagement with the same set of poets – those whose works were published in the 1590s or were circulating in manuscript during that period:

Poetic Work(s)	*Organisational structure or feature*
Astrophil and Stella (1591 edition)	Two bipartite sections; '153' total poems
Astrophil and Stella, *Diana* (MS version)	Schematic use of the number 63
Delia (1594), *Idea* (1599)	Schematic use of the number 55
Ovid's Banquet of Sense	Pyramidal structure, perspective conceits
Parthenophil and Parthenophe, *Amoretti*	Schematic use of mirror poems
Amoretti	Schematic use of repeated sonnets

Coupled with parallels to Shakespeare's plays and narrative poems, these similarities suggest that much of *Sonnets* was written in the mid-1590s. They may also indicate that Shakespeare completed a version of *Sonnets* by 1600. This last possibility merits investigation: it squares with Elizabethan practices of making coterie references and circulating manuscripts among friends. Shakespeare's sequence exhibits both manuscript and print features, which speak to concerns with private and public expression.

Parallels between *Sonnets* and Shakespeare's life similarly speak to private concerns. While autobiographical allusions are conventional in sonnet sequences, Shakespeare's rhetoric of intimacy and evocations of infidelity and scandal are far from typical: *Sonnets* hints intensely at secret truths and in doing so warrants investigation of biography and hidden schemes. And while such explorations must prove themselves through interpretive results, the pay-offs do not have to assume the form of textual explication. Some hypotheses have straightforward pay-offs: postulating that the fair youth was modelled on Southampton leads to analysis of *Sonnets* as the third of three related works and enhances claims about number symbolism and numeric schemes; identifying Daniel as the rival poet clarifies Sonnet 87's parody. But most of my discussion of rival-poet candidates develops a framework for understanding poetic rivalry in the 1590s, in relation to styles and careers available to poets. While this too can lead to textual explication (of Sonnet 76's allusions to verse satire, for example), the more essential pay-off is less utilitarian: gaining a feel for the environment in which Shakespeare wrote his sonnets.

Mining for biographical ore also plays an ancillary role in interpreting *Sonnets*' narrative or dramatic situations. The poet's sufferings in Sonnet 33, for instance, can be linked to Shakespeare's tribulations in his thirty-third year; the poet's infidelities in Sonnets 109–22 can be connected to Shakespeare's 'abandonment' of Southampton after the Essex rebellion. These contexts can help us understand the poetry if we do not reduce the poems to their occasions, and if we give due allowance to the poet's allegorising tendencies. Their value does not really lie in decoding one event with another, which is limiting and literal, or even in adding local and emotional colour to the poetry. But they can help us understand the selection and arrangement of events, and the allegories attendant on them. For example, if the poet-youth separation of Sonnets 97–9 refers to two periods – Southampton's 'three season' absence in the late 1590s and Southampton's 'three year' imprisonment in the early 1600s – we may infer that Shakespeare constructed or adapted his sequence to allow for both allusions: in *Sonnets*' allegory, the two times are redeemed. We do not need biographical specifics to deduce the allegory of redemption or to sense that Shakespeare speaks from personal experience when he depicts the poet playing with 'figures' during the beloved's absence, but evidence that he wove together different periods of his life – perhaps revising his poetry to do so – tells us something about the degree of his investment in his allegory, if not his devotion to Southampton. (It is as if he was preparing for a third and final separation.) It also tells us something about how he and his age viewed love's ideal qualities and idealising tendencies, which may be different from how we see them or how we like to think we see them. For all the ways in which *Sonnets* deflates its ideal image of the beloved and offers an allegory of accepting human imperfections, it remains Platonic at heart.

A Matter of Perspective

Invoking two basic meanings of 'perspective' – a representational technique in the visual arts, and a way of considering, knowing, or evaluating – I asserted in the Introduction that my interpretation of *Sonnets* was grounded in a Renaissance understanding of perspective, and that the poet's evolving perspectives (on his beloved, himself, and more) are figured in the pyramidal scheme. Here in the Conclusion I again invoke those meanings, but with the aim of moving from the Renaissance to later periods and present-day concerns. Guiding my discussion are two topics: post-Renaissance views of *Sonnets* and the sonnet sequence, and Shakespeare's modernity. My aim is to provide a more vibrant account of the art and ambitions of *Sonnets*, based on restored familiarity with Shakespeare's milieu and knowledge of the sonnet sequence's afterlife. In my view, *Sonnets* is both of its time and exceptionally modern.

Let us first review some Elizabethan perspectives. Evolving from Italian and French models, the Elizabethan sonnet sequence was typically amatory in content; in the 1590s, it competed with and in some ways replaced pastoral as the genre with which poets began their careers. Instead of a shepherd-lover who sings, sequences feature a poet-lover who writes. And instead of evoking aristocratic competition (leisure-class shepherds participating in impromptu contests), sonneteers register ambition in their craft, which is directed mostly to fellow poets (members of the guild, so to speak). *Sonnets* is unusual not in its display of skill but in its straightforward references to poetic competition, and in its conflation of patron and intimate friend in the beloved: in other sequences, the conflation tends to be confined to dedicatory poems. The rival-poet series moreover portrays non-aristocratic poets competing for aristocratic patronage: it is a late-Elizabethan scenario.

Shakespeare's perspectives are similarly of his time. In Sonnet 24, the word 'pérspective' alludes to a specific kind of perspective image (an anamorphosis) and to a perspective glass (a device for viewing such images). More immediately, it is a shorthand for 'seeing perspectively': looking at a picture in a way that resolves its anamorphic image. In Shakespeare's plays, 'perspective' also points to distortion and optical illusion. In *Richard II*, Bushy compares the image-distorting power of tears to 'pérspectives' that reveal 'nothing but confusion' when we look at them directly but exhibit 'form' when we regard them from an oblique angle. In *Henry V*, Henry jokes that he cannot see the French cities that have come into his possession because a maiden, Catherine, stands in the way; the King of France replies: 'Yes, my lord, you see them perspectively, the cities turned into a maid'. Henry sees the world through the lens of his desire, and what he sees is like a perspective image that can resolve in two ways. These senses of 'perspective' lose currency by the end of the seventeenth century, and 'to see things in perspective' comes to suggest seeing things in an undistorted or true way (*OED*). But for the *Sonnets* poet and (it would seem) Shakespeare, there is no such thing as an undistorted perspective: desires and fears colour our observations; only with difficulty and in limited ways do we see beyond ourselves. This is a feature of *Sonnets* that makes it feel modern, and not just modern in the sense that the sequence highlights triangular desire and other theories of love associated with modernity – after all, such theories are supposedly grounded in human nature – but modern in the sense that it is possible to 'gain perspective' on emotional situations and to 'work through' them.[1] Whether or not Shakespeare invented subjectivity or interiority as we know it (as scholars of different stripes have claimed), *Sonnets* depicts a struggle with perspective that can be usefully characterised as modern.[2]

Along with the expression 'see perspectively', the Elizabethan genre of the sonnet sequence dies out within two decades of *Sonnets*' publication, though sequential schemes linger in works like George Herbert's *The Temple* (1633). Less predominantly amatory, sonnets of Elizabethan and other varieties continue to be written in the seventeenth century. For most of the eighteenth century, the sonnet is seldom cultivated by English-language poets; its renaissance comes with Romanticism. Partly responding to renewed interest in *Sonnets*, sequences that might be called 'pre-Romantic' appear in the last decades of the eighteenth century: Charlotte Smith's *Elegiac Sonnets*, William Bowles's *Fourteen Sonnets*, Mary Robinson's *Sappho and Phaon*, and Anna Seward's *Original Sonnets*.[3] (Of the four, Robinson's is the most Elizabethan in mode, because the sonnets detail the travails of love.) Most sonnets of the early nineteenth century are stand-alone poems, and if there is a common theme among them, it is the sonnet itself, not love: Wordsworth's 'Scorn not the sonnet' and 'Nuns fret not at their convent's narrow room', and Keats's 'If by dull rhymes our English must be chained', are emblematic in this regard. The sonnet is regarded as a confining form, though also the form in which Shakespeare 'unlocked his heart'. Even in what might be called sequences of sonnets – Wordsworth's *Ecclesiastical Sonnets*, *Sonnets in Defence of Capital Punishment*, and *The River Duddon*, or Jones Very's scriptural meditations – the content is not amatory, and organisational schemes are absent or marginally significant.

The situation is different in the Victorian era. This is the period when the term 'sonnet sequence' gains currency, and the novel is the ascendant genre. Three sequences stand out: Elizabeth Barrett Browning's *Sonnets from the Portuguese*, George Meredith's *Modern Love*, and Dante Gabriel Rossetti's *The House of Life*.[4] *Sonnets from the Portuguese* is published in 1850; despite its use of the Petrarchan form and its allusion to the Portuguese poet Luís de Camões, the sequence draws on the Elizabethan sequence if not specifically on Shakespeare ('How do I love thee? Let me count the ways' rewrites 'Shall I compare thee to a summer's day?'). *Modern Love* and *The House of Life* are written in the second half of the nineteenth century (the latter over decades), and both hark back to the Elizabethan sonnet sequence. Working with and against Elizabethan conventions, Meredith creates a sixteen-line sonnet to help him tell his love story, urging the reader to listen for 'a newly-added chord' and depicting modern love as a rebel angel; imitating Petrarch and Shakespeare, Rossetti divides his sequence into two parts and advertises pairs, trios, and other series of sonnets. Both sequences include linked sonnets, and both are more narratively oriented than *Sonnets*, though perhaps not to the degree that 'sonnet sequence' or Meredith's novelistic career might imply: their governing conceit is that each sonnet is 'a moment's monument', as Rossetti says in his introductory sonnet. If they monumentalise something larger than their occasions, it is the poet's emotional experience, not the beloved or the beloved's beauty per se. And poetic competition is more implicit if equally informed by period- and poet-specific factors: Meredith is battling his own reputation as a novelist; Rossetti's most immediate rival is the Tennyson of *In Memoriam*. In literary-historical lore, these sequences are more autobiographical and more narrative than *Shakespeare's Sonnets*. But are they really different in kind, or to what extent are they different?

Here it pays to go outside English-language poetry, to a work that is often synonymous with modern poetry, Charles Baudelaire's *Les Fleurs du mal*. Like Rossetti's and Meredith's works, Baudelaire's poems allude to the Renaissance sequence, albeit to a kind more of the Ronsardian variety than the Shakespearean. Its 1857 version opens with an epigraph from the Renaissance poet Agrippa d'Aubigné and contains exactly 100 poems, about half of which are sonnets and many of which are amatory. And like *Shakespeare's Sonnets* (and *Modern Love*), it questions conventional views of love, particularly the idealisation of the beloved. Baudelaire's sonnets moreover speak to poetic competition: pointedly, the sonnet is not a form cultivated by Victor Hugo, a stylistically expansive poet whom Baudelaire both admired and regarded as a blocking figure.[5] Baudelaire was also cagey about how personal his poems were; like a Renaissance poet, he presented himself more as an allegorist than a diarist, and when his book was tried for offending morality, one defence of it, put forth by the novelist and poet Barbey d'Aurevilly, was that the book was an allegory with a 'secret architecture':

> Artists who can see the lines that are beneath the luxuriance and efflorescence of colour will clearly perceive that there is a secret architecture here, a plan calculated by the poet, premeditated and intentional ... From an aesthetic and experiential perspective, the poems would therefore lose much if they were not read *in the order* in which the poet – who knows what he is doing – has arranged them.[6]

In short, the meaning of the sequence was commonly misconstrued by non-artists, not because they read it biographically (d'Aurevilly invites that mode of interpretation at the start of his review), but because they did not read it holistically, with an eye to its schemes. Something similar might be said of *Sonnets* today: if we wish to read the work in the spirit in which it was written, we would do well to grant that the author constructed a personal allegory, and to read his sonnets in the order that he arranged them – with the understanding that he knew what he was doing. The secret architecture of *Shakespeare's Sonnets* may be more genre-based than that of *Les Fleurs du mal*; the sufferings of Baudelaire's poet may be more 'modern'; but the differences between the works are more of degree than kind. With both sequences, we are dealing with the same fundamental questions. How and why does the poet organise poems? How and why does the poet allegorise personal experience?

The nineteenth-century examples moreover provide perspective on twentieth- and twenty-first-century views of *Sonnets* and the sonnet sequence. In reaction to Victorian bardology and to facile biographical interpretations, modern scholars have mostly followed a modernist script (with some postmodern filigrees), concentrating on ways in which *Sonnets* is not personal and is only organised enough to suggest that the search for overall perspective is a fool's errand. For Shakespeare, however, Love is not Time's fool – this is what makes him both modern and of his time: he believes in ideals in spite of damning evidence to the contrary. With *Sonnets from the Portuguese, The*

House of Life, *Modern Love*, and *Les Fleurs du mal*, we have the licence of post-Romanticism to look into biographical connections, and documentation to boot: we can check our interpretations against letters, diaries, and other extant paratexts. With Barrett Browning, we can point to a marriage as the foundation of the sequence; with Meredith, we can point to marital infidelity; and with Rossetti and Baudelaire we can conjure names – Elizabeth Siddal, Jane Morris, and Fanny Cornforth; Jeanne Duval, Marie Lebrun, and Madame de Sabatier – and identify particular poems with particular women. We can also see how Rossetti and Baudelaire revised their sequences in response to life events. All of this helps us understand better their art and intentions. We can interpret *Sonnets* in a similar spirit, if we have the ability and the will to see what Shakespeare's love hath writ.

Appendix A: Principal English sonnet sequences published between 1582 and 1609

Chronological lists of sonnet sequences can be found in Thomas P. Roche's *Petrarch and the English Sonnet Sequence* (1989) and Michael R. G. Spiller's *The Development of the Sonnet* (1992). My list is selective: it focuses on secular sequences published in the two decades prior to *Shakespeare's Sonnets*; its aim is to highlight trends in amatory sequences. The left column identifies the sequence by year, poet, and title; the right column summarises content, especially the number of sonnets. Items missing from the left include sequences in manuscript during the period, notably Robert Sidney's untitled sequence (thirty-five sonnets), Fulke Greville's *Caelica* (109 poems), and Henry Constable's sixty-three-sonnet *Diana*. Items missing from the right include some dedicatory poems and some poems whose content is difficult to summarise succinctly. Daniel's 1594 *Delia*, for example, is accompanied by his tragedy *Cleopatra*, and Drayton's 1599 *Idea* is followed by three poems of lament.

1582 Thomas Watson, *The Hekatompathia*	100 poems (18-line sonnets)
1591 Philip Sidney, *Astrophil and Stella*	107 sonnets and 10 songs by Sidney, 28 sonnets by Daniel, and 7 songs by others
1592 Samuel Daniel, *Delia* (first 1592 edition)	50 sonnets, a 4-stanza ode, and 'The Complaint of Rosamond'
1592 Henry Constable, *Diana*	Introductory sonnet, 20 numbered sonnets, and 2 additional sonnets
1592 Samuel Daniel, *Delia* (second 1592 edition)	54 sonnets, a 4-stanza ode, and 'The Complaint of Rosamond'

1593 Barnabe Barnes, *Parthenophil and Parthenophe*	Three sections: 'Sonnets', 'Elegies', and 'Odes'. 104 sonnets in the book's first section; 4 dedicatory sonnets at the end
1593 Thomas Lodge, *Phyllis*	20 sonnets, 2 eclogues, 1 elegy, 20 more sonnets, 1 ode, 'The Complaint of Elstred'
1593 Giles Fletcher, *Licia*	52 sonnets, 1 ode, 1 pastoral dialogue, 1 Latin distich, 'A Lover's Maze', 3 elegies, 'The Rising to the Crown of Richard III'
1593 Thomas Watson, *The Tears of Fancy*	60 sonnets
1594 Henry Constable, *Diana*	Introductory sonnet by the publisher, 75 sonnets (8 by Sidney) in groups of ten
1594 Michael Drayton, *Idea's Mirror*	An introductory sonnet, an 18-line sonnet by 'Gorbo il Fidele', 51 sonnets
1594 William Percy, *Sonnets to Coelia*	20 sonnets and 1 madrigal
1594 Samuel Daniel, *Delia*	Introductory sonnet, 55 sonnets, 1 4-stanza ode, and 'The Complaint of Rosamond'
1595 Edmund Spenser, *Amoretti*	89 sonnets, 4 anacreontic poems (9 stanzas), and 1 hymn ('Epithalamion', 24 stanzas)
1596 Bartholomew Griffin, *Fidessa*	62 sonnets
1596 Richard Linche, *Diella*	38 sonnets and 'The Love of Dom Diego and Gynerva'
1596 William Smith, *Chloris*	49 sonnets
1597 Richard Barnfield, *Certain Sonnets*	20 sonnets (part of *Cynthia*)

1598 Philip Sidney, *Astrophil and Stella*	108 sonnets and 11 songs (interspersed)
1599 Michael Drayton, *Idea*	59 poems (55 sonnets, a cansonet, and 3 dedicatory sonnets)
1600 Michael Drayton, *Idea*	66 poems (60 sonnets, a cansonet, and 5 dedicatory sonnets)
1601 Samuel Daniel, *Delia*	57 sonnets, 1 4-stanza ode, and 1 pastoral poem (with an envoy)
1604 Sir William Alexander, *Aurora*	125 poems (106 sonnets, 10 songs, 1 sestina, 4 madrigals, 3 elegies, 1 echo)
1605 Michael Drayton, *Idea*	3 introductory sonnets and 64 numbered sonnets (60 plus 4 dedicatory sonnets)
1605? John Davies of Hereford, *Wit's Pilgrimage*	104 poems in the first section (101 sonnets, 2 other poems, 1 sonnet), 48 poems in the second section (47 sonnets), 2 sonnets in the middle of the third section, and 1 at end

Later sequences include the 1619 edition of *Idea*, which contains an introductory sonnet, sixty-three numbered sonnets, and a cansonet; the 1623 edition of *Delia*, which contains sixty-seven sonnets; and Mary Wroth's *Pamphilia to Amphilanthus* (1620), which mixes twenty songs among eighty-three sonnets.

Appendix B: 'Anagrams, Shakespeare's Sonnets, *and the identity of the fair friend*'

In '"Loe, here in one line is his name twice writ": Anagrams, *Shakespeare's Sonnets*, and the Identity of the Fair Friend' (2009), R. H. Winnick argues that Shakespeare's sequence has more than fifteen and likely more than twenty 'Wriothesley' anagrams, typically embedded in 'short, thematically relevant, interlinear phrases'. Winnick's most compelling examples are in Sonnet 17, whose fourth and ninth lines individually contain all twenty-two letters needed to form 'Wriothesley' twice, and whose final line can be construed to mean 'You will live twice in your child and twice in my rhyme'. Most of his anagrams are in the first half of the fair-youth section:

Sonnet number, line number, and line (with the anagram phrase in boldface)

1.5	But thou contracted to thine **owne bright eyes**	[*L* missing]
2.3	**Thy youthes proud liuery** ſo gaz'd on now	[*W* missing]
9.10	Shifts but his place, for ſtill **the world inioyes it**	
10.2	**Who for thy ſelfe art ſo vnprouident**	[*I* missing]
17.4	**Which hides your life, and ſhewes not halfe your parts**	[double anagram]
17.9	**So ſhould my papers (yellowed with their age)**	[double anagram]
20.14	Mine be thy loue and **thy loues vſe their** treaſure	[*W* missing]
22.9	O therefore loue be of **thy ſelfe ſo wary**	[*I* missing]
29.13	**For thy ſweet loue** remembred ſuch welth brings	[*I* missing]
39.10	Were it not **thy four leiſure gaue ſweet** leaue	
55.13	So til the iudgement **that your ſelfe ariſe**	[*W* missing]
55.14	You liue in **this, and dwell in louers eies**	[*Y* missing]
58.9	Be **where you liſt, your charter is ſo ſtrong**	
69.1	Thoſe parts of thee that **the worlds eye doth view**	
70.4	A Crow that flies in heauens ſweeteſt **ayre**	

81.6	Though I (once gone) to all **the world muſt dye**	[*I* missing]
89.10	**Thy fweet beloued name no more** ſhall dwell	[*I* missing]
108.8	Euen as when firſt I hallowed thy faire name	
126.4	**Thy louers withering,** as **thy fweet felfe grow'ſt**	[double anagram]

At a glance, the anagrams may seem far-fetched, since half of them are missing a letter. For this reason, it pays to follow Winnick and begin with Sonnets 17 and 126. Very few lines of English pentameter verse have all twenty-two letters needed to form 'Wriothesley' twice; with two such lines, 17 is probably unique; and 126's *Wriothesley*'s occur in separate halves of a line. What is more, the anagrams in Sonnets 17 and 126 are thematically relevant: 17 promises the youth a second life in verse; 126 is the final 'Wriothesley' poem and the final fair-youth poem.

Thematic relevance is crucial for the anagrams missing a letter. Sonnets 81 and 89, for example, pun on their missing letter, *I*:

> Your name from hence immortall life ſhall have,
> Though I (once gone) to all **the world muſt dye** . . .
> (Sonnet 81, lines 5–6)

> . . . in my tongue,
> **Thy fweet beloued name no more** ſhall dwell,
> Leaſt I (too much prophane) ſhould do it wronge.
> (Sonnet 89, lines 10–11)

In 81, the poet declares that his name will die with him, but the youth's name will live on; he almost sounds as if he is sacrificing his life (his *I*) for the youth. In 89, the poet pledges to stop uttering the youth's name, lest he wrong the name by bringing it into association with his own unworthy self (his profane *I*). A similar pun informs 22's anagram:

> O therefore loue be of **thy felfe fo wary**,
> As I not for my felfe, but for thee will,
> Bearing thy heart which I will keepe fo chary . . .
> (Sonnet 22, lines 9–11)

Line 10's 'I not for my felfe' hints that the poet is donating an *I* to the previous line, to complete 'Wriothesley'. In evoking the conceit that he will carry and guard the youth's heart in his own heart, the poet associates his 'other *I*' with Wriothesley. Line 11 may also contain an anagram: 'will keepe ſo chary' has all the letters needed to form 'Will Shakespeare' if a second *A* and *S* are borrowed from line 10, whose first word is 'As'. To put it another way: the 'Shakespeare' anagram is mostly contained in 'keepe ſo chary', and the names of the poet and the youth can be assembled with line 9's 'thy ſelfe ſo wary', line 10's 'As I', and line 11's 'will keepe ſo chary'. Along with their hearts, the poet and youth share parts of their names.

Sonnets 10 and 29 also contain anagrams missing an *I*. Each anagram occurs in a four-word phrase at the start of a line, and each *I* can be supplied by the last word of the same line:

> For ſhame deny that thou bear'ſt loue to any
> **Who for thy ſelfe** art ſo vnprouident . . .
> (Sonnet 10, lines 1–2)

> **For thy ſweet loue** remembred ſuch welth brings
> That then I ſkorne to change my ſtate with Kings.
> (Sonnet 29, lines 13–14)

Winnick notes that the anagrams could be replaced with *Wriothesley*'s to make new meanings: '**Wriothesley**, [thou] art so unprovident', '**Wriothesley** remembered such wealth brings'. More crucial, Sonnet 10 introduces the pronoun 'I' to *Sonnets*, and both poems feature change. In 10, the poet pleads with the youth to break from self-destructive behaviour and offers to change his opinion about the youth if the youth changes intentions about fatherhood ('O change thy thought, that I may change my minde'). 'I' and 'change' allude to the anagram, which is missing an *I* and formed from 'changed' letters. Sonnet 10's couplet also emphasises exchange: 'Make thee an other ſelfe for loue of me, / That beauty ſtill may liue in thine or thee'. And in 29's couplet, 'change' means 'exchange' and is preceded by a punning use of 'remembered': 'thy ſweet loue remembered'. Shakespeare hints at reassembling parts or 're-membering'.

Poems with 'Wriothesley' anagrams are often informed by pronominal wordplay. This is true of Sonnet 55, which contains anagrams missing a *W* and a *Y*, respectively:

> So til the iudgement **that your ſelfe ariſe**,
> You liue in **this, and dwell in louers eies**.
> (Sonnet 55, lines 13–14)

The poet is proclaiming or hoping that the fair youth will live in *Sonnets* and the eyes of lovers who read *Sonnets*, until Judgement

Day – when the youth will rise from the dead for eternal life. Since he presents his verse as a monument that will preserve the beloved, allusions to the youth's name would be apt; anagrams are present in 'that your felfe arife' and 'this, and dwell in louers eies'. But the first anagram is missing a *W*; the second, a *Y*. Winnick observes that the *W* could be supplied by two *you*'s – a second 'you' can be understood in '[you] yourself arise', for example – and that the second anagram would not need a *Y* if the name were spelled 'Wrioteslie'. The anagram would not be missing a *Y* if 'eies' were spelled 'eyes', as it is in line 11: like Spenser in Sonnets 35 and 83 of *Amoretti*, as Shakespeare plays with ideas of self and other, he may be employing 'eies' and 'eyes' to link the letters *I* and *Y* with the pronouns 'I' and 'you'. What is more, a complete 'Wriothesley' can be found in 'You liue in this and dwell in louers'; for both anagrams to be complete, they could share the 'you' in line 14. As in Sonnet 23, in which the poet instructs the reader to 'hear with eies', a *Y* may be left out to make a point. In any event, the 'you' at the line's beginning resonates with the 'eies' at the end. *You–I* puns recur in the fair-youth sonnets, and they fit with the theme that the poet sees himself in the youth.

Sonnets 2 and 20 also contain anagrams missing a *W*:

> WHen fortie Winters fhall befeige thy brow,
> And digge deep trenches in thy beauties field,
> **Thy youthes proud liuery** fo gaz'd on now,
> Wil be a totter'd weed of fmal worth held.
>
> (Sonnet 2, lines 1–4)

> But fince fhe prickt thee out for womens pleafure,
> Mine be thy loue and **thy loues vfe their** treafure.
>
> (Sonnet 20, lines 13–14)

Winnick suggests that two *U*'s in 'Thy youthes proud liuery' can be combined to form a *W*, and that the phrase can be shortened to 'youthes' and 'liuery', releasing the word 'proud' to create the line 'Proud **Wriothesley**, so gazed on now'. But combining *U*'s is unnecessary: lines 1 and 4 draw attention to *W* ('when', 'winters', and 'brow'; 'will', 'weed', and 'worth'), and line 3 ends with a *W* and the suggestive phrase 'gaz'd on now'. In Sonnet 20, 'Wriothesley' and *W* are more intensely evoked. There are several unnecessary *W*'s ('rowling' for 'rolling', for example); there are puns on 'use' and 'double use'; and '*Hews*' may be a cipher for 'Henry Wriothesley' or 'Henry Wriothesley, Earl of Southampton'. The missing *W* can be adduced from the poem's play with *W* or taken from 'womens'.

The anagram phrases in Sonnets 39, 69, and 70 may or may not be missing letters:

>Oh abſence what a torment wouldſt thou proue,
>Were it not **thy ſour leiſure gaue ſweet** leaue.
>
>(Sonnet 39, lines 9–10)

>Thoſe parts of thee that **the worlds eye doth view**
>Want nothing that the thought of hearts can mend.
>
>(Sonnet 69, lines 1–2)

>That thou are blam'd ſhall not be thy defect,
>For ſlanders marke was euer yet the faire,
>The ornament of beauty is ſuſpect,
>**A Crow that flies** in heauens ſweeteſt **ayre**.
>
>(Sonnet 70, lines 1–4)

Each five-word phrase has all the 'Wriothesley' letters. But if we follow Winnick by shortening the phrases and replacing the anagrams with *Wriothesley*'s, some letters go missing:

>Oh abſence what a torment wouldſt thou proue,   [thy ſour leiſure]
>Were it not **Wriothesley** gaue ſweet leaue.   ('W' missing)
>
>Thoſe parts of thee that **Wriothesley** doth view   [the worlds eye]
>Want nothing that the thought of hearts can mend.   ('I' missing)
>
>The ornament of beauty is ſuſpect,   [A Crow that flies]
>**Wriothesley** in heauens ſweeteſt ayre.   ('Y' missing)

Sonnet 39's new phrase, 'thy ſour leiſure', lacks a *W*; Sonnet 69's 'the worlds eye' lacks an *I*; and Sonnet 70's 'A Crow that flies' lacks a *Y* (and a second *E*). The *W* in 39's phrase could be formed from the two *U*'s in 'four leiſure', and the *I* in 69's phrase could be supplied via a pun on 'eye'. Without 'ayre', though, 70's phrase would be missing two letters. Even with 'ayre', the 'Wriothesley' letters may well be due to chance, not design.

Sonnet 70 notwithstanding, Winnick builds an impressive case for 'Wriothesley' anagrams. Among his more compelling examples are the following:

>Look what an vnthrift in the world doth ſpend
>Shifts but his place, for ſtill **the world inioyes it.**
>
>(Sonnet 9, lines 9–10)

Be **where you lift**, your charter is ſo ſtrong,
That you your ſelfe may priuiledge your time . . .
                                        (Sonnet 58, lines 9–10)

I muſt each day ſay ore the very ſame,
Counting no old thing old, thou mine, I thine,
Euen as when **firſt I hallowed thy faire** name.
                                        (Sonnet 108, lines 6–8)

In Sonnet 9, 'look what' and 'shifts his place' call attention to the anagram: Shakespeare may be telling the reader to look for scrambled letters. And the anagram phrase, 'the world inioyes it', underscores Wriothesley's importance. In Sonnet 58, 'where you list' has one extra letter, *U*, which potentially puns on 'you': 'You, Wriothesley'. With a touch of irony, perhaps, the poet tells the youth to be where he likes and puts 'Wriothesley' in its/his place – within the confines of a half-line. Sonnet 108's anagram is less economical but more pointed. In the octave, the poet claims that there are no new ways to praise the youth, and that he must therefore say the same old things as if saying daily prayers – he thus harks back to the time when he first evoked the youth's name as something holy. The sum of all his praise is the name 'Wriothesley', which is present on two levels in line 8: 'Wriothesley' and 'name' both occur in 'firſt I hallowed thy faire name'. The anagram may even include 'Hal' (Henry), since 'Wriothesley' can be formed without the 'hal' in 'hallowed'.

Appendix C: Additional 'Wriothesley' anagrams

In building his case for 'Wriothesley' anagrams, Winnick leaves open the possibility that he has overlooked examples. The following list speaks to that possibility:

Sonnet number, line number, and line (with the anagram phrase in boldface)

1.5	But thou contracted to thine **owne bright eyes**	[L missing]
1.8	Thy felfe thy foe, to **thy sweet felfe too cruell**	[I missing]
1.11	**Within thine own bud burieft thy** content	
1.13	**Pitty the world, or elfe** this glutton be	
1.14	To eate **the worlds due, by** the graue and thee	[I missing]
9.5	The **world wilbe thy widdow and ftill weepe**	
9.10	Shifts but his place, for ftill **the world inioyes it**	
13.1	**O That you were your felfe**, but loue you are	[I missing]
13.8	**When your fweet iffue your fweet forme fhould beare**	[double anagram]
13.13	O none but **vnthrifts, deare my loue you know**	
20.5	An eye more bright then theirs, **leffe falfe in rowling**	
20.7	A man in hew all *Hews* **in his controwling**	
20.8	**Which fteals mens eyes and womens** foules amafeth	
20.14	Mine be thy loue and **thy loues vfe their** treafure	[W missing]
23.14	**To heare wit eies belongs** to loues fine whit	[Y missing]
24.5	For through the Painter **muft you fee his skill**	[W missing]
24.6	To finde **where your true Image pictur'd lies**	
24.9	Now fee **what good-turnes eyes for eies** haue done	[L missing]
24.10	**Mine eyes haue drawne thy fhape**, and thine for me	[L missing]
24.11	Are **windowes to my breft, where-through** the Sun	[L missing]
77.1	**THy glaffe will fhew thee how thy** beauties were	
77.2	**Thy dyall how thy pretious mynuits wafte**	
77.5	**The wrinckles which thy glaffe will truly fhow**	
98.11	**They weare but fweet, but figures of delight**	
98.14	As with **your fhaddow I with thefe did play**	

106.12 They had **not ſtill enough your worth** to ſing   [one *E* missing]
106.13 For we **which now behold theſe preſent days**
122.2   Full **characterd with laſting memory**

Other than three items (1.5, 9.10, and 20.14), this is a new list of anagrams.

Sonnets 1, 9, 13, 20, 24, 77, 98, and 106 have at least two anagrams each. Sonnet 13 is striking in that it introduces you-forms to the sequence and contains four *Wriothesley*'s – one at the beginning, two in the middle, and one at the end of the poem:

> **O That you were your ſelfe,** but loue you are
> No longer yours, then you your ſelfe here liue,
> Againſt this cumming end you ſhould prepare,
> And your ſweet ſemblance to ſome other giue.
> So ſhould that beauty which you hold in leaſe
> Find no determination, then you were
> You ſelfe again after your ſelfes deceaſe,
> **When your ſweet iſſue your ſweet forme ſhould beare.**
> Who lets ſo faire a houſe fall to decay,
> Which husbandry in honour might vphold,
> Againſt the ſtormy guſts of winters day
> And barren rage of deaths eternall cold?
>   O none but **vnthrifts, deare my loue you know,**
>   You had a Father, let your Son ſay ſo.

'O That you were your ſelfe' alludes to the first you-forms. It also contains all the 'Wriothesley' letters except *I*. As with other anagrams missing an *I*, Shakespeare may be linking letter with pronoun: the pronoun 'I' is conspicuously absent, and the letter *I* does not come until 'liue' at the end of line 2. In this context, 'here liue' may mean 'live in this world' and 'live in this poem'. Shakespeare may also play with perfection or completeness. In order to live eternally, Wriothesley must become his true self (he must father a child); in order to be complete, 'Wriothesley' needs the *I* in 'liue'. Line 8 contains two potential anagrams: 'When your ſweet iſſue' has every 'Wriothesley' letter except *L*; 'your ſweet forme ſhould beare' has every letter but *I*. Again, the poet suggests that Wriothesley has yet to make himself or his own 'sweet form' complete. He also evokes an analogy: a child is a form of a parent; an anagram is a form of a name. In contrast to the first three examples, line 13's anagram is complete: all eleven letters are in the line's last seven syllables; more economically, they are in 'vnthrifts' and 'loue you know', with an *E* borrowed from 'deare'. The line perhaps hints at 'O none but my dear Wriothesley'.

Sonnet 1 contains an anagram missing an *L* in line 5 and a full anagram in line 8:

> FRom faireſt creatures we deſire increaſe,
> That thereby beauties *Roſe* might neuer die,
> But as the riper ſhould by time deceaſe,
> His tender heire might beare his memory:
> But thou contracted to thine **owne bright eyes**,
> Feed'ſt thy lights flame with ſelfe ſubſtaniall fewell,
> Making a famine where aboundance lies,
> Thy ſelfe thy foe, to **thy sweet ſelfe too cruell**.
>
> (Sonnet 1, lines 1–8)

The poet describes the youth as narcissistic: 'contracted' (betrothed) to his 'owne bright eyes'. He also suggests that the youth is 'contracted' (shrunk) to the small space of his own eyes: 'thou contracted to' points to the anagram. The missing *L* is supplied by line 6, which contains seven *L*'s, two of which are superfluous. We might say that there is a famine of *L*'s in line 5 and an abundance in line 6, and that line 7 alludes to the anagram. The argument about hoarding beauty comes to a head in line 8, when the poet calls the youth an enemy to himself and hides an *I*-less 'Wriothesley' in 'thy sweet ſelfe too cruell'. In keeping his beauty to himself, the youth is being cruel to himself and absenting himself from his self.

With the conceits of dearth and plenty, Shakespeare could have used any 'Wriothesley' letter, so why settle on *L*? To judge from Sonnet 24's anagrams, *L* stands for 'light', and it may hint at 'live' and 'love'. In 24, the poet imagines painting or engraving the youth's form in his heart. In describing the form, the poet mixes thou-forms and you-forms:

> Mine eye hath play'd the painter and hath ſteeld,
> Thy beauties forme in table of my heart,
> My body is the frame wherein ti's held,
> And perſpectiue it is beſt Painters art.
> For through the Painter **muſt you ſee his skill**,
> To finde where **your true Image pictur'd lies**,
> Which in my boſomes ſhop is hanging ſtil,
> That hath his windowes glazed with thine eyes:
> Now ſee **what good-turnes eyes for eies** haue done,
> **Mine eyes haue drawne thy ſhape, and thine for me**

> Are **windowes to my breſt, where-through** the Sun
> Delights to peepe, to gaze therein on thee
>   Yet eyes this cunning want to grace their art
>   They draw but what they fee, know not the hart.

The two you-forms in lines 5–6 allude to *W* and two anagrams: line 5's final six syllables contain every 'Wriothesley' letter except *W*; line 6's final seven syllables contain every letter except *W*. ('Where' completes line 6's anagram, and perhaps line 5's.) Both anagrams reinforce the theme that the poet carries an image of the youth in his heart. The three anagrams in lines 9–11 contain every 'Wriothesley' letter except *L*: 'what good-turnes eyes for eies', 'Mine eyes haue drawne thy ſhape, and thine for me', and 'windowes to my breſt, where-through'. In line 9, 'eyes for eies' is crucial: the different spellings are necessary for the anagram, and they reinforce the conceit of exchange. The second example alludes to the name's form: 'Mine eyes haue drawne thy ſhape'. The third example portrays the youth's eyes as a window to the poet's soul, and it looks to the next line, in which the form of the youth can be seen in the poet's heart. (The enjambment 'where-through the Sun / Delights to peepe' conveys the idea of 'looking through' to the heart and emphasises the word 'delights'.) In short, after three successive anagrams with missing *L*'s, the *L* in 'Delights' emerges like sudden sunlight through a window. Since the first *L* after Sonnet 1's 'owne bright eyes' also involves 'light' ('Feed'ſt thy lights flame'), the poet would seem to associate *L* with 'light' – and perhaps also with the love that he feels when he sees the light of the youth's eyes. Beyond 'light' and 'love', *L* may hint at 'live'. In Sonnet 13, the word 'live' at the end of line 2 completes the 'Wriothesley' anagram begun in line 1, and the two anagrams in line 8 require an *L* and an *I*, respectively – the first letters of 'live'.

The anagrams in Sonnet 106 may allude to a missing *E*:

> WHen in the Chronicle of waſted time,
> I ſee diſcriptions of the faireſt wights,
> And beautie making beautifull old rime,
> In praiſe of Ladies dead, and louely Knights,
> Then in the blazon of ſweet beauties beſt,
> Of hand, of foote, of lip, of eye, of brow,
> I ſee their antique Pen would haue expreſt,
> Euen ſuch a beauty as you maiſter now.
> So all their praiſes are but propheſies
> Of this our time, all you prefiguring,

> And for they look'd but with deuining eyes,
> They had **not ſtill enough your worth** to ſing:
> For **we which now behold theſe preſent dayes,**
> Haue eyes to wonder, but lack toungs to praiſe.

Line 12's 'not ſtill enough your worth' contains ten of the eleven 'Wriothesley' letters: one *E* is missing. Line 13's 'we which now behold theſe preſent dayes' contains all eleven letters, and then some. Shakespeare may be playing with the idea that ancient poets were not able to see 'enough' (E-nough) of the youth to praise him adequately. In the present day, by contrast, poets can see more than enough: line 13 contains seven *E*'s.

Sonnet 20 contains four anagrams:

> A Womans face with natures owne hande painted,
> Haſte thou, the Maſter Miſtris of my paſſion,
> A womans gentle hart but not acquainted
> With ſhifting change as is falſe womens faſhion;
> An **eye more bright then theirs, leſſe falſe in rowling**:
> Gilding the obiect where-vpon it gazeth,
> A man in **hew all Hews in his controwling,**
> **Which ſteales mens eyes and womens** ſoules amaſeth,
> And for a woman wert thou firſt created,
> Till nature as ſhe wrought thee fell a dotinge,
> And by addition me of thee defeated,
> By adding one thing to my purpoſe nothing.
>   But ſince ſhe prickt thee out for womens pleaſure,
>   Mine be thy loue and **thy loues vſe their** treaſure.

The cleanest example is in line 7, whose the opening phrase 'A man in' and the spellings of 'hew' and 'controwling' signal its presence. (The italicised 'Hews' may also evoke Henry Wriothesley.) The anagram in line 5 requires every word except 'An'; without the poem's context, we might attribute it to chance. But Sonnet 20 offers a playful story about how Nature put together the fair youth, belatedly pricking an appendage to his feminine form. The many superfluous *W*'s reinforce the conceit, punning on 'double you' and 'double use'. Sonnet 9 similarly plays with *W* and also contains a fifth-line anagram that requires every word except the first article. And Sonnet 20 contains three anagrams in one quatrain. The third anagram, in line 8, is mostly in 'Which ſteales mens eyes': we merely need to steal an *O* from 'womens'. (The poet may be jesting about sex and astonishment.) The final anagram, in line 14, is missing a *W*, a letter that is otherwise plentiful in the poem. The missing W can be supplied by two U's or (more aptly) may be stolen from 'womens' in line 13.

As the foregoing examples suggest, it pays to consider narrative context. It also pays to consider sequential context. Winnick's foundational examples – the double anagrams in Sonnets 17 and 126 – occur in organisationally prominent poems: in the final sonnet of the first pyramid step and in the fair-youth coda. The same might be said of other examples, such as Sonnet 98's anagrams and allusions to 'figures' of the youth, which are depicted as products of the poet's meditations during a break in writing: the next sonnet, 99, marks a division between the two main parts of the fair-youth sonnets (for details, see Chapter 6). More analysis of sequential context is called for; here I will concentrate on anagrams at the beginning, middle, and end of sequential schemes; and anagrams in mirror poems.

Beyond the opening and closing examples already discussed – the two anagrams in the octave of Sonnet 1, and the double anagrams in Sonnet 126 – there are anagrams in the sestet of the first sonnet, in the middle of the sequence, and at the end of the fair-youth section. The three 'Wriothesley' anagrams in Sonnet 1's sestet occur in the poem's last four lines:

> Thou that art now the worlds fresh ornament
> And only herauld to the gaudy spring
> **Within thine own bud burieft thy** content
> And, tender chorle, makft waft in niggarding:
>   **Pitty the world, or elfe** this glutton be,
>   To eate **the worlds due, by** the graue and thee.

Line 11's anagram requires all but one word; the examples in the couplet are more economical; along with the octave examples, they suggest that Shakespeare made an effort to work anagrams into his sequence's first sonnet. The final anagram notably lacks an *I*; it suggests that the fair youth is devouring himself. It may also account for awkward phrasing: there are easier ways of saying that the youth destroys himself by dying and by not siring a child.

In the sonnet at the midpoint of the 153-poem pyramid, 77, Shakespeare includes three 'Wriothesley' anagrams, in the first five lines:

> THy glaffe **will fhew thee how thy beauties were;**
> Thy **dyall how thy pretious mynuits wafte;**
> The vacant leaues thy mindes imprint will bear;
> And, of this booke, this learning maift thou tafte:
> **The wrinckles which thy** glaffe **will truly fhow** . . .

While none of these anagrams is economical, they occur in a cluster, in a mirror poem, and in the central poem of *Sonnets*' main pyramid: all of this suggests that they are designed. (As in Sonnet 1, they may also account for awkward phrasing.) In line 5, I have put 'The' in boldface rather than 'glaſſe', in order to illustrate that no 'Wriothesley' anagram depends on 'glass' – more on this in a moment. As Sonnets 77 and 126 suggest, anagrams may be present in all mirror sonnets, including in the first lines of a sonnet related to 77, Sonnet 122: 'TThy guift, thy tables, are within my braine, / Full **characterd with la ting memory**'. 'Full characterd' alludes here to a full spelling of a word – the full 'Wriothesley'. Sonnet 122 is the last poem of fair-youth section, other than the 'No' trio and the coda. It registers completion.

Sonnets 77 and 122 are the rule, not the exception: all of the sequence's mirror sonnets have 'Wriothesley' anagrams. Here is a chart of the anagrams in Sonnets 3, 22, 62, and 103:

 3.12   Diſpight of **wrinkles this thy goulden** time
 22.1   MY glaſſe ſhall not perſwade me I am ould
 62.7   And for **my ſelfe mine owne worth** do define
 103.1 ALack what **pouerty my Muſe brings** forth

None of the anagram phrases requires 'glass', the sequence's word for 'mirror'. And while no phrase, except maybe Sonnet 3's, is economical, some make sense when they are replaced with 'Wriothesley', like Sonnet 62's: 'And for **Wriothesley**, [I] do define'. And Sonnet 3's phrase is followed by a suggestive couplet: 'But if thou live remembered not to be, / Die single, and thine image dies with thee'. It is as if Shakespeare was saying that, in spite of the fair youth's 'golden' time, if the name 'Wriothesley' is not reassembled (re-membered), the youth will not achieve immortality.

Appendix D: Marlowe, Barnfield, and 1599

While I discuss many Elizabethan and some Jacobean poets in this book, it should go without saying that more analysis of Shakespeare's contemporaries remains to be done. My emphasis has been on poets who were active or actively read in the 1590s, especially in the mid-1590s. I have not explored in depth Shakespeare's Jacobean milieu: more connections might be made to poets like William Alexander and John Davies of Hereford, for example. Nor have I focused on the seventeenth-century Elizabethan years, except in relation to Southampton's imprisonment and the *Sonnets* poet's separation from the youth. With those years, I advocate analysis of post-1599 plays (especially of *Hamlet* and *Troilus and Cressida*), and investigation of satire and theatrical rivalry (especially of the so-called 'Poets' War' that took place between late 1599 and late 1601).[1] Even among poets who were active in the 1590s, I have not analysed every writer equally: Drayton, for example, receives less attention than Spenser, Daniel, Barnes, and Chapman; I do not discuss the 'Gulling Sonnets' of Sir John Davies (the one not of Hereford). All of these poets and poems, and more, merit attention.

This appendix expands my analysis of two poets, Marlowe and Barnfield, particularly in relation to 1599. Marlowe, of course, was dead in 1599, having been murdered in a tavern room in late 1593, but his poetic presence lingered for decades. Marlowe's posthumous reputation was informed by rumours that he was an atheist and a lover of boys: his sexually suggestive *Hero and Leander*, a poem that influenced Shakespeare's *Venus and Adonis* and the procreation sonnets, was first published with Chapman's continuation in 1598; in 1599, Marlowe's translation of Ovid's *Amores* was one of the works that the Bishops' ban ordered to be burned.[2] Barnfield, meanwhile, had published two works that evoke same-sex love, *The Affectionate Shepherd* (1594) and *Certain Sonnets* (published in *Cynthia*, 1595). Marlowe, Barnfield, and Shakespeare converge in *The Passionate Pilgrim*, a pirated collection of poems attributed to Shakespeare, first published in late 1598 or early 1599.

But let us first focus on Barnfield. *Cynthia* was published in early 1595, around the same time as *Amoretti*.[3] And like *Amoretti*, *Cynthia* contains 122 poetic units. *Cynthia*, moreover, pays homage to Spenser, addressing him by his pastoral name as the best living poet: 'Colin, chief of shepherds all' (Sonnet 20). Besides acknowledging Spenser's pre-eminence, Barnfield is shielding himself from detractors. Sonnet 20 gestures conventionally towards modesty (the poet apologises for not being as witty as Spenser), but much of *Cynthia*'s defensive posture derives from Barnfield's love poems that express homosexual desire – first *The Affectionate Shepherd*'s pastorals and now *Cynthia*'s sonnets. In his introductory letter to 'courteous gentlemen readers', he takes pains to defend his poetry, citing Virgil, whose second eclogue refers to a man's love for a boy, and Spenser, whose conceits he imitates. For this letter alone, *Cynthia* might have caught Shakespeare's attention. By 1595, Shakespeare had dedicated two works to Southampton, and he had likely written many fair-youth sonnets. Since *Cynthia* is the only English sequence other than *Sonnets* in which a male poet addresses a male beloved at length, it may have served as a warning that poetry expressing love between men invited scrutiny if not hostility. If Shakespeare had considered publishing *Sonnets* in the mid-1590s, *Cynthia* may have altered his thinking. And Barnfield, if he was not already an admirer of Shakespeare's poetry, became one in the late 1590s. In his third sonnet in *Poems in Diverse Humours* – a work appended to *The Encomium of Lady Pecunia* (1598) – he praises *Venus and Adonis* and *Lucrece* for putting Shakespeare's name in 'Fame's immortal book'.

Cynthia may also have caught Shakespeare's attention for a mirror poem, Sonnet 11:

> Sighing, and sadly sitting by my love,
> He asked the cause of my heart's sorrowing,
> Conjuring me by heav'n's eternal king
> To tell the cause which me so much did move.
> 'Compelled', quoth I, 'to thee will I confess,
> Love is the cause, and only love it is
> That doth deprive me of my heav'nly bliss;
> Love is the pain that doth my heart oppress'.
> 'And what is she', quoth he, 'whom thou dost love?'
> 'Look in this glass', quoth I, 'there shalt thou see
> The perfect form of my felicity'.
> When, thinking that it would strange magic prove,
>   He opened it, and taking off the cover,
>   He straight perceived himself to be my lover.

Sonnet 11 is the centre poem of 'Certain Sonnets' if the final ode belongs with the sonnets. Centre poem or not, it makes quibbling use of pronouns (especially *she–he*) and pointed use of 'perfect form' and 'Look in this glass'. Like Shakespeare, Barnfield describes a scene in which the speaker asks the beloved to look in a mirror, and he does so with a phrase similar to Sonnet 3's 'Look in thy glass' and Sonnet 103's 'Look in your glass'. But if one poet is drawing on the other, it is unclear who is influencing whom. Perhaps influence goes in two directions: from Shakespeare's 3 to Barnfield's 11, and from Barnfield's 11 to Shakespeare's 3–103 scheme.

In the 1599 edition of *The Passionate Pilgrim*, Shakespeare's and Barnfield's poems mingle with one another. The volume contains twenty poems, starting with versions of Sonnets 138 and 144 and ending with Barnfield's ode 'As it fell upon a day'; its eighth poem is a Barnfield sonnet that praises Spenser. Because *The Passionate Pilgrim*'s publisher, William Jaggard, copied the Barnfield poems from *Poems in Diverse Humours*, he would have known who wrote them, and the volume's twenty-poem arrangement may be informed by his knowledge of the authors.[4] It is conceivable, for example, that Barnfield's sonnet has been positioned as the first poem not by Shakespeare.[5] In the late 1590s, 'sweet Shakespeare' had the reputation of being a love poet, the author of *Venus and Adonis*, *Love's Labour's Lost*, and *Romeo and Juliet*.[6] The inclusion of Barnfield's poems in a work that advertises itself as love poetry by Shakespeare suggests that the editor felt that such poems could pass as Shakespeare's, or that he associated Barnfield with Shakespeare. But neither of Barnfield's poems in *The Passionate Pilgrim* is a love lyric per se, and 'As it fell upon a day' potentially shifts the volume's tone at the end: it is a lament about being abandoned by fortune and friends. Something else may be going on.

Barnfield's ode contrasts with the poems that come before it in *The Passionate Pilgrim*, but it is not incongruous. It may be read as part of a designed arrangement:

Opening poems of *The Passionate Pilgrim*:

1. 'When my loves swears that she is made of truth' (Shakespeare)
2. 'Two loves I have, of comfort and despair' (Shakespeare)

Closing poems of *The Passionate Pilgrim*:

19. '[Come] live with me and be my love' and 'Love's Answer' (Marlowe, Raleigh)
20. 'As it fell upon a day' (Barnfield)

Like Shakespeare's 'When my loves swears that she is made of truth', Raleigh's response to Marlowe portrays lovers as liars through the figure of an urbane woman: Shakespeare's mistress and Raleigh's shepherdess know the ways of the world. And like 'Two loves I have, of comfort and despair', 'As it fell upon a day' discusses betrayal in friendship and distinguishes between true and untrue companions. The ode also contains a subtext of amatory betrayal: its opening lines allude to spring and Philomela's rape. Jaggard's arrangement of poems clarifies this subtext and hints at transgressive love. Jaggard may even be evoking Marlowe's reputation as a lover of boys, since aficionados would have known that 'Come live with me' was Marlowe's poem.[7] In any event, the arrangement of poems might have placed Shakespeare in the company of Barnfield and Marlowe, as might the volume's title, whose 'pilgrim' likely derives from the 'pilgrim' sonnet in *Romeo and Juliet*, and whose 'passionate' could allude to Marlowe and Barnfield. In 1600, 'Come live with me' was published as 'The Passionate Shepherd to His Love'. If Marlowe was already known as the passionate shepherd in 1593, Barnfield's 1594 'affectionate shepherd' may be a nod to him.[8]

Still, the Barnfield-Marlowe-Shakespeare conjunction may have been unwelcome to Shakespeare, even as a marketing device. Privately, perhaps, Shakespeare identified with Marlowe. In the wake of Jaggard's volume and the 1599 banning of Marlowe's translations of Ovid, he alludes to Marlowe twice in *As You Like It* – as a man who had a 'great reckoning in a little room' (Act 3, Scene 3), and as the shepherd of love at first sight (Act 3, Scene 5). The allusions to Marlowe are clear, but their significance is unclear.[9] Is Shakespeare sympathising with the passionate shepherd or distancing himself from him? Maybe both.

Appendix E: Sonnets 69–70 and the boundaries of the fifty-five-poem pyramid

The fifty-five-sonnet pyramid consists of Sonnets 21–75. Like the steps of the 153-poem pyramid, its steps are demarcated by non-linked sonnets at boundaries, except at the boundary between the seventh and eighth steps (Sonnets 69–70). Why the exception? Let us first look at where Sonnets 21–75 fall in the 153-poem pyramid. These fifty-five sonnets take up most of the second step and all of the third through fifth steps. Each of the four steps concludes with a somewhat separate poem because it is anticipatory or retrospective (33, 48, 62, and 75). In some pairs and trios in these steps, non-linked sonnets allow for alternative constructions: Sonnets 25–6, for example, can be regarded as a pair or as two separate sonnets, and Sonnets 46–8 can be seen as a trio or as a pair and a sonnet. In the fifty-five-sonnet pyramid, 46–8 and 69–70 potentially transgress boundaries between steps, but because Sonnet 48 can be regarded as separate from 46–7, 46–8 need not cross a boundary. It is harder to say the same of 69–70, since these sonnets are strongly linked: 69 explains why the youth's deeds make the world judge ill of him; 70 maintains that envy drives such judgements. (The couplet rhymes, *show–grow* and *show–owe*, reinforce the link.) The simplest explanation for the boundary transgression is a competing scheme: Sonnets 69–70, 71–2, and 73–4 are a series of pairs crucial to the main pyramid's fifth step. Shakespeare could not uncouple 69–70 and maintain the scheme.

But like 33–4 in the main pyramid, Sonnets 69–70 are perhaps an exception that proves the rule. The two poems speak of mending faults:

> Sonnet 69
> Those parts of thee that the world's eye doth view
> Want nothing that the thought of hearts can mend.
> All tongues, the voice of souls, give thee that due,

Utt'ring bare truth, ev'n so as foes commend.
Thy outward thus with outward praise is crowned;
But those same tongues that give thee so thine own,
In other accents do this praise confound
By seeing farther than the eye hath shown.
They look into the beauty of thy mind,
And that (in guess) they measure by thy deeds;
Then, churls, their thoughts – although their eyes were kind –
To thy fair flow'r add the rank smell of weeds.
  But why thy odor matcheth not thy show,
  The soil is this: that thou dost common grow.

Sonnet 70
That thou art blamed shall not be thy defect,
For slander's mark was ever yet the fair;
The ornament of beauty is suspect,
A crow that flies in heaven's sweetest air.
So thou be good, slander doth but approve
Thy worth the greater, being wooed of Time;
For canker vice the sweetest buds doth love,
And thou present'st a pure unstainèd prime.
Thou hast passed by the ambush of young days,
Either not assailed, or victor, being charged;
Yet this thy praise cannot be so thy praise,
To tie up Envy evermore enlarged.
  If some suspect of ill masked not thy show,
  Then thou alone kingdoms of hearts shouldst owe.

Understood as a flaw in the pyramid, Sonnets 69–70 can be redeemed in the broader design. In 69's couplet, the poet explains to the youth why he (the youth) has a bad reputation: 'But why thy odor matcheth not thy show, / The soil is this: that thou doth common grow'. ('Soil' means both 'fault/blemish/stain' and 'solution to the riddle'.) Sonnet 69's explanation is also an accusation, and it is meant to sting: the poet risks overstepping bounds of friendship and class by punning on 'common'. As if to forestall an indignant reaction, 70 reassures the youth: 'That thou art blamed shall not be thy defect, / For slander's mark was ever yet the fair'. Now the youth is not at fault. The poet argues that public blame only proves the youth's worth more, and he concludes his argument with hyperbolic flattery: the youth would be too powerful – he would possess 'kingdoms of hearts' – if he were above suspicion. In brief, Sonnet 70 offers a strained explanation for the youth's flaws, and it illustrates a defect in the fifty-five-poem pyramid. In light of *Sonnets*' concerns with perfection and imperfection, such a flaw could be part of the design – or so Shakespeare may have rationalised, making a virtue out of necessity.

But Shakespeare need not have been rationalising, or not merely rationalising: there is evidence that he tried to reconcile his schemes. In Q, there are at least twelve misprints of 'their' for 'thy' in the fair-youth sonnets. As Burrow suggests, these may result from shorthand forms of 'they' and 'thy'; another 'strong possibility' is that 'the copy for Q was revised, with "your" being in some places overwritten with "thy" (or vice versa), and then misread by the compositor as "their"'.[10] And as Evans explains, shorthand forms of 'thy' and 'their' ('y^i' and 'y^r') could easily be mistaken for forms of 'you'.[11] More to the present purpose: the dozen misprints of 'their' occur in the fifty-five-poem pyramid; one is in 70; and the opening line of 70, 'That thou art blamed shall not be thy deféct', has a misprint of 'are' for 'art'. Again, Burrow is helpful:

> Q reads 'thou are' [in line 1]; the only other occasion in which the Sonnets use 'thou are' is in [Sonnet 22's] 'So long as youth and thou are of one date', in which the plural subject ('youth' and 'thou') explains the use of 'are'. This slip, combined with the 'their/thy' error in line 6, suggests that 'you' and 'your' may have been overwritten in the manuscript of this poem.[12]

Because 69–70 are thou-sonnets and 71–2 are you-sonnets, one way to signal that 70 belongs with 71–2 more than with 69 would be to change 70 to a you-sonnet. If 'you' and 'your' were overwritten in the manuscript, the emendations could indicate that Shakespeare tried to change the pronouns, in order to accommodate competing schemes.

This last possibility foregrounds an unexpected application of this book's arguments: establishing an authorial text. While I have noted that details of Q – from spellings that allow for anagrams, to the 'monument' of Sonnet 55 – appear to be authorial, I have not made an inventory of such items. My sense is that most 'misprints' are designed, and that Shakespeare, attuned to differences between manuscript and print culture, is both evoking a conceit of providential error and anticipating errors in a way that aligns with his view that the people in whom we are most invested as ideals – those whom we love the most – are inevitably flawed.

Notes

Introduction

1. For 'pérspective' as an adverbial adjective, see Ingram and Redpath, 62. Booth (173) and Kerrigan, (*"The Sonnets"*, 205) regard it as one of four possibilities. Mowat and Werstine present 'seen perspectively' as the primary meaning of 'pérspective' (66).
2. See Greenblatt, *Renaissance Self-Fashioning*, 17–24.
3. Auden, 'Shakespeare's Sonnets', 88.
4. Duncan-Jones, *Sonnets*, 40–4.
5. Allen, 202.
6. Rollins, Volume 1, v.
7. See the notes of Oram et al. and Prescott and Hadfield.
8. Final sentence of 'Interrogating the *Sonnets*'.

Chapter 1

1. Ferry, 29.
2. Ferry, 27.
3. Jackson, 'Pronouns', 29.
4. Jackson, 'Pronouns', 24.
5. Jackson, 'Pronouns', 24–5.
6. Jackson, 'Aspects', 134 (footnote 49); West, 7–11; Stirling, 16–20; Kerrigan, *"The Sonnets"*, 8; Booth, 546; and Edmondson and Wells, 33.
7. In his first note to 'Essay, Supplementary to the Preface' (1815), Wordsworth provides a list of twenty-seven Shakespeare sonnets that illustrate merits in thought and language.
8. Quoted in Kerrigan (*"The Sonnets"*, 446) and Duncan-Jones (*Sonnets*, 465).
9. Vendler, 488.
10. Kerrigan, *"The Sonnets"*, 53.
11. For 'antanaclasis' and rhetorical repetitions in *Sonnets*, see Ramsey, 104–7.

12. For more on 115's ambiguities, see Booth, 378–84.
13. West, 359.
14. West, 359–60.
15. West, 357.
16. Herman, 32–3.
17. Herman, 43–4.
18. Meres, 317.
19. For details, see Duncan-Jones and Woudhuysen, 489–98.
20. From *An Apology for Actors* (quoted in Duncan-Jones and Woudhuysen, 497).
21. As Duncan-Jones notes, Jonson's dedicatory letter to his *Epigrams* (1616) may be a reply to *Sonnets*: it emphasises the correct use of Pembroke's title and asserts that Jonson's poems need no cipher to be understood (*Sonnets*, 60–3).
22. I reject the theory that 'begetter' means 'procurer': there is little philological support for it, and Thorpe implies that he is following the poet in wishing the 'begetter' happiness and eternity. For 'begetter' as 'procurer', see Caveney.
23. Beeching, xli.
24. Poets who allude to three years include Desportes, Ronsard, and Daniel. Davies of Hereford refers to a seven-year period in *Wit's Pilgrimage*.
25. See Akrigg, 3. It is also unclear whether the 's' is voiced or unvoiced.
26. The motto might also be translated 'one by means of all, and all by means of one' or 'one throughout all, and all throughout one'. It is cognate with 'the part through the whole, and the whole through the part', and it may be related to a commonplace saying about the soul – *The soul is all in all, and all in every part* (see Baldwin, 157 and 176–7).
27. In *Shakespeare, An Ungentle Life*, Duncan-Jones favours Pembroke's candidacy but concedes that some sonnets 'may have been originally written for Southampton' (248). In *Will in the World*, Greenblatt generally favours Southampton's candidacy but allows for the possibility that sonnets may have been written or recycled for Pembroke (232). In *Soul of the Age*, Bate suggests that 'both camps' of scholars may be correct (206).

Chapter 2

1. For 'come to have or receive your memorial', see Evans, *Shakespeare's Sonnets*, 205.
2. For more on etymology in Sonnet 107, see Vendler, 456–7.
3. The elegy to Sidney is the twenty-ninth poem.
4. Scodel, 19–25.
5. Sandys, 128.

6. See Duncan-Jones, *Sonnets*, 25–7.
7. Puttenham, 78–9.
8. Hopper, 35.
9. Smarr, 379.
10. Lomazzo, 140.
11. Wright, *Passions*, 307.
12. Lomazzo, 17.
13. Sylvester, *Divine Weeks* (Week 2, Day 1, Part 1, lines 29–31).
14. Fowler, *Triumphal Forms*, 185.
15. Book 3, Ode 30, lines 1–5. I have translated 'aere' as 'brass' because 'bronze' dates from the eighteenth century.
16. See Burrow, *William Shakespeare*, 626, who cites lines 252–9 of Propertius III.ii.
17. Fowler, *Triumphal Forms*, 185 and 189.
18. Kerrigan, "*The Sonnets*", 42.
19. Graziani, 80.
20. Graziani, 81–2.
21. Graziani, 82.
22. Roche, 48.
23. Roche, 416 and 458.
24. Duncan-Jones, *Sonnets*, 101 and 272.
25. Duncan-Jones, *Sonnets*, 99 and 326.
26. For the prominence of 108, see Fowler, *Triumphal Forms*, 175–6. For divisions in the fair-youth section, see Duncan-Jones, *Sonnets*, 100.
27. Duncan-Jones, *Sonnets*, 236 and 264.
28. Duncan-Jones, *Sonnets*, 100.
29. Roche, 422.
30. Graziani, 80.
31. Duncan-Jones, *Sonnets*, 99.
32. For example, Burrow, *William Shakespeare*, 103–6.
33. See the *OED* entries on 'step', 'degree', and 'ladder'.
34. Kerrigan, "*The Sonnets*", 13.
35. Kerrigan, "*The Sonnets*", 13–14.
36. For 'The Seven Ages of Man', see Bate, *Soul of the Age*, 96.
37. Primaudaye, 563.
38. Wright, *Passions*, 2 and 4.
39. Drayton, 139.
40. Quoted in Roche, 572.
41. Roche, 362.
42. Roche, 363.
43. In the 1598 text, 'bless' and 'bliss' are spelled 'blesse' and 'blisse', respectively. For 'Blissed' instead of 'Blessed', see Ringler, 478.
44. For the Tansillo sonnets, see Lawrence, 75 and 110.
45. Compare Daniel's *sight-sought* with Shakespeare's *sigh-sought* in Sonnet 30.

46. The other sonnets that evoke the myth are 4, 11, and 12. Sonnet 17 is the centre poem of Spenser's sequence, not Du Bellay's.
47. Vendler, 30–1.
48. Dubrow, *Domestic Loss*, 23 and 31.
49. Attridge, 116.
50. Attridge, 115 and 116–17.
51. Fowler, *Triumphal Forms*, 175.
52. Fowler, *Triumphal Forms*, 174–80.
53. Parker, 70. For details, see Parker's introduction and 70–81.
54. For axes of symmetry in formal gardens, see Bird.
55. Fowler, *Triumphal Forms*, 180.

Chapter 3

1. Drayton started publishing poems on heroic subjects in 1593.
2. For an overview of sixteenth-century sonnets, see Spiller, especially chapter 6.
3. Quoted by Spiller, 95.
4. These echoes are noted by A. Kent Hieatt.
5. For the allusion to Christ's age, see Prescott and Hadfield, 600.
6. For the influence of *The Ruins of Time*, see Kerrigan, "The Sonnets", 390–2; for *Prothalamion*, see Jackson, 'Echoes of Spenser's *Prothalamion*', 180–2. For *The Faerie Queene*'s impact on 106, see Cheney, 'Shakespeare's Sonnet 106', 340–62.
7. For the significance of 12×12, see Oram et al., 213.
8. For Chaucer and Langland, see Oram et al., 213.
9. For this traditional view, see Hadfield, *Edmund Spenser*, 235 and 536.
10. For Spenser's troubles with *Mother Hubberd's Tale*, see Prescott and Hadfield, 583, and Hadfield, *Edmund Spenser*, 265–74.
11. Cheney, *National*, 277.
12. Cheney, *National*, 278.
13. Cheney, *National*, 56–7.
14. Cheney, *National*, 57.
15. Cheney, *National*, 9.
16. For the anti-Virgilian reading of *Tamburlaine*, see Cheney, *Counterfeit Profession*, 115–35. For Marlowe's borrowings from *The Faerie Queene*, see Lethbridge, 26–35.
17. Cheney, *National*, 277.
18. For Lucan's epic as anti-Virgilian and anti-imperial, see Quint, 131–57.
19. For Shakespeare's political views, see Hadfield, *Shakespeare and Renaissance Politics*, 1–35. For Spenser's views of monarchy and nobility, see Helgerson, *Forms of Nationhood*, especially 52–9 and footnotes 60 and 64 (312–13).

20. For the view that Daniel was complicit in the 1591 *Astrophil and Stella*, see Woudhuysen, *Sir Philip Sidney*, 371–83, and Lawrence, 68–9.
21. This information is from Hiller and Groves.
22. Besides the seventeen dedicatory sonnets appended to some copies of the 1590 *Faerie Queene*, Spenser wrote at least one Spenserian sonnet before 1595 – a dedicatory poem to Gabriel Harvey's *Four Letters* dated 18 July 1586.
23. For Aetiön as Drayton, see Oram et al., 542, and Fleay, 93–5.
24. My translations of Lucian are based on the Loeb text, 143–51. When Lucian introduces the Aëtiön story, he uses the expression 'ta teleutaia', which can mean 'recently' (as in the Loeb) or 'last of all'. For more on 'ta teleutaia', see Politt, 175.
25. For more on *Colin Clout's Come Home Again* as a volume, see Hadfield, *Edmund Spenser*, 313–16.
26. Hadfield, *Edmund Spenser*, 318.
27. The reciprocal influence of Daniel's *Civil Wars* and the Henriad is well documented. See, for example, Forker's introduction to *Richard II*, and Kastan's introduction to *1 Henry IV*.
28. Varying accounts can be found in the biographies by Greenblatt, *Will in the World* (199–216), Duncan-Jones (*Sonnets*, 48–55), and Ackroyd (187–90).
29. See, for example, Greenblatt, *Will in the World*, 199–216.
30. Quoted in Greenblatt, *Will in the World*, 214–15.
31. For 'o'er-green' as a pun on 'Greene', see, Potter, 100–1.
32. For the 'Spencers of Althorp', see Hadfield, *Edmund Spenser*, 19–22.
33. Hudston, 386.
34. Huntington, 76.
35. See Huntington, 130.
36. Jackson, 'Francis Meres', 244.
37. Jackson, 'Aspects', 128.
38. Booth, *Sonnets*, 265–6.
39. West, 244.
40. West, 245.
41. This is a common comparison. See, for example, Acheson, 144–8.
42. Beeching, 'The Sonnets', 371.
43. Burrow, *William Shakespeare*, 540.
44. Lee, 107.
45. My remarks are based on Doyno's notes (210).
46. For Chapman and 'the school of night', see Woudhuysen, *Love's Labour's Lost*, 70–6.
47. See Waddington, 92.
48. The 1598 dedication of Homer to the Earl of Essex may be the only excessive dedication to an aristocrat that Chapman wrote in the 1590s. For an opposing view, see Acheson, 188 and following.

49. All citations of the plays are from *The Pilgrimage to Parnassus*.
50. Quoted in the appendix of the second Arden edition of *Hamlet*, 573–4.
51. Since stanza 12 of 'Ovid's Banquet of Sense' consists of four lines plus Corinna's fourteen-line song/sonnet, Chapman might be inviting the reader to calculate an extra stanza and nine extra lines. This would bring the total poetic units to 266 (one more than in *Lucrece*) and the total lines to 1,865 (ten more than in *Lucrece*).
52. 'The Amorous Contention' was republished with unnumbered stanzas in 1598 and attributed to 'R. S., Esquire'.
53. All quotations are from Smarr, 369.
54. Smarr, 369.
55. See Fowler, *Triumphal Forms*, 140–6.
56. Boaden, 46–56. Also see Rollins, *The Sonnets*, 2:279.
57. Rollins, 2:280.
58. Creighton, *Shakespeare's Story*, 3.
59. Rollins, 2:280.
60. For Jonson's parody of Daniel's sonnet, see Miola, 17.
61. For the Daniel-Danaïd pun, see Roche, 358.
62. Creighton, *Shakespeare's Story*, 34 and 46.
63. Jackson, 'Francis Meres', 244.
64. Creighton (citing Grossart), *Shakespeare's Story*, 46.
65. See Creighton, *Shakespeare's Story*, 37–44. It is unclear whether Daniel was officially recognised as laureate. In his 1674 history of Oxford, Anthony Wood writes: 'Spenser was Poet Laureate to Queen Elizabeth: when he died Samuel Daniel succeeded him, and him Ben Jonson' (quoted in Creighton, *Shakespeare's Story*, 38). In works published in 1599, 1601, and 1603, Daniel uses blazonry with laurel sprigs and oak leaves on the title pages (Creighton, *Shakespeare's Story*, 42–3). The laureate position was not formalised until 1668.
66. Ringler, lvi.
67. See Phillips, 75 and following.
68. Brooke, 6–7.
69. See the entry for 'rich rhyme' in *The New Princeton Encyclopedia of Poetics*, and Wilson-Okamura, 764–8.
70. Daniel, 224.

Chapter 4

1. To my knowledge, the only commentator who points to Sonnet 33's crucifixion imagery is Booth, who notes that 'heav'n's sun [by punning on "son"] floods the poem with vague and unharnessed suggestions of the incarnation and crucifixion' (188).
2. This tradition was widespread: see Curtius, 503 and following.

3. See Hopper, *Medieval Number Symbolism*, 131.
4. West, 212.
5. Vendler, 308–9.
6. Duncan-Jones, *Sonnets*, 242.
7. Grundy, 61.
8. Paragraph 6 of Chapter 13 of Book 1 of the *New Arcadia* (p. 61 in the 1590 edition).
9. Schaar, 110–17.
10. For more on Barnfield's sonnet and 99, see Kerrigan, *"The Sonnets"*, 48–9. For more on Spenser's sonnet and other sources for 99, see Rollins, *The Sonnets*, 1:244–7.
11. For example, see Greenblatt, *Will in the World*, 229.
12. As Duncan-Jones and Woudhuysen note, 'publisher' had not yet acquired the sense of 'one who issues books', but it was related to 'set forth', which could mean 'publish' (240).
13. The miniature 'Cobbe portrait' was thought to depict a woman until 2002 (see Holden).
14. Winnick, 268.
15. Winnick, 267.
16. For the example from *The Two Gentlemen of Verona*, see Winnick, 267–8.
17. See Shapiro, 133, and Weis, 38.
18. Weis, 38.
19. Weis, 224.
20. Massey links Juliet's witticism to 'Wriothesley' but does not note the play with W and R (471).
21. For the dating of *Romeo and Juliet*, see Weis, 33–43.
22. For more on Wriothesley as a Montague, see Weis, 45.
23. For details on the coat of arms and other information about Southampton, see the opening chapters of Green's *Wriothesley's Roses*.
24. Book XI, Chapter 30. *Concerning the City of God against the Pagans*, translated by Henry Bettenson, 465.
25. From the note to Revelation 13:18 in the 1599 Geneva Bible.
26. For Sidney, see lines 22–4 of Song 6. The title of Constable's sonnet is 'Of the envy others bear to his lady for the former perfections' (I.ii.6).
27. Butler, 75.
28. The chapters begin on pp. 332 and 377, respectively. The translations are mine.
29. *Nicene*, Series 1, Volume VII, 441. All translations of Augustine's sermons are based on Volumes VI and VII of this series.
30. Butler and Fowler, 160.
31. Butler and Fowler, 164–5.
32. Butler and Fowler, 162.
33. For 'non-climatic climax', see Duncan-Jones and Woudhuysen, 16.
34. Duncan-Jones and Woudhuysen, 194.

Chapter 5

1. The symmetry evoked by 22, 77, and 122 is false in the sense that 72, not 77, is halfway between 22 and 122.
2. For 'dial', see Burrow, *William Shakespeare*, 534. For arguments about the number of gifts, see Ingram and Redpath, 178 and Evans, *Shakespeare's Sonnets*, 173.
3. For 'copying and commonplacing', see Zarnowiecki, 140.
4. For reflexive pronouns as two words in Renaissance English, see Booth, 197–8.
5. For 'cóntrary' as 'mirror image', see Booth, 243, and Ferry, 201.
6. Ferry, 202.
7. For 'lover' and 'lovers', see Booth, 431.
8. For 'The rest is silence' and 126's parentheses, see Duncan-Jones, *Sonnets*, 366.
9. Sonnet 43 begins with a 'When I . . . then' phrase but its structure is otherwise different, and it is not a meditation on time.
10. For more on *Aurora*'s organization and themes, see Roche, 275–85.
11. See, for example, Duncan-Jones, *Sonnets*, 214.
12. Fowler, *Forms*, 148.
13. For 8's symbolism, see Fowler, *Forms*, 150–52.
14. For *Arcadia* as a source, see Duncan-Jones, *Sonnets*, 120; Evans, *Shakespeare's Sonnets*, 113; and especially Rollins, 2:119–21.
15. Quoted in Fowler, *Spenser and the Numbers of Time*, 34.
16. For number symbolism in *Julius Caesar*, especially play on the number four and the pairs of four in the assassination scene, see McAlindon, 384–5.
17. For pageants and other examples, see the third chapter of *Triumphal Forms*. The Pentateuch remark is from *Spenser and the Numbers of Time*, 34 (note 2).
18. See Stocker, 161.
19. Sonnet 5 ('Of the Prowess of His Lady') is from the second section of *Diana* (I.ii.5).
20. See Waddington, 164.
21. Waddington, 163.
22. For allusions to Ephesians 5 in *Sonnets*, see Booth, 192.
23. The roses are in the coat of arms of the city of Southampton.
24. Duncan-Jones, *Sonnets*, 132. For the biblical phrase, Duncan-Jones cites Matthew 4:25. Other versions can be found at Matthew 13:12 and 25:29, and Luke 8:18 and 19:26.
25. For 'threescore and ten' as the proverbial limit of life, see Psalms 90:10.
26. Strictly speaking, Sonnet 45's 'ee' rhymes are not Spenserian because the second pair of rhymes is not the first pair of its quatrain.
27. Augustine, Sermons in *Nicene and Post-Nicene Fathers*, VI, 363.
28. Augustine, Sermons in *Nicene and Post-Nicene Fathers*, VI, 364–5.

310   *The Secret Architecture of Shakespeare's Sonnets*

29. Augustine, Sermons in *Nicene and Post-Nicene Fathers*, VI, 258–9.
30. For more on doubling in 88, see Vendler, 385, and Blick, '"Duble Vantage"', 83–90.
31. For parallels to Sonnet 33–4, see Baldwin, 232–7, and Evans, *Shakespeare's Sonnets*, 136.
32. Kastan, 76.
33. See Ferry, 182–3.
34. See Ringler, 436–7.
35. For more on the number of lines in speeches, see Huntington, 230–40.
36. Act 2, Scene 1, lines 112–3. For Richard's birthdate, see Corbin and Sedge, 82.
37. Weis, 43.
38. Weis, 38.
39. Weis, 43.
40. Duncan-Jones, *Ungentle Life*, 96.
41. Duncan-Jones, *Ungentle Life*, 104–5. Since August was the sixth month in the Elizabethan calendar, the date 'August 11' could have been 11/6 or 6/11.

Chapter 6

1. For 'look what' as 'whatever', see Booth, 147–8.
2. For the belief that sexual emission shortened life, see Duncan-Jones, *Sonnets*, 128.
3. Vendler, 85.
4. For a description of *serio ludere*, see Logan and Adams, xxi.
5. For a description of Erasmus's *Copia* and its place in Renaissance curricula, see George A. Kennedy, 244–5.
6. See, for example, Burrow, *Shakespeare and Classical Antiquity*, 39–41.
7. Vendler, 84.
8. West, 40.
9. West, 40.
10. For the orthography of W, see Duncan-Jones, *Sonnets*, 37.
11. For puns on 'you's', 'hues', and 'use', see Booth, 164.
12. Davies's 'VV' poem is from *Microcosmus*. It is the second of two sonnets dedicated to Pembroke and appears near the end of the volume.
13. See Winnick, 268.
14. In Amour 39, the sestet's you-forms may denote a plural.
15. In the second edition of *Delia*, Daniel uses you-forms in Sonnet 28's couplet.
16. The six you-sonnets are 5, 8, 10, 13, 21, and 22; 18 was a thou-sonnet in the earlier edition. In the three thou-sonnets added to the 1599 *Idea* (12, 30, and 43), the forms are arguably determined by rhyme.
17. Desportes's sonnet is number 18 in *Les Amours d'Hippolyte*.

18. For more on Daniel and Tebaldeo, see Lawrence, 83–4.
19. Desportes says 'gaze at yourself' ('vous mirer'). Tebaldeo uses 'figura', a word that is potentially close in meaning to 'form'. Neither Desportes nor Tebaldeo uses a word like 'form' earlier in their sonnets, and neither stresses the danger of viewing the lady too much.
20. The phrase 'best painters' art' (in Q, 'best Painters art') might be construed as 'the art of the best Painter' (God's art or Nature's art), but the lack of a definite article argues against it.
21. Such devices could come in different shapes (including pyramids) and could contain mirrors and multifaceted lenses. See Shickman, 217–18.
22. My assertions about rarity are based on Schaar's survey (52–4).
23. Schaar, 52–4.
24. For the spelling and pronunciation of '-ed', see Booth, 175.
25. Wright, 50–1.
26. Tyler, 151.
27. By 'broken rhymes', I mean multisyllabic rhymes in which the rhyming syllables extend across two words in at least one of the rhyming lines.
28. Sonnet 26's alternation of masculine and feminine rhymes is not strictly in the French style because the *show it–bestow it* rhyme comes after two consecutive masculine rhymes.
29. For 'enduring memorial', see Thomson and Taylor, 432. For 'life-like statue', see Jenkin, 393. For 'surviving mourner', see William Browne of Tavistock, 'An Elegy on Mr William Hoptwon': 'Since I (his living monument) indite / And moulder into dust the while I write'.
30. For alchemical imagery in *Sonnets*, see Healy, especially 67–8.
31. For 'quaint' and 'no thing', see Booth, 163–5.
32. For 'control' as 'call to account' and 'refute', see the notes on 58, 66, and 125 in Booth and in Kerrigan, *"The Sonnets"*. For 'control' as 'point out faults' or 'find fault with', see Hiller and Groves's note to line 50 of Daniel's *Musophilus*, and line 901, in which Daniel spells 'controls' with a 'w'.
33. For 'hue' as *sprezzatura* and *je ne sais quoi*, see Burrow, *William Shakespeare*, 420 and Baldwin, 165.
34. For the sexual meaning of 'use', see Booth, 137 and 142.
35. For 'Hews' as a cipher for Southampton, see Rollins 2:183–5.
36. See, for example, Schaar, 97, and Grundy, 219.
37. For the identity of 'Grace', see Grundy, 219.
38. Schaar, 93–7.
39. Schaar, 97.
40. Booth, 184.
41. For 'equipage', see Booth, 186, and Burrow, *William Shakespeare*, 444.
42. Tyler, 37–8.
43. For Nashe and Lee, see Rollins, *The Sonnets* I, 93–4.
44. For satire as an antidote to love poetry, see Helgerson, *Self-Crowned Laureates*, 104–11.

45. See, for example, Duncan-Jones, *Sonnets*, 12.
46. See, for example, Vendler, 336.
47. Burrow, *William Shakespeare*, 576.
48. Vendler, 419.
49. Evans, *Shakespeare's Sonnets*, 195.
50. From Ledger's notes (www.shakespeares-sonnets.com/sonnet/99).
51. For more on *Julius Caesar*, Elizabethan calendars, and 1599, see Sohmer, *Shakespeare's Mystery Play*, and Shapiro, chapter 8.
52. Weever's satire was first published in 1600 in *Faunus and Melliflora*.
53. My range of creation dates is based on a chart assembled by Nolen Jones, 26. Some Anno Mundi calendars begin with the world's 're-creation' after the flood.
54. Butler, *Number Symbolism*, 108–9.
55. Akrigg, 69–73.
56. Akrigg, 78 and 93–6.

Chapter 7

1. For 'Ver' as an allusion to the Earl of Oxford, see Chatterly, 352.
2. For a modern edition that questions whether the repetition of the sonnets may be a printer's error, see Prescott and Hadfield, 650. For commentators who question *Sonnets*' repeated couplet, see Rollins, 1:238.
3. Roche makes a similar argument (xv).
4. Variants include 'fairest' and 'fayrest'.
5. For 'report' as 'reputation', see Duncan-Jones, *Sonnets*, 183 and 302.
6. Burrow, *William Shakespeare*, 596.
7. Duncan-Jones, *Sonnets*, 336.
8. Sequences with roughly 108 sonnets include: Greville's *Caelica*, Barnes's *Parthenophil and Parthenophe*, and Davies of Hereford's *Wit's Pilgrimage*.
9. For 108 and the suitors, see Fowler, *Triumphal Forms*, 175.
10. For Southampton's imprisonment and the poem's date, see Kerrigan, *"The Sonnets"*, 308, 313, and 319.
11. For 'still' and 'skill', see Kerrigan, *"The Sonnets"*, 313.
12. Q prints 'beauties best'.
13. Cheney, 'Shakespeare's Sonnet 106', 351. The line is from *The Faerie Queene*, Book 5, Canto 3, Stanza 40.
14. Cheney, 'Shakespeare's Sonnet 106', 350–1.
15. Quoted in Cheney, 'Shakespeare's Sonnet 106', 355 and 361.
16. Cheney, 'Shakespeare's Sonnet 106', 349.
17. For details about Constable's life, I draw on Grundy's introduction.
18. For 'auténtique' and subject-object reversibility, see Hiller and Groves, 54.
19. For more connections between these poems, see Schaar, 29–31.

20. For the performance of *Love's Labour's Lost* during the 1604–5 Christmas seasons, see Woudhuysen, introduction to the Arden edition of *Love's Labour's Lost*, 83–4.
21. From the 1549 edition of *The Book of Common Prayer*, 65.
22. For Sonnet 116 and the Corinthians passage, see Callaghan, 63.
23. Duncan-Jones, *Sonnets*, 21–6.
24. Lever, 263.
25. Booth, 429–30.
26. For Gascoigne's use of 'by' for 'concerning', see Larsen, 187.
27. For 'assured' as 'betrothed', see Bell, *Elizabethan Women*, 170–3.
28. See the notes on these poems in Oram et al. and Prescott and Hadfield.
29. Hadfield, *Edmund Spenser*, 299. For more on Spenser's and Boyle's ages, see Blick, 'Spenser's *Amoretti* and Elizabeth Boyle', 309–15.
30. Burrow, *William Shakespeare*, 602.
31. Duncan-Jones, *Shakespeare, An Ungentle Life*, 118.
32. Duncan-Jones, *Shakespeare, An Ungentle Life*, 118.
33. The 1608 quarto of *King Lear* prints 'Love is not love'; the 1623 folio, 'Love's not love'.
34. In adopting 'The Phoenix and the Turtle' as the title, and in describing the poem as bipartite, I am following scholarly tradition. See Bednarz, *Shakespeare and the Truth of Love*.
35. The other poets are Jonson, Chapman, Marston, and 'Ignoto'. For Salisbury and *Love's Martyr*, see Duncan-Jones and Woudhuysen, 97–111.

Chapter 8

1. Mackail, 116.
2. For an alternative view on 'bed-vow' and the mistress's marital state, see Bell, 'Rethinking Shakespeare's Dark Lady'.
3. Duncan Sakeld, as quoted in a *Daily Mail* interview in 2012. For more details on Lucy Negro, see Sakeld, 'Black Luce'.
4. For details of Lanier's biography, see Green, 545–53.
5. Bate, *Genius*, 56–7.
6. Bate, *Genius*, 56.
7. Green, 555 and 561.
8. For precedents for 'black beauty', see Schaar, 111–12. For poems that attack cosmetics, see Green, 573.
9. For parallels, see McClumpha, 168–74, and Furness, 338–41.
10. For 'fire him out' and bawdy phrases in 144, see Kerrigan, *"The Sonnets"*, 60–1.
11. Q's text repeats line 1's 'my sinful earth' at the beginning of line 2. With 'Pressed by', I am following Stephen Orgel in his edition of *Sonnets*.
12. Jackson, 'Rhyme', 220.

13. Jackson, 'Rhyme', 221.
14. The fair-youth examples are Sonnets 3–4, 93–4, 113–14, and 121–2.
15. They occur sixteen to seventeen times in each of the first group's plays, and ten to twelve times in each of the second group's plays (www.opensourceshakespeare.org).
16. Alden, 366.
17. For Sonnet 150's parallels to 116 and *The Book of Common Prayer*, I am indebted to G. R. Ledger (www.shakespeares-sonnets.com/sonnet/150).
18. Schaar, 110–13.
19. Greville's 58 may be echoed in Shakespeare's 132. See Schaar, 114–15.
20. Schaar, 77.
21. Schaar, 74–8.
22. The image is so unusual that modern editors have erroneously emended 'in my bosom make thy resting place' to 'in thy bosom make my resting place' (Schaar, 106).
23. Muir, 33–4.
24. See Booth, 504, and Beeching, 129.
25. Cited by Beeching, 129.
26. In Renaissance English, 'array' can mean 'clothe', 'dress', 'afflict', and 'bring low'; 'marshal troops for battle' is atypical for the period. See Booth, 504, and Beeching, 129.
27. The passage occurs in Cleopatra's last speech, near the end of the play. See Duncan-Jones, *Sonnets*, 408.
28. In substituting 'eye' for 'eyes' at the end, the poet evokes a bawdy pun on 'nether eye'. See Duncan-Jones, *Sonnets*, 424.
29. For the references to venereal disease and the 'hot bath' cure, see Duncan-Jones, *Sonnets*, 422–7.
30. Quoted by Duncan-Jones, *Sonnets*, 422 (translation by Emily Wilson).
31. Hutton, 399.
32. See Booth, 536.

Chapter 9

1. See Duncan-Jones, *Sonnets*, 431.
2. For 'moody', 'agitated', and 'distraught', see Kerrigan, "*The Sonnets*", 395. For the seducer as fickle, see Duncan-Jones, *Sonnets*, 94. For 'flickering', see the *OED* entry on 'fickle' (in some Renaissance uses, 'fickle' refers to the changeable appearance of things and natural agents).
3. 'Shore's Wife' also begins with a preposition: 'Among the rest by Fortune overthrowen, / I am not least that most must wail her fate'.
4. For details, see Weis, 326.
5. Duncan-Jones and Woudhuysen, 194–5 (notes to stanzas 122–3).
6. Duncan-Jones and Woudhuysen, 48, 248, and 338 (notes).

7. Duncan-Jones, *Sonnets*, 17.
8. Sidney, *Arcadia*, 336. Dido's rhetoric may be echoed in Sonnet 75, especially lines 5–10.
9. For 'characterisation and mood', see Rees, 165; for the comparison of Dido and the maid, see Rees, 163–4.
10. Rees, 166.
11. Duncan-Jones, *Sonnets*, 445.
12. Kerrigan, *"The Sonnets"*, 390–1.
13. Kerrigan, *"The Sonnets"*, 391.
14. For the allusions to historical figures, see McCabe's edition of Spenser's shorter poems, 586–7.
15. See Jackson, 'Echoes of Spenser's *Prothalamion*', 180–2.
16. For the view that the poem's refrain sometimes functions as a counter-current to celebration, see Prescott and Hadfield, 676–7 (notes).
17. For the 'Willow Song' and other parallels in Shakespeare's work, see Kerrigan, *"The Sonnets"*, 393–4 and Sharon-Zisser and Whitworth, 25–33.
18. Duncan-Jones, *Sonnets*, 93.
19. Duncan-Jones, *Sonnets*, 94.
20. Duncan-Jones, *Sonnets*, 431.
21. Booth, 224.
22. Kerrigan, *"The Sonnets"*, 247.
23. Plato's *Timaeus and Critias*, 24–5.
24. For Ficino's influence on English writers, see Sears, 238.
25. My translations of Ficino are based on those of Farndell's edition.
26. The line about the individual soul and the World Soul is from the end of the chapter entitled 'Why the soul is compared to a compound and to musical harmony'.
27. This passage comes from near the end of the chapter entitled 'On the spirit of the world'.
28. Parker, 75.
29. Parker, 120–1.
30. The third of three sonnets with that title, this poem is in *Diana*'s third part (III.ii.6).
31. *Ovid's Banquet of Sense* perhaps also alludes to the World Soul in the 'The Amorous Contention of Phyllis and Flora', when the stanza count skips from 53 to 56. (Chapman may have deliberately left out 54 and 55.)
32. The 55-poem *Idea's Mirror* is a Huntington Library copy, available through Early English Books Online (Reel number 381:04, UMI Collection 'STC'). Though the numbering of poems in the 1599 *Idea* continues past 55, the post-55 poems are not sonnets.
33. The probability would be $(27!\cdot 18!)/(54!\cdot 45!)$ or .00088. In a fifty-five-poem series, there are potentially fifty-four linked pairs; in a ten-step pyramid, there are nine 'boundary pairs'.
34. See Evans, *Shakespeare's Sonnets*, 172.

35. 'Jesus, son of Mary, savior of the world'. My information about the Rushton Lodge is from the guidebook published by the English Heritage.

Conclusion

1. Generally associated with the work of Réne Girard, the concept of triangular or mimetic desire has been applied to *Sonnets* by Eve Sedgwick. For an overview of Sedgwick's arguments and a more productive application of Girard, see Barber.
2. Claims about Shakespeare's modernity are legion. Anne Ferry's *The "Inward" Language* and Joel Fineman's *Shakespeare's Perjured Eye* are two examples that focus on *Sonnets*.
3. These volumes were published in (respectively) 1784, 1789, 1796, and 1799. Of the four, Robinson's is the most Elizabethan in mode, because the sonnets are amatory (evoking 'Lesbian' love), despite the Petrarchan form. For more on the eighteenth-century sonnets, especially Smith's sonnets, see Roberts.
4. My quotations of and information on Rosetti's and Meredith's sequences are from Cecil Y. Lang's *The Pre-Raphaelites and their Circle*.
5. See my discussion in *Invisible Fences*, especially 72–5.
6. Quoted in Baudelaire's *Oeuvres completes*, I:1196. My translation.

Appendices

1. For 'The Poet's War', see Bednarz, *Shakespeare & The Poets' War*.
2. For Marlowe and 1599, see Shapiro, 217–18.
3. The *Amoretti* entry in the Stationers' Register is under '19 November [1594]'; the *Cynthia* entry is under '17 January [1595]'.
4. In treating Jaggard as the presumed editor, I am following Duncan-Jones and Woudhuysen (90).
5. Poems 1, 2, 3, and 5 of *The Passionate Pilgrim* are confidently ascribed to Shakespeare; there is no scholarly consensus about the authorship of poems 4, 6, and 7. See Duncan-Jones and Woudhuysen, 387–95.
6. For Shakespeare's reputation as a love poet, see Duncan-Jones and Woudhuysen, 4–9.
7. For Marlowe's reputation as a lover of boys, see Orgel's introduction to Marlowe's poems, viii.
8. The 'pilgrim' sonnet begins with 'If I profane with my unworthiest hand' (Act 1, Scene 5). For the title of *The Passionate Pilgrim*, see Duncan-Jones and Woudhuysen, 386; Potter, 259–60; and Shapiro, 192–3.

9. In *Shakespeare for the Wiser Sort*, Sohmer argues that Shakespeare is following an Elizabethan custom of recognising the 'seven-years' day' anniversary of a death (133).
10. Burrow, *William Shakespeare*, 432.
11. Evans, *Shakespeare's Sonnets*, 263.
12. Burrow, *William Shakespeare*, 520.

Bibliography

This is a bibliography of works cited and noted, not of all works consulted; as such, it represents the literature most relevant to my arguments. Few scholars pursue the idea that *Shakespeare's Sonnets* is organised, let alone highly organised. In the last half-century, three books have examined organisation in English sequences: Alastair Fowler's *Triumphal Forms* (1970), Thomas P. Roche's *Petrarch and the English Sonnet Sequence* (1989), and Tom W. N. Parker's *Proportional Form in the Sonnets of the Sidney Circle* (1998). These studies help me place Shakespeare and his *Sonnets* in literary-historical context, as do Richard Helgerson's *Self-Crowned Laureates* (1983), Raphael Falco's *Conceived Presences* (1994), and Gavin Alexander's *Writing After Sidney* (2006), which analyse literary careers in Renaissance England. And while there is a tradition of rearranging the order of *Sonnets*' poems – as studies by Brents Stirling (1968), S. C. Campbell (1978), and John Padel (1981) illustrate – it is in an entirely different spirit than my analysis, which argues that the 1609 order is authorial. Neil L. Rudenstine's *Ideas of Order* (2014) bucks the scholarly trend somewhat in outlining a thematic organisation of *Sonnets*, but his scheme is a loose structure, not an allusive and intricate one.

In detailing Shakespeare's dialogue with contemporaries, I draw on comparative studies, most of which were published decades ago. These include: Anne Ferry's chapters on Sidney and Shakespeare in *The "Inward" Language* (1983), which depicts Sidney-Shakespeare connections as deep and centred on 'language of the heart'; Paul Ramsey's discussion of Samuel Daniel and Shakespeare in *The Fickle Glass* (1979), which details verbal, thematic, and cadential parallels; and Patrick Cheney's studies of Spenser and Shakespeare, which portray Shakespeare's idea of authorship as 'counter-Spenserian'. Cheney's thesis in *Shakespeare, National Poet-Playwright* (2004) is akin to mine, as I also see Shakespeare's poetry as integral to his artistic career. For rhetorical connections between *Sonnets* and Shakespeare's narrative poems, Heather Dubrow's *Captive*

Victors (1987) has been helpful, and her 'The Politics of Plotting *Shakespeare's Sonnets*' (1996) has been a trusty guide to pitfalls of narrative approaches. MacDonald P. Jackson's articles on pronouns, rhymes, and other aspects of organisation in *Sonnets*, published over the last four decades, have broadened my analysis of the sequence's structure. One recent trend with which my book accords is epitomised by Lukas Erne's *Shakespeare as Literary Dramatist* (2003) and *Shakespeare and the Book Trade* (2013). Like Erne and scholars in his vein, I dispute the idea that Shakespeare was unconcerned about literary authorship, and I promote the idea that Shakespeare cared about the afterlife of his works.

The works that I cite most are editorial commentaries. The modern ones include those of Booth (1977), Kerrigan (1986), Evans (1996), Vendler (1997), Burrow (2002), West (2007), Duncan-Jones (2010), and Shrank and Lyne (2018). Among these, West pays the most attention to *Sonnets* as a sequence. For earlier commentary, my main resource is Hyder Edward Rollins's compendium (1944); I also draw on the editions of Tyler (1890), Beeching (1906), Alden (1916), and Brooke (1936). (The earlier commentators are more likely to offer suggestions about source texts and to consider biography.) For Shakespeare's allusions to other Elizabethan writers, the most useful studies are Rollins's commentary, T. W. Baldwin's *On the Literary Genetics of Shakespeare's Poems and Sonnets* (1950), and Clas Schaar's *Elizabethan Sonnet Themes* (1962).

Commentaries/Editions of Shakespeare's Sonnets

Alden, Raymond MacDonald. *The Sonnets of Shakespeare*. Houghton Mifflin. 1916.

Atkins, Carl D. *Shakespeare's Sonnets*. Fairleigh Dickinson University Press. 2007.

Beeching, H. C. *The Sonnets of Shakespeare*. Athenaeum. 1906.

Booth, Stephen. *Shakespeare's Sonnets*. Yale University Press. 1977.

Brooke, Tucker. *Shakespeare's Sonnets*. Oxford University Press. 1936.

Bullen, A. H. *The Works of Shakespeare*, Volume X. Shakespeare's Head Press. 1907.

Burrow, Colin. *William Shakespeare: The Complete Sonnets and Poems*. Oxford University Press. 2002.

Dover Wilson, John. *The Sonnets*. Cambridge University Press. 1966.

Duncan-Jones, Katherine. *Shakespeare's Sonnets*. Arden. 1997, 2010.

Evans, G. Blakemore. *Shakespeare's Sonnets*. Cambridge University Press. 1996.

Ingram, W. G., and Theodore Redpath. *Shakespeare's Sonnets*. Hodder and Stoughton. 1978.
Kerrigan, John. *"The Sonnets" and "A Lover's Complaint."* Penguin. 1986.
Mowat, Barbara A., and Paul Werstine. *Shakespeare's Sonnets and Poems*. Folger Shakespeare Library. Simon and Shuster. 2006.
Orgel, Stephen. *The Sonnets* (Pelican Shakespeare). Revised edition. Penguin. 2001.
Rollins, Hyder Edward. *New Variorum Shakespeare: The Sonnets*. 2 vols. Lippincott. 1944.
Rowse, A. L. *Shakespeare's Sonnets*. Harper & Row. 1964.
Shrank, Cathy, and Raphael Lyne. *The Complete Poems of Shakespeare*. Routledge. 2018.
Tyler, Thomas. *Shakespeare's Sonnets*. David Nutt. 1890.
Vendler, Helen. *The Art of Shakespeare's Sonnets*. Harvard University Press. 1997.
West, David. *Shakespeare's Sonnets*. Duckworth Overlook. 2007.

Unless otherwise noted, citations of Renaissance poetry are based on the first published editions. Unless otherwise noted, citations of Shakespeare's plays are based on the Third Arden Series.

Secondary Works

Acheson, Arthur. *Shakespeare and the Rival Poet*. John Lane: The Bodley Head. 1903.
Ackroyd, Peter. *Shakespeare: The Biography*. Random House. 2005.
Akrigg, G. P. V. *Shakespeare and the Earl of Southampton*. Harvard University Press. 1968.
Alexander, Gavin. *Writing After Sidney: The Literary Response to Sir Philip Sidney 1586–1640*. Oxford University Press. 2006.
Allen, Vivien. Introduction and notes to *Dear Mr Rossetti: The Letters of Dante Gabriel Rossetti and Hall Caine 1878–1881*. Sheffield Academic Press, Ltd. 2000.
Attridge, Derek. *Well-Weighed Syllables: Elizabethan Verse in Classical Metres*. Cambridge University Press. 1974.
Auden, W. H. 'Shakespeare's Sonnets' in *Forewords and Afterwords*. Vintage Books, Random House. 1973.
Augustine. *Concerning the City of God against the Pagans* (Pelican Classics). Trans. Henry Bettenson. Penguin. 1972.
Augustine. Sermons in *Nicene and Post-Nicene Fathers*, Series 1, Volumes VI and VII. Trans. Rev. William Findlay, revised by Rev. D. S. Schaff. Originally published by The Christian Literary Company. 1888.
Baldwin, T. W. *On the Literary Genetics of Shakespeare's Poems and Sonnets*. University of Illinois Press. 1950.

Barber, Benjamin. 'Mimetic Drama in Shakespeare's Sonnets and Byron's Historicizing Lyricism'. *Anthropoetics*. Vol. 21. No. 2. Spring 2016.
Bate, Jonathan. *The Genius of Shakespeare*. Picador Books. 1997.
Bate, Jonathan. *Soul of the Age: A Biography of the Mind of William Shakespeare*. Random House. 2009.
Baudelaire, Charles. *Oeuvres complètes*. Collection Bibliothèque de la Pléiade. Ed. Claude Pichois. 1975. Volume I.
Bednarz, James P. *Shakespeare and the Poets' War*. Columbia University Press. 2001.
Bednarz, James P. *Shakespeare and the Truth of Love: The Mystery of 'The Phoenix and the Turtle'*. Palgrave Macmillan. 2012.
Bell, Ilona. *Elizabethan Women and the Poetry of Courtship*. Cambridge University Press. 1998.
Bell, Ilona. 'Rethinking Shakespeare's Dark Lady' in *A Companion to Shakespeare's Sonnets*, ed. Michael Schoenfeldt. Wiley-Blackwell. 2010.
Bird, Sarah, John Edmondson, Susan Nicholson, Katherine Stainer-Hutchins, and Christopher Taylor. 'A Late Sixteenth-Century Garden: Fact or Fantasy'. *Garden History*. Vol. 24, No. 2. 1996.
Blick, Fred. '"Duble Vantage": Tennis and Sonnet 88'. *The Upstart Crow*. 2009.
Blick, Fred. 'Spenser's *Amoretti* and Elizabeth Boyle, Her Names Immortalized'. *Spenser Studies*. Vol. 23. 2008.
Boaden, James. *On the Sonnets of Shakespeare*. Thomas Rodd. 1837.
Burl, Aubrey. *Shakespeare's Mistress: The Mystery of the Dark Lady Revealed*. Amberely Publishing. 2012.
Burrow, Colin. *Shakespeare and Classical Antiquity*. Oxford University Press. 2013.
Butler, Christopher. *Number Symbolism*. Routledge. 1970.
Butler, Christopher and Alastair Fowler. 'Time-Beguiling Sport: Number Symbolism in Shakespeare's *Venus and Adonis*' in *Shakespeare 1564–1964: A Collection of Modern Essays by Various Hands*, ed. Edward A. Bloom. Brown University Press. 1964.
Callaghan, Dympna. *Shakespeare's Sonnets*. Wiley. 2008.
Campbell, S. C. *Only Begotten Sonnets*. Bell & Hyman. 1978.
Caveney, George. 'Mr. W.H.: Stationer William Holme (d. 1607)'. *Notes and Queries*. 1 February 2015.
Chatterly, Albert. Introduction and notes to *Thomas Watson: English Poems*. Marion Hopkins. 2003.
Cheney, Patrick. *Marlowe's Counterfeit Profession: Ovid, Spenser, Counter-Nationhood*. University of Toronto Press. 1997.
Cheney, Patrick. 'Perdita, Pastorella, and the Romance of Literary Form: Shakespeare's Counter-Spenserian Authorship'. Chapter in Lethbridge, *Shakespeare and Spenser: Attractive Opposites*. Manchester University Press. 2008.

Cheney, Patrick. *Shakespeare, National Poet-Playwright*. Cambridge University Press. 2004.

Cheney, Patrick. *Shakespeare's Literary Authorship*. Cambridge University Press. 2008.

Cheney, Patrick. 'Shakespeare's Sonnet 106, Spenser's National Epic, and Counter-Petrarchism'. *English Literary Renaissance*. Vol. 31, No. 3. 2001.

Cheney, Patrick. 'Spenser's Pastorals'. Chapter 4 of *The Cambridge Companion to Spenser*, ed. Andrew Hadfield. Cambridge University Press. 2006.

Cook, Albert S. 'The Elizabethan Invocations to Sleep'. *Modern Language Notes*. Vol. 4, No. 8. 1889.

Corbin, Peter, and Douglas Sedge. Introduction and notes to 'The Revels Plays' edition of *Thomas of Woodstock*. Manchester University Press. 2002.

Cousins, A. D. *Shakespeare's Sonnets and Narrative Poems*. Longman. 2000.

Creighton, Charles. *Shakespeare's Story of His Life*. Grant Richards. 1904.

Curtius, Ernst Robert. *European Literature and the Latin Middle Ages*. Trans. Williard R. Trask. Princeton University Press. 1973.

Daniel, Samuel. *Samuel Daniel: Selected Poetry and A Defense of Rhyme*. Ed. Geoffrey G. Hiller. Pegasus Press. 1998.

Danson Brown, Richard. *'The New Poet': Novelty and Tradition in Spenser's 'Complaints'*. Liverpool University Press. 1999.

Davies, John. *Microcosmos: The Discovery of the Little World*. Printed by Joseph Barnes. Ireland. 1611.

Doyno, Victor A. Introduction and notes to *Parthenophil and Parthenophe*. South Illinois University Press. 1971.

Drayton, Michael. *Poems: by Michael Drayton Esquire: The Baron's Wars, England's Heroical Epistles, Idea, Odes*, etc. Printed by W. Stansby for John Swethwicke. 1619.

Dubrow, Heather. *Captive Visitors: Shakespeare's Narrative Poems and Sonnets*. Cornell University Press. 1987.

Dubrow, Heather. *Shakespeare and Domestic Loss: Forms of Deprivation, Mourning, and Recuperation*. Cambridge University Press. 2004.

Dubrow, Heather. '"Uncertainties now crown themselves assured": The Politics of Plotting *Shakespeare's Sonnets*'. *Shakespeare Quarterly*. Vol. 47. 1996.

Duncan-Jones, Katherine. *Shakespeare, An Ungentle Life*. Arden. 2001.

Duncan-Jones, Katherine, and H. R. Woudhuysen. Introduction and notes to *Shakespeare's Poems*. Arden. Third Series. 2007.

Edmonson, Paul, and Stanley Wells. 'Interrogating the *Sonnets*'. A conference paper delivered in 2007 and printed in 2010 (http://shakespeare.revues.org/1021).

Erne, Lukas. *Shakespeare and the Book Trade*. Cambridge University Press. 2013.

Erne, Lukas. *Shakespeare as Literary Dramatist*. Second edition. Cambridge University Press. 2003, 2013.
Evans, G. Blakemore. Introduction and notes to the New Cambridge Shakespeare edition of *Romeo and Juliet*. Updated edition. Cambridge University Press. 2003.
Evans, Maurice, and Race Booth. Introduction and notes to *Elizabethan Sonnets*. Orion Publishing. 2003.
Exequiae Illustrissimi Equitis, D. Philippi Sidnaei, Gratissimae Memoriae ac Nomini Impensae. Dana F. Sutton's hypertext version, which includes translations and notes, can be found at http://www.philological.bham.ac.uk/exequiae/
Falco, Raphael. *Conceived Presences: Literary Genealogy in Renaissance England*. University of Massachusetts Press. 1994.
Ferry, Anne Davidson. *The "Inward" Language: Sonnets of Wyatt, Sidney, Shakespeare, Donne*. University of Chicago Press. 1983.
Ficino, Marcilio. *All Things Natural: Ficino on Plato's Timaeus*. Ed. Arthur Farndell. Shepheard-Walwyn. 2010.
Fineman, Joel. *Shakespeare's Perjured Eye: The Invention of Poetic Subjectivity in the Sonnets*. University of California Press. 1986.
Fleay, F. G. *Guide to Chaucer and Spenser*. Collins' School and College Classics. Leopold Classics Library. 2015.
Fletcher, Giles. *Licia*. Printed by John Legat. Cambridge. 1593.
Forker, Charles R. Introduction and notes to *King Richard II*. Arden. Third Series. 2002.
Fowler, Alastair. *Literary Names: Personal Names in English Literature*. Oxford University Press. 2014.
Fowler, Alastair. *Spenser and the Numbers of Time*. Routledge & Paul. 1964.
Fowler, Alastair. *Triumphal Forms Structural Patterns in Elizabethan Poetry*. Cambridge University Press. 1970.
Furness, Horace Howard. Introduction and notes to *Love's Labour's Lost*. A New Variorum Edition of Shakespeare. J. B. Lippincott Company. 1904.
Graziani, René. 'The Numbering of Shakespeare's Sonnets 12, 60 and 126'. *Shakespeare Quarterly*. Vol. 35. 1984.
Green, Martin. *Wriothesley's Roses in Shakespeare's Sonnets, Poems, and Plays*. Clevedon Books. 1993.
Greenblatt, Stephen. *Renaissance Self-Fashioning*. University of Chicago Press. 1980.
Greenblatt, Stephen. *Will in the World: How Shakespeare Became Shakespeare*. Norton. 2004.
Grundy, Joan. Introduction and notes to *The Poems of Henry Constable*. Liverpool University Press. 1960.
Hadfield, Andrew. *Edmund Spenser: A Life*. Oxford University Press. 2012.
Hadfield, Andrew. *Shakespeare and Renaissance Politics*. Thomson Learning. 2004.

Healy, Margaret. *Shakespeare, Alchemy, and the Creative Imagination: The Sonnets and A Lover's Complaint*. Cambridge University Press. 2011.

Helgerson, Richard. *The Elizabethan Prodigals*. University of California Press. 1976.

Helgerson, Richard. *Forms of Nationhood: The Elizabethan Writing of England*. University of Chicago Press. 1992.

Helgerson, Richard. *Self-Crowned Laureates: Spenser, Jonson, Milton and the Literary System*. University of California Press. 1983.

Herman, Peter C. Introduction and Notes to *Philip Sidney's Apology for Poetry and Astrophil and Stella*. College Publishing. 2001.

Hieatt, A. Kent. 'The Genesis of Shakespeare's Sonnets: *Spenser's Ruines of Rome: By Bellay*'. PMLA. Vol. 98, No. 5. 1983.

Hieatt, A. Kent, Charles W. Hieatt, and Anne Lake Prescott. 'When Did Shakespeare Write Sonnets 1609?' *Studies in Philology*. Vol. 88. 1991.

Hiller, Geoffrey G., and Peter L. Groves. Introduction and notes to *Samuel Daniel, Selected Poetry and A Defense of Rhyme*. Pegasus. 1998.

Holden, Anthony. 'That's no lady, that's . . .'. *The Guardian. The Observer Review*. 21 April 2002.

Hopper, Vincent Foster. *Medieval Number Symbolism: Its Sources, Meaning and Influence*. Columbia University Press. 1938.

Hudston, Jonathan. Introduction and notes to *George Chapman: Plays and Poems*. Penguin. 1998.

Huntington, John W. *Ambition, Rank, and Poetry in 1590s England*. University of Illinois Press. 2001.

Hutton, James. 'Analogues of Shakespeare's Sonnets 153–54: Contributions to the History of a Theme'. *Modern Philology*. Vol. 38. May 1941.

Jackson, M. P. 'Aspects of Organization in Shakespeare's Sonnets'. *Parergon*. Vol. 17. 2002.

Jackson, M. P. 'The Distribution of Pronouns in *Shakespeare's Sonnets*'. *Journal of the Australasian Universities Language and Literature Association*. Vol. 97, No. 1. 2002.

Jackson, M. P. 'Echoes of Spenser's *Prothalamion*'. *Notes and Queries*. Vol. 37. 1990.

Jackson, M. P. 'Francis Meres and the Cultural Contexts of Shakespeare's Rival Poet Sonnets'. *The Review of English Studies*. Vol. 56, No. 224. 2005.

Jackson, M. P. '*Shakespeare's Sonnets:* Rhyme and Reason in the Dark Lady Series'. *Notes and Queries*. Vol. 46. 1999.

Jackson, M. P. 'Vocabulary and Chronology: The Case of Shakespeare's Sonnets'. *The Review of English Studies*. Vol. 52, No. 205. 2001.

Jenkin, Harold. Introduction and notes to *Hamlet*. Arden. Second Series. 1982.

Kastan, David Scott. Introduction and notes to *Henry IV, Part 1*. Arden. Third Series. 2002.

Kennedy, George A. *Classical Rhetoric and its Christian and Secular Tradition, from Ancient to Modern Times.* Second Edition. University of North Carolina Press. 1999.

Kennedy, William. *Petrarchism at Work: Contextual Economies in the Age of Shakespeare.* Cornell University Press. 2016.

Kerrigan, John. Introduction and notes to *Motives of Woe Shakespeare and 'Female Complaint'* (a critical anthology). Oxford University Press. 1991.

Lang. Cecil Y. *The Pre-Raphaelites and their Circle.* University of Chicago Press. 2014.

Larsen, Kenneth J., ed. *Edmund Spenser's Amoretti and Epithalamion: A Critical Edition.* Medieval & Renaissance Texts & Studies. 1997.

Lawrence, Jason. *'Who the Devil Taught Thee so much Italian?': Italian Language Learning and Literary Imitation in Early Modern England.* Manchester University Press. 2005.

Lee, Sidney. *A Life of William Shakespeare.* Macmillan. 1898.

Leishman, J. B. *Themes and Variations in Shakespeare's Sonnets.* Routledge. 1961.

Lethbridge, J. B. 'Spenser, Marlowe, Shakespeare: Methodological Investigations'. Introduction to *Shakespeare and Spenser, Attractive Opposites.* Manchester University Press. 2008.

Lever, J. W. *The Elizabethan Love Sonnet.* Methuen & Co. 1956.

Logan, George, and Robert M. Adams. Introduction and notes to Thomas More's *Utopia.* Cambridge University Press. 1989, 2002.

Lomazzo, Giovanni Paolo. *A Tract Containing the Arts of Curious Painting, Carving, Building.* Trans. Richard Haydock. Joseph Barnes. 1598

Lucian. *Lucian Volume VI.* Trans. K. Kilburn. Loeb Classical Library. Harvard University Press. 1959.

McAlindon, Thomas. 'The Numbering of Men and Days: Symbolic Design in "The Tragedy of Julius Caesar"'. *Studies in Philology.* Vol. 81. No. 3. 1984.

McCabe, Richard, ed. *Spenser: The Shorter Poems.* Penguin Books Limited. 2006.

McClumpha, C. F. 'Parallels between *Sonnets* and *Love's Labour's Lost*'. *Modern Language Notes.* Vol. 15, No. 6. 1900.

McDonald, Russ. '"Pretty Rooms": Shakespeare's Sonnets, Elizabethan Architecture, and Early Modern Visual Design'. Chapter 27 of *The Oxford Handbook of Shakespeare's Poetry*, ed. Jonathan F. S. Post. Oxford University Press. 2013.

Mackail, John W. *The Approach to Shakespeare.* Clarendon Press. 1930.

Macray, W. D. Rev. Introduction and notes to *The Pilgrimage to Parnassus* (with the two parts of *The Return from Parnassus*). Oxford University Press. 1886.

Marotti, Arthur. '"Love Is Not Love": Elizabethan Sonnet Sequences and the Social Order'. *ELH.* Vol. 49, No. 2. 1982.

Martindale, Charles, and Colin Burrow. 'Clapham's *Narcissus*: A Pre-Text for Shakespeare's *Venus and Adonis*?' (text, translation, and commentary). *English Literary Renaissance*. Vol. 22, No. 2. 1992.

Massey, Gerald. *Shakespeare's Sonnets Never Before Interpreted: His Private Friends Revealed*. Longmans and Co. 1866.

Meres, Francis. *Palladis Tamia: Wits Treasury*. Printed by P. Short, for Cuthbert Burbie. London. 1598.

Miola, Robert S. Introduction and notes to Ben Jonson's *Every Man in His Humour*. Manchester University Press. 2000.

Monte, Steven. *Invisible Fences: Prose Poetry as a Genre in French and American Literature*. University of Nebraska Press. 2000.

Muir, Kenneth. *Shakespeare's Sonnets*. George Allen and Unwin. 1979.

Neil, Michael. Introduction and notes to *The Tragedy of Antony and Cleopatra*. Oxford University Press. 1994.

Nolen Jones, Floyd. *The Chronology of the Old Testament*. Master Books. 1993.

Norman, Arthur M. Z. 'Daniel's *The Tragedy of Cleopatra* and *Antony and Cleopatra*'. *Shakespeare Quarterly*. Vol. 9. No. 1. 1958.

Oram, William A, Einar Bjorvand, Ronald Bond, Thomas H. Cain, Alexander Dunlop, and Richard Schell, eds. *The Yale Edition of Spenser's Shorter Poems*. Yale University Press. 1989.

Orgel, Stephen. Introduction and notes to *Christopher Marlowe: The Complete Poems and Translations*. Penguin. 2007.

Padel, John. *New Poems by Shakespeare: Order and Meaning Restored to the Sonnets*. Herbert. 1981.

Parker, Tom W. N. *Proportional Form in the Sonnets of the Sidney Circle: Loving in Truth*. Oxford University Press. 1998.

Phillips, Wendy. 'No More *Tears*: Thomas Watson Absolved'. *Comitatus: A Journal of Medieval and Renaissance Studies*. Vol. 20. No. 1. 1989.

Plato. *Timaeus and Critias*. Ed. and Trans. Desmond Lee and Thomas Johansen. Revised Edition. Penguin. 2008.

Politt, J. J. Introduction and notes to *The Art of Ancient Greece: Sources and Documents*. Cambridge University Press. 1990.

Potter, Lois. *The Life of William Shakespeare*. Wiley-Blackwell. 2012.

Prescott, Anne Lake, and Andrew Hadfield. Introduction and notes to *Edmund Spenser's Poetry*. Norton Critical Editions. Fourth edition. Norton. 2013.

Primaudaye, Pierre de la. *The French Academy*. Printed by Edmund Bollifant for G. Bishop and Ralph Newbery. London. 1586.

Puttenham, George. *The Art of English Poesy*. Critical edition. Ed. Frank Whigham and Wayne A. Rebhorn. Cornell University Press. 2007.

Quint, David. *Epic and Empire: Politics and Generic Form from Virgil to Milton*. Princeton University Press. 2021.

Ramsey, Paul. *The Fickle Glass*. AMS Press. 1979.

Rees, Joan. 'Sidney and A Lover's Complaint'. *Review of English Studies*, New Series. Vol. 42. May 1991.

Ringler, William A., Jr. Introduction and notes to *The Poems of Sir Philip Sidney*. Oxford University Press. 1962.
Rivers, Isabel. *Classical and Christian Ideas in English Renaissance Poetry*. Routledge. 1994.
Roberts, Bethan. *Charlotte Smith and the Sonnet: Form, Place and Tradition in the Late Eighteenth Century*. Liverpool University Press. 2019.
Roche, Thomas P. *Petrarch and the English Sonnet Sequence*. AMS Press. 1989.
Rudenstine, Neil L. *Ideas of Order: A Close Reading of Shakespeare's Sonnets*. Farrar, Straus, and Giroux. 2014.
Sakeld, Duncan. 'Black Luce and the "curtizans" of Shakespeare's London'. *Signatures*. Vol. 2. 2000.
Sakeld, Duncan. Interview by Dalya Alberge and Claire Ellicot. *The Daily Mail*. 27 August 2012.
Sams, Eric. 'Who was the Rival Poet of Shakespeare's Sonnet 86?' *Connotations*. Vol. 8. No. 1. 1998.
Sandys, George. *A Relation of a Journey Begun [in] 1610*. W. Barrett. 1615.
Schaar, Claes. *Elizabethan Sonnet Themes and the Dating of Shakespeare's Sonnets*. Lund Studies in English. Vol. 32. AMS. 1962.
Schoenfeldt, Michael, ed. *A Companion to Shakespeare's Sonnets*. Wiley-Blackwell. 2010.
Scodel, Joshua. *The English Poetic Epitaph: Commemoration and Conflict from Jonson to Wordsworth*. Cornell University Press. 1991.
Sears, Jayne. 'Ficino and the Platonism of the English Renaissance'. *Comparative Literature*. Vol. 4. 1 January 1952.
Shapiro, James. *1599: A Year in the Life of Shakespeare*. HarperCollins. 2005.
Sharon-Zisser, Shirely, and Stephen Whitworth. 'Generating Dialogue on Shakespeare's *A Lover's Complaint*'. Introduction to *Critical Essays on Shakespeare's A Lover's Complaint*. Ed. Shirley Sharon-Zisser. Routledge. 2006.
Shickman, Alan. 'The "Perspective Glass" in Shakespeare's *Richard II*'. *Studies in English Literature*, Vol. 18, No. 2. 1978.
Sidney, Philip. *The Countess of Pembroke's Arcadia*. Ed. Hugh Sanford. Printed by John Windet for William Ponsonbie. London. 1593.
Smarr, Janet Levarie. 'The Pyramid and the Circle: "Ovid's Banquet of Sense"'. *Philological Quarterly*. Vol. 53. 1984.
Sohmer, Steve. *Shakespeare for the Wiser Sort: Solving Shakespeare's Riddles*. Manchester University Press. 2007.
Sohmer, Steve. *Shakespeare's Mystery Play: The Opening of the Globe Theatre 1599*. Manchester University Press. 1999.
Spiller, Michael R. G. *The Development of the Sonnet: An Introduction*. Routledge. 1992.
Stirling, Brents. *The Shakespeare Sonnet Order: Poems and Groups*. University of California Press. 1968.
Stocker, Margarita. 'Remodeling Virgil: Marvell's New Astraea'. *Studies in Philology*. Vol. 84. No. 2. 1987.

Thomson, Ann and Neil Taylor. Introduction and notes to *Hamlet*. Third Series. Arden. 2006.
Waddington, Raymond B. *The Mind's Empire: Myth and Form in George Chapman's Narrative Poems*. Johns Hopkins University Press. 1974.
Weis, René. Introduction and notes to *Romeo and Juliet*. Third Series. Arden. 2012.
Wilders, John. Introduction and notes to *Antony and Cleopatra*. Third Series. Arden. 1995.
Wilson-Okamura, 'The Aesthetics of Spenser's Feminine Rhyme'. In Prescott and Hadfield, pp. 764–8.
Winnick, R. H. '"Loe, here in one line is his name twice writ": Anagrams, *Shakespeare's Sonnets*, and the Identity of the Fair Friend'. *Literary Imagination*. Vol. 11. No. 3. 2009.
Woudhuysen, H. R. Introduction and notes to *Love's Labour's Lost*. Third Series. Arden. 1998.
Woudhuysen, H. R. *Sir Philip Sidney and the Circulation of Manuscripts: 1558–1640*. Oxford University Press. 1996.
Wright, George T. *Shakespeare's Metrical Art*. University of California Press. 1991.
Wright, Thomas. *The Passions of the Mind in General. With a Treatise Thereto Adjoining of the Climacterical Year, Occasioned by the Death of Queen Elizabeth*. Printed by Valentine Simmes and Adam Islip for Walter Burre and Thomas Thorpe. London. 1604.
Yeats, W. B. 'Anima Hominis' in *Mythologies*. Simon and Shuster. 1959.
Zarnowiecki, Matthew. *Fair Copies: Reproducing the English Lyric from Tottel to Shakespeare*. University of Toronto Press. 2014.

Individual Sonnets and 'A Lover's Complaint'

Sonnet 1: 112, 216, 249, 282, 288, 290, 293
Sonnet 2: 218, 282, 285
Sonnet 3: 113, 294
Sonnet 5: 139–40, 271
Sonnet 7: 270
Sonnet 8: 217
Sonnet 9: 154–7, 194, 282, 286, 288
Sonnet 10: 15, 64, 282, 283
Sonnet 11: 87, 113, 142–3
Sonnet 12: 15, 113, 270
Sonnet 13: 15, 32, 112, 288, 289–90, 291
Sonnet 14: 203
Sonnet 15: 64, 271
Sonnet 17: 33, 114, 208, 266, 271, 282, 283, 293
Sonnet 18: 10, 15–16, 50–1, 56, 157, 171–2, 199, 266
Sonnet 19: 172, 266
Sonnet 20: 11, 114, 172–3, 266, 282, 285, 288, 292–3
Sonnet 21: 88, 93–4, 173–4, 211, 263, 265, 266
Sonnet 22: 87, 142, 174, 262–3, 282, 283, 294
Sonnet 23: vi, 117, 174, 285, 288
Sonnet 24: 1, 15, 33, 166–8, 174, 196–7, 271, 288, 290–1
Sonnet 25: 16, 136, 168–9, 174
Sonnet 26: 136, 168–70, 174
Sonnet 29: 99, 174, 282, 283
Sonnet 30: 174, 271, 304

Sonnet 31: 174, 175–6, 208–9, 228, 271
Sonnet 32: 56, 174, 176–7, 271
Sonnet 33: 56, 64, 102–4, 143, 147–53, 178, 227, 269, 270, 271
Sonnet 34: 56, 87
Sonnet 36: 13, 197–9
Sonnet 39: 282, 286
Sonnet 40: 57
Sonnet 41: 203
Sonnet 43: 258, 309
Sonnet 44: 102, 143
Sonnet 45: 143–4, 309
Sonnet 48: 56, 110, 113–14, 186, 228, 264–5
Sonnet 49: 181, 185
Sonnet 52: 87, 186, 270
Sonnet 53: 259
Sonnet 54: 181–2
Sonnet 55: 36, 145, 181, 262, 282, 284, 301
Sonnet 56: 182
Sonnet 58: 282, 287
Sonnet 59: 259
Sonnet 60: 218, 270
Sonnet 61: 110
Sonnet 62: 130–1, 294
Sonnet 63: 61, 64, 110–11, 183, 271
Sonnet 64: 36, 185
Sonnet 66: 145, 145–6
Sonnet 69: 282, 286
Sonnet 70: 282, 286

Sonnet 71: 45
Sonnet 73: 184–5, 218
Sonnet 74: 185
Sonnet 75: 87, 110, 183, 185–6, 263, 265
Sonnet 76: 77–8, 79–80, 186, 201, 211
Sonnet 77: 33, 61, 78, 84–5, 87, 132, 216–17, 288, 293–4
Sonnet 78: 77, 80–1, 85, 95
Sonnet 79: 82, 110
Sonnet 80: 78, 82–3, 101
Sonnet 81: 33, 45, 77–9, 83, 115, 138, 186, 270, 283
Sonnet 82: 83–4
Sonnet 83: 83–4
Sonnet 84: 84
Sonnet 85: 84
Sonnet 86: 76–8, 85, 88, 101, 109, 186
Sonnet 87: 77, 98–101, 186–7, 266, 273
Sonnet 88: 98, 146
Sonnet 89: 283
Sonnet 96: 194, 197–9
Sonnet 98: 249, 288
Sonnet 99: 4, 87, 107–9, 137, 146, 190–3, 194–5, 199, 202, 240, 247, 271
Sonnet 100: 61, 132
Sonnet 103: 133, 294
Sonnet 104: 27, 202–4
Sonnet 106: 65, 202, 204–7, 209, 269, 271, 289, 291–2, 312
Sonnet 107: 27, 36, 43, 202, 204, 219, 259
Sonnet 108: 5, 45, 47, 200–2, 219, 283, 287
Sonnet 109: 47, 211, 214, 259
Sonnet 111: 211
Sonnet 112: 72, 211, 259
Sonnet 115: 19–20
Sonnet 116: 10, 11, 16, 17–18, 212–13, 217, 221, 239–40, 272
Sonnet 117: 20–1, 213
Sonnet 118: 210–11, 213
Sonnet 119: 211, 213, 219–20
Sonnet 120: 211, 213
Sonnet 122: 115, 217, 289, 294
Sonnet 123: 36, 43
Sonnet 125: 36, 43, 214, 218
Sonnet 126: 12, 65, 111, 114–15, 122, 131–2, 138, 201, 223, 283, 293, 294
Sonnet 127: 223, 226, 272
Sonnet 128: 224
Sonnet 131: 223
Sonnet 133: 227–8
Sonnet 135: 11
Sonnet 136: viii, 43
Sonnet 138: 10, 24, 297
Sonnet 142: 224
Sonnet 144: 11–12, 24, 241–2, 297
Sonnet 145: 122, 223, 234
Sonnet 146: 45–6, 234, 242–3, 272
Sonnet 147: 234
Sonnet 148: 234
Sonnet 150: 235, 236–7, 239–40
Sonnet 151: 237–8
Sonnet 152: 115, 224, 238–9
'A Lover's Complaint': 6, 9, 30, 46, 48, 65, 223, 248–67, 268

Groups of Sonnets

Basic pyramidal scheme (all sonnets): 29–30, 42–8, 268–9
Sonnets 1–17 ('procreation sonnets', step 1 of pyramid): 3, 42, 46, 57, 158–61, 268
Sonnets 1–25: 136–7, 140
Sonnets 1–98 (first part of the 'fair youth' sonnets): 9, 29, 46–7, 154–93, 268
Sonnets 1–126 ('fair youth' sonnets): 12, 268
Sonnets 2, 22, and 62: 132–3
Sonnets 3, 22, 62, 77, 103, and 126 (mirror sonnets): 126–33
Sonnets 3 and 103: 126–7
Sonnets 12, 15, 29, 30, 64, and 106 ('When I' sonnets), 133–4, 204
Sonnets 12, 52, and 60 (temporal sonnets): 49
Sonnets 14, 41, and 104: 202–4
Sonnets 15–17 (trio): 16–21, 55–6, 157
Sonnets 18–33 (step 2 of pyramid): 57, 58–9, 170–1
Sonnets 21–75 (the 55-sonnet 'pyramid within the pyramid'), 258–67, 299–301
Sonnets 22, 62, and possibly 126: 130–2
Sonnets 22, 77, and 122 (trio): 127–30
Sonnets 25–6: 170–1
Sonnets 27–8: 174
Sonnets 31–2: 175–6
Sonnets 33–4 (boundary sonnets): 11, 47, 56, 126–7, 133, 179, 227–8, 231, 299
Sonnets 33, 66, and 99: 102–7, 141–2, 192
Sonnets 34–48 (step 3 of pyramid): 57, 59, 157–8, 178–80, 268
Sonnets 36 and 96: 197–9
Sonnets 40–2 (trio): 11, 59, 179
Sonnets 49, 63, and 81 (climacteric sonnets): 50–1, 180–1, 270
Sonnets 49–62 (step 4 of pyramid): 57, 180–3
Sonnets 49, 64, 81, and 100 ('square number' sonnets): 134–6
Sonnets 50 and 51: 174
Sonnets 52–75 ('So am I' to 'So are you'; 24 sonnets, allusions to a day and a year), 137–8
Sonnets 55, 81, and 107 ('monument' trio): 30–33
Sonnets 63–8 (third-person sonnets): 15
Sonnets 63–75 (step 5 of pyramid): 57–8, 180–6
Sonnets 67–8: 184
Sonnets 69–70: 264, 299–301
Sonnets 71–2: 184, 299
Sonnets 76–87 ('rival poet' series, step 6 of pyramid): 58, 75, 77–85, 186
Sonnets 77–80 (pointing mostly to one rival): 77–83

Sonnets 82–3: 83–4
Sonnets 82–5 (pointing mostly to more than one rival): 77–9, 83–5
Sonnets 84–5: 84
Sonnets 88–90 (trio): 187
Sonnets 88–98 (step 7 of pyramid): 58, 187–90
Sonnets 91–3 (trio): 187
Sonnets 94–6 (trio): 187–8
Sonnets 97–8 (pair): 12, 188–90, 194–5
Sonnets 97–9: 194–9, 201, 271, 273
Sonnets 97–122 (365 lines, representing a year), 137–8, 195, 209
Sonnets 99–108 (step 8 of the pyramid): 58, 199–209
Sonnets 99–126 (second part of the 'fair youth' sonnets): 9, 29, 46–7, 268
Sonnets 99, 126, and 145 (formally irregular sonnets): 29, 42, 46–7, 268
Sonnets 109–17 (step 9 of the pyramid): 209–13
Sonnets 109–21 ('infidelity group'): 21, 209–14
Sonnets 109–25: 222, 273
Sonnets 110 and 111: 146
Sonnets 111–21 (transgression series): 211–14, 233–4, 239
Sonnets 115–17 (trio): 17–21, 210

Sonnets 118–25 (step 10 of the pyramid): 209–14
Sonnets 121 and 122: 146–7
Sonnet 122–5 (perfection/imperfection), 125
Sonnets 122–6 ('thou' sonnets): 15
Sonnets 123–5 ('No' trio): 137, 213
Sonnets 127–44 (first part of the 'mistress' sonnets): 29, 46–7, 223, 268
Sonnets 127–54 ('mistress' sonnets): 9, 45, 223–47, 268
Sonnets 127–33 (eleventh step of the pyramid): 227–31, 234
Sonnets 133–4 (boundary sonnets): 47, 126–7, 133, 179, 231
Sonnets 134–9 (twelfth step of the pyramid): 231–40
Sonnets 134–44 (possible 11-sonnet series): 231, 233, 234
Sonnets 135–6: 233
Sonnets 139–40: 232–3
Sonnets 140–4 (thirteenth step of the pyramid): 231–40
Sonnets 143–4: 233
Sonnets 146–54 (second part of the 'mistress' sonnets): 29, 46–7, 223, 234–40, 268
Sonnets 149–50: 234–5
Sonnets 151–2: 235
Sonnets 153–4 (Cupid sonnets): 45, 48, 243–7, 257, 272

Index

Acheson, Arthur, *Shakespeare and the Rival Poet*, 7, 306
Ackroyd, Peter, 306
Aetiön, 69, 306
Akrigg, G. P. V., 312
Alberti, Leon Battista, 60
Alexander, William, *Aurora*, 105, 136, 139, 281, 295, 309
anamorphosis, 2
Anno Mundi calendar, 191–2, 267, 269, 312
Attridge, Derek, 60–1, 305
Aubigné, Agrippa d', 276
Auden, W. H., 5, 302
Augustine (of Hippo), 44, 118, 120–1, 308, 309
Aurevilly, Barbey d', 277

Baldwin, T. W., 319
Barnes, Barnabe, 85–8, 105, 193, 202, 240, 272, 295
  Parthenophil and Parthenophe, 22, 62, 63, 85–7, 99–100, 108–9, 119–20, 245–7, 272, 280, 312
Barnfield, Richard, 295–8, 308
  Cynthia, 22, 48, 63, 105, 109, 280, 296–7, 316
Barozzi da Vignola, Giacomo, *Two Rules of Practical Perspective*, 36
Bassano, Emilia *see* Lanier, Emilia
Bate, Jonathan, 224–5, 303, 304, 313

Baudelaire, Charles, 276–8, 316
Bednarz, James, 313
Beeching, H. C., 26, 306
Bell, Ilona, 313
Benson, John, *Poems Written by William Shakespeare, Gent*, 6
Bettenson, Henry, 308
biblical references
  Corinthians 13:4–6, 213, 313
  Daniel 2:31–45, 141
  Ephesians 5:1–20 and 5:21–33, 141, 309
  Genesis 6:3, 49
  John 21:1–11, 120–1
  Luke 8:18 and 25:29, 145, 309
  Matthew 4:25, 13:12, and 25:29, 309
  Matthew 18:21, 145–6
  Psalm 6, 118
  Psalm 85, 141
  Psalm 90, 45, 309
  Revelation 13:18, 308
Boaden, James, 94, 307
Bongo, Pietro, 103–4, 118, 120
Book of Common Prayer, 18, 212–13, 239, 313, 314
Booth, Stephen, 16, 79, 259, 292, 303, 306, 307, 309, 311, 314, 315
Bowles, William, 275
Boyle, Elizabeth, 217–18
Browne, Thomas, *Garden of Cyrus*, 140–1

Browning, Elizabeth Barrett, 276–8
Burrow, Collin, 189, 301, 304, 309, 311, 312, 317
Butler, Christopher, 121–2, 308

Chapman, George, 7, 66, 72–7, 82, 88–94, 96–7, 295, 306
  Achilles' Shield, 73
  Blind Beggar of Alexandria, 73
  Hero and Leander, 72, 74, 119, 139, 141
  Humourous Day's Mirth, 73
  Ovid's Banquet of Sense, 63, 72–3, 74–5, 81–2, 89–94, 262, 272, 307, 315
  Seven Books of the Iliad, 73
  Shadow of Night, 62, 72–3, 74–5, 88
  Sonnet in *Nennio*, 73–4
Cheney, Patrick, 65–7, 205–6, 305, 312, 318
Chester, Robert, *Love's Martyr*, 221–2
Chettle, Henry, 71–2
Churchyard, Thomas, 250
Clapham, John, *Narcissus*, 113
climacteric (major and minor), 27, 45, 49–50, 180–1
Constable, Henry, 4, 107, 193, 202, 205, 206–7, 240, 272, 279, 308, 312
  Diana, 14, 64, 141, 162, 167–8, 262, 272, 279–80, 309, 315: 'Grace full of grace', 175, 208; 'Miracle of the world!', 206–7; 'Of his mistress upon occasion of her walking in a garden', 4, 107–8; 'To Sir Philip Sidney's Soul', 262
Cornforth, Fanny, 278
Creighton, Charles, 94–5, 307
Curtius, Ernst Robert, 307

Daniel, Samuel, 28, 66, 68, 70–2, 76, 82, 94–8, 105, 166–7, 202, 205, 207, 224–5, 240, 242–3, 272, 273, 295, 307
  Civil Wars, 63, 67, 71, 101, 243
  Cleopatra, 51, 62, 67, 82, 96, 243
  Delia, 14, 48, 51–2, 62, 63, 67, 81–2, 96–7, 99, 100–1, 163–8, 262, 272, 279–81, 310: 'Complaint of Rosamond', 97, 249–50, 253, 254; 'Let others sing of knights and paladins', 207–9; 'Raising my hope on hills of high desire', 54–5; 'The star of my mishap imposed this paining', 100–1
  Defence of Rhyme, 67, 100–1
  Musophilus, 97, 311
  sister (possible model for Shakespeare's mistress), 224–6
  Sonnet in *Nennio*, 70–1
Davidson, Francis, 94
Davies, Sir John (author of 'Gulling Sonnets'), 295
Davies of Hereford, John, 105, 295, 303, 310
Desportes, Philippe, 164–5, 310, 311
Devereux, Penelope (also Penelope Rich), 13, 23, 150
Devereux, Robert *see* Essex, Second earl of
Drayton, Michael, 66, 69, 76, 100, 207, 241, 304, 306
  Barons' Wars, 63
  Idea, 50, 63, 64, 105, 163–4, 241–2, 262, 272, 279–81
  Idea's Mirror, 14, 62, 100, 262
  'Upon the Death of Lady Penelope Clifton', 49–50
Drummond of Hawthornden, William, Elegy for the Prince of Wales in *Tears on the Death of Meliades*, 33–5
Du Bartas, Guillaume de, *La Sepmaine*, 39–40; *see also* Sylvester, Joshua

Du Bellay, Joachim, 55, 64, 305
Dubrow, Heather, 305, 318–19
Duncan-Jones, Katharine, viii, 24, 44–5, 46, 106, 153, 214, 220–1, 256, 302, 303, 304, 309, 312, 313, 314, 315
Duncan-Jones (Katherine) and Woudhuysen (H. R.), 122, 303, 308, 313, 314, 316
Duval, Jeanne, 278

Edmondson, Paul, and Stanley Wells, 9, 16
Elizabeth I (Queen of England), 27, 205, 221–2
Erasmus, 155–6, 310
Erne, Lukas, 319
Essex, Second earl of (Robert Devereux), 71, 94, 191, 222, 273, 306
Evans, G. Blakemore, 189–90, 301, 309, 315, 317

Falco, Raphael, 318
Ferry, Anne, *The 'Inward' Language*, 13–14, 302, 309, 316, 318
Ficino, Marsilio, 260–2, 315
Fletcher, Giles, *Licia*, 23, 105, 162, 244–5, 280
Florio, John, 224–5
Fowler, Alastair, 8, 42–4, 46, 61, 121–2, 138–9, 304, 305, 307, 309, 312, 318

Gascoigne, George, 63, 313
Graziani, René, 44–5, 304
Green, Martin, 308, 313
Greenblatt, Stephen, 302, 303, 306
Greene, Robert, 71–2, 81, 178
Greville, Fulke, 22, 63, 241, 262, 279, 312, 314
Griffin, Bartholomew, *Fidessa*, 105, 242–3, 280
Grundy, Joan, 108, 308, 311

Hadfield, Andrew, 305, 306, 313
Hall, Joseph, *Virgidemiarum*, 35–6
Harrington, Sir John, 95–6
Harvey, Gabriel, 89
Hathaway, Anne (wife of Shakespeare), 224
Haydocke, Richard, *The Art of Pictorial Representation*, 37–9
Hayward, Sir John, 191
Helgerson, Richard, 305, 311, 318
Herbert, George, 266, 275
Herbert, Mary (Countess of Pembroke), 28
Herbert, William *see* Pembroke, Third earl of
Hereford, John Davies of, 156, 166–7, 225, 281, 295, 312
Heywood, Thomas, 24
Hieatt, A. Kent, 305
Hogarth, William, *The Analysis of Beauty*, 38–9
Holbein, Hans, *The Ambassadors*, 2
Holinshed's Chronicles, 192
Homer (author of *Iliad* and *Odyssey*), 60, 88, 202, 306
Hopper, Vincent, 44–5, 304, 308
Horace (Quintus Horatius Flaccus), 43, 65, 105
Howard, Henry (Earl of Surrey), 63
Hugo, Victor, 277
Hunsden (Lord), 224
Huntington, John, 74, 306
Hutton, James, 244–5, 314

Jackson, MacDonald P., 14, 16, 76–7, 302, 305, 307, 313–14, 315, 319
Jaggard, William, 24, 190, 297–8
James I (King of England), 27, 209, 214
Jones, William, *Nennio, A Treatise on Nobility*, 70–1
Jonson, Ben, 24, 66, 76, 94, 96, 303
Volpone, 24
Joyce, James, *Ulysses*, 7

Kastan, David Scott, 310
Keats, John, 275
Kennedy, George A., 310
Kerrigan, John, 16, 18, 44, 253, 302, 304, 305, 308, 312, 313, 315

Lanier, Emilia, 224–6, 313
Lawrence, Jason, 304
Lebrun, Marie, 278
Ledger, G. R., 190, 314
Lee, Sydney, 306, 311
Leicester, First earl of (Robert Dudley), 254
Lever, J. W., 214
Linche, Richard, *Diella*, 48, 105, 280
Lintott, Bernard, publisher of Shakespeare's works, 6
Lodge, Thomas, *Phyllis*, 105, 162–3, 166, 280
Lomazzo, Giovanni, *Trattato dell'arte della pittura*, 37, 304; see also Haydocke, Richard
Lucan (Marcus Annaeus Lucanus), 66, 305
Lucian, *Herodotus*, 69

Mackail, J. W., 223, 313
Malone, Edward, publisher of Shakespeare's works, 6
Marlowe, Christopher, 66–7, 72, 74, 76, 85, 295–8, 316
  Amores (translation of Ovid), 66
  Dido, Queen of Carthage, 66
  Doctor Faustus, 73
  Hero and Leander, 66, 74, 119, 295
  Tamburlaine the Great, 55, 66, 73, 305
Marotti, Arthur, 4
Marston, John, 86, 177–8, 240
Meredith, George, 276–8, 316
Meres, Francis, *Palladis Tamia*, 24, 66, 77, 97, 303, 307

Michelangelo, 37–9
Milton, John, 'On Shakespeare', 33
Mirror for Magistrates, 249–50
Monte, Steven, *Invisible Fences*, 316
Morris, Jane, 278
Muir, Kenneth, 242, 314

Nashe, Thomas, 71, 87, 151, 178, 311
Negro, Lucy ('Black Luce'), 224–5, 313
Nenna, Giovanni Battista, *Il Nennio*, 70–1, 73–4; see also Jones, William
Neoplatonism, 39–40, 258–67, 273
Newman, Thomas, 22
Niçeron, Jean-François, *La Perspective curieuse*, Jean-François, 38

Ovid (Publius Ovidius Naso), 40, 43, 65–6, 74, 206, 295
Oxford, Seventeenth earl of (Edward de Vere), 7, 196, 312

Parker, W. N., 61, 262, 305, 315, 318
Peele, Robert, 72
Pembroke, Countess of (Mary Sidney), 22, 67, 97
Pembroke, Third earl of (William Herbert), 7, 26–8, 67, 88, 94, 156–7, 220–2
Percy, Walter, *Coelia*, 87, 105, 280
Persius (Aulus Persius Flaccus), 92
perspective, 1–2, 274–8
Petrarch, Francesco (and Petrarchan), 3, 45–6, 63, 81, 206, 226, 247
Platonic World Soul, 9, 192, 258–67
Platonism see Neoplatonism
Plutarch, 138–9

Prescott (Anne Lake) and Hadfield (Andrew D.), 305, 313
Primaudaye, Peter de la, *The French Academy*, 49, 304
Propertius (Sextus Propertius), 43
pyramids (in Renaissance culture), 33–42
Puttenham, George, *The Art of English Poesy*, 36, 304

Raleigh, Sir Walter, 297–8
Ramsey, Paul, 318
Rees, Joan, 251, 315
Rich, Penelope *see* Penelope Devereux
Ringler, William A., 304, 307
Robinson, Mary, 275, 316
Roche, Thomas P., 44–5, 46, 51, 279, 304, 309, 312, 318
Rollins, H. E., 7, 95, 178, 302, 307, 309, 311
Romanticism, 5, 6, 7
Ronsard, Pierre de, 28
Rossetti, Dante Gabriel, 7, 276–8, 316
Rudenstine, Neil L., 318

Sabatier, Madame de, 278
Sakeld, Duncan, 313
Salisbury, Sir John, 221–2, 313
Sams, Eric, 85
Sandys, George, 36, 303
Scaliger, Julius Caesar, 191
Schaar, Claes, 308, 311, 312, 314
Scodel, Joshua, 303
Seneca the Younger (Lucius Annaeus Seneca), 66
Seward, Anna, 275
Shakespeare, William
    LIFE
    1599, Sonnet 99, and the turn of the century, 190–3; writing poems when the theatres were closed, 102; the mid-1590s and Sonnet 33, 147–53

LITERARY WORKS (other than the sonnets and 'A Lover's Complaint')
Antony and Cleopatra, 51, 236–7, 243
As You Like It, 191, 298
Coriolanus, 236
Cymbeline, 116, 192, 236, 250, 254
Hamlet, 89, 295, 307
1 Henry IV and *2 Henry IV*, 27, 45, 149–50, 151, 152–3, 176, 201–2, 236
Henry V, 71, 274–5
3 Henry VI, 81
Henry VIII, 236
Julius Caesar, 141, 190–1
King John, 148–9
King Lear, 221, 313
Love's Labour's Lost, 75, 88, 93, 209, 226, 236, 297, 306, 313
Lucrece, 9, 24, 62–3, 87–8, 89, 102, 111–14, 116, 121–5, 147, 190–1, 250, 254–5, 256, 267, 269, 296, 307
Merchant of Venice, 103
Othello, 254
Passionate Pilgrim, 6, 24, 190, 241, 295–8, 316
Pericles, 236
'Phoenix and the Turtle', 6, 221–2, 313
Richard II, vi, 71, 148–9, 150–1, 274
Romeo and Juliet, 71, 116–17, 147–8, 151, 153, 297, 308, 316
Troilus and Cressida, 93, 244, 295
Two Gentlemen of Verona: 115–16
Venus and Adonis, 9, 24, 26, 40, 74, 75, 85–6, 87, 89, 102, 111–14, 116, 121–5, 147, 178, 191, 255–6, 267, 269, 295, 296
Winter's Tale, 236

Shapiro, James, 308, 316
Siddal, Elizabeth, 278
Sidney, Mary *see* Pembroke, Countess of
Sidney, Philip, 22, 40, 65, 119, 266, 272, 303, 308
  Arcadia, 22, 69, 109, 140, 250–3, 308, 315
  Astrophil and Stella (individual poems): Sonnet 7, 240–1; Sonnet 33, 150–1; Sonnet 60, 52–4, 61; Sonnet 93, 13
  Astrophil and Stella (sonnet sequence), 3, 13, 14, 22–3, 51–2, 55, 60–1, 62–4, 67, 68, 104–5, 119, 120, 140, 155, 202, 224, 234, 240, 272, 279–81
  Defence of Poetry, 67
  Elegies for, in *Exequiae illustrissimi equitis*, 33–4
Sidney, Robert, 262
Smarr, Janet Levarie, 92–3, 304, 307
Smith, Charlotte, 275
Smith, William, *Chloris*, 280
Sohmer, Steve, 312, 317
'sonnet sequence' as a term, viii, 12, 60–1
Southampton, Third earl of (Henry Wriothesley), 5, 7, 26–8, 62, 85–6, 88, 94, 102, 111–14, 117, 153, 168, 173, 190, 196, 204, 209, 219, 220, 222, 273, 285–7, 312
Spenser, Edmund, 65–7, 69–72, 76, 97–8, 193, 202, 204–5, 240, 272
  Amoretti, 3, 8, 14, 48, 63, 67–8, 97–8, 105, 107, 109, 144, 197–9, 205, 214–19, 224, 262, 272, 285, 316; Sonnets 58–60, 215–18, 254, 280
  Complaints, 65

  Colin Clout's Come Home Again, 63, 65, 68, 69, 70
  'Doleful Lay of Clorinda', 70
  Faerie Queene, 64–5, 66, 67, 69, 92, 107, 141, 205, 262, 312
  Four Hymns, 65
  Mother Hubberd's Tale, 65
  Prothalamion, 65, 254
  Ruins of Rome, 55, 64–5
  Ruins of Time, 65, 253–4
  Shepherd's Calendar, 65
  Sonnet in *Nennio*, 70–1
Spiller, Michael R. G., 279
Steevens, George, publisher of Shakespeare's works, 6
Stirling, Brents, 318
Sylvester, Joshua, *Divine Weeks*, 39–42, 262, 304

Tansillo, Luigi, 54
Tebaldeo, Antonio, 311
Tennyson, Alfred (Lord), 276
Thorpe, Thomas, 24–6
Tofte, Robert, 105
Tresham, Thomas (Rushton Triangular Lodge), 267
triangular number (compared to square number), 42, 120
Tyler, Thomas, 178, 311

Ussher, James, 191

Vendler, Helen, 6, 18, 106, 155–6, 302, 303, 308, 312
Vere, Edward de *see* Oxford, Seventeenth earl of
Vernon, Elizabeth, 191
Very, Jones, 275–6
Virgil (Publius Vergilius Maro), 40, 65–6, 68, 205–6, 296, 305

Waddington, Raymond B., 306, 309
Watson, Thomas, 14, 100, 193, 202, 280

Sonnets 46–8 of *The Tears of Fancy*, 195–7
Weever, John, 191
Weis, René, 308, 314
West, David, 16, 21, 80–1, 105, 303, 306, 308
Wilson, Emily, 314
Wilson, Thomas, 155
Wilson-Okamura, 307
Winnick, R. H., 114–17, 282–7, 288, 308, 310
Wood, Anthony, 307
Wordsworth, William, 14, 275–6, 302

Woudhuysen, H. R., 306, 313
Wright, Thomas, *The Passions of the Mind* (with climacteric treatise), 37, 49, 304, 311
Wriothesley, Henry *see* Southampton, Third earl of.
Wroth, Mary, *Pamphilia and Amphilanthus*, 6, 162, 221, 262, 281
Wyatt, Sir Thomas, 63

Yang, Cecil Y., 316

Zarnowiecki, Matthew, 309